Practicing Feminist Ethics in Psychology

Edited by

Mary M. Brabeck

American Psychological Association

Washington, DC

Published by
American Psychological Association
750 First Street, NE
Washington, DC 20002

Copies may be ordered from
APA Order Department
P.O. Box 92984
Washington, DC 20090-2984

In the U.K., Europe, Africa, and the Middle East, copies may be ordered from
American Psychological Association
3 Henrietta Street
Covent Garden, London
WC2E 8LU England

Typeset in Goudy by WorldComp, Sterling, VA

Printer: Port City Press, Baltimore, MD
Dust jacket designer: Minker Design, Bethesda, MD
Technical/Production Editor: Amy J. Clarke

Library of Congress Cataloging-in-Publication Data
Practicing feminist ethics in psychology / edited by Mary M. Brabeck.
    p.   cm.
    Includes bibliographical references and indexes.
    ISBN 1-55798-623-1 (cloth : acid-free paper).—ISBN 1-55798-635-5 (pbk. : acid-free paper).
    1. Feminist psychology. 2. Feminism. 3. Women—Psychology. I. Brabeck, Mary M.
BF201.4.P73   1999
174'.915'082—dc21
                                    99-41175
                                       CIP

British Library Cataloguing-in-Publication Data
A CIP record is available from the British Library.

Printed in the United States of America
First Edition

CONTENTS

CONTRIBUTORS

Mary M. Brabeck, PhD, Professor and Dean, School of Education, Boston College, Chestnut Hill, MA

Laura S. Brown, PhD, independent practice, Seattle WA

Jeanne D. Day, PhD, Chair, Department of Psychology, University of Notre Dame, Notre Dame, IN

Cynthia de las Fuentes, PhD, Department of Psychology, School of Education and Clinical Studies, Our Lady of the Lake University, San Antonio, TX

Celia B. Fisher, PhD, Center for Ethics Education, Department of Psychology, Fordham University, Bronx, NY

Jennifer J. Freyd, PhD, Department of Psychology, University of Oregon, Eugene

Karen Strohm Kitchener, PhD, Counseling Psychology, School of Education, University of Denver, Denver, CO

James R. Mahalik, PhD, Counseling, Developmental, and Educational Psychology, School of Education, Boston College, Chestnut Hill, MA

Alice McIntyre, PhD, Graduate School of Education and Allied Professions, Fairfield University, Fairfield, CT

Naomi M. Meara, PhD, Department of Psychology, University of Notre Dame, Notre Dame, IN

David L. Miller, PhD, Director of Academic Computing, Bristol Community College, Fall River, MA

Danielle R. Oakley, MS, Department of Educational and Counseling Psychology, University of Kentucky, Lexington

Aileen H. Park, MA, Counseling, Developmental, and Educational Psychology, School of Education, Boston College, Chestnut Hill, MA

Kathryn Quina, PhD, Department of Psychology, University of Rhode Island, Kingston

Nicole L. Simi, MA, Counseling, Developmental, and Educational Psychology, School of Education, Boston College, Chestnut Hill, MA

Elizabeth E. Sparks, PhD, Counseling, Developmental and Educational Psychology, School of Education, Boston College, Chestnut Hill, MA

Kathleen Ting, PhD, Counseling, Developmental, and Educational Psychology, School of Education, Boston College, Chestnut Hill, MA

E. Alice Van Ormer, MA, Counseling, Developmental, and Educational Psychology, School of Education, Boston College, Chestnut Hill, MA

Melba J. T. Vasquez, PhD, independent practice, Austin, TX

Judith Worell, PhD, Department of Educational and Counseling Psychology, University of Kentucky, Lexington

ACKNOWLEDGMENTS

This work began in 1996 as a task force on feminist ethics and psychological practice within the Division of the Psychology of Women (Division 35) of the American Psychological Association. I thank all of the writers in this collection, especially Kathleen Ting, who stayed with me during the many interruptions of the work caused by my "day job." It is a rare joy to work with gifted feminist psychologists whose challenging work expands one's ways of thinking, being, and doing. Throughout the long process of my editing of this collection, the contributors were steadfastly supportive and collegial friends. A number of anonymous reviewers gave all of us useful feedback on our chapters; one reviewer in particular read the complete manuscript in an earlier version and gave us many useful suggestions. Cheryl Brown Travis, senior editor of the Division 35 book series, provided encouragement, support, and a quick response to email inquiries. Jennifer Henderson and Angela Shartrand were my able graduate assistants through the various stages of production of this volume; I am very grateful to them for their generous and gifted assistance. My daughter Kalina read and critiqued all my work and gave me insightful suggestions, posed challenging questions, and provided loving support during an editing getaway week. Finally, Mike, David, Karen, and Grampa kept me going. I am profoundly grateful for the wonderful people who accompanied me on this journey.

Practicing Feminist Ethics in Psychology

INTRODUCTION

MARY M. BRABECK AND KATHLEEN TING

Feminist theory has been defined as a distinct theoretical perspective, involving a unique history, set of assumptions, pedagogy, research methods, and psychological practice (Worell & Johnson, 1997). Similarly, feminist ethicists have drawn from women's experience (e.g., Baier, 1994; Eugene, 1989; Shogan, 1988; Tronto, 1987) and from feminist theory to describe the unique domain of feminist ethics (e.g., Andolsen, Gudorf, & Pellauer, 1985; Held, 1987). This book describes feminist ethics and applies feminist ethics to psychological practice in a variety of settings.

As described at the National Conference on Education and Training in Feminist Practice at Boston College, July 8–11, 1993, the tenets of feminist theory served as a common core for the writers of this volume (Brabeck & Brown, 1997). Seventy-seven feminist psychologists met over a 4-day national working conference to outline the fields of feminist theory, assessment, therapy, research, curriculum, pedagogy, supervision and post-doctoral training, and the role of diversity in advancing an inclusive feminist psychology. This work was published by the American Psychological Association as part of the Psychology of Women Book Series (Worell & Johnson, 1997). The Theory Group articulated nine central tenets that inform feminist theory and are at the core of feminist practice. Most of the chapter authors in this book apply these tenets to their discussions of feminist ethics. The nine tenets are listed in Exhibit I.1.

EXHIBIT I.1
Summary of Tenets of Feminist Theory of Psychological Practice

1. Feminist theory of psychological practice is consciously a political enterprise, and its goal is social transformation in the direction of feminist consciousness.

2. We are trying to change women's understanding of their reality to include the oppression of the patriarchal society and to create feminist consciousness. *Feminist consciousness* is a process of becoming, a way of seeing and sensing the world, a familiar lens, "another mother tongue." Feminist consciousness leads one to be response-able to self and others, attend to one's own and collective well-being; is unnumbing and re-integrating of all experiences and leads to social transformation. A goal of feminist practice is the creation of a feminist consciousness that becomes as unconscious as patriarchal consciousness is currently.

3. The capacity to create theory comes from experience and human connections through any form or medium: human communication, written word, political action, group solidarity, community activism. In this way, the personal is political because experience is connected to transformation and change.

4. Gender is an important locus of women's oppression and intersects with other important loci of oppression including but not limited to ethnicity, culture, class, age, sexual orientation, ability, and linguistic status. The practitioner of feminist theory is self-reflective regarding her positions in these various hierarchies.

5. Feminist theory of feminist practice embraces human diversity as a requirement and foundation for practice. Diversity (ethnicity, sexual orientation, able-bodiness, religion, language) not only is a goal in its own right but also is necessary for feminist theory to be complete and reflective of the total range of human experience.

6. Feminist theory affirms, attends to, and authorizes the experience of the oppressed in their own voices. This is an interactive process in which our role as oppressor must be considered a part. Feminist therapists–psychologists are self-reflective about their own experience, which informs this process.

7. Feminist practitioners expand the parameters of conceptions of identity or person-hood. Feminist theorists and practitioners seek models of human growth and development that describe a variety of ways that people have a sense of identities and multiple subjectivities.

8. Feminist theory of practice leads to an appreciation of the complex and multideter-mined causations of distress, with particular attention to the sociopolitical context. Within this context, persons are viewed as capable of acting (response-able) to effect change, and each person is viewed as responsible for participating in the process of change. As part of the process of change, those practicing a feminist theory contextualize behavior as occurring within a patriarchal system. Women are viewed as agentic and powerful but not entirely responsible for the pathology of sexism. Feminist theory of practice challenges assumptions of men as whole and center and women as broken and marginalized.

9. Feminist theory building is not static. Feminist theory of psychological practice is evolving and in process.

Note. From "Feminist Theory and Psychological Practice" (p. 32), by M. M. Brabeck and L. Brown, with L. Christian, O. Espin, R. Hare-Mustin, A. Kaplan, E. Kaschak, D. Miller, E. Phillips, T. Ferns, and A. Van Ormer, 1997, in J. Worell and N. G. Johnson (Eds.), *Shaping the Future of Feminist Psychology,* Washington, DC: American Psychological Association. Copyright 1997 by the American Psychological Association. Reprinted with permission.

Following recommendations from the Theory Group of the National Conference (Brabeck & Brown, 1997), *feminist practice* is described broadly as including therapy, teaching, research, writing, communication, activism, supervision, and forensic work. Although other texts describe feminist ethics in psychology within the therapeutic context (Lerman & Porter, 1990; Rave & Larsen, 1995), no other book has attempted to apply feminist theory and ethics to the broad number of arenas within which feminist psychologists practice. The authors of this book's chapters describe feminist ethics in teaching, cases of dual or overlapping relationships, antiracist and multicultural education, research, forensic work, and technology. In so doing, the authors as a group attempt to illustrate the contribution of feminist theory and ethics to psychological practice. We invite others to apply the ethical lenses presented here to additional arenas of psychological practice, such as public schools, mental health clinics, nursing homes, and hospitals. By identifying and applying feminist tenets and principles articulated at the national conference (see Exhibit I.1) to specific areas of psychological practice, this book's chapter authors advance the knowledge regarding feminist ethics of psychological practice. We hope that the book is useful to psychologists in practice, ethicists, students, and researchers.

Feminist ethics of psychological practice present a mandate for moral action that empowers individuals, creates just social structures, and ensures that all people are attentively cared for so as to nurture and develop each person's potential within the contexts in which each lives (see Tenets 1 and 2 in Exhibit I.1). By focusing on a variety of current problems that confront feminist practitioners, the authors in this book indicate how we might attain this feminist moral vision.

An overview of the emerging field of feminist ethics is presented in chapter 1 by Mary Brabeck and Kathleen Ting. Given the many different ideological positions within feminism described in chapter 1 and the fact that feminist ethics as a field is in its beginning stages, it is not surprising that there is no explicit consensus among feminists regarding the defining attributes of feminist ethics. However, in this introduction, we introduce each of the subsequent chapters by highlighting five broad themes common to feminist ethics that are discussed in the chapters that follow:

(1) the assumption that women and their experiences have moral significance
(2) the assertion that attentiveness, affective responses, and subjective knowledge can illuminate moral issues
(3) the admonition that feminist ethics engage in analysis of the context and of the power dynamics inherent in that context

(4) the claim that a feminist critique of male oppression must be accompanied by a critique of racist, classist, homophobic distortions

(5) the injunction that feminist ethics require action directed at achieving systemic social justice.

Each of these themes is supported in the chapters that follow. Each is also claimed by feminist ethicists, the tenets of feminist psychological theory as described by the Theory Group at the national conference (Brabeck & Brown, 1997), and the tenets of feminist therapy as described by members of the Feminist Therapy Institute (Lerman & Porter, 1990; Rave & Larsen, 1995; Rosewater & Walker, 1985). The foundation for these five insights, derived from feminist work in philosophy, ethics, and psychology is further elaborated in chapter 1.

THEME 1: WOMEN AND THEIR EXPERIENCES HAVE MORAL SIGNIFICANCE

All feminist ethicists begin with the assumption that women and their experiences have moral significance (Cole & Coultrap-McQuin, 1992). Although this may seem self-evident, it has not always been viewed as a valid assertion. The personhood of women (vs. of men) has been debated since Aristotle (Shields, 1975). Virtues and roles associated with women have continually been devalued (Miller, 1976), and paradoxically women have been both elevated beyond what is humanly possible and degraded to what is subhuman (Brabeck, 1989). Historically, women have been infantilized and legally regarded as property. The rigid, narrow roles to which women are assigned are often transformed into pervasive caricatures of women (the good mother, the temptress, the virgin, the whore, etc.). Because the male constructions of "woman" efface individuality and difference, they fail to capture the complexity of what it means to be a woman. To achieve a more adequate understanding of the complexities and diversities of women, feminist ethicists begin by attending to the experiences of women (see Tenets 3 and 6 in Exhibit I.1).

Experiences with children, students, and research participants, and the particularities of their own lives, lead chapter authors to question the ethical limitations of abstract ethical principles. In this volume, Celia Fisher (chap. 6) develops her insights into feminist ethics that arose from her experiences of parenting and her work with college students. Other authors describe their experiences as practitioners in classrooms (Kitchener, chap. 2; McIntyre, chap. 3; Worell & Oakley, chap. 8), research programs (Fisher, chap. 6; Freyd & Quina, chap. 5); courtrooms (Brown, chap. 4), therapy settings (Mahalik, Van Ormer, & Simi, chap. 9; Sparks & Park, chap. 10), cyberspace (Quina & Miller, chap. 7), and with the media (Vasquez & de las Fuentes, chap. 11).

For example, in chapter 2, Karen Kitchener focuses on the everyday ethical issues that arise between faculty members and college students. She applies a feminist ethical analysis to the responsibilities and ethical challenges professors encounter when students make ethical errors. Kitchener describes the tension between not abdicating power of the professor and empowering her students. She describes the conflict between the responsibility to facilitate the development of students and the duty to protect the public from incompetent psychologists. Kitchener reminds readers of the five ethical principles, namely, beneficence, nonmaleficence, autonomy, justice, and fidelity, and how despite the fact that these can help guide one through one's ethical decision-making process, they are insufficient. She cautions that a morality built solely on principles, abstract theory, and rules can lead to a dangerous self-righteousness. In her chapter, she identifies virtues and ethical character traits that are central to a feminist perspective. Kitchener suggests how the ethical character of moral agents can lead to moral responses that are more adequate than those that rely on principles or moral rules alone. She suggests four virtues that are relevant to ethical responses informed by feminist consciousness: respectfulness, trustworthiness, willingness to take responsibility, and caring or compassion. Kitchener also tentatively explores a fifth virtue, prudence, and demonstrates how each virtue is informed by a woman's experiences in personal relationships.

An examination of her experiences as a white teacher and administrator informs Alice McIntyre's discussion of feminist ethics. In chapter 3, McIntyre discusses the role of antiracist practices in feminist pedagogy and illuminates the need for reflexivity and power analyses and for acknowledging and attending to one's own privileged position when teaching for social change. McIntyre highlights the importance of making the experience of one's privilege—in this case, whiteness—public. McIntyre's feminist pedagogy is anchored in her experiences of deconstructing whiteness with white students who aspire to be teachers. Her antiracist and feminist work presents a model of self-interrogation regarding one's own racist and oppressive practices as essential for ethical action. McIntyre explores the ethical conflicts and personal difficulties that arise for her as a feminist and antiracist professor. In particular, she discusses the ethical issues of self-disclosure (an issue also addressed in the context of therapy by Mahalik, Van Ormer, and Simi in chap. 9) and the challenges of overcoming student resistance to antiracist teaching. Her work is an argument for an ethic of social justice; she offers a challenging agenda for feminist ethical action and recommendations for sustaining oneself while engaging in social justice work.

THEME 2: ATTENTIVENESS AND SUBJECTIVE KNOWLEDGE CAN ILLUMINATE MORAL ISSUES

Because feminist ethicists place great value on grounded knowledge (i.e., knowledge derived from lived experience), they examine the cognitive, affective, and subjective realities of women's experiences (Fox, 1992). Over the past 3 decades, feminist ethicists have described how honest attention, clear sightedness, and loving perception can reveal truth and the moral good (Frye, 1983; Noddings, 1984; Weil, 1951). Subjectivity, the result of reflection on personal experience, is not objectively verifiable and is informed by both cognition and affect. It has been a proper object of study for feminist theorists (see Tenets 2 and 7 in Exhibit I.1).

In chapter 4, Laura Brown suggests that objectivity is the name given to the subjectivities of the dominant group. She highlights the important distinction between the awareness of bias, which is congruent with feminist ethical norms for forensic psychology, and the so-called "absence of bias," which is how those norms are operationalized in the law. Whereas mainstream ethics of forensic practice assume the possibility of objectivity and neutrality and celebrate the distance between practitioner and the "case" as evidence of the highest virtue, feminist ethics require practitioners to identify their values, subjective beliefs, and biases (Lerman & Porter, 1990, p. 38). Brown demonstrates how feminist legal and ethical insights have led to changes in legal theory and greater protection for battered women in the courts. She also demonstrates how assertions of objectivity can mask ignorance and result in incompetence. Throughout her chapter, Brown offers a respectful critique of the ethical choices made by a friend who worked as a feminist forensic psychologist on the O. J. Simpson murder trial. Brown's critique is informed by reflections on her own subjective experience in forensic work.

Feminist attention to subjectivity as a source of knowledge has been, in part, a response to the hegemony of objective rational science (Harding & Hintikka, 1983). In chapter 5, Jennifer Freyd and Kathryn Quina use the false memory controversy as an example of how feminist ethical science raises questions about the values, interpretations, and intended uses of science. According to Freyd and Quina, feminist ethical science is a process whereby one constantly analyzes the research process and outcomes from a gendered sociocultural perspective. They discuss some of the ways in which science has been misapplied in the debate over the delayed memory recall of child abuse. They also suggest guidelines that may be useful in minimizing further misapplications of science through careful applications of feminist ethical principles. Freyd and Quina describe the limitations of objectivity and the importance of recognizing the influence of our own values as feminists—including power and authority—on the science that we research and the knowledge we promote.

According to Celia Fisher in chapter 6, subjectivity enters the research relationship when the ethical feminist researcher is obliged to understand the research participant's point of view. Although Fisher acknowledges that social and personal biases influence the way science is conducted, she maintains that the scientific method is a viable method for feminists to follow to understand ethically relevant perspectives of research participants. She discusses the *scientist–citizen dilemma*: the need to reconcile the researcher's professional commitment to the production of scientific knowledge with her or his humanitarian commitment to participant welfare. Fisher also cautions that whereas participant perspectives can inform ethical deliberations of individual scientists, participant views do not remove scientists' ethical responsibilities. In her view, scientists must integrate their caring and understanding of participant perspectives with a realistic sense of the researcher's own competencies to take responsibility for ethical decisions. Fisher further examines how feminist ethics enable scientists to integrate their rational and caring selves in ways that enhance their ability to engage research participants as partners in creating experimental procedures that reflect both scientific and interpersonal integrity.

THEME 3: FEMINIST ETHICISTS ENGAGE IN ANALYSIS OF THE CONTEXT AND OF THE POWER DYNAMICS INHERENT IN THAT CONTEXT

Feminist ethicists recognize that all experiences are profoundly shaped by the contexts of people's lives (Spelman, 1988). People develop within the constant interplay of internal phenomenological experience and external sociopolitical realities. A feminist model assumes that the etiology of all behavior is complex and multidetermined and that the politics of the social milieu profoundly influence the expression and meaning of human behavior. As ethical feminist practitioners, we are obliged to interrogate ourselves regarding our motives for our choice of action and to attend to how our position of power affects our ethical choices (see Tenets 4 and 8 in Exhibit I.1).

Self-interrogation of our own relative power within a particular context and our unavoidable embeddedness in the status quo can reveal ethical dilemmas. For example, Laura Brown (chap. 4) enjoins feminist forensic psychologists to question themselves as to whether functioning as a forensic expert in a masculine system—where justice is "blind"—encourages the legal system to continue unchanged or whether such participation is necessary as an avenue for creating social change. She offers some guidelines for making these decisions.

In a similar vein, Alice McIntyre (chap. 3) argues that white feminists have a responsibility to engage in self-analysis and self-critique about their own positionalities as white women, to develop a pedagogy that engages all students in dialogue, and at the same time to critique that dialogue. She also suggests that white feminists have the responsibility to be in solidarity with people of Color and other white allies who are committed to dialoguing about racism. Together, feminists and multiculturalists must find ways to make changes to attain societal justice.

A concern for a balance of power is central to the issues that Kathryn Quina and David Miller (chap. 7) raise regarding the cultural and ethical structure of cyberspace. Quina and Miller envision a cybersociety, which is "anti-domination in its goals, empowering in its interactions, multicultural in its scope, and transformational in every act." The authors envision computer-mediated communication (CMC) as a potential source of power, a political enterprise, and a place for potential "evolution and revolution." They discuss some of the challenges (access, accountability, abuse, and activism) in bringing feminist organizations into the "information superhighway" and how the feminist revolution could be expanded into the new structures created by CMC through feminist ethics. They describe the skills that would make such ethical practice possible. Quina and Miller further discuss how CMC can become a very effective medium for dispersing feminist ethical thinking.

Judith Worell and Danielle Oakley in chapter 8 present the ethical dilemmas facing feminist teachers in their efforts to implement feminist principles within traditional academic contexts. Although they recognize that the faculty is primarily responsible for instructional planning and strategies, they also maintain that the perspectives of students are relevant and valid. Drawing from principles and strategies of feminist pedagogy, they reveal the ethical dilemmas that inevitably occur when feminist teachers confront inequalities of power and authority while working in a traditional, hierarchical, and patriarchal context. They present different ethical dilemma scenarios to illustrate ways in which the feminist teacher can ensure that the professor retain the feminist ethical injunction to honor all voices, encourage activism to attain social justice, and maintain principles of equality and equity.

An attention to power inequities is also central to feminist therapy. According to the Code of Ethics of the Feminist Therapy Institute (1990) and Tenets 1 and 2 of the National Conference on Education and Training in Feminist Practice, feminist therapists are committed "to political and social change that equalizes power among people. Feminism strives to create equal valuing of all people by recognizing and reducing the pervasive influences and insidious effects of patriarchy on people's lives" (p. 37). Consequently, one of the Feminist Therapy Institute's ethical principles states that feminist therapists stay actively engaged in the understanding, exploration, and analyses of power in people's lives. In chapter 9 of this book, James Mahalik, Alice Van Ormer, and Nicole Simi describe the context in which self-disclosure can be used in the service of empowering clients in the practice of therapy. Because of the higher prevalence of feminist therapists' self-disclosures, the authors revisit principles of feminist theory and ethics to define guidelines for the appropriate and effective use of self-disclosure. They report findings that therapist self-disclosure is beneficial and examine the ethical issues of underdisclosing information to clients. They provide an example of the application of feminist ethics to examine self-disclosure in the therapeutic context.

THEME 4: FEMINIST CRITIQUES OF MALE DISTORTIONS MUST BE ACCOMPANIED BY A CRITIQUE OF RACIST, CLASSIST, HOMOPHOBIC DISTORTIONS

Whereas feminist ethicists view gender oppression as a unit of analysis and view empowerment of girls and women as a goal of feminist practice, a number of feminists have called attention to the danger of essentialism and false universals (Greene & Sanchez-Hucles, 1997; hooks, 1993; Spelman, 1988). As Calhoun (1988) wrote, "unless moral theory shifts its priority to knowledgeable discussions of human differences—particularly differences tied to gender, race, class and power—these lists are likely to be sexist, racist, and classist" (p. 456).

As feminist practitioners, we acknowledge the limits of our own standpoint and know that we are affected by our own ethnicity, able-bodiness, class, sexual orientation, and culture. We try to be self-conscious about our own positions of privilege and to acknowledge the effects that our own positions of dominance have on our constructions of ourselves and others. Ethical feminist practice requires us to engage in self-interrogation regarding the ways in which our context causes us to oppress others (Applebaum, 1997). The Ethical Guidelines for Feminist Therapists of the Feminist Therapy Institute (1990) assert that

> a feminist therapist is aware of the meaning and impact of her own ethnic and cultural background, gender, class, and sexual orientation, and actively attempts to become knowledgeable about alternatives from sources other than her clients. The therapist's goal is to uncover and respect cultural and experiential differences. (p. 39)

In a similar vein, Tenet 4 (Exhibit I.1) notes that whereas gender is an important unit of analysis for feminists, other loci of oppression must also be examined.

In their chapter, Sparks and Park (chap. 10) point out that much of feminist theory was developed within a Western, individualistic cultural context. They highlight how in its theoretical development, feminism failed to acknowledge that notions of the self and gender are influenced by social constructions. Moral convictions, they point out, reflect individuals' belief systems, which are influenced by race, ethnicity, class, and multiple other contextual factors. Sparks and Park discuss how some of psychology's and feminism's ethnocentric assumptions are evident in an emphasis on individualism. For them, multicultural ethics can be a corrective to the ethnocentrism of feminist ethics. They use clinical vignettes about battered women to examine how minimizing the influences of culture in the lives of these women may contribute to misunderstandings and culturally insensitive clinical interventions. They further point to the similarities and differences between the fundamental tenets of both feminist theory of practice and those of multicultural counseling and therapy—both are endeavors that seek to improve the human condition.

THEME 5: FEMINIST ETHICS REQUIRE ACTION DIRECTED AT ACHIEVING SOCIAL JUSTICE

Feminist ethics go beyond moral awareness of particulars, ethical principles, and knowledge of the good to advocate for action to achieve social justice. The Feminist Theory Group (Brabeck & Brown, 1997) wrote that "feminist theory of psychological practice is consciously a political enterprise, and its goal is social transformation in the direction of feminist consciousness" (p. 32; see Tenet 1 in Exhibit I.1). Furthermore, when one becomes aware of moral wrongs within oneself or within society, one is required to act to change these wrongs. "Good intentions," Applebaum wrote (1997), "are not enough" (p. 409).

Feminist consciousness encompasses responsibilities for the well-being of one's self and others and leads the ethical feminist practitioner to work toward social transformation. Feminist ethics require feminist practitioners to work to change society to improve it for all members of society. Moreover, according to the Feminist Therapy Institute, "a feminist therapist seeks multiple avenues for impacting change, including public education and advocacy within professional organizations, lobbying for legislative actions, and other appropriated activities" (Lerman & Porter, 1990, p. 40).

As leaders in promoting social responsibility, feminist psychologists have long been concerned with advocating for oppressed groups. Melba Vasquez and Cynthia de las Fuentes (chap. 11) examine hate speech and verbal violence from the perspective of feminist and traditional ethics. They expose the traumatic impact of hate speech and other forms of racism, sexism, ageism, and homophobia; they warn that hate speech and hate crimes are predicted to rise with increasing racial, ethnic, and cultural diversity. According to Vasquez and de las Fuentes, moral exclusion accounts for much of exploitation, discrimination, and forms of genocide. Moral exclusion occurs when individuals or groups are perceived to be outside the boundary in which moral values, rules, and considerations of fairness apply. Those who are morally excluded are perceived as nonentities, expendable, or underclass. Consequently, harming or exploiting them appears to be appropriate and acceptable. Hate speech poses both legal and ethical dilemmas and raises particular issues for feminist psychologists. Vasquez and de las Fuentes discuss the legal and ethical conflicts that arise within the feminist and multicultural communities, when the issue of protecting oppressed groups against various forms of demeaning and verbally violent forms of expression is interpreted as censorship. To resolve these issues, the authors explore the application of "virtue ethics" in the process of decision making regarding policy about hate speech.

With the requirement that feminist educators take action against dominant practices that marginalize particular groups of people, Alice McIntyre points out how feminist pedagogy intersects with feminist principles and ethics to achieve justice. In a similar vein, Worell and Oakley suggest that whereas ethical principles clearly present ideals toward which to strive, the ideals must be realized by deliberate action. Kitchener enjoins feminists to take ethical stands against the societal structures that create inequitable health care systems. Sparks and Park believe that feminists must work to bring about change in the sociopolitical context that supports the victimization of women; they present suggestions for reweaving multicultural and feminist theories. Vasquez and de las Fuentes believe that feminist practitioners have the skill and ought to facilitate the broadening of the boundaries of moral inclusion in American society. Quina and Miller envision the boundless possibilities for social justice work in cyberspace. Fisher and Freyd and Quina urge psychology researchers to use knowledge to attain social justice. Mahalik, Van Ormer, and Simi suggest psychologists in clinical practice should adopt "aspirational ethics," which focus on behavior that ought to be encouraged in any ethical professional. For Brown, the struggle to attain social justice determines how a feminist ethicist ought to judge Walker's decision to act as an expert witness for the defense in the O. J. Simpson murder trial. Social justice also is the mark against which she weighs her own decision about whether to continue as an expert witness in a case against a Caucasian lesbian brought by a heterosexual African American woman.

All the chapter authors hold the view that feminist practitioners have the mandate to use their knowledge to bring about individual, familial, communal, educational, institutional, legal, and social change—to move beyond "social justice noise" (Grant & Zozakiewicz, 1995, p. 271) to create social justice. At the end of this volume, Naomi Meara and Jeanne Day (in the Epilogue) reflect on these chapters from the perspectives offered by professional psychology and virtue ethics. They offer their insights into the ways in which feminist ethics in general and the chapters in this volume in particular expand one's understanding of ethics and psychological practice.

Although the chapters in this book do not resolve all ethical dilemmas or present a formula for achieving social justice, we hope that they provoke new ways of thinking about ethical issues from the perspectives offered by feminist ethics. We hope that the ideas in this book point to new ways of being and practicing as ethical psychologists.

REFERENCES

Andolsen, B. H., Gudorf, C. E., & Pellauer, M. D. (1985). *Women's consciousness, women's conscience: A reader in feminist ethics*. Minneapolis, MN: Winston Press.

Applebaum, B. (1997). Good liberal intentions are not enough! Racism, intentions and moral responsibility. *Journal of Moral Education, 26*(4), 409–421.

Baier, A. (1994). *Moral prejudices: Essays on ethics*. Cambridge, MA: Harvard University Press.

Brabeck, M. M. (Ed.). (1989). *Who cares? Theory, research and educational implications of the ethic of care*. New York: Praeger.

Brabeck, M., & Brown, L. (With Christian, L., Espin, O., Hare-Mustin, R., Kaplan, A., Kaschak, E., Miller, D., Phillips, E., Ferns, T., & Van Ormer, A.). (1997). Feminist theory and psychological practice. In J. Worell & N. Johnson (Eds.), *Shaping the future of feminist psychology: Education, research, and practice* (pp. 15–35). Washington, DC: American Psychological Association.

Calhoun, C. (1988). Justice, care, and gender bias. *Journal of Philosophy, 85*, 451–463.

Cole, E. B., & Coultrap-McQuin, S. (Eds.). (1992). *Explorations in feminist ethics: Theory and practice*. Bloomington: Indiana University Press.

Eugene, T. (1989). Sometimes I feel like a motherless child: The call and response for a liberational ethic of care. In M. M. Brabeck (Ed.), *Who cares? Theory, research and educational implications of the ethic of care* (pp. 45–62). New York: Praeger.

Feminist Therapy Institute. (1990). Feminist Therapy Institute code of ethics. In H. Lerman & N. Porter (Eds.), *Feminist ethics in psychotherapy* (pp. 37–40). New York: Springer.

Fox, E. L. (1992). Seeing through women's eyes: The role of vision in women's moral theory. In E. B. Cole & S. Coultrap-McQuin (Eds.), *Explorations in feminist ethics: Theory and practice* (pp. 111–116). Bloomington: Indiana University Press.

Frye, M. (1983). *The politics of reality: Essays in feminist theory*. Trumansburg, NY: Crossing Press.

Grant, C. A., & Zozakiewicz, C. A. (1995). Student teachers, cooperating teachers, and supervisors: Interrupting the multicultural silences of student teaching. In J. Larkin & C. E. Sleeter (Eds.), *Developing multicultural teacher education curricula* (pp. 259–278). Albany: State University of New York Press.

Greene, B., & Sanchez-Hucles, J. (With Banks, M., Civish, G., Contratto, S., Griffith, J., Hinderly, H. H., Jenkins, Y., & Robertson, M. K.). (1997). Diversity: Advancing an inclusive feminist psychology. In J. Worell & N. Johnson (Eds.), *Shaping the future of feminist psychology: Education, research, and practice* (pp. 173–202). Washington, DC: American Psychological Association.

Harding, S., & Hintikka, M. B. (Eds.). (1983). *Discovering reality: Feminist perspectives on epistemology, metaphysics, methodology and philosophy of science*. Boston: D. Reidel.

Held, V. (1987). Feminism and moral theory. In E. F. Kittay & D. T. Meyers (Eds.), *Women and moral theory* (pp. 111–128). Totowa, NJ: Rowman & Littlefield.

hooks, b. (1993). Black women: Shaping feminist theory. In M. Pearsall (Ed.), *Women and values: Readings in recent feminist philosophy* (pp. 165–174). Belmont, CA: Wadsworth.

Lerman, H., & Porter, N. (Eds.). (1990). *Feminist ethics in psychotherapy*. New York: Springer.

Miller, J. B. (1976). *Toward a new psychology of women*. Boston: Beacon Press.

Noddings, N. (1984). *Caring: A feminine approach to ethics and moral education*. Berkeley: University of California Press.

Rave, E. J., & Larsen, C. (1995). *Ethical decision making therapy: Feminist perspectives*. New York: Guilford Press.

Rosewater, R., & Walker, L. (1985). (Eds.). *Handbook of feminist therapy: Women's issues in psychotherapy*. New York: Springer.

Shogan, D. (1988). *Care and moral motivation*. Toronto, Ontario, Canada: OISE Press.

Shields, S. (1975). Functionalism, Darwinism, and the psychology of women. *American Psychologist, 30,* 739–754.

Spelman, E. (1988). *Inessential woman: Problems of exclusion in feminist thought*. Boston: Beacon Press.

Tronto, J. (1987). Beyond gender difference to a theory of care. *Signs, 12,* 644–661.

Weil, S. (1951). *Waiting for God* (E. Craufurd, Trans.). New York: Putnam.

Worell, J., & Johnson, N. G. (Eds.). (1997). *Shaping the future of feminist psychology: Education, research, and practice*. Washington, DC: American Psychological Association.

1

FEMINIST ETHICS: LENSES FOR EXAMINING ETHICAL PSYCHOLOGICAL PRACTICE

MARY M. BRABECK AND KATHLEEN TING

In 1991, the political scientist Jean Bethke Elshtain wrote, "feminism without ethics is inconceivable" (p. 126). According to Elshtain, all feminisms offer an ethical position that accompanies a political, activist agenda to achieve social justice and improve women's lives. However, ethicists only recently have begun to examine the unique contributions that feminism makes to the field of ethics. Thirty years ago, there was no field called "feminist ethics" (Cole & Coultrap-McQuin, 1992; Tong, 1993). In contrast, today feminist philosophers are joined by psychologists, sociologists, educators, lawyers, and theologians in defining and applying feminist ethics to practical problems that challenge practitioners. Feminist moral theory informs thinking about how to define the morally good from a feminist perspective and how to use this perspective to resolve ethical dilemmas (Baier, 1994; Cole & Coultrap-McQuin, 1992; Noddings, 1984; Shogan, 1988). Feminist ethicists claim that ethical action is required for the feminist enterprise and describe the moral obligations of feminist thought and action (Card, 1991; Spelman, 1988).

Feminist ethics involves much of what traditional ethics includes.

Traditional ethicists have carefully examined (1) the *nature* of actions (are they required, forbidden, or merely permitted?); (2) the *consequences* of actions (are they good, bad, or merely indifferent?); and (3) the *motives* behind action (are they self-directed, other-directed, or both?). (Tong, 1993, p. 15)

However, feminist ethics go beyond this. Feminist ethical theories provide unique lenses for determining what one ought to do and deciding on a course of action in the face of competing ethical principles.

In this chapter, we return to the five overlapping themes of feminist ethics identified in the introduction of this book. These themes are discussed and illustrated in the chapters that follow in this volume and in the work of feminist ethicists, theorists, and psychologists discussed in this chapter. Here we provide the theoretical base for each of the five overarching themes that characterize feminist ethics:

1. the assumption that women and their experiences have moral significance
2. the assertion that attentiveness, subjective knowledge, can illuminate moral issues
3. the claim that a feminist critique of male distortions must be accompanied by a critique of all discriminatory distortions
4. the admonition that feminist ethics engage in analysis of the context and attend to the power dynamics of that context
5. the injunction that feminist ethics require action directed at achieving social justice.

Of course, like all psychologists, feminists also are aided in making ethical judgments by the American Psychological Association's (APA) Ethical Principles of Psychologists and Code of Conduct (APA, 1992) and by moral philosophy, which provides the foundation for descriptions of ethical principles and moral dispositions or virtues. Kitchener (1999) offered an excellent overview of the major philosophical traditions that inform ethical thought, in general, and ethics of psychological practice, in particular. Some of these major traditions are briefly referred to here, along with some of the major insights of feminist ethicists who work within these perspectives and challenge them (Andolsen, Gudorf, & Pellauer, 1985; Baier, 1994; Card, 1991; Cole & Coultrap-McQuin, 1992; Held, 1987).

A concern with ethics should be a central aspect of all feminist dialogue (Elshtain, 1991); however, feminist thought is not unitary. There are multiple feminisms, such as liberal, Marxist, radical, relational, and postmodern (see, e.g., Enns, 1993; and Tong, 1989, 1993, for discussions of different feminisms and feminist ethics). Thus, it should be no surprise that within feminism, there are disputes about issues. Whereas each feminist perspective offers ethical insights, competing and sometimes contradictory ethical ideas are associated with different feminisms. In this chapter, we aim to reveal some of those disputes. We discuss the debate over the relative importance of reason and experience in ethical thought and action; we describe the different moral views offered by an ethic of care and an ethic of justice; we examine the postmodernism challenge to ethics, in general, and feminist ethics, in particular; and we identify the tension between individualism and collectivism in achieving the feminist agenda of social justice.

Even though there are disputes among feminist ethicists and theorists, there are also agreements. In our discussion of the five common and overlapping themes of feminist ethics, we describe the unique contributions of feminist ethics to understanding ethical psychological practice. This chapter provides a backdrop for the subsequent chapters in which feminist ethics and theory are applied to diverse settings of psychological practice.

WOMEN AND THEIR EXPERIENCES HAVE MORAL SIGNIFICANCE

Arguing that moral philosophy has been largely a male enterprise, feminists seek to expose the individual and institutional practices that have denied women access to jobs and education and have devalued and suppressed women. As philosopher Patricia Ward Scaltsas (1992) wrote,

> the project of criticizing, analyzing and when necessary replacing the traditional categories of moral philosophy in order to eradicate the misrepresentation, distortion and oppression resulting from the historically male perspective is, broadly speaking, the project of feminist ethics. (p. 16)

According to many feminist writers, the problem with our "understandings" of women is that they have been developed within a patriarchal society that privileges male insights, experiences, and beliefs. To rectify errors in constructing and understanding the "nature of woman," feminists argue that we must begin experientially with the particulars of women's lives. In so doing, they have developed the field of feminist ethics.

An attention to women's experiences has led many feminist philosophers and theorists to examine the roles most associated with women, such as mothering, care giving, women's friendships, and peace making (Flax, 1990). For example, from the experiences of mothering, Sara Ruddick (1980) identified maternal thinking as involving a particular attentiveness to the needs of children; maternal thinking, she argued, is expressed in an ethical stance characterized by "attentive love." Through an historical examination of women's friendships and female groups, Janice Raymond (1986) explored a philosophy of friendship that was both ethical and feminist and rooted in women's connections to each other. Nel Noddings's (1984) ethic of care theory was grounded in the examination of women's relationships, particularly the mother–child relationship, and is an ethical theory of responsibility to and for others. Carol Gilligan (1982) examined the moral reasoning of women who were faced with a decision about whether to have an abortion and illustrated how moral thinking is informed by the ethic of care.

Such feminist work reveals that the experiences of women are important sources for identifying ethical concerns and issues. In this way, mothering, women's friendships, peace making, and collective and collaborative ways of decision making and organizing (Lykes, Brabeck, Ferns, & Radan, 1993) are claimed by feminist ethicists and moral theorists as belonging in the moral domain. Their work expands the arenas of ethical concerns to include women's issues. Furthermore, feminist ethicists articulated moral critiques of acts and policies that keep women subordinate, and they envisioned emancipatory moral alternatives (Jaggar, 1991). For example, they used feminist ethical lenses to examine the evils of racism (e.g., Cannon, 1988), problems of violence against women (e.g., Bell, 1993), and social policies regarding immigration, people with disabilities, pornography, and health care (e.g., DiQuinzio & Young, 1997).

Feminist ethicists also focused attention on feminine ethical values, such as the ethic of care. The most well-known work on the ethic of care is by Carol Gilligan (1982), who originally claimed that the ethic of care was a moral orientation that could be identified by examining the experiences of women and girls and the ethical dilemmas they face. She argued that the experiences of inequality and subordination that circumscribe the lives of women and girls also give rise to a moral self grounded in human connections and characterized by concerns with relationships. Emphasizing the differences between men and women, Gilligan and her colleagues (e.g., Miller, 1976; Noddings, 1984; Ruddick, 1980) celebrated that which they saw as the "feminine self" and the feminine values associated with what they characterized as the "feminine voice." This voice, claimed Gilligan (1982), "emerges with great clarity, defining the self and proclaiming its worth on the basis of the ability to care for and protect others" (p. 79). Gilligan's feminine moral voice develops because women are encouraged to define their identity through relationships of intimacy and care (p. 164). In contrast, Gilligan argued, the masculine voice is socialized to be concerned with abstract rules of justice. The male identity, she claimed, is defined by separation (p. 161), and "instead of attachment, individual achievement rivets the male imagination and great ideas or distinctive activity defines the standard of self-assessment and success" (p. 163). Women, she claimed, are more likely to be guided by the ethic of care, whereas men are more likely to be guided in moral thinking by the ethic of justice (Gilligan, 1982; Hoagland, 1991; Noddings, 1984).

Relational feminists, like Gilligan, Noddings, and Miller, have generally advanced three assertions. First, they offered a critique of Kantian moral theory that holds abstract reasoning as the pinnacle of human thought. Relational theorists claim that women's subjective knowing, revealed in discussions about moral issues (Belenky, Clinchy, Goldberger, & Tarule, 1987; Gilligan, 1982) is equally valid. They argue that women's experiences, informed by reflection and emotional responses, are important sources of knowledge. In contrast, Kant (1785/1988) believed that the morally autonomous man is innately capable of using reason alone to apprehend the morally right and wrong. For Kant, moral law is universal and has the same absolute validity as the physical laws (e.g., time and space). Kant (1798/1974) also viewed women as kind and benevolent but less able to reason abstractly than men. He, therefore, concluded that women should be excluded from the realm of full moral responsibility. Relational feminists have accepted that women have a more subjective epistemology but have argued that this gives them a greater ethical sensibility than men. They have claimed that the ethic of care provides a valid, if not superior, guide for discerning what is right and wrong. Although relational feminists did not argue that women are incapable of abstract, principled reasoning, they asserted that their attention to others also provides them access to subjective knowledge that is informed by both rationality and affect. Some feminists have turned to Hume's moral theory (Baier, 1994) to identify the processes of attention and reflection as being critical to the ethical process (Noddings, 1984).

Hume (1817) believed that moral sentiment leads one to choose good and to avoid evil and that moral sentiment is innate and based on feelings rather than reason alone. Because moral sensibility is innate, people have the capacity for compassion, apprehension of the morally good, and care for the welfare of others. According to Hume, if one is to become a good person, one must go beyond the use of one's reason alone and deepen one's feelings for others. Similarly, feminists (e.g., Noddings, 1989) noted that focusing solely on one's reasoning capacity is a fundamentally flawed approach, which can result in evil. For example, one may not question the reasoning of Adolf Hitler or a mass murderer. Instead these individuals are believed to be affectively flawed: They lack the empathy for their victims or a concern for their victims' welfare.

Second, relational feminists have emphasized the value of empathy, nurturance, and caring over, or in addition to, justice, rights, and moral rules. They have argued that qualities associated with women must be as fully valued as those associated with men. Thus, what society calls "woman's passivity" may be thought of as peacefulness. Her maternal work may be associated with the ethic of care or beneficence. Her attention to particularities might be thought of as concern for the welfare of others.

Third, relational feminists have challenged the notions of individualistic moral choice derived from universal Kantian moral imperatives. They have emphasized relationships and connections to others (Scaltsas, 1992).

They have argued against the human ideal of autonomous, independent, and separate individuals and have suggested instead that we develop a new ethical lens that recognizes our interdependence on each other, our connections to others, and our responsibilities for each other (Whitbeck, 1989). In place of the autonomous man as the moral ideal, they have proposed that the mother–child relationship is paradigmatic. As an alternative to a rights-based morality that ensures one's individual rights are guaranteed, relational feminists have offered a relationship-based morality, grounded in one's connections to others (Held, 1987; Whitbeck, 1989).

Subsequent empirical research (Brabeck, 1996) shows that whereas the ethic of care can be identified in individuals' moral responses, gender differences are not found to the degree originally asserted by Gilligan and her colleagues. Indeed, some have argued (e.g., Hare-Mustin & Marecek, 1990) that the "women = care, men = justice" dichotomy is a dangerous stereotype that maintains women as subordinate to men and fails to attend sufficiently to the diversity among women (e.g., Addelson, 1987; Applebaum, 1997; Scaltsas, 1992). These philosophers have argued that the trouble with dividing the moral world between the masculinist individualism of justice and reason and the feminine relational ethics of care and compassion relegates women to the private sphere and men to the public sphere. Furthermore, this division essentializes gender differences, privileging men and disadvantaging women, and offers no legitimate avenue for effecting changes that might result in benefits for all (Applebaum, 1997; Houston, 1989, 1990). In addition, these philosophers have asserted that the ethic of care is an equally valid moral perspective for both women and men and that both the ethic of care and the ethic of justice need to be integrated into a complete moral theory (Houston, 1989).

Instead of pointing to women as the inherent source of the ethic of care, critics of what is often called a "feminine" rather than "feminist" ethical theory have examined the oppressive and sexist context for the virtues associated with women (e.g., Applebaum, 1997; Houston, 1990; Puka, 1989). Philosopher Betty Sichel (1991) distinguished between feminine and feminist ethics with the following:

> "Feminine" at present refers to the search for women's unique voice and most often, the advocacy of an ethic of care that includes nurturance, care, compassion, and networks of communications. "Feminist" refers to those theorists, whether liberal or radical in other orientation, who argue against patriarchal domination, for equal rights, a just and fair distribution of scarce resources, etc. (p. 90)

Although still affirming the intrinsic value of an ethic of care, those who move the feminine ethic to a feminist theory advocate that the oppressive structures that relegate women to private spheres and limit women's access to public life should be changed (Applebaum, 1997). Clearly, individuals and societies need men and women who are caring and just citizens and who are able to create moral communities in which all people are free from the threat of uncaring and unrestrained violence.

Gilligan (1982), and other relational feminists (e.g., Noddings, 1984; Ruddick, 1980), asserted that an examination of the experiences of women reveals an ethic of care that is different from what is revealed by examining men's experiences. However, she saw these gender differences as attributable to the differences in gender socialization, the societal constructions of gender, and one's individual social constructions of reality. In contrast, other feminist ethical theorists who start with women's experiences have concluded that "feminist consciousness," a way of being and seeing the world, is associated more particularly with women and may be an aspect of women's essential nature. These ideas are taken up next.

ATTENTIVENESS AND SUBJECTIVE KNOWLEDGE CAN ILLUMINATE MORAL ISSUES

In placing greater value on women's experiences rather than on pre-ordained categories (e.g., right and wrong, good and evil), feminist ethics places great value on grounded knowledge. Some feminists argue that experiences inform one's ethical understanding through feminist consciousness and subjective knowing.

In 1951, Simone Weil laid the philosophical foundation for a subjectivist moral view that was later developed by feminist philosophers. Weil believed that pure attentiveness or attentive seeking was a form of prayer that could reveal God. Later, Iris Murdoch (1970–1971) developed Weil's ideas and argued that loving regard, patience, and just discernment are the "characteristic and proper mark of the active moral agent" (p. 34). Concerned that women not be limited or suppressed in the role of caring for others, Marilyn Frye (1983) saw attention as active. She distrusted the dualistic division that was characteristic of men writing about women, which equated men with rationality and women with subjectivity. For Frye, attention involves not only perceiving reality but also constructing it. Because one can construct people through one's perceptions of them, proper attentiveness may be understood as a moral and instrumental–agentic act. Consequently, according to Frye, one must be careful about how one is attentive to others and to how one attends to oneself. For Frye, loving attention to others must be accompanied by an equally careful subjective attention to one's self. As Frye (1983) wrote,

> the loving eye is one that pays a certain sort of attention. This attention can require a discipline but not a self-denial. The discipline is one of

self-knowledge, knowledge of the scope and boundary of the self. What is required is that one knows what are one's interests, desires, and loathings, one's projects, hungers, fears, and wishes, and that one knows what is and what is not determined by these. In particular, it is a matter of being able to tell one's own interests from those of others and knowing where one's self leaves off and another begins. (p. 75)

Whereas relational feminists urge feminists to celebrate women's values, relationships, and unique moral perspectives, they do not claim that men cannot attain these virtues; nor do they devalue male virtues and attributes. However, other feminists—often called "radical feminists" (e.g., Daly, 1978, 1984; Marks & de Courtivron, 1981; Raymond, 1986)—view women's attributes, moral sensibilities, and affective relational skills as innately different or arising from biologically based experiences, such as woman's ability to give birth and nurse (Marks & de Courtivron, 1981). They argue that women's values and virtues are unique to women and not available to men. They urge people to build on their understanding of the moral domain by paying attention to the subjectivities of women that arise out of their experiences. However, this proves difficult because women's experiences and subjectivities have been constructed within a patriarchy. How can one know what women's nature, ethics, and epistemologies really are, separate from these constructions? How can a woman save her moral self from the pollution of patriarchy? Radical feminists envision the moral course as women collectively living separate from men and as far away from patriarchy as possible.

From a radical feminist perspective, women may not be able to dismantle patriarchy, but they can save themselves through feminist–womanist ways of being, knowing, and doing that are separate from men and masculine ways (Daly, 1978). Mary Daly exhorted women to free themselves from oppressive socioeconomic, political, and linguistic patriarchy. She created an emancipatory language for resurrecting women from oppression into self-creation, hence liberating them from patriarchy. Radical feminists reject assertions of value neutrality, explaining that behind any claims to neutrality lie the values of the dominant group. Radical feminists denounce patriarchal attempts to name and thereby assert power over and determine the limits and boundaries of women's experiences and knowledge. For example, Daly rejected (1984) equating women with the heart—care and compassion as "mush-headed sentimentality requiring control by The Head" (p. 281). She placed a woman's heart in her own head and urged women to act courageously: "It is only by Taking Heart again, by Courage-ing the Sin of reuniting her passion and intellect, that a woman can Realize her powers. Pyrosophical Crones, wrenching the Heart back into our own semantic context, make Courage the core of [the] Women's Movement" (p. 281).

Radical feminists denounce assertions of "truth" and "the good" because they are irredeemably masculine and, therefore, flawed. In their place, radical feminists assert as normative women's subjective ways of knowing and deconstructing prevailing knowledge claims. They advocate that women forge special relationships with other women and encourage them to form women's groups as a way to protect, preserve, and develop women's unique virtues (Daly, 1984; Raymond, 1986). This is a radical, lesbian, and separatist rewriting of traditional ethics. Radical feminists have argued from Audre Lorde's (1984) provocative assertion that "the master's tools will never dismantle the master's house" (p. 110). If patriarchy is at the root of all oppressions, radical feminists try to save themselves by separating from the flawed patriarchal social systems. As Hoagland (1989) wrote, "we may withdraw from a particular situation when it threatens to dissolve into a relationship of dominance and subordination. And we may withdraw from a system of dominance and subordination in order to engage in moral revolution" (pp. 54–55).

Although recognizing the value of the critique of patriarchy, many feminists (Brabeck & Brown, 1997; Cocks, 1984; Brown, 1994, chap. 4, this volume; Lerman & Porter, 1990) view separatism as counterproductive. They have argued that engagement with oppressive structures is necessary to achieve the feminist social justice agenda. They (Brabeck & Larned, 1996; Weisstein, 1997) have noted that embracing subjectivity as "women's ways of knowing" may in fact be reinforcing stereotypes of women. This is especially the case when people are not simultaneously working toward transforming the institutional and cultural landscape in ways that support and enhance the lives of women. For example, Weisstein (1997) discussed the importance of science in its capacity to overturn existing paradigms, regardless of the interests that may support them. She criticized social constructivism and postmodernism for rejecting objective knowledge and focusing on the subjective as "leading us back into the cave, away from reality and away from an understanding of our world and how to change it" (p. 146). Weisstein agreed that these ideas are indeed

> filtered through our cultural and social categories, the ongoing social context and our social rank, but filters do indeed pass information, and science is one of the intellectual procedures that holds open the possibility of constructing a model of reality that works and predicts and that others can replicate. (p. 149)

Similarly, if the legal system does not recognize the equal rights of women and if attitudes and social standards for acceptable male behavior fail to protect women from male violence, people must engage in work to change these unjust structures and to rid individuals of oppressive practices and the attitudes that support them (Faludi, 1991).

Such engagement for the collective good is consistent with feminist ethics. Furthermore, radical separatist theories, based on ideas about the essential nature of women, may also support an analysis that decontextualizes women and may create a false universalism: the claim that all women share a "common nature," regardless of race, ethnicity, class, or the attributes that influence how their identities are constructed.

FEMINIST CRITIQUES MUST BE ACCOMPANIED BY A CRITIQUE OF ALL DISCRIMINATORY DISTORTIONS

Feminist philosophers have cautioned against focusing only on gender oppression, privileging the experiences of Caucasian heterosexual middle-class women over that of women of Color, lesbians, poor women, or any woman who lives outside the North American and North European dominant contexts (hooks, 1993; Spelman, 1988). Feminist ethicists have argued that treating women as a unitary group may unwittingly endorse a restrictive rather than an emancipatory view of women (Applebaum, 1997; Houston, 1990). For example, claiming that the ethic of care is a virtue for all women may lead some women to believe they must provide care to others, even if they are damaged in the process (Puka, 1989). Some women might falsely believe that even if battered, they are morally obligated to continue to care about the batterer and maintain the relationship (Applebaum, 1997; Houston, 1990).

The Feminist Theory Group (Brabeck & Brown, 1997) located gender at the intersection of other important loci of oppression (e.g., ethnicity, culture, class, age, sexual orientation, ability, linguistic status). However, for most women, gender is not the most salient variable on which they experience interpersonal and sociopolitical oppression. Out of an ethical concern for liberating oppressed people, feminists embrace human diversity as a requirement and foundation for practice. In a similar vein, the Feminist Therapy Institute (1987) asserts that feminist therapists are obligated to value each individual, to work for empowerment as an ethical imperative, and to strive to reduce the effects of sexism, racism, classism, homophobia, ageism, and anti-Semitism on themselves and others (Lerman & Porter, 1990; Smith & Douglas, 1990).

This view is akin to standpoint theory that uses marginalized lives as the starting point from which to frame concepts. Based on the work of such philosophers as Flax (1990), Hartsock (1983), and Jaggar (1991), standpoint theory seeks to understand the distinctive features of women's experiences as they take place in a gender-stratified culture and are interpreted by women. Standpoint theory is interested in subjective, interpretive capacities. It can be traced back to Hegel's (Bell, 1993) reflection on the slave–master relationship. Hegel (1807/1977) realized that the distinct standpoints occupied by slave and master produce radically different understandings of both their relationship and the world. Hegel contended that the viewpoints of oppressed and dominant groups are not merely distinct but qualitatively unequal. Those in positions of power have substantial interest in preserving their hierarchical place. They invest considerable effort in making their standpoint the dominant reality. Feminist standpoint theory (Collins, 1986) extends this to ask the following: How do various standpoints arise out of conditions surrounding them, and how are these construed within subjective consciousness? According to Wood (1992), standpoint theory is capable of meeting the challenge of examining differences among women without falling into essentialism. By grounding claims to women's virtues in women's lives and the unique particularities of each woman's experiences, standpoint theory can account for differences among women as well as between men and women. Thus, nothing in the logic of standpoint theory precludes analysis of the intersections among conditions that structure race, class, and gender relations in any given culture (Wood, 1992).

Narrative is the metaphor that most frequently captures the idea that individual lives must be understood from their standpoint and within their context. Any individual's reality is located at the intersection of time and place and forms an ongoing narrative. Feminist ethics recognize that any moral obligation to act arises out of a person's or a community's story and will continue into that person's or community's future. The past, present, and future are affected complexly by individuals and their social, psychological, relational, and political contexts. For feminist ethicists, moral adequacy depends on paying loving attention to the particularities of individuals' and a community's narratives while examining these particularities in light of their unique sociocultural contexts. When one attends lovingly to others by entering into their perspectives and examining the contexts of their lives, one is engaging in feminist ethics. Such attention raises questions about the ways in which people's lives are affected by bigotry, prejudice, and other distortions. The goal of feminist ethics is not simply to show that women are an oppressed group but rather to rid the world of oppressions, including those to which women are subjected. Because women are oppressed, they are in a good position for engaging in analysis of how power is used to oppress individuals and groups. We next address the ethical obligation of feminists to engage in this analysis.

FEMINIST ETHICS ENGAGE IN ANALYSIS OF THE CONTEXT AND OF THE POWER DYNAMICS INHERENT IN THAT CONTEXT

When the process of knowing is informed by care, one attends to the particular circumstances of individuals and groups, not only to individual rights and privileges. Simultaneously rational and affective, caring knowing both perceives and constructs realities. Because loving attention reveals the power hierarchies inherent in each particular situation, feminist ethics require practitioners to critique the ways in which one's own positions in the hierarchy of power within any context affects one's perceptions and moral sensitivities. This self-critique must occur in all ethical psychological practices. For example, in conducting ethical research, an ethical feminist would raise questions regarding power relationships that might influence the research process. Does the researcher or participant determine what questions to ask and what questions to answer? Should the author of the research be the university-based person, or are others who are participants the major contributors? Whose needs are served by the research? Is tenure, money, reputation, or prestige the motivation behind the work? Ethical feminist researchers must engage in such an analysis of the power relationships in the work to develop new knowledge.

As Barbara Applebaum (1997) noted, it is ethically imperative to make dominant people aware of how their dominance subordinates others. Postmodernism offers feminists important tools for analyzing power and a method for deconstructing how "woman" has been constructed within patriarchal society. Postmodernism challenges the assertion of absolute objective reality, uncovers power inequities in definitions of reality, and insists on viewing the critical analysis of all knowledge as historically and politically situated. Such critiques of the injustices of the hegemonic "canon" of beliefs, including beliefs about morality and ethics, are in accord with feminist ethics. Most feminist ethicists assert that because ethical principles are situated contextually, all ethical acts must be understood within sociopolitical contexts. Most agree with postmodernists that certainty about truth is not attainable and assume that alternative ways of knowing and constructing reality (e.g., subjectivity) always exist. Both feminists and postmodernists interrogate ways of knowing and the inherent power hierarchies that affect what is accepted as "knowledge."

Postmodernism, nevertheless, poses some dilemmas for the feminist ethicist. If one believes one's realities to be only constructions arising out of specific contexts, it follows that no universal experience may be claimed. Within this epistemological stance, neither universal truth nor moral absolutes exist. How then are we to develop a moral argument against heinous acts, such as torture, female genital mutilation, and battering? How are we to decide on the ethical action required of an ethical feminist practitioner? Under the radical relativism of postmodernism, how do we even justify the question of what the feminist researcher (or feminist therapist, teacher, activist, administrator) ought to do? Without a conscious ideological and epistemological position, we may get lost easily in a multiplicity of stories— what postmodernists call "texts."

Although feminists agree that no one text should be regarded as absolutely more "true" or "ethical" than the next, feminists (e.g., Harding & Hintikka, 1983) have pointed out that postmodernism may lead to radical relativism. Postmodernism rejects the grand narrative, which provides a theoretical explanation for forces such as patriarchy and sexism. Ultimately, postmodernism leaves one with a philosophy of negation (Alcoff, 1989): One can say what is not (woman, truth, virtue) but not what is (e.g., women, truths, virtues). The radical relativism of postmodernism is a dangerous framework for the feminist enterprise, not because it legitimizes oppression but because it helps maintain it. As Hawkesworth (1989) noted, "in a world of radical inequality, relativistic resignation supports the status quo" (p. 351). For feminists committed to making the world more just and those working to identify ethical responses to complex situations, the status quo is not an option. We assert that an analysis of gender oppression can illuminate oppression and dominance over other groups; once revealed, feminist practitioners have a responsibility to act (Applebaum, 1997).

FEMINIST ETHICS REQUIRE ACTION DIRECTED AT ACHIEVING SOCIAL JUSTICE

When an ethical person discerns a wrong against an individual or a group, he or she is obligated to act. Feminist ethics is concerned not only with what ought to be but also with how to bring what *is* more in line with what *ought to be* (Bell, 1993). As Prilleltensky (1997) put it, "discourse without action is dangerous because it creates the impression that progress is taking place when in fact only the words have changed" (p. 530). Similarly, Jaggar (1991) argued that any feminist approach to ethics must include action to achieve equity for women within existing political, social, and economic structures. When such structures are not amenable to equity, they must be altered to be made more just.

As a prerequisite of ethical action, feminist virtue ethicists (e.g., Kitchener, 1999; Meara, Schmidt, & Day, 1996) have argued that moral character or virtue is necessary. Virtue ethicists have suggested that when moral virtues of autonomy, nonmaleficence, beneficence, justice, and fidelity inform the process of decision making, more sensitive ethical conduct results. Virtue ethics intersect with both principle ethics and feminist consciousness to form the characteristics of a virtuous agent of change. Although at first glance, this position appears highly individualistic, it is nevertheless paradoxically grounded in connections to others. In other words, feminist virtue ethicists seek to root individual virtues in a community's wisdom and moral sense (Meara & Day, chap. 12, this volume; Meara et al., 1996).

Nevertheless, other feminist ethicists (e.g., Jakobsen, 1998) have argued that virtue ethics represents a position that is too highly individualistic. They have pointed out that liberal ideals of virtue ethics perpetuate the status quo of a meritocracy in which men and Caucasian women have the most advantage and access to society's resources and rewards (Eisenstein, 1981). Liberals have been criticized for failing to adequately analyze the patriarchal structure of capitalism and its inherent economic and social injustices to women and all people of Color and social classes (e.g., Jaggar, 1991). Whereas liberal philosophies are profoundly affected by capitalism, racism, and patriarchy, their focus remains on the promotion of self-determination and rugged individualism (Prilleltensky, 1997). It is not surprising then that liberalism inevitably fails to deliver on its promise of equal access, equal opportunities, and equal rights for women and other people of Color. As some feminists claim, individual moral action is not sufficient to address structural wrongs (Jakobsen, 1998; Lykes et al., 1993), even when one embraces feminist virtues and principles (Tong, 1993). For example, caring has been claimed by some feminists as an important virtue traditionally associated with womanhood. Yet how can we discern whether women's seemingly inherent "superior ability to care" has to do with gender (sex) or with their subordinate status? There is a political pitfall in the claim to women's superior caring: If the relationship between women and caring is glorified, then the relationship between women and oppression may be supported and justified (Puka, 1989). Some feminists (e.g., Bell, 1993; Jakobsen, 1998) maintain that despite the important contributions made by Gilligan, Noddings, and virtue ethicists, their theories remain fundamentally individualistic and apolitical because they fail to look beyond the personal relationships within families to the institutions and structures that create them.

Linda Bell (1993) invited readers to expand their feminist awareness of the political and take a revolutionary stance against the status quo. She asked that people realize that *feminine* is a construction within a system where women are dominated by men, "so no ethic, especially no ethic of nurturance, can be realized without a supporting politic change" (Kuykendall, as cited in Bell, 1993, p. 38). One's personal experiences are ultimately a road to political change (hence the often-quoted "the personal is political"). One ought to question one's limiting individual solutions and to hold each other accountable to, and for, a larger moral community. As feminists, we ought to place more importance on the shared process of discovery, expression, interpretation, and adjustment between people and seek out solutions that affect entire communities rather than only individuals and occur in collaborations rather than competitions (Lykes et al., 1993).

Bell (1993) noted the paradox inherent in working toward political change. Everyone is embedded in one's social context; as one critiques and strives to change the status quo, one must confront the same system that gives one privileges. Changing that system will change people. Thus, according to Bell (1993), it is not surprising that this is the juncture where many people walk away from the challenge of change and avoid confronting institutional and structural moral considerations. Yet, she urged, without such an analysis and accompanying agendas for change, the larger systems of repression will remain intact.

Similarly, Elshtain (1991) claimed that feminist ethics must move beyond individual moral action to where ethics intersect with political action:

> All feminisms share an explicit political urge—to reform or to remake the world in line with a deeply held conviction that women have been the victims of faulty and exploitative social institutions. One cannot separate feminist politics from ethics; they are entangled at each and every point, from the assumptions that undergird alternative feminist theories to the explicit projects that feminists endorse. This holds whether one is addressing radical, [relational,] liberal, Marxist or social-ist, or what is now called ecofeminism. (p. 128)

Such a change suggests that feminist ethics may entail as much political action as ethical action. However, this need not be interpreted negatively. Tong (1993) noted that in classical times, politics and ethics were joined. For Plato, the virtues of the individual and those of the city were isomorphic; for Aristotle, ethics and politics together led to the human good. As Tong (1993) wrote,

> to say that feminist approaches to ethics are "political" in the classical sense of the term is to say . . . that feminists pay attention to issues of power because in so doing they liberate themselves and others. Politics is indispensable to ethics in the sense that only an empowered person has the capacity to self-reflectively make this a better world. (p. 183)

Feminist ethics must be involved in creating the structural and cultural conditions for self-determination. Like any ethical theory, feminist ethics ought to move people from "thinking the good" to "doing the good" to enhance the human condition and create a more just and caring world.

The work of feminist ethicists and feminist theorists provides a foundation for reading the chapters that follow in this volume. The authors in the chapters attempt to apply feminist ethical theory and analysis to everyday problems that feminist psychologists face. In so doing, they demonstrate the application of the ideas described in this chapter.

REFERENCES

Addelson, K. P. (1987). Moral passages. In E. F. Kittay & D. T. Meyers (Eds.), *Women and moral theory* (pp. 87–110). Totowa, NJ: Rowman & Littlefield.

Alcoff, L. (1989). Cultural feminism versus post-structuralism: The identity crisis in feminist theory. In M. R. Malson, J. F. O'Barr, S. Westphal-Wihl, & M. Wyer (Eds.), *Feminist theory in practice and process* (pp. 295–326). Chicago: University of Chicago Press.

American Psychological Association. (1992). Ethical principles of psychologists and code of conduct. *American Psychologist, 47*, 1597–1611.

Andolsen, B. H., Gudorf, C. E., & Pellauer, M. D. (1985). *Women's consciousness, women's conscience: A reader in feminist ethics*. Minneapolis, MN: Winston Press.

Applebaum, B. (1997). Good liberal intentions are not enough! Racism, intentions and moral responsibility. *Journal of Moral Education, 26*(4), 409–421.

Baier, A. (1994). *Moral prejudices: Essays on ethics*. Cambridge, MA: Harvard University Press.

Belenky, M. F., Clinchy, B. M., Goldberger, N. R., & Tarule, J. M. (1987). *Women's ways of knowing: The development of self, voice, and mind*. New York: Basic Books.

Bell, L. (1993). *Rethinking ethics in the midst of violence: A feminist approach to freedom*. Lanham, MD: Rowman & Littlefield.

Brabeck, M. (1996). The moral self, values and circles of belonging. In K. F. Wyche & F. J. Crosby (Eds.), *Women's ethnicities: Journeys through psychology* (pp. 145–165). Boulder, CO: Westview Press.

Brabeck, M., & Brown, L. (With Christian, L., Espin, O., Hare-Mustin, R., Kaplan, A., Kaschak, E., Miller, D., Phillips, E., Ferns, T., & Van Ormer, A.). (1997). Feminist theory and psychological practice. In J. Worell & N. Johnson (Eds.), *Shaping the future of feminist psychology: Education, research, and practice* (pp. 15–35). Washington, DC: American Psychological Association.

Brabeck, M. M., & Larned, A. G. (1996). What we do not know about women's ways of knowing. In M. R. Walsh (Ed.), *Women, men and gender: Ongoing debates* (pp. 261–269). New Haven, CT: Yale University Press.

Brown, L. (1994). *Subversive dialogues: Theory in feminist therapy*. New York: Basic Books.

Cannon, K. G. (1988). *Katie's canon: Womanism and the soul of the Black community*. New York: Continuum.

Card, C. (1991). *Feminist ethics*. Lawrence: University Press of Kansas.

Cocks, J. (1984). Wordless emotions: Some critical reflections on radical feminism. *Politics and Society, 13*(1), 27–58

Cole, E. B., & Coultrap-McQuin, S. (Eds.). (1992). *Explorations in feminist ethics: Theory and practice*. Bloomington: Indiana University Press.

Collins, P. H. (1986). Learning from the outsider within. *Social Problems, 33*, 514–532.

Daly, M. (1978). *Gyn/ecology: The metaethics of radical feminism*. Boston: Beacon Press.

Daly, M. (1984). *Pure lust: Elemental feminist philosophy*. Boston: Beacon Press.

DiQuinzio, P., & Young, I. M. (1997). *Feminist ethics and social policy*. Bloomington: Indiana University Press.

Eisenstein, H. (1981). *Contemporary feminist thought*. Boston: G. K. Hall.

Elshtain, J. B. (1991). Ethics in the Women's Movement. *Annals of the American Academy, 515*, 126–139.

Enns, C. Z. (1993). Twenty years of feminist counseling: From naming biases to implementing multifaceted practice. *The Counseling Psychologist, 21*, 3–87.

Faludi, S. (1991). *Backlash: The undeclared war against American women*. New York: Crown.

Feminist Therapy Institute. (1987). *Feminist Therapy Institute ethical code*. Denver, CO: Author.

Flax, J. (1990). *Thinking fragments: Psychoanalysis, feminism and postmodernism in the contemporary West*. Berkeley: University of California Press.

Frye, M. (1983). *The politics of reality: Essays in feminist theory*. Trumansburg, NY: Crossing Press.

Gilligan, C. (1982). *In a different voice: Psychological theory and women's development*. Cambridge, MA: Harvard University Press.

Harding, S., & Hintikka, M. B. (Eds.). (1983). *Discovering reality: Feminist perspectives on epistemology, metaphysics, methodology and philosophy of science*. Boston: D. Reidel.

Hare-Mustin, R. T., & Marecek, J. (Eds.). (1990). *Making a difference: Psychology and the construction of gender*. New Haven, CT: Yale University Press.

Hartsock, N. (1983). The feminist standpoint: Developing the ground for a specifically feminist historical materialism. In S. Harding & M. B. Hintikka (Eds.), *Discovering reality: Feminist perspectives on epistemology, metaphysics, methodology and philosophy of science* (pp. 283–310). Boston: D. Reidel.

Hawkesworth, M. (1989). Knowers, knowing, known: Feminist theory and the claims of truth. In M. Malson, J. F. O'Barr, S. Westphal-Wihl, & M. Wyer (Eds.), *Feminist theory in practice and process* (pp. 327–352). Chicago: University of Chicago Press.

Hegel, G. W. F. (1977). *Phenomenology of spirit* (A. V. Miller, Trans.). New York: Oxford University Press. (Original work published 1807)

Held, V. (1987). Feminism and moral theory. In E. F. Kittay & D. T. Meyers (Eds.), *Women and moral theory* (pp. 111–128). Totowa, NY: Rowman & Littlefield.

Hoagland, S. L. (1989). *Lesbian ethics*. Palo Alto, CA: Institute of Lesbian Studies.

Hoagland, S. L. (1991). Some thoughts about 'caring.' In C. Card (Ed.), *Feminist ethics* (pp. 146–264). Lawrence: University Press of Kansas.

hooks, b. (1993). Black women: Shaping feminist theory. In M. Pearsall (Ed.), *Women and values: Readings in recent feminist philosophy* (pp. 165–174). Belmont, CA: Wadsworth.

Houston, B. (1989). Prolegomena to future caring. In M. M. Brabeck (Ed.), *Who cares? Theory, research and educational implications of the ethic of care* (pp. 84–100). New York: Praeger.

Houston, B. (1990). Caring and exploitation. *Hypatia, 5*(1), 115–120.

Hume, D. (1817). *A treatise of human nature.* London: Thomas & Joseph Allman.

Jaggar, A. M. (1991). Feminist ethics: Projects, problems, prospects. In C. Card (Ed.), *Feminist ethics* (pp. 78–106). Lawrence: University Press of Kansas.

Jakobsen, J. R. (1998). *Working alliances and the politics of difference: Diversity and feminist ethics.* Bloomington: Indiana University Press.

Kant, I. (1974). *Anthropology from a pragmatic point of view* (M. J. Gregor, Trans.). The Hague, the Netherlands: Martinus Nijhoff. (Original work published 1798)

Kant, I. (1988). *Fundamental principles of the metaphysics of morals* (T. K. Abbot, Trans.). Buffalo, NY: Prometheus Books. (Original work published 1785)

Kitchener, K. S. (1999). *The foundations of ethical practice, research and teaching in psychology.* Mahwah, NJ: Erlbaum.

Lerman, H., & Porter, N. (Eds.). (1990). *Feminist ethics in psychotherapy.* New York: Springer.

Lorde, A. (1984). *Sister outsider.* New York: Crossing Press.

Lykes, M. B., Brabeck, M. M., Ferns, T., & Radan, A. (1993). Human rights and mental health among Latin American women in situations of state sponsored violence: Bibliographic resources. *Psychology of Women Quarterly, 17,* 525–544.

Marks, E., & de Courtivron, I. (Eds.). (1981). *New French feminisms.* New York: Schocken Books.

Meara, N. M., Schmidt, L. D., & Day, J. D. (1996). Principles and virtues: A foundation for ethical decisions, policies, and character. *The Counseling Psychologist, 24,* 4–77.

Miller, J. B. (1976). *Toward a new psychology of women.* Boston: Beacon Press.

Murdoch, I. (1970–1971). *The sovereignty of good.* New York: Schocken Books.

Noddings, N. (1984). *Caring: A feminine approach to ethics and moral education.* Berkeley: University of California Press.

Noddings, N. (1989). *Women and evil.* Berkeley: University of California Press.

Prilleltensky, I. (1997). Values, assumptions, and practices: Assessing the moral implications of psychological discourse and action. *American Psychologist, 52,* 517–535.

Puka, B. (1989). The liberation of caring: A different voice for Gilligan's "different voice." In M. M. Brabeck (Ed.), *Who cares? Theory, research and educational implications of the ethic of care* (pp. 19–44). New York: Praeger.

Raymond, J. (1986). *A passion for friends*. Boston: Beacon Press.

Ruddick, S. (1980). Maternal thinking. *Feminist Studies, 1*, 342–367.

Scaltsas, P. W. (1992). Do feminist ethics counter feminist aims? In E. B. Cole & S. Coultrap-McQuin (Eds.), *Explorations in feminist ethics: Theory and practice* (pp. 15–26). Bloomington: Indiana University Press.

Shogan, D. (1988). *Care and moral motivation*. Toronto, Ontario, Canada: OISE Press.

Sichel, B. A. (1991). Different strains and strands: Feminist contributions to ethical theory. *Newsletter on Feminism, 90*(2), 90.

Smith, A. J., & Douglas, M. A. (1990). Empowerment as an ethical imperative. In H. Lerman & N. Porter (Eds.), *Feminist ethics in psychotherapy* (pp. 43–50). New York: Springer.

Spelman, E. (1988). *Inessential woman: Problems of exclusion in feminist thought*. Boston: Beacon Press.

Tong, R. (1989). *Feminist thought: A comprehensive introduction*. Boulder, CO: Westview Press.

Tong, R. (1993). *Feminine and feminist ethics*. Belmont, CA: Wadsworth.

Weil, S. (1951). *Waiting for God* (E. Craufurd, Trans.). New York: Putnam.

Weisstein, N. (1997). Power, resistance and science. *New Politics, 6*(2), 145–151.

Whitbeck, C. (1989). A different reality: Feminist ontology. In A. Garry & M. Pearsall (Eds.), *Women, knowledge and reality: Explorations in feminist philosophy*. (pp. 51–76). Boston: Unwin Hyman.

Wood, J. T. (1992). Gender and moral voice: Moving from woman's nature to standpoint epistemology. *Women's Studies in Communication, 15*, 1–24.

2

RECONCEPTUALIZING RESPONSIBILITIES TO STUDENTS: A FEMINIST PERSPECTIVE

KAREN STROHM KITCHENER

What does it mean for feminists to be ethical with their students? What is an ethical faculty–student relationship from a feminist perspective? To answer these questions, one must identify the assumptions at the core of feminist ethics. Reflecting on a conference on feminist ethics, Allison Jaggar (1991) found a general lack of consensus about its nature. She did, however, identify some themes that seemed to be consistent in the works of feminists, for example, attention to contemporary ethical issues, criticism of the limits of traditional ethical theories, and a common assumption that the subordination of women is morally wrong and the moral experience of women is worthy of respect. Since then, other voices particularly in psychology have identified additional themes that play a central role in feminist ethical concerns. Others have raised the issue of power, its uses and misuses, arguing that power is always an ethical issue (Brabeck & Brown, 1997; Brown, 1990). Hannah Lerman and Natalie Porter (1990) added that feminist ethics involves committed social action that moves beyond help for the individual;

An earlier version of this chapter was presented in August 1996 at the 104th Annual Convention of the American Psychological Association in Toronto, Ontario, Canada.

some (Brabeck & Brown, 1997) have emphasized the concern with oppression and embracing human diversity. Jaggar concluded that any relativistic stance toward ethics, in other words, any ethical stance built on the assumption that ethical truths are totally dependent on the individuals and groups that hold them, that condones moral subordination, devaluation, or both of women and their experience, is incompatible with feminism. The view that feminism embraces diversity yet rejects a radical relativism that does not allow judgment between conflicting moral claims has been reiterated by the feminist theory of the feminist practice group (Brabeck & Brown, 1997), noting that it is one of the difficult paradoxes of feminist ethics.

This chapter begins with similar assumptions: Feminists can validate the experience of women, embrace diversity, value the connections between themselves and others, and consider the context in which moral decisions and actions take place. Yet feminists can condemn actions or policies that harm or demean students, judge faculty whose relationships with students are marked with dishonesty, and assert that faculty members have an ethical responsibility to engage students in ways that will empower them and help them develop. Although discussions of sexual relationships between faculty members and students have received some attention in the literature, little has been written on the day-to-day ethical issues that arise between feminist faculty members and students. Those everyday relationships are the focus of this chapter.

Feminist psychology educators are faced with a variety of ethical tensions in their work with students. For example, there is the tension between not abdicating power and wanting to empower students (Richardson, 1982) and between the responsibility to facilitate the development of students and to protect the public from incompetent psychologists. There are pitfalls on both sides of these issues. For example, one way to facilitate the development of students is through a mentoring relationship. Those relationships themselves have an inherent tension. They place students and faculty members in overlapping roles, for example, as a research assistant–employee as well as a student who is graded in their classes. Consequently, there are opportunities for misunderstanding and exploitation (Kitchener, 1988). At the same time, however, they may provide enriching learning experiences and professional development opportunities that might not be open to students, particularly women students, in other circumstances. Similarly, abdicating or denying a faculty member's power in the classroom is tantamount to lying to students and denying their perceptions of the real authority that society and a faculty member's place in the academic institution gives them (Lerman & Rigby, 1990). However, by failing to empower students, feminist faculty members may fail to fulfill one of their more important ethical obligations.

In addition, the responsibility to protect the public arises, particularly, in applied areas like clinical, counseling, and school psychology because the graduates of these programs will have career options that involve serving the public. Because as feminists we embrace human diversity and are committed to developing models that acknowledge diverse realities (Brabeck & Brown, 1997), we must be concerned that graduate programs neither condone nor graduate students who exploit women or are insensitive to the racial, ethnic, and other differences that exist both between and among men and women. As a result, we have an ethical obligation not to graduate students whom we know are inept or lack ethical sensitivity and are likely to harm the consumers they have sworn to help (Kitchener, 1992).

Take the following case as an example of the conflict between the responsibility to help students develop and to protect the public from psychologists who are unethical.

> Over several years, a professor had given a similar assignment to students in one of her graduate seminars. It involved designing a research study for a particularly difficult issue that the class had been studying. When the papers were turned in, she noticed that one was similar to a paper she received last year. Fortunately, she had requested a copy of the earlier paper to keep as an example of outstanding work. She confronted Marion, the student who turned in the paper, with the possibility that she had cheated. Marion indicated that recently there had been a death in her family, and she had been having difficulty concentrating. As a result, she read a former student's paper to start thinking about the task. She claimed she had designed the study herself, however, and did not think the paper she read had influenced her very much. When the faculty member pointed out the similarities between the papers, Marion seemed genuinely surprised at the amount of overlap. The faculty member was perplexed because she had been impressed by Marion's integrity. She was one of the best students in her cohort, and plagiarizing another's work seemed out of character for her.

In cases like these or when balancing the overlapping roles that mentoring sometimes involves, questions arise about how feminists should ethically respond. Should they act on a sense of compassion or care for the student? Should their primary responsibility be to protect the public from a potentially dishonest professional? How should they take into consideration the context that surrounded the student's actions?

ETHICAL PRINCIPLES: A FEMINIST PERSPECTIVE

Elsewhere, I suggested that five ethical principles, beneficence (do good), nonmaleficence (do no harm), respect for autonomy, justice, and fidelity, can be used to help psychologists think through and make decisions about ethical problems, such as the one described above (Kitchener, 1984, 1992). However, some feminists have criticized a principled approach to ethics. For example, Sarah Hoagland (1991) and Nel Noddings (1984) argued that principles provide little help when considering a particular situation. As Hoagland (1991) succinctly put it, "principles don't tell us when to apply them, and in the long run, they work only when we really don't need them" (p. 248). Similarly, Marcia Hill, Kristen Glaser, and Judy Harden (1995) suggested that the meaning of the principles is unclear and is shaped by a person's place in the social culture. As an example, they pointed to the effects that power and culture may have on how principles are defined. I would agree with both of these criticisms; yet as Hoagland (1991) pointed out in a discussion of Nodding's work, "this does not mean, however, that we reject moral principles altogether. It is just that we regard them as guidelines, not the ultimate arbiters of behavior" (p. 248).

In other words, principles can provide guidance, even when they are difficult to define; I believe they implicitly underlie many of the ethical decisions feminists make and the beliefs they hold. Furthermore, principles can help psychologists, feminists or not, move beyond thinking that if they do not break the American Psychological Association's (APA) Ethical Principles of Psychologists and Code of Conduct (1992), they have acted in an ethical way. Thus, in the following pages, I illustrate how the principles noted above underlie many feminist ethical assumptions, particularly as relationships with students are considered, and how a feminist ethical stance provides a unique understanding of them. Then I suggest that principles are insufficient guides for ethical action and that issues of ethical character are central to a feminist ethical stance with students and others. Good ethical character allows for nonrule-bound responses to the particulars of a situation.

Beneficence, the responsibility to help others, and nonmaleficence, the responsibility to refrain from harming them, are two of the most straightforward ethical requirements of faculty (Kitchener, 1992). As Hill et al. (1995) pointed out, however, defining what it means to benefit and harm students is difficult and must be influenced by the characteristics of the situation and the people involved. Brabeck and Brown (1997) posited that feminists must be sensitive to the complex and multidetermined causes of distress. Thus, culture and context are critical in defining what constitutes either harm or help in a particular situation. In fact, part of what a feminist perspective adds to the understanding of these principles is an awareness of the role that culture and power play in providing definitions of ethical terms. For example, what constitutes harm to a highly acculturated, middle-class, Latina student may be quite different from what constitutes harm to an European American woman student from an impoverished background.

The theme of empowering others is another one that runs through many feminist writings, particularly in psychology (Brown, 1990; Lerman & Rigby, 1990; Smith & Douglas, 1990). For example, Adrienne Smith and Mary Ann Douglas argued that empowerment is an ethical imperative in feminist therapy. They distinguished between "power over" others and the "power within." Power over, they suggested, is inherent in the therapeutic relationship; thus, feminists must learn to deal with power in a way that is respectful and helpful rather than harmful. By contrast, power within is a "feeling of strength and control centered in an individual" (Smith & Douglas, 1990, p. 43). If these observations are translated into an educational setting, feminist faculty members need to similarly learn how to use their power over students in a way that is beneficial and particularly in a way that helps students develop the power within. In fact, feminists know that not harming others involves not disempowering them. Disempowerment is not the only harm about which feminist faculty members should be concerned, however; any activity that subordinates or devalues women and their experience is ethically unacceptable.

Benefiting students from a feminist perspective involves authorizing their experience of the world and recognizing how faculty members' power affects them (Brabeck & Brown, 1997). In other words, being beneficent with Marion would include not engaging in activities that would cause her harm and asking what led her to feel so little power that she could not approach her instructor for help. It would also mean asking whether the instructor or others in her past used power over her in some kind of coercive way, so that she felt powerless to approach anyone except another (equally powerless) student. Women of all cultures and social backgrounds have experienced having their work ignored, devalued, and sometimes stolen. Because of this experience, honestly reporting and valuing others' work is a way of empowering them. Valuing students' work and teaching students, like Marion, to value the work of others can have such an effect.

Another part of the moral obligation to "do good" is the responsibility to transform society. Again, the theme that runs through the writings of many feminist ethicists is the necessity of addressing oppression, not just with individuals but with social support systems, political units, governments, and so on (Brabeck & Brown, 1997; Feminist Therapy Institute, 1990; Hoagland, 1991; Jaggar, 1991; Smith & Douglas, 1990). Thus, feminist theories of psychological practice focus on the moral obligation to be involved in social and political transformation (Brabeck & Brown, 1997). Additionally, the Feminist Therapy Institute (1990) Code of Ethics requires that "a feminist therapist seek multiple avenues for impacting change, including public education and advocacy within professional organizations, lobbying for legislative action, and other appropriate activities" (p. 40). With students, feminists need to identify ways that the institutional system devalues women or others and establish ways to change them (McIntyre, chap. 3; Worell & Oakley, chap. 8, this volume). In Marion's case, it may lead the faculty member to try to change her own way of interacting with students and to intervene with individuals, departments, or the institution to provide students with support, so that they do not end up feeling powerless. For example, women faculty at my institution have helped to establish a women's undergraduate and graduate student caucus to address these kinds of problems. It may also lead faculty to advocate for changes in the university's policy regarding plagiarism and to clarify that policy with each incoming cohort of students.

A third principle is fairness or justice. Issues of fairness or justice include assuring fair treatment of others and a fair distribution of goods and services. When justice is visually represented, it is usually as a woman blindfolded with scales, implying that justice is impartial to the irrelevant characteristics of the person being judged. The difficulty, of course, is in deciding which are ethically relevant and which are ethically irrelevant characteristics. Many feminists insist, however, that context and the diversity of human experience must be considered when defining them (Brabeck & Brown, 1997; Brabeck & Ting, chap. 1, this volume).

Although feminist writers have sometimes maligned justice as a singular ethical principle, fair treatment of women is at the core of feminist beliefs. In essence, other things being equal, gender ought not to be a consideration in making hiring decisions, providing access for services or education, determining pay scales, having a voice in social policy questions, and so on. When "other things" are not equal, as they often are not for women and men and women of Color, then gender or ethnicity may be considered relevant characteristics. This is the basis, for example, of arguments for affirmative action. Similarly, other things being equal, someone in a wheelchair has an equal need for education, as does someone who is not. Thus, justice demands providing equal access to educational institutions, even though doing so may involve special accommodations like wheelchair ramps. In other words, in a system that has been oppressive, justice may require special treatment of those who have been oppressed.

Additionally, feminism adds that meeting the moral minimum in providing for a fair distribution of psychological services is not enough in light of the oppression of women and others. As an example, the Feminist Therapy Institute (1990) Code of Ethics requires that feminist therapists "increase their accessibility to and for a wide range of clients from her own and other identified groups through the delivery of services" (p. 39).

Issues of justice enter educational settings in a variety of ways from grading and evaluation procedures, as in Marion's case, to the treatment of subject matter. Feminist theory suggests that faculty can never be totally unbiased in their evaluation and presentation of subject matter. However, justice from a feminist perspective demands that feminist faculty must honestly examine how their biases affect their work and share that information with their students; this includes a feminist bias. In Marion's case, these issues lead to raising such questions as the following: To what extent is her cultural and educational background relevant or irrelevant to her actions? Are the faculty member's biases affecting her response to Marion? From a feminist perspective, the definition of fair treatment for Marion should not involve a predetermined application of a university or departmental policy on plagiarism without considering her history in the department and her current situation.

Respect for autonomy or respect for the rights of people to make decisions about their own lives as long as their decisions do not infringe on similar rights of others is a fourth principle. Feminists have long recognized that self-determination and autonomy are central ingredients in a moral world (Lerman & Porter, 1990). One tenet of the feminist theory of practice, for example, affirms the experience of those who are oppressed and the importance of how they experience the world (Brabeck & Brown, 1997; Brabeck & Ting, chap. 1, this volume).

Acting autonomously means being able to act intentionally with the understanding of a situation and without controlling influences that unduly pressure the person to make particular decisions (Beauchamp & Childress, 1994). In teaching, one way to respect autonomy is to provide students with adequate information to make reasonable decisions about their own lives whether as professionals or students. For example, the instructor of the class might have asked Marion whether she knew that when she used the other student's paper to "start her thinking" that she needed to acknowledge the other student's ideas if they provided her with substantial insight and that not to do so would be plagiarism.

A substantial contribution that feminism makes to the understanding of autonomy is the observation that oppression in and of itself is a controlling influence that limits choice and voice. Feminist faculty may have to nurture feelings of autonomy in students who have felt powerless as decision makers and be sensitive to undue influences, which may interfere with a student's ability to make choices and act on them. In particular, faculty must be careful that their position in the university's power structure does not undermine students' growing authority and voice (Brabeck & Brown, 1997). This implies that the instructor should talk with Marion and evaluate the extent to which her decisions were free from controlling influences.

The fifth principle, fidelity, is also central to a feminist ethical stance because it includes issues such as faithfulness, honesty, and promise keeping. Lying and dishonesty contribute to the disempowerment of women because they distort reality and imply that a woman's perception of the situation is in error rather than the lie itself (Smith & Douglas, 1990). Other issues of honesty are critical for educational settings. Plagiarism, for example, is a form of dishonesty. By not accurately reporting her sources, Marion participated in an activity that devalued a peer's work, violating the principle of beneficence, and was dishonest, violating the principle of fidelity.

Based on the principles of beneficence and fidelity, Marion's actions could be seen as wrong. Additionally, they could be seen as unjust because they would have denied the fair benefits of credit to the original author. However, the faculty member must decide how to weigh the fact that Marion's decision may not have been fully autonomous because her thinking may have been clouded by her grief. The dilemma arises when feminist faculty must consider how to balance these issues and respond to the situation after making a judgment. At one extreme, Marion could be expelled from the university on the basis of her dishonesty and out of a concern that she may act in a similar way in the future when she is under stress. Some faculty may feel pulled toward this conclusion when students plagiarize because universities have codes of conduct that may require specific actions in these kinds of cases. They might argue on the basis of justice that because Marion is a student, she ought to be treated like any other student. At the other extreme, some feminists might want to excuse her actions, arguing that they resulted from her particular situation in the moment and feminist ethics emphasizes attending to the context of the decision (Brabeck & Brown, 1997; Hill et al., 1995). Neither extreme seems ethically defensible from a feminist perspective. If the instructor takes the first position, she risks sacrificing the person for the principle and perpetrating an unnecessary harm. If she takes the second position, she risks glossing over behavior that might be problematic for Marion and her clients in the future. She would also risk treating the student whose ideas were "borrowed" unjustly and reinforcing unethical behavior.

As noted, justice demands that Marion be treated like similar students insofar as the particular characteristics she brought to the situation were ethically irrelevant to her actions. However, feminists take the position that context must be considered. How might these positions be balanced? To develop an answer, faculty must ask other ethically relevant questions: To what extent did Marion feel powerless to access other alternatives, and to what extent did her own disorientation lead her to misperceive the situation? If she did misperceive the situation, it may be unfair to apply the university's plagiarism policy in an absolutistic way. Based on principles, this analysis could be taken further on the basis of Marion's answers to the questions and the costs and benefits of each potential solution (Haas & Malouf, 1989).

LIMITATIONS OF PRINCIPLES AND RULES

Even if an analysis of relevant ethical principles were conducted, however, it would be limited in its approach. Although I once thought so, ethical principles along with strong ethics codes are not a panacea for the ethical problems in the field of psychology whether one argues from a feminist perspective or not. They do not explain, for instance, why a student who was familiar with APA's Ethics Code and thus knew the right thing to do did not act on that knowledge and cut ethical corners (Kitchener, 1996). Furthermore, a moral system that focuses on principles and rules sometimes gives the impression that there is more consistency in moral decision making than is the case. For example, how would a system built on principles and ethics codes accommodate the information that the student in the above case had recently been dealing with a death in her family or with the instructor's observation that her actions seemed out of character?

Noddings (1984) suggested that in moral situations, the uniqueness of human encounters must be considered, along with how to maintain moral relationships. She maintained that principles and codes should never be used as an excuse to treat others as objects. Elaborating on this idea, Churchill (1994) noted that principles can be abused when they are valued above real concerns for people. In his words, it is an error to deify principles so that they have an "intrinsic value, as things to be protected, rather than a means to respect and protect persons" (p. 326). The feminist view adds that this is especially dangerous given the patriarchal system in which *right* is often defined from the perspective of the most powerful person or group. In situations like these, principles and rules—like ethics codes or the law—can be wielded as weapons to rally like-minded others to causes that oppress others rather than provide enlightened discourse. One has only to look as far as President Clinton's impeachment process to see how the rules of law and the cry of moral righteousness were used for political gain. Ultimately, the process diminished rather than enhanced a concern with an ethical solution. In other words, a morality built entirely on principles and rules can sometimes lead to a dangerous self-righteousness: the view that a certain group or person knows the right way to behave and others who fail to live up to these standards should be expelled, scorned, or otherwise disregarded. There are other limits to a moral system built entirely on principles, but they are beyond the scope of this discussion (Hill et al., 1995; Hoagland, 1991).

I am not recommending that principles or rules like the APA Ethics Code be discarded. Ethics codes allow psychologists to take a moral stance when they might be feeling a "weakness of will" and to respond to situations that otherwise might appear confusing. Similarly, principles provide clarity of thought and consistent guidelines when ethical codes are silent. They also provide a rationale for the items in the Ethics Code itself and a common vocabulary within the mental and physical health fields with which to consider ethical issues.

Some feminists have suggested that what is missing in ethics built on principles and rules, however, is an appreciation of a person's values and the more affective aspect of an ethical response (Hill et al., 1995). Others have talked about this as the "character" issue in ethics because it deals with questions about what constitutes good moral character and what values are better ones to hold (Beauchamp & Childress, 1994; Frankena, 1963; Meara, Schmidt, & Day, 1996). Among ethicists, this issue is usually discussed under the topic of virtue ethics.

The assumption of virtue ethics is that people with good moral character will be better able to understand moral problems and to make better moral decisions about them. It is more likely that a student with good moral character will use moral principles and understand ethical rules than will a student with poor moral character, for example.

Although concerns about virtuous behavior may sound outdated to 20th century feminists, they can be translated into a question such as the following: What would a feminist acting with good moral sense do in a real-world situation? A virtue from this perspective is a disposition or character trait to act in the best moral way under the circumstance and to have the feelings and emotions that are consistent with those actions (Annas, 1993; Kitchener, 1999). In psychological terms, a *virtue* is a personal trait that leads someone to take a moral position. It may include aspects of moral motivation, ego strength, and moral sensitivity, which have all been investigated as psychological constructs (Rest, 1994). Values, then, are an outgrowth of character. If someone has a strong moral character, her or his values are consistent with it.

Virtue or character is linked to the motivation for moral action; thus, for every ethical principle, there is a corresponding character trait that predisposes a person to act on the principle (Beauchamp & Childress, 1994; Frankena, 1963). For example, to act on the principle of beneficence, one must be benevolent. Upholding autonomy is dependent on respectfulness. However, some virtues may not correspond to principles. For example, it might be suggested that feminists need to be courageous in order to take unpopular social action, but there is no corresponding moral principle.

The question feminists must ask is this: What kind of moral character can and should be encouraged and nurtured in each other and in our students? Some (Brabeck & Brown, 1997; Jaggar, 1991) have argued, for example, that feminists should not condone values that encourage the subordination, disempowerment, or devaluation of women or others or values that lead to torture, rape, or other explicitly harmful acts. In other words, they have identified the values feminists should not hold. Identifying the positive ethical values that feminists should hold is equally critical to better understand feminists' responsibilities toward students and may help clarify their responsibilities to students such as Marion.

In the remainder of this article, I identify virtues or ethical character traits that seem central to a feminist perspective and suggest how they might guide relationships with students. The values that follow from these virtues will more likely be consistent with a feminist mission.

WHAT VIRTUES ARE CONSISTENT WITH A FEMINIST RELATIONSHIP TO STUDENTS?

Although there is a corresponding virtue for each principle discussed earlier, some such as being benevolent or nonmalevolent seem so defensible that they need no further discussion. Other virtues, however, are implicit in writings of feminist ethicists in psychology or philosophy and are at the core of feminist consciousness—these bear some discussion. They are respectfulness, trustworthiness, willingness to take responsibility, and caring or compassion. These four seem particularly relevant to understanding the kind of character feminists need to develop to ethically work with students. The first two are related to principles discussed earlier, whereas the latter two are not.

Respectfulness

Most accounts of respectfulness suggest it is an attitude marked by a willingness to take another person's or group's perspective on an issue into account, particularly when one's actions might affect that person or group (Darwell, 1992; Meara et al., 1996). Respectfulness is central to a feminist perspective. Jaggar (1991), for example, suggested that one goal for feminist ethics is to treat women's moral experience with respect but not without criticism. As noted earlier, it underlies the ability to act on the principles of respect for autonomy. It is clearly foundational for embracing human diversity. Respectfulness requires feminists to listen to and for differences among women (Lugones, 1991). Respectfulness is required when feminists implore that women's experiences as Chicanas, Latinas, European Americans, African Americans, lesbians, heterosexuals, and so on be taken into account and valued. Some have called respectfulness a central tenet of feminist therapy (Siegel & Larsen, 1990; Smith & Douglas, 1990), arguing that it is essential to acknowledge that therapist and client share a common humanness because not doing so would accentuate the power differential. Respectfulness from this perspective means listening to students and their perspective, although not necessarily agreeing with them.

In Marion's case, it means carefully considering her perceptions of the events and trying to understand how her unique background may have influenced her actions. As the feminist theories of practice suggest (Brabeck & Brown, 1997), respectfulness also means including her to the extent that it is possible in discussions regarding the meaning of her actions. In other words, an ethically defensible solution should be made in response to both her voice and the voice of the student whose ideas she plagiarized.

Trustworthiness

Annette Baier (1993) argued that trustworthiness is at the core of the virtues that women see as absent from moral discourse focused on rules and principles. Trust, she suggested, provides the central component of binding human relationships, such as those between parent and child, teacher and pupil. Trust always involves taking a risk because people make themselves vulnerable to other people; appropriate trustworthiness suggests others' trust will not be misplaced. Trustworthiness underlies the principle of fidelity. Feminists may ask students to trust them with their budding ideas and growing sense of self. In the case of therapy, clients trust their therapists not to knowingly engage in activities that would put them at risk of long-term harm. A trustworthy faculty member would neither misuse her or his power to exploit students nor would she or he use the pretense of authority to get by with inadequate preparation or knowingly engage in other activities that might harm students.

In many ways, the addition of new standards to the APA Ethics Code regarding dual relationships, plagiarism, and others speaks to a lack of trustworthiness on the part of some psychologists. If psychologists were more trustworthy, they would be less likely to engage in exploitative activities and there would be less need for standards like the one on multiple relationships. In fact, Standard 1.17, Multiple Relationships, requires that psychologists refrain from entering into multiple relationships if it appears that those relationships might impair their objectivity, harm the consumer, or otherwise interfere with their professional effectiveness. In essence, it says psychologists should be trustworthy, thoughtful, and prudent when considering those relationships.

I now turn to the issue of mentoring raised earlier in this chapter. In essence, it often involves a nonsexual, nonromantic dual relationship. A faculty member who is already in a position of power because of his or her responsibility to evaluate students enters into a second relationship in which a student takes on another role, such as coauthor or employee. In the second relationship, the student may develop products such as research studies or papers for which the faculty member could claim credit. In cases like these, students have little recourse if their efforts are not fully acknowledged or if unreasonable demands are placed on them (Kitchener & Harding, 1990). Feminists have touted such relationships because of the good they can do; however, such confidence is often based on the belief that those who interact with students in such roles are trustworthy. In other words, the presumption is that faculty members will act as trusted guides rather than as deceptive exploiters. This implies that if the profession is going to avoid an ongoing proliferation of ethical standards that further restrict the nature of relationships between faculty and students, feminists must lobby for greater consideration of character development in graduate programs.

Willingness to Take Responsibility

The importance of taking and accepting responsibility for one's actions permeates discussions of feminist ethics. This is at the core of the theories of feminist practice (Brabeck & Brown, 1997) because feminist practice assumes people are responsible for participating in the change process and that being "response-able" is at the core of a feminist consciousness. In addition, the Feminist Therapy Institute's (1990) Code of Ethics requires that feminist therapists accept responsibility for monitoring the "complexity and conflicting priorities inherent in multiple overlapping relationships" (p. 40). Others (Siegel & Larsen, 1990; Smith & Douglas, 1990) have argued that feminists must deal with power responsibly. Similarly, Adrienne Smith and Mary Ann Douglas (1990) suggested that an ethical feminist must help clients emphasize responsibility for their own behavior. Thus, feminists are expected both to exhibit this virtue and to nurture it in others.

From this perspective, being responsible means being accountable for one's own actions, accepting that one's actions can help or hurt others, and answering for whatever consequences one's actions cause. Being responsible also means entering interactions with forethought because feminists (myself included) know their actions can and do affect others. As the theory of feminist practice suggests, feminists must be particularly sensitive to the responsible use of power, including their own (Brabeck & Brown, 1997; Brabeck & Ting, chap. 1, this volume). Similarly, the willingness to be answerable for one's own conduct in a social arena is also critical. Earlier, I suggested that social activism was an aspect of beneficence. Here, I suggest that developing the character trait of responsibility may help feminists take the steps necessary to intervene in the social system to benefit others, particularly those who are oppressed.

On a microlevel, being responsible with students means being accountable for what is taught and for how one's power is used with students. Thus, in Marion's case, the faculty member should ask whether her use of power in the classroom left Marion feeling like she had few choices or whether she implied that conferring with former students was acceptable. If so, she should consider whether she needed to take some of the responsibility for Marion's ethical error. A faculty member who values responsibility should also ask whether she or he modeled acting responsibly to her or his students. On a macrolevel, however, willingness to take responsibility means more, such as intervening in the university system so it becomes a more humane one. It is in such cases that responsibility overlaps with the virtue of courage.

Caring or Compassion

Noddings (1984), Gilligan (1982, 1993), and others focused on the virtue of care, whereas others have labeled it "compassion" (Beauchamp & Childress, 1994; Drane, 1994). Noddings in particular suggested that being ethical implies being caring in relationships with others. Caring, she suggested, is a special kind of love, which requires a commitment from the "one-caring" to act on behalf of the other person or at least to reflect on what should be done. Acting out of care, she argued, is not the same as responding to fixed rules and principles. Instead it means acting out of regard for another who is in a particular circumstance. Tom Beauchamp and James Childress (1994) similarly suggested compassion includes an active concern for another's welfare and empathy for the other person's situation or suffering. It is not difficult to think of faculty who meet the moral minimum in terms of the APA Ethics Code but never treat a student or research participant with compassion or care.

Care, as Noddings (1984) conceived it, is not a simple notion; it requires a mental toughness that allows the one-caring to feel the other's pain and to see the situation through the eyes of the other, but it does not mean giving up the responsibility to set limits on the other and to say *no* when it is appropriate. It requires that the one-caring maintain the ability to enter a rational–objective mode to decide how to act. For example, if the faculty member in Marion's case decided that she cheated on her paper, thus violating the principles of fidelity and beneficence and the APA Ethics Code, the responsibility to treat Marion with care remains. Acting with care or compassion means trying to understand the student's pain and to perceive the situation through her or his eyes. It also may initially imply a commitment to remediation. As Noddings (1984) maintained, "an ethic of care is likely to be stricter in its judgment, but more supportive and corrective in following up its judgment, than ethics otherwise grounded" (p. 93). This does not mean that feminists should abrogate the responsibility to consider the possibility that Marion might have a serious deficit in her character that could undermine her ability to be an ethical professional and ultimately place others at risk of harm. It does suggest, however, that faculty must try to preserve the possibility of future care until that alternative is no longer available. In this case, requiring the student to take some kind of remedial action would provide an alternative to either severing the ties with the student (by expelling or failing her) or excusing her actions. Thus, it would provide a way to preserve the possibility of caring, while not ignoring the fact that she made an ethical error. However, if Marion makes a similar error in the future or in some other way leads the faculty member to believe that she cannot become an ethical and competent professional, there may be no alternative to dismissing her. Ultimately, the lack of an alternative diminishes the ethical ideal but does not rescind the responsibility of the faculty member to act (Noddings, 1984). Others (Nozick, 1968; Ross, 1930) have suggested such acts often leave one with a feeling of moral regret that a more fully moral solution might have been found.

Note that some character traits that feminists consider to be virtues when carried to their extreme become vices. Thus, Hoagland (1991) argued that taking caring to its extreme could create dependency. It could disempower rather than empower by justifying an inequality in relationships, a kind of maternalism, and it could lead to idealizing relationships in which there is neither reciprocity nor mutual responsibility. In other words, caring without respect for the other as a full human being, who does and can make choices and must take responsibility for those choices, would be a diminished form of a feminist ethical ideal. Similarly, respectfulness and trustworthiness carried to the extreme can become excuses for blind obedience to authority (Beauchamp & Childress, 1994) and could lead to an unwillingness to be critical when criticism is needed. Because criticism of systems that degrade women is central to feminism (Brabeck & Brown, 1997), such blind obedience would undermine the feminist ideal.

Although it is seldom discussed in feminist literature, the virtue of prudence or practical wisdom also seems important to a feminist ethical stance. Briefly, prudence involves the ability to evaluate complex situations in a way that is clear and firm but flexible; it also involves integrating information derived from emotions and the intellect into good moral decisions (Annas, 1993; Meara et al., 1996). Prudence is necessary for operating in complex multicultural situations where it may be important to identify that others' definitions of a good outcome or even the variables involved may not agree. It also underlies the observation that the application of ethical principles to any situation involves good judgment (Kitchener, 1999; Meara et al., 1996). Prudence is essential for responsible social action; thus, it is critical to feminist practice when practice is considered broadly (Brabeck & Brown, 1997). In essence, the ethical feminist is a prudent one who acts carefully and wisely, evaluating the feelings and perceptions of others and knowing when it is time to challenge and confront and when it is time to listen.

CONCLUSION

Feminism does not allow an easy ethical stance regarding relationships to students or others. It implies that students should not be deceived about faculty members' real power and that faculty have a responsibility to help students identify and claim their own power. It means providing students with the tools, knowledge, and freedom to make their own choices, while understanding that perceived choice may be influenced by culture, values, and society. It means making a commitment to hear students' differences and helping them become aware of others' differences. It means taking responsibility to develop systems that value both differences and fair treatment. It also means developing the kind of character that will allow one to meet these demands with respectfulness, responsibility, trustworthiness, and compassion. If feminists are untrustworthy and fail to model responsible caring to students, they will ultimately fail to fulfill the feminist mission to develop good psychologists who also know how to be good people, who cannot condone the subordination of others, who do not devalue others' experiences just because they are different, and who can critically evaluate ethical dilemmas and take action in a way that promotes a feminist perspective.

REFERENCES

American Psychological Association. (1992). Ethical principles of psychologists and code of conduct. *American Psychologist, 47,* 1597–1611.

Annas, J. (1993). *The morality of happiness.* Oxford, England: Oxford University.

Baier, A. (1993). What do women want in a moral theory? *Nous, 19*(1), 53–63.

Beauchamp, T. L., & Childress, J. F. (1994). *Principles of biomedical ethics* (4th ed.). Oxford, England: Oxford University Press.

Brabeck, M., & Brown, L. (With Christian, L., Espin, O., Hare-Mustin, R., Kaplan, A., Kaschak, E., Miller, D., Phillips, E., Ferns, T., & Van Ormer, A.). (1997). Feminist theory and psychological practice. In J. Worell & N. Johnson (Eds.), *Shaping the future of feminist psychology: Education, research, and practice* (pp. 15–35). Washington, DC: American Psychological Association.

Brown, L. S. (1990). Feminist framework for ethical theory. In H. Lerman & N. Porter (Eds.), *Feminist ethics in psychotherapy* (pp. 1–3). New York: Springer.

Churchill, L. R. (1994). Rejecting principlism, affirming principles: A philosopher reflects on the ferment in U.S. bioethics. In E. R. DuBose, R. P. Hamel, & L. J. O'Connell (Eds.), *A matter of principles? Ferment in U.S. bioethics* (pp. 321–331). Valley Forge, PA: Trinity Press International.

Darwell, S. L. (1992). Two kinds of respect. In J. Deigh (Ed.), *Ethics and personality: Essays in moral psychology* (pp. 65–78). Chicago: University of Chicago Press.

Drane, J. F. (1994). Character and the moral life: A virtue approach to biomedical ethics. In E. R. DuBose, R. P. Hamel, & L. J. O'Connell (Eds.), *A matter of principles? Ferment in U.S. bioethics* (pp. 284–309). Valley Forge, PA: Trinity Press International.

Feminist Therapy Institute. (1990). Feminist Therapy Institute code of ethics. In H. Lerman & N. Porter (Eds.), *Feminist ethics in psychotherapy* (pp. 38–40). New York: Springer.

Frankena, W. K. (1963). *Ethics.* Englewood Cliffs, NJ: Prentice Hall.

Gilligan, C. (1982). *In a different voice: Psychological theory and women's development.* Cambridge, MA: Harvard University Press.

Gilligan, C. (1993). A reply to critics. In M. J. Larrabee (Ed.), *An ethic of care* (pp. 207–214). New York: Routledge. (Original work published 1986)

Haas, L. J., & Malouf, J. L. (1989). *Keeping up the good work: A practitioner's guide to mental health ethics.* Sarasota, FL: Professional Resource Exchange.

Hill, M., Glaser, K., & Harden, J. (1995). A feminist model for ethical decision making. In E. J. Rave & C. C. Larsen (Eds.), *Ethical decision making in therapy: Feminist perspectives* (pp. 18–37). New York: Guilford Press.

Hoagland, S. L. (1991). Some thoughts about "caring." In C. Card (Ed.), *Feminist ethics* (pp. 146–264). Lawrence: University Press of Kansas.

Jaggar, A. M. (1991). Feminist ethics: Projects, problems, prospects. In C. Card (Ed.), *Feminist ethics* (pp. 78–106). Lawrence: University Press of Kansas. (Original work published 1990)

Kitchener, K. S. (1984). Intuition, critical evaluation and ethical principles: The foundation for ethical decisions in counseling psychology. *The Counseling Psychologist, 12*(3), 43–55.

Kitchener, K. S. (1988). Dual role relationships: What makes them so problematic? *Journal of Counseling and Development, 67,* 217–221.

Kitchener, K. S. (1992). Psychologist as teacher and mentor: Affirming ethical values throughout the curriculum. *Professional Psychology: Research and Practice, 23,* 190–195.

Kitchener, K. S. (1996). There is more to ethics than principles. *The Counseling Psychologist, 24,* 92–97.

Kitchener, K. S. (1999). *Ethical decisions in psychology: Practice, research, and teaching.* Mahwah, NJ: Erlbaum.

Kitchener, K. S., & Harding, S. S. (1990). Dual role relationships. In B. Herlihy & L. Golden (Eds.), *AACD ethical standards casebook* (pp. 146–154). Alexandria, VA: American Association for Counseling and Development.

Lerman, H., & Porter, N. (1990). The contribution of feminism to ethics in psychotherapy. In H. Lerman & N. Porter (Eds.), *Feminist ethics in psychotherapy* (pp. 5–13). New York: Springer.

Lerman, H., & Rigby, D. N. (1990). Boundary violations: Misuse of the power of the therapist. In H. Lerman & N. Porter (Eds.), *Feminist ethics in psychotherapy* (pp. 51–59). New York: Springer.

Lugones, M. C. (1991). On the logic of pluralism feminism. In C. Card (Ed.), *Feminist ethics* (pp. 35–44). Lawrence: University Press of Kansas.

Meara, N. M., Schmidt, L., & Day, J. D. (1996). Principles and virtues: A foundation for ethical decisions, policies and character. *The Counseling Psychologist, 24,* 4–77.

Noddings, N. (1984). *Caring: A feminine approach to ethics and moral education.* Berkeley: University of California Press.

Nozick, R. (1968). Moral complications and moral structures. *Natural Law Forum, 13,* 1–50.

Rest, J. R. (1994). Background: Theory and research. In J. R. Rest & D. Narvaez (Eds.), *Moral development in the professions* (pp. 1–26). Hillsdale, NJ: Erlbaum.

Richardson, M. S. (1982). Sources of tension in teaching the psychology of women. *Psychology of Women Quarterly, 7,* 45–54.

Ross, W. D. (1930). *The right and the good.* Oxford, England: Clarendon Press.

Siegel, R. J., & Larsen, C. C. (1990). The ethics of power differentials. In H. Lerman & N. Porter (Eds.), *Feminist ethics in psychotherapy* (pp. 41–42). New York: Springer.

Smith, A. J., & Douglas, M. A. (1990). Empowerment as an ethical imperative. In H. Lerman & N. Porter (Eds.), *Feminist ethics in psychotherapy* (pp. 43–50). New York: Springer.

3

ANTIRACIST PEDAGOGY IN THE UNIVERSITY: THE ETHICAL CHALLENGES OF MAKING WHITENESS PUBLIC

ALICE McINTYRE

Over the past 3 decades, the scholarship related to feminist ethics, feminist theory, and their relationship to feminist practice has become diversified, multifaceted, and sharply debated. Many feminist psychologists have enhanced and made more complex traditional ways of theorizing and conducting research by deliberately inserting and foregrounding race (see, e.g., Collins, 1990; Essed, 1991; Helms, 1993; and Sparks, 1996), reflexivity (see, e.g., Hurd, 1998; Hurd & McIntyre, 1996; McIntyre & Lykes, 1998; and Morawski, 1994), activism (see, e.g., Fine, 1992; Lykes, 1997; and Pastor, McCormick, & Fine, 1996), sexuality (see, e.g., Cruikshank, 1981; Griffin & Zukas, 1993; and Wilkinson & Kitzinger, 1993), social class (see, e.g., Jones, 1998; Ostrove & Stewart, 1998; Reay, 1996; and Walkerdine, 1996), and ethnicity (see, e.g., Olson & Ceballo, 1996; and Unger, 1998) as fundamental to the formulation of ethical principles, theories, and practices. These scholars have challenged white,[1] European American feminists, in

---

[1] *The Publication Manual of the American Psychological Association* (1994) states that "racial and ethnic groups are designated by proper nouns and are capitalized. Therefore, use *Black* and *White* instead of

particular, to become and remain equally conscious of racism, classism, ageism, anti-Semitism, homophobia, ableism, and other forms of oppression that are directly linked to the underlying tenets of feminism and feminist ethics.

Similarly, white feminist educators and psychologists have been criticized by feminist educators and psychologists of Color for specifically failing to illuminate some of the problematic policies and practices that maintain racism in academia. Academics of Color have repeatedly told white feminists, myself included, to rethink, reform, and restructure exclusionary practices that exist in the institutions in which they work (see, e.g., hooks, 1990, 1994; Ng, Staton, & Scane, 1995; and Tatum, 1992, 1994). They have also challenged them to be more reflective about their own privileged positions as white feminists and to attend to the ways in which they are implicated in the norms, standards, and educational models set by white academics and institutions.

In response, many white feminists have become adept at using the language of "diversity" in the belief that modifying their syllabi and supporting programs on campus that address racism, sexism, homophobia, and so forth take care of their commitment to institutional change. In addition, many of them have become quite clever at naming their raced, classed, and gendered positions, assuming that because they name them, they are addressing the power they imbue. Rather than reflecting on their privilege and taking action about the ways in which they reproduce the very practices of domination that many of them are seeking to challenge (Patai, 1991), they focus on cultural difference and sensitivity to "the other." Thus, they fail to address the ways in which interlocking systems of oppression weave their way through the development and implementation of institutional practices and policies.

These issues have particular significance for those feminist antiracist educators teaching white students, especially white students from privileged backgrounds. On the one hand, as a white educator, I have legitimacy due to my skin color. Students do not dismiss me or the content of my courses

---

black and *white* (colors to refer to other human groups currently are considered pejorative and should not be used)" (p. 52). As I note in this chapter, the ethics feminists define, redefine, and use to frame theory and practice not only have been "deeply patriarchal, embodying firmly entrenched double standards of behavior for men and women" (Andolsen, Gudorf, & Pellauer, 1985, p. xi) but also have been shaped and influenced by entrenched beliefs about the dominance of whites and subjugation of people of Color. Thus, I use the uppercase B for Black and the lowercase w for white because, as Harris (1993) argued, both have "a particular political history. Although 'white' and 'Black' have been defined oppositionally, they are not functional opposites. 'White' has incorporated Black subordination; 'Black' is not based on domination . . . 'Black' is naming that is part of the counterhegemonic practice" (p. 1710). In keeping with Harris's position, I also use the uppercase C for people of Color.

because of the color of my skin. I also have experience "being white" and, therefore, can identify with students' resistance, denial, and aversion to looking at issues of white racism and skin color privilege. On the other hand, white homogeneity within a classroom (and institution) can all too easily mute self- and collective critique. Being seduced by sameness can prevent white faculty members from critically examining the ways in which they perpetuate racist practices (see Hurd & McIntyre, 1996). They become blind to their complicity in the structural arrangements of their institutions and are often unable to notice, name, and challenge white students' racist assumptions and beliefs.

In this chapter, I argue that it is essential for white feminists to make whiteness a "central, self-reflective topic of inquiry within the academy" (Scheurich, 1993, p. 8) and within discussions of feminist ethics. Feminists have invested heavily in dismantling patriarchy and hegemonic practices that oppress (white) women by, among other things, defining and redefining characteristics of feminist ethics, theory, research, and practice. The guiding principles threaded throughout the above areas evolved out of a refusal to accept theory, research, and ethical perspectives that were "deeply patriar- chal, embodying firmly entrenched double standards of behavior for men and women" (Andolsen et al., 1985, p. xi). Equally important, these princi- ples have been shaped and influenced by entrenched beliefs about the superiority of whites and the inferiority of Blacks and other people of Color as well as immigrants, poor people, gay men and lesbians, people with disabilities, and other disenfranchised groups. As feminists work to dismantle patriarchal systems that oppress women, they need also to invest in disman- tling racist practices in the institutions in which they work. They need to develop ethical processes that promote transformation and "include an analysis of power and the multiple ways people are oppressed and oppressing" (Brabeck & Brown, 1997, p. 23).

In this chapter, I examine the links between feminist ethics and femi- nist antiracist teaching—both of which are "guided by and reflect the central concerns of feminism" (Bell, 1993, p. 17). I provide examples of my experi- ences both as an educator and an administrator to illuminate three main areas that I believe are essential for engaging in ethical antiracist teaching.

First, I view teaching as a site for social critique. I believe that antiracist educators, myself included, need to address racism by providing students with an analysis of whiteness as a system and ideology of white dominance that marginalizes and oppresses people of Color and ensures existing privi- leges for white people in this country (see, e.g., Fine, Weis, Powell, & Wong, 1997a; Frankenberg, 1993; Helms, 1993; Lopez, 1996; McIntyre, 1997a, 1997b; Roediger, 1994; and Sleeter, 1996, for further discussions of white- ness). Examining how whiteness informs and influences people's ways of being in the world raises questions about power, privilege, sexism, racism, oppression, and a host of other issues with which most of the white students I encounter are unfamiliar.

Second, I believe that educators have a responsibility to engage in self- and collective analysis and critique about their positions as white feminist educators and how their histories, social locations, and university positions intersect with their pedagogical practices. Third, I believe that they have an ethical responsibility to be in solidarity with people of Color and other white allies who are committed to addressing racism and finding ways for making institutional change. Feminists in academia have a responsibility to pay attention to—and take action from—the "privileged positions we currently occupy" (Sleeter & McLaren, 1995, p. 22) and to commit themselves to making "social justice noise" (Grant & Zozakiewicz, 1995, p. 271) as they develop pedagogies of and for justice and social change.

Below, I describe ways in which I make—or at least try to make—social justice noise. The examples I share are informed by feminist theorizing that suggests that feminist researchers and educators need to "look for what's been left out . . . overlooked, unconceptualized, and not noticed" (Stewart, 1994, p. 13).

The examples I present are based on my experience as the director of the graduate program in elementary education at a private northeastern university and my years of teaching education and psychology courses to predominantly white middle- and upper middle-class students. I discuss one exercise I conducted with over 400 students during the past 5 years. Some of the students I refer to here were enrolled in an undergraduate class of 45 1st-, 2nd-, and 3rd-year students. The class consisted of 37 white students (30 women and 7 men) and 8 students of Color: 1 African American woman, 1 biracial woman who identified herself as half white and half Black, 1 Filipino man, 1 Arab American woman, 2 Chinese American women, 1 Filipino woman, and 1 Korean American woman.[2] Other students discussed throughout the chapter were—and are—enrolled in master's programs in psychology and education.[3]

---

[2] Although I focus on the experiences of mostly white students in this chapter, I do so with a clear understanding that students of Color have had their own struggles with the content of my classes as they, too, grappled with the intersection of gender, race, sexuality, and social class during the semester. I am not dismissing their experiences. Their presence in the class both constrained and facilitated dialogue among the white students. Yet in this chapter, I want to focus on the more pressing problems I experienced in the class that centered on how white students made meaning of whiteness and how I, as a white educator, addressed white student resistance.

[3] I audiotape many of my classes and explain to my students that I analyze class discussions to both assist me in my teaching and to analyze the content for research purposes, which includes writing for publication. I invite students to provide feedback and critique, letting them know that the tapes and drafts of papers I am working on are always available to them. I also explain to them that I change the names of the courses, the students, and any other descriptors that would identify them.

TEACHING AS A SITE FOR SOCIAL CRITIQUE

Many feminist ethicists (see, e.g., Bell, 1993; Card, 1991b; Cole & Coultrap-McQuin, 1992; and Koehn, 1998) and feminist antiracist educators (see, e.g., Ellsworth, 1989; hooks, 1994, 1995; McIntyre, 1997b; Ng et al., 1995; Tatum, 1992, 1994; and Weiler, 1988) believe that "feminist ethics begins with or assumes a criticism of the historical" (Robb, 1985, p. 212). Thus, their criticism begins with an analysis of the "interlocking matrix of relationships" (Collins, 1990, p. 20) that exist within systems of privilege and oppression. The courses I teach are designed to explore those relationships, focusing on how systems of racism, sexism, classism, and other forms of oppression—along with history, theoretical principles, and political ideologies—function both to conceal and illuminate one's understandings of oneself and others.

Two years ago, I began an undergraduate course in education and psychology by asking my students the following question: What does it mean for you to be a member of a racial group? I prefaced that question with my "introduction to this course" presentation in which I explained the requirements of the course I was teaching, outlined how I saw the course evolving, and invited the students to make comments, give feedback, suggest changes, and ask other questions they might have regarding the class. They usually do not have many. First-day jitters, a certain amount of uncertainty about whether they registered for the "right" course, and a "reserved respect" for authority usually inhibit much interactive dialogue. I accept that arrangement during the initial class meetings and use the silence as a point of departure for what I always hope will become a more participatory experience.

After I posited the above question, I asked the students to write (anonymously) for 10 minutes describing what it means for them to be *raced*: acknowledging the implications of labeling oneself, or being labeled, by one's skin color and calling attention to the relationship between skin color and social positions. Entertaining the idea that they are raced challenges the white students, in particular, to view themselves as members of a "racial" group—a new and unexplored area for many of them.[4]

Many of the white students' responses to what it means for them to be raced were comparable with much of the literature regarding how white

---

[4]Hacker (1995) suggested, "having a [sic] white skin does not immunize a person from misfortune or failure. Yet even for those who fall to the bottom, being white has worth" (p. 35). Although I am not dismissing the significance of ethnicity, gender, social class, and differences to access to wealth and power among whites, I chose to focus the students' attention on the worth of being white in this country. In addition, I recognize that "race is more of a social category than a reliable biological classification. . . . The danger," as Campbell (1996) suggested, ". . . is not race, but racism, the oppression of a group of people based on their perceived race" (p. 49).

students perceive themselves as racial beings (see, e.g., King, 1991; McIntyre, 1997a, 1997b; Roman, 1993; Sleeter, 1993, 1996; Tatum, 1992, 1994; and Wellman, 1993). The following is an example of some of the students' comments: "I do feel that affirmative action has played a major role in the decline of white's authority in the workplace." "It is simply a skin color, nothing more. Being a member of the white race has no special meaning to me. . . . I do not see myself as being different from others because of the color of my skin." "I don't understand this constant emphasis on color or race. Who cares? Does it really matter what the color of your skin is? I wish people would look at each other as human beings and respect each other for that." "When competing with minorities in some situations, I am denied certain opportunities because I am white and, therefore, not culturally diverse."

Many of the students colluded with present-day rhetoric by positioning themselves as victims, as the ones who were "denied certain opportunities because I am white." This type of victimization talk seemed quite logical to the students. They had grown up and been educated during 2 decades marked by, among other things, a backlash to the Civil Rights Movement. Like many other white people living in the United States, they believe that "racial discrimination is no longer a serious problem in the United States" (Feagin & Vera, 1995, pp. 153–154) and that "all things considered, things aren't so bad for Blacks" (Hacker, 1995, p. 35).

In addition, many of the white students in this class—and in other classes I have taught—chose to ignore the implications of skin color and, instead, universalized their collective humanness. In doing so, they invoked a way of thinking about racial identity that says the following: "It's simply a skin color, nothing more." Invoking a color-blind approach to one's racial identity relieves white people from having to deal with the fundamental issue of skin-color privilege afforded to whites in this country. In addition, suggesting that "it's only a skin color, nothing more" relieves whites of having to deal with how white supremacy functions in the United States and how institutional, societal, cultural, and legal structures maintain and sustain racial inequities based on skin color.

REPRESENTING WHITENESS

To illuminate some of the misconceptions the students had about what it means to be white, I followed up the written exercise by asking the students to form small groups and create group collages "representing whiteness." Most of the students had never heard the term *whiteness* before and were unsure of how to proceed. I purposely refrained from defining whiteness for them because I was concerned that if I defined it for them, they would give me back, in the collages, what I defined. That was not the point of the exercise.

The point of the exercise was for them to leaf through magazines and, as a group, create a collage that best represented their conceptualization of whiteness.[5] The students had about 40 minutes to work on their collages. Once completed, each group presented their collage to the entire class. Before they described it, the rest of the students interpreted it and, when necessary, made inquiries about particular words, symbols, and photographs.

The major themes that emerged in the students' collages (and that have also emerged in the 80 other collages I analyzed across similarly populated classes) are whites (a) as "rich," "beautiful," "bold," "dazzling," "free from worry," and "living high on the horse above everyone else"; (b) as the ones in positions of power (e.g., in the areas of politics, entertainment, and business); and (c) as "living fit" and being able to live "a very comfortable, well-off life." Through the images represented on the collages, the students described white people as basically thinking that they are the center of the universe and everything revolves around them. They talked about the nonexistence of people of Color in mainstream media and questioned the power of the media in shaping people's beliefs and attitudes. The students rarely addressed whiteness as it relates to social class, gender, sexuality, nationality, and so forth, which were issues explored during the remainder of the semester.

As the students began to make collective meaning of the collages, they found themselves confronted with images that were disturbing, contradictory, and quite challenging. They saw images of themselves, vis-à-vis members of the dominant group, that disturbed them and challenged their sense of themselves as white. They uncovered aspects of white U.S. culture that were unsettling and challenged their assumptions and beliefs about race, racism, and skin-color privilege. The students' responses to the collages were quite different from their reflections on race as written in their earlier essays.

---

[5]The students were asked to bring magazines to class for the collage exercise. These could be magazines they subscribe to, borrow from friends, or find at home or at work. Thus, the magazines reflect the reading material of a particular group of young, white, middle- and upper middle-class people living in the United States and their families, friends, and coworkers: *Time, Newsweek, Elle, Glamour, GQ, Family, Good Housekeeping, People, Us, Seventeen, Brides, Sports Illustrated, National Geographic,* and the like. Given some of the shared characteristics of the students in the classes I teach, there is a tendency for them to "read" the collages in ways that produce an agreed-on singular meaning to the multidimensionality of whiteness. Therefore, it is essential—once the collages are presented, interpreted, read, and discussed—to deconstruct the natural, universal aspects of whiteness that are created among the groups. We critically examine the use of images in advertising, the "power" of the media, and the relationship among the message, the messengers, and the active receivers of the messages. Without a deeper, critical, sustained critique of the relationship between advertising and whiteness, the activity itself could lead to a reification of stereotypes and a privilege of the dominant discourse. My aim here is not to measure the effect of advertisements and images on students' meaning-making processes. Instead, I suggest that even with its limitations, the collage activity can be used in conjunction with a critical perspective that disrupts a reductionist, essentialist, relativistic approach to examining whiteness.

I wrote elsewhere about the methodological implications of using collages to examine whiteness (McIntyre, 1997b). Here, I want to examine some of the ethical dilemmas I face as I address white students' resistance to problematizing whiteness and racism. First, I explore the ethical dimensions of self-disclosure and why I believe it is necessary to disclose aspects of my own experiences as a white person to students. Second, I describe the moments of contestation that emerge for me when students make racist comments in class.

ETHICAL DECISION MAKING:
SELF-DISCLOSURE AND NAMING RACISM

In my previous work (McIntyre, 1997a, 1997b), I suggested that attempting to critique the ideology of whiteness with white students invites resistance, denial, feelings of discomfort, and occasional moments of insight. The students in this class experienced similar feelings and reactions. They had little or no previous experience with critically examining their racial locations or with problematizing the multiple levels of racism and oppression that function in U.S. society.

It is an essential aspect of antiracist teaching and feminist ethics to accompany students through the emotional jolts that occur when they engage in critique. Therefore, I do not discourage students from expressing their feelings, but I do ensure that the remainder of the course is not spent trying to assuage their discomfort. Instead, I suggest that they make constructive use of their feelings. Given the culture of niceness that pervades many educational institutions, that is not easy for them. This current constituency of students is so accustomed to "being polite" that they find it difficult to muster up enough anger at what they have discovered to be able to work through their feelings and be self-reflective about their privileged racial and social positions.

After the interpretation of the collages, students typically feel like they have been had, that I "set them up," made them look like "bad white people," and left them unable to defend themselves against charges that they are members of a dominant racial group that benefits from racist practices. Subsequently, the rest of the semester becomes a "contest of the white wills." I try to link the myriad discussions to the sociopolitical climate and to the historical legacy of whiteness. They try to deny any participation in a racial group that benefits from racist practices and policies. I suggest that as whites, they move beyond the resistance and actually restructure their worldviews. They suggest to me that they are not racists; therefore, their worldviews are not in need of being restructured.

The students' resistance to examining whiteness is predictable and makes sense, given their life experiences. Some white students get sick of hearing about "it" and wonder why everything has to be related to race. Some white students remain silent during problematic discussions that make them uncomfortable. Some continually reformulate what they mean by trying to find the right way to articulate their thoughts and feelings to keep everybody feeling good. Others are very willing to risk confrontation and engage in critical debates that facilitate change. In addition, some white students just refuse to budge and decide, as one of my students did, that I was "brainwashing the class about racism," and I ought to "have a more open mind to those who are Republican."

The students' resistance to speaking openly about whiteness is partly due to their lack of opportunity to do so in academic settings. Similarly, they have been presented with misinformation about the history of whiteness in their educational experiences. In addition, many of the students do not trust that I, as one of the gatekeepers in the university, will not use my authority to penalize them for remarks I find offensive. They fear that if they really talk about how they feel, I (and their peers) will label them as "racists" and I will give them a bad grade. Addressing power imbalances in the professor–student relationship is fundamental to feminist teaching and a core component of feminist ethics. Therefore, I attend to the hierarchies of power that exist in the classroom environment.

Making My Whiteness Public

One way I try to "level the playing field" and alleviate the anxiety that students have about "talking race" is by disclosing aspects of my own history as a white person. Like feminist therapists who grapple with the ethical dilemmas associated with self-disclosure, I question how much I need to tell students about my experiences with racism (see, e.g., Feminist Therapy Institute, 1987; Jordan & Meara, 1990; Lerman & Porter, 1990; and Mahalik, Van Ormer, & Simi, chap. 9, this volume, for further discussions of self-disclosure). Equally important, I question the motives behind my decision to tell students particular stories about my life as a white, working-class, Irish adolescent growing up in Boston (MA) during the 1970s (McIntyre, 1997b; McIntyre et al., 1998). Am I engaging in self-disclosure because nothing else seems to be working and a story may evoke a response from my students? Will my self-disclosure put the focus on me and other whites in ways that yet again obfuscate the effect of racism on people of Color? Will my self-disclosure evoke what Friedman (in Fine et al., 1997b) called "narrative[s] [from students] of guilt, accusation, or denial, and by so doing . . . dispense with the real work of organizing for racial justice and engaging in antiracism pedagogies" (p. xii)?

Feminist ethicists provide guidelines for negotiating the difficult terrain of creating boundaries and dealing with self-disclosure. Yet hard and fast rules governing ethical practices cannot (and should not) be universalized across various contexts. Much depends on the "unresolved . . . alive and embodied questions" (Brown, 1994, p. 30) generated in daily teaching practice. Therefore, although I do not question the need for a set of principles that guide educators through ethical dilemmas that occur in teaching, I do question how and under what circumstances I address those dilemmas. I believe that self-reflection and self-critique are essential aspects of developing strategies to combat racism. I also believe that students need to have classroom opportunities for those experiences. Thus, I feel a need to describe certain life experiences that shaped my views and contributed to my commitment to antiracist education.

I tell students about my experiences as a white adolescent fighting (verbally and physically) with Black girls in the neighborhood over who owned the street corner and who had the better basketball team—the Black girls or the white girls. I describe the struggles I went through at age 16 when my older sister came home to Boston from New York with her new African American boyfriend. I tell students what it was like to participate in St. Patrick's Day parades in Boston. I speak about the years I stood by silently as white people shouted racial slurs at people of Color as they marched through the streets of South Boston. Then I talk about the decision I made one year to leave the parade after seeing people who are white like me and Irish like me harass people of Color. At that moment, I no longer wanted to identify with my own people.

Speaking to students about my ethnicity, social class background, experiences of racism, and the ways in which I worked to undo my beliefs and commit myself to antiracist work allows a space for them to do the same. Some students continue to hesitate when speaking about themselves and about the issues that get raised in class. Yet others find that they can identify with parts of my story and are less fearful of speaking about their own experiences with racism.

Space prohibits me from describing the path the students and I take in class, the moments of rupture we experience as we explore in depth the multiple issues that emerge in our discussions, and the strategies I use to keep the students "coming back to the table." Yet through readings, films, assignments, class activities, critical questioning, and graphic portrayals of the effects of whiteness, I try to help white students, in particular, construct a different perspective about society than the one they bring to class.

Almost without exception, the white students told me—and each other—that they were more aware of the meaning of whiteness by the end of the term. They repeatedly commented on the fact that they "had never thought about it before," "skin color privilege had never occurred to me," and "I never realized the impact of racism before." Numerous students talked about valuing the opportunity to discuss issues of race and racism, even if the discussions were difficult and made them feel angry, guilty, and confused. As one student said, "I was angry at first, but now . . . I recognize privilege and that's a start."

As a white educator whose goal is to address white racism in academia, I appreciate their "start." I am under no illusion that a one-semester course can undo a white student's views about him- or herself and others' white racism. I know that engaging white students in dialogue about white racism is not necessarily going to result in those students constructing an identity that is free of white-privileged consciousness. I also do not believe that because some students experienced a racial awakening that that experience is going to result in a life-long commitment to work against racial injustice, not just be aware of it. Nonetheless, I believe that feminist educators, committed to pedagogies of transformation and hope, have an ethical obligation to start somewhere; the somewhere for me is the classroom and the institution in which I work.

Naming Racism

In addition to speaking about my racial identity, the ways racism informs my life, and the subsequent actions I take to address racism, I also negotiate the ethical dimensions of naming racism and other forms of oppression during class discussions. I teach a graduate course in multicultural education for predominantly white middle- and upper middle-class students in education and psychology programs. Last semester, the students and I were engaged in a discussion about a set of collages the students had created representing whiteness. One of the student groups commented on the "lack of people of Color displayed in any of the advertisements dealing with business people and professionals." At one point in the discussion, a white female student said, "Well, come on. They do it to themselves. They don't care if they get ahead. You can see that in the schools. Those parents just don't care about their kids' education. So how will they ever be a professional anything!"

This kind of experience happens quite often in the classes I teach. A student makes a racist, sexist, homophobic comment. I wait for another student to question, challenge, or inquire. No one does. The conversation continues, and I think about how I am going to stop the flow of the discussion and address the student's remark. The ethical response is to "pause" the class and revisit the remark. The easy thing to do is ignore it and keep going with the discussion. I have never been a person who is afraid of conflict, angry students, or disgruntled administrators. So it is not the fear of reprimand that causes me to hesitate before I address racism in the classroom. I believe it has more to do with how discouraged I get at the lack of student-initiated responses and challenges. I struggle with the expectations I have of and for white students, always hoping that one of them will come through and question, challenge, confront, and assist in the reformulation of how others think about themselves as whites and how they view racism and other forms of oppression. When the students do not live up to my expectations, I get angry and discouraged. My initial response, which has its genesis in an Irish working-class modus operandi that prefers fighting to intellectual debates (see McIntyre & Lykes, 1998), is to enter into battle with the student. Yet quick responses from me fueled by my own frustrations are not always the most effective entry point into critical dialogue. The dilemma is this: I encourage students to talk about their experiences. Yet I am not always clear when the appropriate moment is to critique those experiences when they maintain a "dysconsciousness" about racism "that justifies inequity and exploitation by accepting the existing order of things as given" (King, 1991, p. 135).

In the above example, I let about 3 minutes pass before I finally went back to the student's remark. I repeated to her what I heard her say and asked if I had heard her correctly. She said that I had. I then asked her—and the class—how she would define *caring*, which led to a lengthy discussion about justice, morality, and relation and caring in teaching. By the end of the discussion, the student who made the racist remark told the class that she had spoken too soon "jumping to conclusions based on my own assumptions." (Later, the student told me that she did not want me to think she was a racist and hoped that her comments would be forgotten.)

One of the students in the above class was also enrolled in a teaching methods course I taught last semester. In a discussion with the students in the methods course about the benefits of teaching in an urban school, one of the white female students asked the following: "I don't understand why we have to focus on multicultural education so much. I don't want to teach in an urban school, and I think white kids need good teachers too. How come all the good teachers have to go to the inner city?" I was about to question the student, and the rest of the class, about both the implicit and explicit assumptions and beliefs that were evident in her comments when the student who was enrolled in both classes intervened. She has been a student in the elementary education program for 2 years and described to the class her own process of undoing beliefs about race, racism, and privilege and their relationships to education. She spoke about the challenges she faces as she addresses her own racism as well as the insights gleaned from engaging in fieldwork and coursework aimed at antiracist teaching.

This was a significant moment because it was the first time in this class that a student voluntarily and without any input from me addressed another student about a racist remark and publicly defended the policies of the elementary education program. In my experience, students can be very effective in generating critiques with each other when they initiate the exchange and challenge one another about issues that get raised in class. I also believe that if I am expecting students to critique one another, the readings, and other class activities, then I need to model that behavior. In addition, I need to do so regardless of the consequences, which range from students shutting down completely, to increased tension in the group, to students walking out of the classroom, to negative evaluations that appear to focus more on my politics than on my teaching practices.

Administration: An Ethical Approach

Like other feminist educators, I have my fair share of student evaluations that comment on "my agenda," arguing that I spend "too much time on minorities," declaring that I "lack compassion for graduate students," and suggesting that I "should concentrate less on racism." I also have occasional visits from and meetings with colleagues and administrators who are concerned about my refusal to change, or at least be flexible about, certain requirements in the elementary education program. I struggle with my role in the university and am constantly humbled by the slow progress I seem to make in teaching white students about whiteness and engaging white colleagues and administrators in a purposeful discourse about individual, institutional, and societal racism. As the director of the graduate program in elementary education, I am in a position to carve out spaces—however cramped they might be—where issues of racism and other forms of oppression can be intentionally and explicitly addressed and critiqued. I have decision-making powers regarding the development of the program, course requirements, hiring and admissions processes, and framing of the student teaching experience.

I have made it a requirement for students to conduct their student teaching in an urban school with a racially diverse student body. This is also a requirement for the fieldwork the students are required to do in some of their methods courses. I am very concerned that teaching in an urban environment can reify stereotypes rather than eliminate them, so I make sure that the coursework and the fieldwork are tightly interwoven throughout the program.

Currently, we are beginning the 3rd year of the program and already some of the students are "making waves" about the fieldwork and student teaching requirements. Although I am clear about the requirements in the initial interview for acceptance into the program and some students appear to willingly embrace that opportunity, once admitted some balk at the requirements and by whatever means possible try to undo my decision about their fieldwork and student teaching placements. In one case, a student went to another professor in the department asking that professor to speak to me about letting her teach elsewhere. My colleague spoke to me; after an informed discussion, my colleague supported my decision to place the student in an urban school. The student was not so supportive. She decided to forego the chair of the department and meet with an administrator higher up. The student complained about the way I handled the program and requested permission to be waived from student teaching in an urban school. I was visited by the administrator who wanted clarification about some of the student's statements. I reiterated the program's mission and its commitment to urban schools, suggesting that the administration continue to support the program by reminding students of the requirements and by assisting students in working through their resistance to teach in inner-city schools.

The student came to my office shortly thereafter, where again I explained the program's commitment to working with urban schools and communities. She became very angry and told me quite loudly that she was going to go as far as she had to go to get what she wanted: "I am going to live in the suburbs. When I get married, my children will go to school in the suburbs. And I intend to teach in the suburbs!"

There are moments during experiences like this when I want to succumb to the feeling of hopelessness and resignation that can often accompany ethical decision making and antiracist teaching. Part of me wanted to simply say, "Fine. Go teach in the suburbs." Another part of me wanted to say, "You're out of the program." I did neither. Instead, I continued to work with the student in developing strategies for unraveling the layers of resistance and fear that were blocking her from what might prove to be a worthwhile experience in her process of becoming a teacher. The student did conduct some of her prestudent teaching fieldwork in an urban school last semester and found the experience to be exciting, challenging, and "great. . . . I got to do some really creative things with the students."

My hope is that this student's experience in her field placement—which she enthusiastically talks about now—contributes to her current process of rethinking earlier stereotypical assumptions about urban schools. I also hope that her peers, some of whom are also trying to have their urban placements changed so they can teach in a school where they feel "more comfortable," will pause and rethink their assumptions.

BEING IN SOLIDARITY

For some feminists, myself included, working for institutions that are hierarchical and populated by predominantly white students and faculty can be a challenging experience. They often find themselves, as the above examples illustrate, "needing to challenge the very social systems to which we belong and by which we are likely to be privileged in many ways" (Bell, 1993, p. 20). Therefore, I have to be conscious of my privilege and use the authority that comes with my position to speak out against discriminatory practices, speak up for those who are usually marginalized in academic settings, and make sure that I "stay alert to the dangers of becoming what [I] despise" (Card, 1991a, p. 26). It is difficult for colleagues of Color, students, and other members of the university community to perceive me as an ally and to judge me as an honorable and ethical practitioner if I remain silent or passive in the face of discrimination. Engaging in critical dialogue with other people who are committed to developing antiracist policies and teaching practices reminds me that there is still much to do in the fight to end racial injustice and that there are a variety of ways for me to take up that challenge.

CROSS-RACIAL DIALOGUE

I have been a participant in a cross-racial dialogue group of academic women (four African American and four European American) for well over 3 years (McIntyre et al., 1998). We come to the table with varied agendas, shifting levels of trust and mistrust, high hopes for racial breakthroughs, and a deep desire to address racial injustices in our personal lives and in the workplace. We grapple individually and collectively with our personal histories and our membership in our respective racial groups and push and pull each other across the chasm that exists between many white and Black women. Sometimes we argue vehemently with each other about our interpretations of whiteness and racism. Other times, we withdraw in silence, change the subject, crack a joke, eat, or simply accept that we agree to disagree. Recently, we have begun sharing teaching dilemmas, requesting feedback and critique in hopes of developing ethical pedagogical practices explicitly aimed at dismantling racism and promoting social transformation. We share our fears and anxieties, acknowledge our failures, and celebrate with one another our successes in addressing racism and other forms of oppression in our personal and professional lives. We have not reached total agreement on certain issues that get raised in the group, and we tentatively approach others. Yet our willingness to engage in candid discourse and speak with one another about what many whites think is the unspeakable represents an important framework for how white people can better understand—and do something about—whiteness and racism. As Christensen (1997) argued,

> as only the experiences of diverse groups of women can give us an accurate account of the impact of gendered power relations in this society, only the experiences of those who are oppressed by racism—

women and men of color—can form the basis for a liberatory knowledge of racism. (p. 620)

CONCLUDING REFLECTIONS

Feminist educators, psychologists, and ethicists call for social transformation and the development of feminist consciousness through practice (Brabeck & Brown, 1997). This requires that they be open to uncertainty, take responsibility for their actions, and collaborate with others in developing strategies for transformative practices. How they negotiate those processes depends on the experiences of those involved and the conditions that frame specific events (Noddings, 1984). Therefore, what I do as a teacher and as an administrator is linked to the multiple contexts in which I live. Many of the practices that have been used by feminist educators have contributed to my ability to make those links.

Nonetheless, I do not believe that antiracist pedagogies necessarily lead to critical transformation or to white students developing racial consciousness. Nor am I convinced that making ethical decisions, engaging in reflective practice, inviting feedback from students, developing syllabi that provide opportunities for critical thinking and learning, and committing oneself to a "pedagogy of possibility" (Luke & Gore, 1992, p. x) will, in and of themselves, result in consciousness-raising experiences. Equally important, I do not believe that they will result in an educational experience that leads to individual change, social change, or both. I engage in all of the above methods of teaching and find them invaluable for the kinds of learning that I like to see happen in my classrooms. However, I also discovered that for these practices to be more than blind attempts at alternative approaches to learning, I need to link them to a way of thinking about education that positions teaching and learning as tools for social justice and the classroom as a site of critique. Framing education as a site for critique inevitably leads to ethical dilemmas. To assist me in addressing those dilemmas in ways that create possibilities for transformative realities, I continue to make my whiteness public, to engage in self-critique with "critical friends" (Tripp, 1993), and work in solidarity with people who tirelessly work for the same.

REFERENCES

American Psychological Association. (1994). *Publication manual of the American Psychological Association* (4th ed.). Washington, DC: Author.

Andolsen, B. H., Gudorf, C. E., & Pellauer, M. D. (Eds.). (1985). Introduction. In B. H. Andolsen, C. E. Gudorf, & M. D. Pellauer (Eds.), *Women's consciousness, women's conscience: A reader in feminist ethics* (pp. xi–xxvi). Minneapolis, MN: Winston Press.

Bell, L. (1993). *Rethinking ethics in the midst of violence: A feminist approach to freedom.* Lanham, MD: Rowman & Littlefield.

Brabeck, M., & Brown, L. (With Christian, L., Espin, O., Hare-Mustin, R., Kaplan, A., Kaschak, E., Miller, D., Phillips, E., Ferns, T., & Van Ormer, A.). (1997). Feminist theory and psychological practice. In J. Worell & N. Johnson (Eds.), *Shaping the future of feminist psychology: Education, research, and practice* (pp. 15–36). Washington, DC: American Psychological Association.

Brown, L. S. (1994). Boundaries in feminist therapy. In N. K. Gartrell (Ed.), *Bringing ethics alive: Feminist ethics in psychotherapy practice* (pp. 29–38). New York: Haworth Press.

Campbell, D. (1996). *Choosing democracy: A practical guide to multicultural education.* Englewood Cliffs, NJ: Prentice Hall.

Card, C. (1991a). The feistiness of feminism. In C. Card (Ed.), *Feminist ethics* (pp. 3–31). Lawrence: University Press of Kansas.

Card, C. (Ed.). (1991b). *Feminist ethics.* Lawrence: University Press of Kansas.

Christensen, K. (1997). "With whom do you believe your lot is cast?": White feminists and racism. *Signs: Journal of Women in Culture and Society, 22,* 617–648.

Cole, E. B., & Coultrap-McQuin, S. (Eds.). (1992). *Explorations in feminist ethics: Theory and practice.* Bloomington: Indiana University Press.

Collins, P. H. (1990). Women's studies: Reform or transformation? *Sojourner: The Women's Forum, 10,* 18–20.

Cruikshank, M. (Ed.). (1981). *Lesbian studies: Present and future.* Old Westbury, NY: Feminist Press.

Ellsworth, E. (1989). Why doesn't this feel empowering? Working through the repressive myths of critical pedagogy. *Harvard Educational Review, 59*(3), 297–324.

Essed, P. (1991). *Understanding everyday racism: An interdisciplinary theory.* Newbury Park, CA: Sage.

Feagin, J. R., & Vera, H. (1995). *White racism.* New York: Routledge.

Feminist Therapy Institute. (1987). *Feminist Therapy Institute ethical code.* Denver, CO: Author.

Fine, M. (1992). *Disruptive voices: The possibilities of feminist psychology.* Ann Arbor: University of Michigan Press.

Fine, M., Weis, L., Powell, L. C., & Wong, L. M. (Eds.). (1997a). *Off white: Readings on race, power, and society.* New York: Routledge.

Fine, M., Weis, L., Powell, L. C., & Wong, L. M. (1997b). Preface. In M. Fine, L. Weis, L. C. Powell, & L. M. Wong (Eds.), *Off white: Readings on race, power, and society* (pp. vii–xii). New York: Routledge.

Frankenberg, R. (1993). *White women, race matters: The social construction of whiteness*. Minneapolis: University of Minnesota Press.

Grant, C. A., & Zozakiewicz, C. A. (1995). Student teachers, cooperating teachers, and supervisors: Interrupting the multicultural silences of student teaching. In J. Larkin & C. E. Sleeter (Eds.), *Developing multicultural teacher education curricula* (pp. 259–278). Albany: State University of New York Press.

Griffin, C., & Zukas, M. (Eds.). (1993). Coming out in psychology: Lesbian psychologists talk. *Feminism & Psychology, 3*(1), 111–133.

Hacker, A. (1995). *Two nations: Black and white, separate, hostile, unequal*. New York: Ballantine Books.

Harris, C. (1993). Whiteness as property. *Harvard Law Review, 106*(8), 1709–1791.

Helms, J. E. (Ed.). (1993). *Black and white racial identity: Theory, research and practice*. Westport, CT: Praeger.

hooks, b. (1990). *Yearning: Race, gender, and cultural politics*. Boston: South End Press.

hooks, b. (1994). *Teaching to transgress: Education as the practice of freedom*. New York: Routledge.

hooks, b. (1995). *Killing rage ending racism*. New York: Holt.

Hurd, T. L. (1998). Process, content, and feminist reflexivity: One researcher's exploration. *Journal of Adult Development, 5*(3), 195–203.

Hurd, T., & McIntyre, A. (1996). The seduction of sameness: Similarity and representing the other. *Feminism and Psychology, 6*(1), 86–92.

Jones, S. (1998). Subjectivity and class consciousness: The development of class identity. *Journal of Adult Development, 5*(3), 145–162.

Jordan, A. E., & Meara, N. M. (1990). Ethics and the professional practice of psychologists: The roles of virtues and principles. *Professional Psychology: Research and Practice, 21*, 107–114.

King, J. E. (1991). Dysconscious racism: Ideology, identity, and the miseducation of teachers. *Journal of Negro Education, 60*(2), 133–146.

Koehn, D. (1998). *Rethinking feminist ethics: Care, trust, and empathy*. London: Routledge.

Lerman, H., & Porter, N. (Eds.). (1990). *Feminist ethics in psychotherapy*. New York: Springer.

Lopez, I. F. H. (1996). *White by law: The legal construction of race*. New York: New York University Press.

Luke, C., & Gore, J. (1992). *Feminisms and critical pedagogy*. New York: Routledge.

Lykes, M. B. (1997). Activist participatory research among the Maya of Guatemala: Constructing meanings from situated knowledge. *Journal of Social Issues, 53*, 725–746.

McIntyre, A. (1997a). Constructing an image of a white teacher. *Teachers College Record, 98*(4), 653–681.

McIntyre, A. (1997b). *Making meaning of whiteness: Exploring the racial identity of white teachers.* Albany: State University of New York Press.

McIntyre, A., Bilics, A., Colley, B., Jones, S., Smith-Mumford, P., Weaver, B., Weaver, M., & Wilson, C. (1998). Engaging in cross-racial dialogue: Does/can it lead to action? *Transformations, 9*(2), 81–99.

McIntyre, A., & Lykes, M. B. (1998). Who's the boss? Confronting whiteness and power differences within a feminist mentoring relationship in participatory action research. *Feminism & Psychology, 8*(4), 427–444.

Morawski, J. G. (1994). *Practicing feminisms, reconstructing psychology: Notes on a liminal science.* Ann Arbor: University of Michigan Press.

Ng, R., Staton, P., & Scane, J. (Eds.). (1995). *Anti-racism, feminism, and critical approaches to education.* Westport, CT: Bergin & Garvey.

Noddings, N. (1984). *Caring: A feminine approach to ethics and moral education.* Berkeley: University of California Press.

Olson, S. L., & Ceballo, R. E. (1996). Emotional well-being and parenting behavior among low-income single mothers: Social support and ethnicity as contexts of adjustment. In K. F. Wyche & F. J. Crosby (Eds.), *Women's ethnicities: Journeys through psychology* (pp. 105–123). Boulder, CO: Westview Press.

Ostrove, J., & Stewart, A. (1998). Representing Radcliffe: Perceptions and consequences of social class. *Journal of Adult Development, 5*(3), 183–194.

Pastor, J., McCormick, J., & Fine, M. (1996). Makin' homes: An urban girl thing. In B. J. R. Leadbeater & N. Way (Eds.), *Urban girls: Resisting stereotypes, creating identities* (pp. 15–34). New York: New York University Press.

Patai, D. (1991). U.S. academics and third world women: Is ethical research possible? In S. B. Gluck & D. Patai (Eds.), *Women's words: The feminist practice of oral history* (pp. 137–154). New York: Routledge.

Reay, D. (1996). Dealing with difficult differences: Reflexivity and social class in feminist research. *Feminism & Psychology, 6*(3), 443–456.

Robb, C. S. (1985). A framework for feminist ethics. In B. H. Andolsen, C. E. Gudorf, & M. D. Pellauer (Eds.), *Women's consciousness, women's conscience: A reader in feminist ethics* (pp. 211–234). Minneapolis, MN: Winston Press.

Roediger, D. (1994). *Towards the abolition of whiteness: Essays on race, politics, and working class history.* London: Verson.

Roman, L. (1993). "On the ground" with antiracist pedagogy and Raymond Williams's unfinished project to articulate a socially transformative critical realism. In D. L. Dworkin & L. Roman (Eds.), *Views beyond the border country: Raymond Williams and cultural politics* (pp. 134–158). New York: Routledge.

Scheurich, J. (1993). Toward a white discourse on white racism. *Educational Researcher, 22*(8), 5–10.

Sleeter, C. E. (1993). How white teachers construct race. In C. McCarthy & W. Crichlow (Eds.), *Race identity and representation in education* (pp. 157–171). New York: Routledge.

Sleeter, C. E. (1996). *Multicultural education as social activism*. Albany: State University of New York Press.

Sleeter, C. E., & McLaren, P. (1995). Introduction: Exploring connections to build multiculturalism. In C. E. Sleeter & P. McLaren (Eds.), *Multicultural education, critical pedagogy, and the politics of difference* (pp. 5–32). Albany: State University of New York Press.

Sparks, E. E. (1996). Overcoming stereotypes of mothers in the African American context. In K. F. Wyche & F. J. Crosby (Eds.), *Women's ethnicities: Journeys through psychology* (pp. 67–86). Boulder, CO: Westview Press.

Stewart, A. J. (1994). Toward a feminist strategy for studying women's lives. In C. E. Franz & A. J. Stewart (Eds.), *Women creating lives: Identities, resilience, and resistance* (pp. 11–36). Boulder, CO: Westview Press.

Tatum, B. (1992). Talking about race, learning about racism. *Harvard Educational Review, 62*(1), 1–24.

Tatum, B. (1994). Teaching white students about racism: The search for white allies and the restoration of hope. *Teachers College Record, 95*, 462–476.

Tripp, D. (1993). *Critical incidents in teaching: Developing professional judgment.* London: Routledge.

Unger, R. (1998). Positive marginality: Antecedents and consequences. *Journal of Adult Development, 5*(3), 163–170.

Walkerdine, V. (1996). Working-class women: Psychological and social aspects of survival. In C. Kitzinger (Ed.), *Feminist social psychologies: International perspectives* (pp. 145–162). Buckingham, UK: Open University Press.

Weiler, K. (1988). *Women teaching for change: Gender, class and power.* South Hadley, MA: Bergin & Garvey.

Wellman, D. (1993). *Portraits of white racism* (2nd ed.). New York: Cambridge University Press.

Wilkinson, S., & Kitzinger, C. (Eds.). (1993). *Heterosexuality: A 'feminism & psychology' reader.* London: Sage.

4

FEMINIST ETHICAL CONSIDERATIONS IN FORENSIC PRACTICE

LAURA S. BROWN

Forensic psychology is defined as the practice of psychology by "any psychologist, experimental or clinical, who specializes in producing or communicating psychological research or assessment information intended for application to legal issues" (Grisso, 1987, p. 831). In practice, psychologists and other mental health professionals are called on by the courts for a myriad of reasons. These include, among others, assessment of mental competency of criminal defendants, evaluation of parental capacities in custody cases, education of juries and judges as to human memory capacity, and analysis of psychological harm arising from trauma or discrimination. Forensic psychologists may also practice outside of the courtroom, consulting on jury

I give credit and thanks to those colleagues who have been my mentors and consultants in feminist forensic practice and with whom I have had the chance to develop my thinking on ethics in this field. Lenore Walker and Lynne Bravo Rosewater were initial and ongoing mentors and role models, and both contributed directly to the development of this chapter, with frank input on their conflicting views about the Simpson case. I thank them both for their candor and their trust in my ability to treat this issue fairly. Shirley Feldman-Summers, Susan (Shaul) Raab-Cohen, Deborah Frank Murray, and Rebecca Saltonstall were members of my initial feminist forensic consultation group, and Shirley remains my ongoing consultant. Nancy Lynn Baker, Louise Fitzgerald, Mary Ann Dutton, Maria P. P. Root, and Andrea Jacobson are other feminist forensic practitioners whose ongoing input has enlightened my forensic practice and contributed to my observations in this chapter.

selection, assisting with research, or coaching an attorney on effectively cross-examining the other side's witnesses.

Each state or province has its own law; there is yet another code for the federal courts in both the United States and Canada, and differing rules for juvenile and family court systems or regulatory settings. Criminal and civil cases have different standards and practices from the others. Nonetheless, a psychologist's role in all of these settings, regardless of task, remains roughly the same: educator to the psychologically lay public, juries, and judges regarding psychological knowledge. Because of their interface with the law and the often highly public and visible nature of their work, forensic psychologists have long been specifically concerned with ethics and standards of conduct (Bersoff, 1995; Committee on Ethical Guidelines for Forensic Psychologists [CEGFP], 1991). Misconduct by a forensic practitioner is rarely invisible. It also has potential real-world consequences, such as loss of a child for a parent seeking custody, loss of liberty or heightened severity of sentencing in a criminal case, loss of money in a civil suit, or—in the most profound case—loss of life itself in a capital murder case.

Commentators on ethical issues in forensic practice have been many (see Bersoff, 1995, for a review of these resources). Such analysis tends to focus on the ethical risks inherent in the forensic arena. These risks are seen as stemming from the adversarial model that prevails in the legal system. There, *truth* is required to be defined in terms that often exceed or even violate the knowledge bases of psychology. For example, a psychologist is often called on to testify about a sex offender's risk to reoffend in the context of both sentencing and probation or parole hearings. Courts and sentencing boards are more likely to release those people identified as a lower risk. Making such probabilistic statements may go beyond what the science of psychology can currently support.

But the pull from both prosecution and defense to ignore such limits in giving testimony is often great. The offender's sentence—going into community treatment versus being sent to prison for many years—may turn on the psychologist's words. Psychologists know that their predictive capacities have limits, yet the legal system attempts to seduce psychologists to ignore or understate such limits (see Grisso & Appelbaum, 1992). As Anderten, Staulcup, and Grisso (1980) put it,

> our basic concern is that the ethical standards of the psychologist can be jeopardized in the courtroom setting because of the psychologist's failure to recognize that the basic tenets of the legal system and the science of psychology are often at odds. (p. 764)

For feminist practitioners, another set of ethical complexities is also present in forensic practice. In this chapter, I examine how feminist ethics can inform forensic psychological practice and, in turn, the particular jeopardies to feminist ethics in that context.

SPECIAL ETHICAL CHALLENGES OF FEMINIST FORENSIC PRACTICE

Feminist practitioners have recently entered the forensic arena. Lenore Walker's (1989a, 1989b) and Lynne Bravo Rosewater's (1985) work for the defense of battered women and Phyllis Chesler's (1987) testimony for women in contested custody cases likely represent some of the earliest applications of feminist psychological scholarship to forensic practice. These authors set the parameters for an emerging paradigm of feminist forensic practice. Most self-identified feminist forensic practitioners appear to be either researchers or clinicians (or both), with expertise in such topics as battered women, sexual abuse and assault, sexual harassment, gender discrimination, misconduct by therapists, and child custody. These topics often engage the interest of feminist psychologists because these legal issues arise from the realities of women's lives at the points where those lives come into contact and conflict with the legal system.

The feminist practice of forensic psychology raises particular ethical challenges above and beyond those that are inherent in forensic practice itself. Much of this challenge arises from a potential fundamental conflict of values between mainstream forensic psychological practice and feminist ethical considerations. Feminist practitioners regard all of their work as inherently political. One of the strategies used by forensic psychologists to create an ethical bottom line for nonfeminist–standard practice has been to assume a stance of "objectivity" or "neutrality" as regards to matters at issue in a given case. Departures from this stance of objective neutrality are seen as potentially problematic, if not inherently unethical. The Specialty Guidelines for Forensic Psychologists, developed by the Division of Psychology and Law of the American Psychological Association (APA), speak indirectly to this: "Forensic psychologists recognize that their own personal values, [and] moral beliefs . . . may interfere with their ability to practice competently" (CEGFP, 1991, p. 658).

The assumptions contained in this statement are frequently interpreted by forensic practitioners and attorneys to mean that one should avoid practicing in any realm where one's values and beliefs may apply. For example, Stanley Brodsky (1990), a leading forensic psychologist, argued that if a psychologist is morally opposed to the death penalty, then she or he should ethically refrain from assessing a person's mental competency for execution because her or his beliefs about the death penalty per se would preclude the conduct of an objective, and thus ethical, evaluation of the person's ability to be put to death. In practice, this assumption of moral neutrality translates into the willingness of forensic practitioners to work on any side of any issue where they are minimally competent to practice and to be retained as experts for whichever attorney first calls on them for their services. Forensic psychologists and psychiatrists who have reputations for almost never serving one or the other side are frequently referred to in conversation (and the occasional Internet posting) in unflattering terms by attorneys and colleagues alike, suggesting that the expert is for sale rather than an independent decision maker. Two inherent assumptions in the forensic practice mainstream are that justice is blind and fair; another assumption is that psychologists who are critical of the legal system should not be working in it, judging by the tenor of discussion at psychology–law meetings and on Internet forensic psychology lists.

At least initially, this standard regarding the awareness of one's values and the impact of values on one's work would appear not to be problematic for feminist practitioners. For example, in the Feminist Therapy Institute (FTI; 1990) Code of Ethics, which represents the best known codification of feminist ethics in psychology, the feminist practitioner is adjured that "feminist therapists recognize that their values influence the therapeutic process and clarify with clients the nature and effect of those values" (p. 38). This standard requires that the feminist practitioner be self-reflective regarding values and offer informed consent to clients about how those values will translate into the professional relationship. The notion that any practitioner might be free of personal values and completely objective, however, is considered unlikely in feminist ethical thinking.

Previously, I described objectivity as the name given to the subjectivities of a dominant group (Brown, 1994). To define oneself as a feminist and then claim neutrality is perceived by both feminists and nonfeminists alike as oxymoronic because to be a feminist is an overt values stance. In consequence, feminist practitioners, myself included, frequently find themselves faced in the courtroom with challenges to their right to testify simply because they elucidate that values stance. Such attempts to exclude testimony by feminist practitioners argue that they are precluded from the expert role by having espoused a feminist theory of psychology. Feminist practitioners are also challenged because they assert that objectivity takes second place to the importance of clarity and honesty about values in their communications with juries and judges. Feminist practitioners have not found an embrace of values to bar forensic practice; however, feminist forensic psychologists try to distinguish for the courts between *awareness of bias*, which is defined in feminist practice as congruent with the ethical norms for forensic psychology, and so-called *absence of bias*, which is usually how those norms are operationalized.

It is not surprising that when feminist practitioners began to pioneer the field of forensic work in the defense of battered women who kill their abusers, they immediately ran into the difficulties of a value-free legal theory in the form of legal definitions of self-defense. Prior to the introduction of feminist psychological testimony, the doctrine of self-defense in common law assumed that an attacker would be of about equal size and strength to her or his victim and that the weapons of self-defense would consequently be roughly equivalent. In this paradigm, fists are self-defense against fists, but weapons are not. Early battered women's self-defense cases faced the problem of challenging this standard in a situation where the attacker, the battering man, was larger and more powerful with his fists and feet alone. The battered woman's reach for a gun, knife, scissors, or other lethal instrument was in such cases a necessary leveling of the playing field. Initially, many battered women were sentenced to prison because they had been unable to defend themselves with the unequal "equal force" of their own hands and feet and were consequently defined by the legal system as going beyond the common law doctrine of self-defense (see Walker, 1989a, and 1989b, for in-depth descriptions of this issue).

Feminist psychologists who attempted to explicate these women's behaviors were considered by many in the mainstream of forensic psychology to be reaching past the norms of forensic practice by asserting that self-defense, rather than revenge, was the woman's motive in killing. Such psychologists were tagged "advocates" rather than experts. Yet it was precisely such testimony that by educating judges finally led to a change in case law, namely, in the matter of *State of Washington v. Yvonne Wanrow* (1977; see Jones, 1980, for an in-depth treatment of these changes in case law). In this trial, the feminist expert testimony convinced the appellate court that a woman could be in fear for her life even when not under direct attack and that fighting back with a weapon was equal force and self-defense. As a consequence of such education by feminist forensic practitioners, legal practices regarding battered women who killed began to change.

Despite victories such as these, the legal system in the United States, and in most industrialized countries, continues to reflect profoundly patriarchal ethics. Consequently, the most fundamental ethical dilemmas for the feminist forensic practitioner continue to be found in this clash of ethical cultures, which occur each time a feminist psychologist takes the witness stand. Mainstream ethics of forensic practice assume the possibility of objectivity and neutrality, in tandem with the culture in general. It celebrates the distance of the practitioner from the issue as the evidence of highest virtue. Feminist ethics, as described by the FTI code and elsewhere, require the practitioners to identify values, practice self-awareness, and engage in the empowerment of the client through informed consent (Brown, 1994). When the "client" is the jury, which is ultimately the case for any forensic practitioner, the delivery of this informed consent and the explication of the psychologist's biases and their impact on testimony become more complex than simply handing an informed consent statement to a psychotherapy client. It is a challenge to imagine how an expert can create an egalitarian, empowering relationship with the jury. Yet it can be a possible challenge to meet, with highly satisfying results.

Mainstream forensic practitioners may argue, and sometimes have argued, that by taking a feminist stance, the feminist forensic practitioner ceases to be an educator, whether to attorneys or triers-of-fact. She or he steps into the position of an advocate, which is assumed to be a violation of forensic psychology ethics (because the role of advocate is reserved for the attorney whose task it is to advocate). This sort of challenge is frequently raised to feminist educators in more usual settings, such as the university classroom (Caplan, 1994). The underlying yet misleading assumption in such challenges is that one can only educate when one is detached from the information delivered and that no bias adheres to the choices of what information is chosen to be delivered or the manner in which the information is framed to the students (see Kitchener, chap. 2, this volume).

In consequence, feminist psychologists who choose to practice in the forensic arena must come prepared to argue that education is always values based and that specialized knowledge arising from feminist psychology can and ought to be presented, so as to inform the legal process. Additionally, feminist forensic psychologists must have in mind a clear feminist strategy for empowering and educating the jury and develop that strategy with the attorney who calls them to the stand. Feminist forensic psychologists have an ethical obligation to weave into their testimony a challenge to false dichotomies between education and advocacy. A feminist forensic ethic states that all forensic practitioners bring a bias and politic to their work, whether it is conscious and explored, as should be true for the feminist practitioner, or nonconscious and unaware, as appears frequently true for nonfeminist forensic psychologists. One task for feminist forensic practitioners, then, is to expose this reality to triers-of-fact by responding to challenges regarding their bias with straightforward education regarding the differences between unacknowledged and stated biases.

Feminist practitioners in pursuit of this ethic of jury empowerment should encourage the attorney who is qualifying them to the court to ask them to explain feminist psychology and to define how it is their theoretical orientation. The feminist psychologist has an ethical obligation to inform the court that all mental health professionals have a theoretical perspective and biases that might arise from that perspective. All need to acknowledge such bias. It would then be incumbent on the feminist psychologist to describe steps taken to be aware of bias and make it transparent to the jury. The feminist practitioner can then invite the jury to use its own skills at critically analyzing her, and other experts', testimony in light of this en-hanced knowledge about bias. Courts frequently rule that certain information can be used by juries to enhance or diminish the weight of evidence given; an explication of bias by the feminist expert witness falls within the purview of such weight.

Feminist forensic practitioners should focus on the ethics of how they can present testimony in a manner that empowers the jury in their roles as decision makers, avoiding more than necessary the creation of a false sense of the "expert" as infallible. It is useful and humbling for experts to remind themselves that theirs are only opinions and that the jury holds the ultimate power of decision making as a means of deconstructing the dominant model of the psychologist as expert witness. My metaphor for this ethical stance is that a feminist expert does not hide behind the mask of professionalism, like *The Wizard of Oz* behind his smoke and mirrors, but she or he instead steps out from behind the curtain, revealing her or his information in a respectful form that educates and empowers jurors and makes them a part of a collaborative thought process with the psychologist.

A feminist ethic would lead a feminist forensic evaluator to feel obli-gated to have familiarity with research that is pertinent to a particular topic. This contrasts with the behavior of some nonfeminist forensic practitioners, who, especially in areas such as harassment and discrimination, seem to be ignorant of or even avoidant of knowledge about that topic. Whereas it would seem intuitively obvious that an expert testifying in court should have in-depth knowledge of the topic being litigated, anecdotal evidence from discussions among feminist forensic practitioners suggests that this is rarely the case when matters of interest to feminist forensic psychology are at hand. Based on my interviews with a number of feminist forensic experts, I think that it is not unusual for a nonfeminist expert in these sorts of cases to claim greater objectivity on a topic based on her or his ignorance of it. However, basing expertise on ignorance violates a feminist ethic. To be able to opine that a person's behavior is consistent with what would be expected in a given situation, one must know the research on how people in that situation behave. In this context, competence to testify is defined in terms of knowledge and familiarity with a topic rather than by absence of the same.

An example of this contrast in the definition of competence as an expert witness comes from my own forensic practice. In the case of *Samantha Johnson v. Boeing* (1989), I was retained as the plaintiff's damages expert in a case of sexual harassment. The defense expert testified that he found the research literature on sexual harassment and other forms of sexual victimization overly political and consequently had avoided reading it be-cause he feared it would interfere with his objectivity in the assessment of a woman alleging sexual harassment in a mostly male work environment.

He defined his expertise by his many years of clinical and assessment experience and by his disinterest in and lack of knowledge of the entire topic of sexual harassment. He was critical of me for having a feminist "bias" in my work. I countered in my testimony that my feminist perspective led me to an ethical obligation to be extremely familiar with that research, up to the point of regular personal consultation with the psychological researchers who generated it, and to evaluate the plaintiff and her claims in the context of that research. I also opined that my ethics required me to make my bias explicit and visible to the jurors, so that they could decide for themselves what it meant to them in their weighing of my opinions. The jury found in favor of the plaintiff, awarding her more than $100,000 as well as all of her attorney fees and other costs.

FEMINIST FORENSICS: PART OF THE SOLUTION OR PART OF THE PROBLEM?

In addition to challenges from dominant legal and psychological cultures to the presence of feminist practitioners in the courtroom, ethical challenges emerge from within feminist psychology itself. Feminist psychologists can legitimately ask whether it is ethical at all for them to participate in a system that some scholars have described as misogynist or whether their engagement with the justice system simply upholds this particular patriarchal institution. This sort of self-questioning mirrors feminist psychological critiques of feminist therapy (Kitzinger & Perkins, 1993). Feminist practice in psychology is a theoretical orientation that maintains a clear values stance regarding social arrangements, one which critiques many of the assumptions underpinning both civil and criminal justice systems.

In the legal realm, feminist scholars are among the foremost critics of the legal system as it currently functions; as one commentator, Ruthann Robson (1992), noted, the U.S. system of jurisprudence is based on English common law, which in turn was designed by and for White male property owners for the protection of their rights to that property, with *property* defined at various times as including White women, children, and all people of Color. Patricia Williams (1991), an African American feminist legal scholar and critic, commented on the irony of her teaching legal concepts whose basis was the enslavement of other African American women and of the contradictions embedded in her participation as a lawyer and legal scholar in a system still haunted by the ghosts of legally imposed and legally supported oppression. Feminisms of all varieties have worked to undermine the construction of White women, children, and people of Color as property.

In consequence of this inherently critical stance, a feminist politic, in law and psychology alike, is at heart subversive to the core values of American and other Europeanized systems of jurisprudence. This is true despite the fact that over time, White women and women and men of color have been formally removed from the property category (although children continue to be placed there both explicitly and implicitly) because the standards and norms that inform the civil and criminal legal systems presuppose the realities of a dominant group membership. The net effect of this sort of underlying assumption is that frequently the insights of feminist psychology and the standards of law clash, as described earlier in the discussion of bias and values in forensic practice.

The feminist practitioners must thus question themselves as to whether functioning as a forensic expert in this flawed and oppressive system only operates to create illusions of justice or fairness when in fact none may exist. A purely radical and separatist feminist ethic, as argued by such authors as Daly (1978) or Hoagland (1988) or by such feminist psychologists as Perkins (1991), suggests that when feminist psychologists work forensically, they encourage the legal system to continue unchanged in its attitudes and values. In turn, they may be corrupted from their own feminist ethics by their participation. Other feminist ethical thinkers, myself included, in turn have argued that such participation is necessary as one aspect of the feminist commitment to social change. They argue that to ignore any possible avenue for creating social change might ultimately undermine the feminist project of justice making (Brabeck & Brown, 1997; Brown, 1994; FTI, 1990).

But there is no clearly defined feminist ethical stance on the matter of participation, and debates within and among feminist psychologists are likely to continue on this topic. Also in reality a feminist expert does not control which facets of her knowledge will be allowed into the courtroom by a judge. For example, in a racial discrimination case, a feminist expert on systemic racism was precluded from testifying; lacking information to place the employer's behaviors into context, the jury were only able to see "personality conflicts," not the subtle systemwide racism visible to the expert.

IF FORENSIC, THEN HOW IS ONE TO BE FEMINIST AND ETHICAL?

For feminist psychologists choosing to participate in the legal system, the questions then become those of how their forensic practice can be both feminist and in feminist terms ethical. If the core ethic of feminist practice is to advance social justice and feminist consciousness (Brabeck & Brown, 1997) and the goal of feminist psychology is to be one aspect of feminist revolution (Brown, 1994), then what considerations must a feminist psychologist undertake before becoming a forensic practitioner? Just as being a therapist who specializes in treating women does not make one a feminist therapist (Brown, 1991; Caplan, 1992), so being a forensic expert who testifies on so-called "women's issues," such as custody, battering, sexual abuse, or sexual harassment, does not make one a feminist forensic practitioner. Neither is direct testimony the only clearly feminist means of effecting change in the justice system.

It would seem that the primary ethical requirement for feminist forensic practice is that the practitioner question herself or himself as to how and whether the decision to participate in a given case in a particular manner will advance or undermine more general feminist principles. In legal settings, relevant principles include the empowerment of consumers of services, enhancement of women's dignity and the well-being of other oppressed group members, support for ongoing social justice struggles inherent in a particular case, and impact of the specific instance of forensic practice on oppressed groups in the broader culture.

THE O. J. SIMPSON CASE: A MODEL FEMINIST FORENSIC ETHICAL DILEMMA

Answering questions such as these is never simple because there are often competing ethical demands and layers of complexity inherent in the facts of a particular case. An extreme and public example of the potential for complexity was illustrated by the O. J. Simpson case, where a man with an established history of battering was accused, found not guilty criminally, but later was held responsible under civil law of murdering his former wife whom he had battered during their marriage. A well-known feminist forensic practitioner, Lenore Walker, who had testified frequently for battered women who killed batterers in self-defense, was engaged as an expert witness for the defense. She had communicated in a number of public forums her intention to testify as to the unlikelihood that a man with Simpson's psychological characteristics, which she reported that she had determined through scores of hours of careful evaluation, would be the sort of batterer who would escalate to murder.

Her participation in this case evoked enormous controversy among feminists, some of which still simmers. Some feminist groups (e.g., National Coalition Against Domestic Violence, 1994) condemned the choice as clearly a violation of feminist ethics because Walker's actions were perceived by many formerly battered women as a personal betrayal and her testimony as undermining to what she had previously said in court in defense of battered women who killed in self-defense. Other feminists (e.g., Freyd, 1995) have suggested that by seizing control over how information about battered women and battering was presented in this trial and by advising defense attorneys against character assassination attempts on the battered murder victim, the forensic psychologist was taking a difficult yet clearly ethical feminist stance.

Walker and her collaborator on this project (Stahley & Walker, 1997), also a feminist psychologist, asserted that their decision to become involved for the defense reflected their decision to make primary a feminist antiracist ethic of undermining assumptions about African American men in relationships with White women as well as their desire to educate the defendant and his attorneys about the errors of the defendant's well-established battering behaviors (it is of note that Stahly, although also long involved in the movement against domestic violence, has not been the target of the kinds of attacks sustained by Walker during and since the Simpson case). Stahley (Stahley & Walker, 1997) wrote that "it would be my job, if I accepted it, to educate the defense about domestic violence" (p. 427). As Walker (Stahley & Walker, 1997) wrote,

> the opportunity for misunderstanding and backlash [in this case] endangered the hard-fought gains over the past 20 years, especially if research data taken out of context . . . were presented to confuse rather than fully educate the jury. Had the prosecutors called on me for consultation, I would have provided it. (p. 428)

Walker added that "an important aspect of this work has been to assure that the media and legal community understand the psychological dynamics of relationship abuse and not blame the victim" (p. 428). She described getting a commitment from the lead defense attorney that there would be no negative publicity about the murdered woman and told him that she would walk off the case if this happened.

Walker described her sense that the ethical imperative for her was to ensure that no one—defense, prosecution, or the media—distort the research data on battering or lethal violence. She also described her difficulties with the unanticipated negative responses that her decision to work as a defense expert engendered, primarily among feminists and battered women's advocates. Stahley and Walker (1997) jointly discussed a dynamic tension between the perceived feminist ethic of loyalty to battered women as a group as an overriding ethical standard presumed by others as inviolable and their perception that feminist ethics in this matter were more specifically concerned with truth telling about the nature of violence in relationships, questions of racism, and the scientific support, or lack thereof, for the prosecution theory that the defendant's history of battering made him per se a murderer. They also commented on the issue of combining an antiracist ethic with their core feminist commitment to stopping violence against women, highlighting the ethical complexities that emerge when a historical racist pattern of an African American man being accused of the murder of a White woman is entangled in the historical misogynist pattern of violent men murdering wives and former wives.

Rosewater (1999), commenting on Stahley and Walker's (1997) analysis, argued that to frame the ethical dilemma as one of combating abuse versus combating racism presents a false dichotomy. She commented that to join the debate at that level was ethically problematic. She argued that Walker, in particular, paid insufficient attention to the ethical principal of nonmalfeasance in regard to the impact of her decision on battered women, the consumer group who were most powerfully negatively affected by the choice of their long-time advocate to testify in defense of a self-confessed batterer. Rosewater agreed that antiracism is an important ethical consideration for feminists and that it is valuable to undermine assumptions that African American men are dangerous to White women. She suggested that in this case, the strategy chosen by Stahley and Walker to address this dilemma was problematic because it ultimately was harmful to many women, while not clearly disrupting racist discourse.

This case illustrates the quandary faced by feminist forensic practitioners: Are there cases that feminists ethically cannot take? Did any good from Walker and Stahley's participation in the defense case (neither were ever called to testify in either the criminal or civil trial) outweigh any harm done? Examining the matter in the light of the outcomes of both the criminal and civil cases and in terms of feminist ethical considerations, the answers remain somewhat unclear. Nonetheless, my current assessment is that feminists' participation in the Simpson case did not advance feminist goals of social justice, either around issues of violence against women or antiracism.

Neither feminist psychologist was afforded an opportunity to challenge the notion, which was repeatedly presented as a primary defense strategy in the criminal trial, that justice for a murdered White woman and justice for an accused African American man were ultimately in competition. The feminist data about battering were never presented to the jury or the public in this case. In the civil case, serious victim blaming directed at Nicole Brown Simpson occurred on the part of the defense as well as outright denials by Simpson that he had battered his former wife. Both feminist psychologists, particularly Walker, were ultimately used by the defense team for impression management yet were silenced in the most important setting; namely, the defense never called either to the witness stand. Many formerly battered women experienced betrayal by Walker, who had been an important icon to battered women and their allies; relationships between and among feminist forensic practitioners became strained.

Of greatest concern to me is the possibility that Walker's strength as a forensic expert in the future for women who kill may have been undermined because her testimony about the reasonableness of a woman's fear for her life (a core of the battered women's self-defense legal strategy) is now challenged by Walker's public statements in the Simpson case that few batterers will be killers—a stance that belies the reasonableness of a woman's fear for her life. Such conflicting information may also undermine the testimony of other feminist experts for battered women, who may now find themselves cross-examined in the context of these apparent contradictions.

None of this suggests that either Walker or Stahley acted in anything but an entirely ethical manner, and clearly from their discussion, at each stage of the process they carefully weighed these risks and believed them worth the effort that they each made. The problematic outcome of their decision to work for the Simpson defense illustrates how, with the clearest of feminist ethical analyses, consultation, and input from colleagues, a feminist forensic practitioner can find her or his politics overrun by the realities of the patriarchal legal system and her or his effectiveness as an educator silenced by the voices of the dominant culture as well as the decisions of lawyers to include or exclude her or his presence from the courtroom.

PATHWAYS THROUGH COMPLEXITY OR ANOTHER COMPLICATED OUTCOME?

So what could have made this case a win for feminist principles? Is there any one overarching feminist value that should guide forensic psychologists in this sort of complex case? In the above example, if the accused had been a woman and the case involved battering in a lesbian relationship, would the questions and dilemmas have been any different? Is it inherently feminist to defend lesbians, for instance, or sexual abuse survivors no matter what they have done? Chesler (1993) suggested as much in her defense of Aline Wuornos, a lesbian and survivor of sexual abuse who was convicted of murdering a number of men who were her prostitution customers. Had Simpson not been such a celebrity but merely an unknown African American man would that have made the decision to participate as a defense witness any more or less ethically complex or supportable? Or would it simply have shielded the psychologist in question from the criticisms of her colleagues and demands of the media because few forensic practitioners have the sort of spotlight thrown on their work as occurred in this case? What if the defendant had been Caucasian and the murdered woman of Color? Would questions of challenging racist biases and assumptions been as important to raise in that instance? No clear answers to these questions will apply in every legal case; instead, the questions illustrate that feminists, in making ethical decisions regarding forensic practice, must consider the web of complexity that each case offers rather than attempting to prematurely simplify the ethical dilemmas involved.

To simply say that a feminist forensic practitioner can never work for an X sort of client or on a Y side of a case or cause, although appearing to simplify the argument through the foreclosure of possibilities, fails to adequately take into account the possible fine details on which the meaning of a legal case for feminist ethics might turn. However, such cases highlight the kinds of questions that a feminist forensic practitioner must confront for ethical practice. There continues to be no consensus about which ethical principles must be paramount for a feminist practitioner, and collectivist versus individual case scenario paradigms for conceptualizing the ethics of an issue remain in tension with one another.

There is no one clearly overarching feminist ethical principle guiding the feminist forensic practitioner in her or his decision making. Even an ethical stance of choosing the path of the greatest good for the greatest number cannot ensure an outcome consistent with feminist political principles because the forensic practitioner controls so little about the outcomes emerging from her or his forensic participation. This clash of ethical primacy is not unique to feminist mental health practitioners. For example, this case evoked fierce debate among the feminist political community, particularly in Los Angeles (CA) where the case was taking place, over whether violence against women or antiracism was more important to attend to. From my perspective a clearly feminist ethical stance would be to attempt to find a strategy that addresses both issues in tandem, seeing them as joined at the root in the history of patriarchy (Lerner, 1993) and its construction of White women and women and men of Color alike as "legitimate" targets of ownership and random violence. The ethical forensic feminist psychologist finds herself or himself having to explore complex and nuanced meanings of power, oppression, and social justice to arrive at a decision about where to lend her or his expertise.

WHEN THE EXPERT'S IDENTITY BECOMES AN ETHICAL ISSUE

In a much less public manner, this sort of ethically complex question is faced constantly by feminist forensic practitioners. In another case, as a lesbian forensic practitioner, I was asked to serve as an expert witness by the plaintiff's attorney in a case where a heterosexual African American woman alleged that she had been sexually harassed by her work supervisor, a Caucasian lesbian. One of the attorney's stated agendas in engaging my services, aside from the fact that he had previously worked with me and apparently respected my work, was that he believed that my presence as a plaintiff's expert would immunize the plaintiff's case against claims of anti-lesbian bias. It was less likely that a lesbian psychologist would have a priori biases against the alleged harasser simply on the basis of her sexual orientation. What was potentially ethically problematic for me was whether I might be used to victimize a lesbian or enable homophobia on the part of the plaintiff. Would my presence be providing a cover for discrimination by creating an appearance of a lack of bias? That is, what if the plaintiff were simply biased against lesbians and bringing sexual harassment charges was seen as a way of actually lesbian bashing her former supervisor?

Because it is not unknown for lesbians and gay men to face the unfair assertion that the simple fact of their being "out" is a sexual harassment of heterosexist coworkers, the potential ethical dilemmas in taking this case were large and complex. I had to begin by discussing with the attorney that I was unwilling to be used as the "good" lesbian testifying against the "bad" lesbian and that as in most legal cases, I would consider any discussion of my sexual orientation to be off limits in the courtroom. In so doing, I had to risk my relationship with (and continued employment by) the attorney. In conducting my assessment, I needed to carefully examine all possible potential avenues for my bias to affect my judgment. As a White lesbian, I was evaluating an African American heterosexual woman who was accusing another White lesbian. I was also a psychologist who in my work role needed to explore all the possible competing hypotheses that might be present in a sexual harassment case.

In this particular instance, I told the attorney that I believed it was important that he inform his client that I was a lesbian and offer her the opportunity to request that he engage a different expert. She did not do so, but at the time of the actual interviews, I raised the issue with her again, wanting to be certain that she felt that she was receiving a fair hearing. I also reminded the attorney that as is always the case for a forensic psychologist, I could arrive at opinions that were not helpful to his client's case and that as a feminist I believed that a weak or unfounded charge of sexual harassment undermines feminist goals of social justice in the legal context. Because this attorney and I had previously had the experience of my arriving at findings that were adverse to the case, this discussion was perhaps easier than it might have been with an attorney for whom I had not previously worked.

When I conducted the assessment of the plaintiff, the question of the accuser's possible antilesbian bias was one of the factors I scrutinized. This emerged as a nonissue in the face of her many close and positive relationships with lesbian friends and relatives. In fact, the problem was more one of the plaintiff's prolesbian feelings and how they had been affected by her work-place experience. A part of her distress emerged because she felt that her supervisor had violated what she believed to be a shared ethic among lesbians of not engaging in boundary-violating behaviors and that she had initially trusted the supervisor more than she would other White women because of the latter's lesbian identity. In this instance, a prolesbian bias in the plaintiff was an aspect of her upset at what had happened in the workplace, an important aspect of my analysis of damages. Ultimately, the case emerged as one with many layers of complexity and was settled before trial.

In this example, the competing feminist ethical considerations did not tell me in advance whether I could ethically work on this case; however, they did function to heighten my awareness of possible biases and problem areas. I was required to critically examine the apparently competing factors to find the core principles of feminist practice that would guide me. Antiracism and the empowerment of victims of sexual harassment are feminist ethical considerations, as is combating antilesbian bias. Assuming such bias in a nonlesbian would have led me astray; ignoring its potential would have equally misguided my understanding of the matter.

The meaning of oppressed group membership and, for this particular plaintiff, the violation by her supervisor of her assumptions of connection and shared values was at heart most important to understanding this case. It illustrates how simplistic or dichotomous paradigms for understanding feminist ethical dilemmas can be profoundly wrongheaded. The ethical charge to a feminist forensic practitioner here is to develop a strategy that does not privilege one social justice goal over another but finds when possible the places where they connect. The only certainty is that simplistic solutions or decision rules can rarely ensure feminist outcomes.

WHERE THERE ARE NO SIMPLE SOLUTIONS, SOME DECISION-MAKING STRATEGIES

Always and only working for the plaintiff's side of a civil case in matters involving discrimination or violation does not ensure a feminist ethical stance because plaintiffs may be advancing bias or oppression by the pursuit of their particular claims or may have fabricated a claim. Neither can a feminist stance in criminal law be embodied by working only for the defense, not the prosecution, in matters where there are questions of abuse or discrimination introduced as possible mitigating factors. The feminist forensic psychologist must be ethically guided by the overarching question of how her or his behavior is likely to influence feminist goals of social justice. Empowering a particular person from an oppressed group, for example, may not empower that group or undermine cultural oppression; not all oppressed people have an identification with their group or a consciousness of the relatedness of their experience to collective experiences. The relationship of the individual case to the overall social and political context must be taken into account as a guide to ethical decision making.

Although feminist forensic activity in certain forums has been reasonably noncontroversial to feminists, some topics evoke fierce debate in regards to appropriate feminist involvement. Recently, the controversy over delayed recall of childhood sexual abuse has led to feminists staking out positions on both sides of the issue. Some (e.g., Tavris, 1993) have argued that for feminists to encourage belief in recovered memories infantilizes women and cements them in a victim position. Some advocates for the so-called "false memory" movement have even asserted that to credit delayed recall of childhood trauma is antifeminist because of the implied criticism of mothers as negligent (Michelle Gregg, personal communication, March 1996). Other feminists have argued that the only ethical stance that can be taken is in complete solidarity with sexual abuse survivors (Steinem, 1995). I argued that the position of the false memory movement silences survivors (Brown, 1997) and at the metalevel upholds patriarchal conceptualizations of paternal control over children, particularly daughters.

Forensically, these arguments can crystallize when an adult survivor sues her or his alleged perpetrator, creating dilemmas for the feminist practitioner (Brown, 1995). For instance, in many jurisdictions, a nonoffending mother must be sued and legally declared negligent for a survivor to collect monetary damages. Can a feminist psychologist participate forensically in a case where mother blaming is at the core of the legal strategy? When the competing empowerment and rights of two women are at stake, who does one empower? Is it ever impossible to empower one woman at the expense of another, or does this create a situation in which one woman's individual dignity will be disrespected (Lerman & Porter, 1990)? What if the survivor is a man? Or what if the evidence demonstrates that the mother has clearly, in fact, behaved in an abusive or negligent manner?

Here, again, complexity is best responded to by a search for core feminist concepts that would inform a particular case. Assuming that the gender (or race, social class, or sexual orientation) of the actors in a particular legal drama will answer the questions avoids the more basic ethical question of what strategy will best potentially undermine patriarchal understandings and realities.

In the matter of child custody, feminist ethical dilemmas may be even more agonizing. Evidence suggests that many contested cases of child custody arise from relationships in which the husband has been violent against the wife and is now using the legal system to continue a reign of coercion and control over her, even after she has attempted to leave the marriage (Walker & Edwall, 1987). Despite this, even fathers with a documented history of violence are more likely to obtain custody in the minority of cases where there is a custody battle (Chesler, 1987). Yet in a custody evaluation, the role of the mental health expert is to be allied neither with the father nor the mother but to assess what constitutes the best interest of the child or children involved (APA, 1994). What does this mean if the father is, when all is said and done, the better parent? What if there has been no abuse or violation and the battle over custody represents a good father's genuine concern for the well-being of his children?

Chesler (1987) seemed to argue that mothers are always the better parents simply because of their gender and having given birth to the child; she is harshly critical of "good fathers." But is her stance consistent with a feminist ethic? If a mother appears weaker as a parent, is the feminist ethical obligation to search for feminist psychological scholarship to explain or excuse her deficits, so as to empower the woman? For example, is it possible that the "poor mothering" judgment reflects racist or classist stereotypes or an overvaluation of certain skills in the assessment of good parenting not inherent to the task but more tied to factors founded in power differentials such as access to financial or educational resources? Or is the empowerment of the child in this instance an overriding consideration?

What about a custody dispute between two women parents? What is the ethical feminist position to take when the mother who did not give birth is judged by the evaluator to be the more effective parent than the mother who did? Questions of essentialism in feminist thought (Hare-Mustin & Marecek, 1990) and the notion that biology makes a "real" mother enter powerfully into these questions because an ethic founded in essentialism will likely provide decisions for a biological mother, whereas an ethic founded elsewhere will not point toward such assumptions. Even though there is no clear feminist ethical guideline regarding essentialist thinking—which frequently informs some schools of feminist psychological scholarship—I would argue that essentialism is linked at the root to racism because both assume biologically inherent behavioral traits and, in consequence, a dangerous foundation on which to base ethical considerations. In matters such as these, an examination of contextual factors can assist in informing the forensic practitioner. That is, how will the most vulnerable person be empowered and patriarchal values most challenged in this particular family?

Most cases where feminist forensic psychologists get involved are likely to be equally rich in ethical questions and quandaries as the ones described above. Rarely is a case presented in which the ethical feminist stance for the forensic psychologist is immediately clear and apparent. Thus, the initial ethical stance that must be taken by feminist practitioners is one of willingness to question their assumptions within the broader framework of feminist values, ethics, and politics and to seek for overarching feminist values that will tie apparently competing issues in the case more closely together. Such an approach will likely arise from a basic assumption that any choice will have both risks and benefits to feminist goals, given the vicissitudes of forensic practice, and that there is unlikely to be consensus among feminist psychologists regarding the right choice in more highly charged and complicated legal cases. However, there must also be a basic assumption that even in the highly chaotic world of the courtroom, there is usually some core feminist value that can be identified and expressed in the work of the feminist practitioner and that feminist forensic psychologists have the ethical responsibility to search for that core value before proceeding with their work on a case.

FEMINIST ETHICAL STRATEGIES IN FORENSIC PRACTICE CONSULTATION

As with other varieties of feminist ethical challenges, those that evolve from forensic practice may lend themselves to resolution through decision-making strategies that enhance the likelihood of an outcome that satisfies feminist ethical norms. Chief among these is the use of consultation among feminist forensic practitioners. Although the risks and benefits of involvement in a particular case from a given perspective may seem intuitively obvious, frequently angles to complex cases are more easily seen by one's colleagues than by oneself. This is not a call for consensus but instead a valuing of more collective, collaborative decision making in the realm of ethical dilemmas. Whereas consultation should be an aspect of any forensic (or other) practitioner's usual strategies for self-care and continuing professional education, certain types of situations should raise warning flags for the feminist practitioner and lead directly and quickly to an ethics consult with a feminist colleague or colleagues. Pursuit of competing opinions is especially valuable, so that the feminist forensic psychologist is required to weigh and resolve dynamic tensions in a relational context with colleagues before putting them into the public sphere of the courtroom.

1. *Cases where there is the actual or potential risk of notoriety and media exposure*. Rarely does the media represent the facts of a notorious legal case adequately, and even more unusually does the role of the forensic expert in such a case appear in anything but highly condensed "sound bite" forms in the press. In such situations, the pulls on the forensic psychologist to make statements that are risky or at odds with feminist principles grow exponentially. Consultation prior to taking a case and during the course of one's involvement in this sort of matter reduces the risk to the feminist forensic practitioner of her or his work being distorted or herself or himself becoming isolated or exploited.
2. *Cases where there are competing feminist ethical principles at stake*. As described above, in situations where there is less than the

usual clarity regarding feminist ethical considerations in the case, consultation can help the forensic practitioner to clarify her or his values and ascertain a set of priorities regarding participation. The necessity of synthesizing apparently competing ethical demands may become more focused on core feminist goals when the voices of several feminist practitioners are engaged in the ethical decision-making process.

3. *Cases for the "other side."* However one defines the other side of cases, it is becoming more common for feminist forensic psychologists to be called on by that side as a consultant or testifying expert. I have, for instance, begun to work selectively as a defense expert in some sexual harassment cases, as have a number of my feminist forensic colleagues. The seduction of this can be great indeed; it aides one's reputation in the forensic practice community to be known as working both sides of the legal aisle. Feminists are also not immune from narcissistic fantasies about how their contact with a particular corporate lawyer will transform the evil entity that has been oppressing women, only to find themselves utterly coopted and used to further that oppression. It is entirely possible for a feminist practitioner to function in an ethical feminist manner working for the "wrong" side of a case, and a consultation with colleagues can increase this likelihood. It is especially important in this kind of case to ensure that you are not hired simply as a strategy for intimidating the other side of the case; you should have sufficient information for evaluating the case before agreeing to serve in such a role.

ROLE CREATIVITY AND ROLE CHANGE IN THE FORENSIC ARENA

Another feminist strategy for ethical forensic practice involves creativity in the development of roles for feminist forensic psychology. A testifying expert is, after all, not the only type of forensic psychologist and, from a feminist perspective, may ultimately be the least effective in creating social change, unless the case in question is likely to change case law. For example, some feminist forensic practitioners work largely as educators for judges and attorneys, teaching directly on topics such as gender roles and behavior as they interface with the law, domestic violence, sexual assault, and so on. Judges' colleges and continuing legal education seminars put on by lawyers' associations afford the opportunity to reach large numbers of legal practitioners and raise awareness and knowledge about the potential for both harm and help to oppressed people that are inherent in the legal system.

The jurist who has already learned of research about rape victims' difficulties with reporting the crime is more likely to act in ways in her or his courtroom to empower future rape victims who come through that venue, which in turn advances feminist goals of social change in a very broad fashion. Because judges have extremely broad discretion regarding what kind of information can be placed in front of a jury, the judge who has already had feminist education may be more likely to allow similar education to the jury, leading in turn to outcomes that are more likely to advance feminist political and social goals.

Others have taken up the explicit role of advocacy in forensic situations, clearly differentiated from that of a testifying expert–educator. In this instance, the forensic psychologists serve as nontherapist advisors to, for example, victims of violence or women in a custody struggle. They offer psycholegal information on dealing with the exigencies of the justice system; facilitating communication between the woman and her attorney, police, or the courts; making referrals for feminist therapy or forensic assessment as needed; and suggesting other advocacy strategies that use the special training and knowledge of a psychologist in such a manner as to empower directly the woman who may be a plaintiff, complainant, or victim–witness in a legal matter. In some instances, the feminist psychologist may offer training or coaching to women going into custody evaluation situations, giving information about common biases held by custody evaluators, so as to improve a woman's chances of a good outcome. The feminist forensic expert can prepare a victim–witness for a criminal trial, using knowledge of what happens in the courtroom in tandem with various resiliency-enhancing interventions, so that the victim–witness feels empowered rather than used by the prosecuting attorney. Feminist forensic experts can assist people abused by a therapist to frame and file a regulatory complaint, using knowledge of therapy ethics to enhance the effectiveness of the client's presentation.

These examples illustrate how, when forensic practice is broadly defined, the potential for creative application of feminist concepts and knowledge in psychology becomes visible. A feminist ethic requires openmindedness to this range of options. It is particularly important to keep possible role options in mind because in some complex legal matters, the feminist ethical choice will not be among those traditionally construed as forensic practice (e.g., the role of the testifying or consulting expert) but may lie among these other possibilities. By considering forensic involvements that depart from traditional roles, more feminist psychologists may become involved in forensic practice and the ultimate goals of feminist psychology may be better served.

PSYCHOLEGAL ASSESSMENT STRATEGIES

When a feminist practitioner serves as a testifying damage expert and conducts a damage assessment, there may be feminist ethical considerations to the engagement of assessment strategies. For example, Fitzgerald (1995) argued that in evaluations of plaintiffs in cases of sexual harassment, the ethical feminist evaluator is careful about how history of sexual abuse and assault is considered in the overall assessment picture. I (Brown, 1992, 1994) argued that certain psychometric instruments may pose ethical risks for feminist practitioners because they embody assumptions so inherently sexist or misogynist that they cannot accurately assess a woman's functioning. Rosewater (1995), however, discussed the risks of use of computerized test interpretations in cases where there are questions of abuse.

Even though there is no one ethical feminist standard for the conduct of assessment in such matters, feminist ethics may assist the forensic practitioner in the weight given to various sorts of information. For instance, a feminist ethic might lead an evaluator to consider how power dynamics between parties in a case might have affected the sort of witness statements given to corroborate or refute various allegations leading to a careful power analysis of the credibility of statements rather than simply taking all information as equally meaningful in a decontextualized manner. A feminist evaluation process also examines the resiliency and coping skills of a person, not just their distress. This can become particularly important in cases where the defense may be alleging that no damages exist, so no harm must have been done. As the U.S. Supreme Court, led by Justice Sandra Day O'Connor, noted in the case of *Harris v. Forklift Systems* (1993), a woman need not have been driven to despair for sexual harassment to have happened and harm to have befallen its targets.

Being able to describe the superior resiliency or coping skills of a given individual may also assist the judge and jury in comprehending the age-old question of "Why did she stay," whether it was in a battering marriage or a job in which harassment was an everyday event. It can also help the triers-of-fact to understand why a person's response to an event has a particular magnitude. This approach to psycholegal assessment places the individual in a social context, asking how a person with similar values, skills, social supports, and shared meanings might respond to certain life events, not just enabling an oppressive norm in which a person is contrasted to a generic human who little resembles the individual's realities or may in fact character-ize few "normal" people.

CONCLUSION

Because the field of feminist forensic practice is still in its youth, there is the potential for most feminist forensic practitioners to encounter ethical dilemmas that were previously unknown to and not addressed by others in the field. This apparent difficulty is also a rich possibility because as feminist practitioners begin to consciously pursue work in the forensic realm, they have the opportunities to transform mainstream forensic practice in a manner parallel to what has occurred in the field of psychotherapy over the past 2 decades. This transformation of forensic practice as a whole and the advancement of feminist challenges to mainstream values is the ultimate ethical struggle for feminist forensic practitioners. In the end, they cannot ethically allow feminist forensic practice to become a marginalized adjunct to forensic psychology; they have an ethical obligation to seek strategies for systemic transformation. Feminist psychology has much to offer mainstream forensic practice. These offerings include enhanced understandings of in-formed consent to participate in a forensic evaluation; the expanded knowl-edge base available from feminist scholarship regarding common catalysts to litigation, such as discrimination, abuse, and harassment; and, ultimately, a richer and more complex vision of the role of the forensic psychologist. They also bring a different model of the relationship of the psychological expert to the jury, one that is respectful in fact and reality of the expertise and authority of these decision makers. My experience is that most forensic practitioners currently offer only *pro forma* lip service to the notion that "juries know best." Because feminist forensic practice arises from the feminist therapy tradition of empowering the expertise of the client, feminist psychol-ogists have a stance that truly does see juries and lay decision makers as their equals in value, which enhances their effectiveness as communicators to those people.

The establishment of a task force on feminist forensic practice in APA's Division of Psychology of Women in 1995 and the development of outreach by that group to interested people in the APA Division of Psychol-ogy and Law represent initial concrete steps in the direction of bringing feminist insights to mainstream forensic psychology. In some places, feminist values have already begun to permeate; for example, APA's child custody evaluation guidelines state that "the psychologist is aware of personal and societal biases and engages in nondiscriminatory practice" (Committee on

Professional Practice and Standards, 1994, p. 677). The current ethical task for feminist forensic practitioners is to expand on and develop these first steps.

REFERENCES

American Psychological Association. (1994). Guidelines for child custody evaluations in divorce proceedings. *American Psychologist, 49,* 677–680.

Anderten, P., Staulcup, V., & Grisso, T. (1980). On being ethical in legal places. *Professional Psychology: Research and Practice, 11,* 764–773.

Bersoff, D. (Ed.). (1995). *Ethical conflicts in psychology.* Washington, DC: American Psychological Association.

Brabeck, M., & Brown, L. S. (1997). Feminist theory and psychological practice. In J. Worell & N. Johnson (Eds.), *Shaping the future of feminist psychology: Education, research, and practice* (pp. 15–36). Washington, DC: American Psychological Association.

Brodsky, S. (1990). Professional ethics and professional morality in the assessment of competence for execution. *Law and Human Behavior, 14,* 91–97.

Brown, L. S. (1991). Ethical issues in feminist therapy: Selected topics. *Psychology of Women Quarterly, 15,* 323–336.

Brown, L. S. (1992). Psychological assessment in cases of sexual harassment. In *Proceedings of the Sex and Power in the Workplace Conference* (pp. 75–80). Seattle WA: Author.

Brown, L. S. (1994). *Subversive dialogues: Theory in feminist therapy.* New York: Basic Books.

Brown, L. S. (1995, August). Feminist issues in evaluation and testimony in recovered memory cases. In L. S. Brown (Chair), *Feminist forensic psychology: An emerging field of feminist practice.* Symposium conducted at the 103rd Annual Convention of the American Psychological Association, New York, NY.

Brown, L. S. (1997). The private practice of subversion: Psychology as *tikkun olam*. *American Psychologist, 52,* 449–462.

Caplan, P. (1992). Driving us crazy: How oppression damages women's mental health and what we can do about it. *Women and Therapy, 12,* 5–28.

Caplan, P. (1994). *Lifting a ton of feathers: A woman's guide to surviving the academic world.* Toronto, Ontario, Canada: University of Toronto Press.

Chesler, P. (1987). *Mothers on trial: The battle for child custody.* Seattle, WA: Seal Press.

Chesler, P. (1993, Summer). An update on Aileen Wuornos. *On the Issues,* p. 22.

Committee on Ethical Guidelines for Forensic Psychologists. (1991). Specialty guidelines for forensic psychologists. *Law and Human Behavior, 15,* 655–665.

Committee on Professional Practice and Standards. (1994). Guidelines for child custody evaluations in divorce proceedings. *American Psychologist, 49,* 677–680.

Daly, M. (1978). *Gyn/ecology: The metaethics of radical feminism*. Boston: Beacon Press.

Feminist Therapy Institute. (1990). Feminist Therapy Institute code of ethics. In H. Lerman & N. Porter (Eds.), *Feminist ethics in psychotherapy* (pp. 37–40). New York: Springer.

Fitzgerald, L. (1995, August). Evaluations in sexual harassment cases. In L. S. Brown (Chair), *Feminist forensic psychology: An emerging field of feminist practice*. Symposium conducted at the 103rd Annual Convention of the American Psychological Association, New York, NY.

Freyd, J. J. (1995, February 25). O. J. trial a chance to explain battered-women syndrome. *The Oregonian*, p. M3.

Grisso, T. (1987). The economic and scientific future of forensic psychological assessment. *American Psychologist, 42*, 831–839.

Grisso, T., & Appelbaum, P. S. (1992). Is it unethical to offer predictions of future violence? *Law and Human Behavior, 16*, 621–633.

Hare-Mustin, R., & Marecek, J. (Eds.). (1990). *Making a difference: Psychology and the construction of gender*. New Haven, CT: Yale University Press.

Harris v. Forklift Systems Inc., 114 S.Ct. 367 (1993).

Hoagland, S. L. (1988). *Lesbian ethics: Toward new value*. Palo Alto, CA: Institute for Lesbian Studies.

Johnson v. Boeing Co., King County Superior Ct. Cause No. 89-2-246-52-0 (1989).

Jones, A. (1980). *Women who kill*. New York: Holt Rinehart Winston.

Kitzinger, C., & Perkins, R. (1993). *Changing our minds: Lesbian feminism and psychology*. New York: New York University Press.

Lerman, H., & Porter, N. (1990). The contribution of feminism to ethics in psychology. In H. Lerman & N. Porter (Eds.), *Feminist ethics in psychology* (pp. 5–13). New York: Springer.

Lerner, G. (1993). *The creation of feminist consciousness*. New York: Oxford University Press.

National Coalition Against Domestic Violence. (1994). [Untitled press release].

Perkins, R. (1991). Therapy for lesbians? The case against. *Feminism and Psychology, 1*, 325–338.

Robson, R. (1992). *Lesbian (out)law: Survival under the rule of law*. Ithaca, NY: Firebrand.

Rosewater, L. B. (1985). Feminist interpretation of traditional testing. In L. B. Rosewater & L. E. A. Walker (Eds.), *Handbook of feminist therapy: Women's issues in psychotherapy* (pp. 266–273). New York: Springer.

Rosewater, L. B. (1995). The use and abuse of the MMPI in the forensic evaluation of women survivors of interpersonal violence. In L. S. Brown (Chair), *Feminist forensic psychology: An emerging field of feminist practice*. Symposium conducted at the 103rd Annual Convention of the American Psychological Association, New York, NY.

Rosewater, L. B. (1999). [Forensic practice with battered women who kill]. Manuscript in preparation, Beachwood, OH.

Stahley, G. B., & Walker, L. E. A. (1997). What are nice feminists like you doing on the O. J. defense team? Personal ruminations on the "Trial of the century." *Journal of Social Issues, 53*, 425–440.

State v. Wanrow, 88 Wash. 2nd 221, 559 P.2d 548 (1977).

Steinem, G. (1995, August). *Opening address*. Presented at the 103rd Annual Convention of the American Psychological Association, New York, NY.

Tavris, C. (1993, January 3). Beware the incest survivor machine. *New York Times Book Review*, pp. 1, 16–17.

Walker, L. E. A. (1989a). Psychology and violence against women. *American Psychologist, 44*, 695–702.

Walker, L. E. A. (1989b). *Terrifying love: Why battered women kill and how society responds*. New York: Harper & Row.

Walker, L. E. A., & Edwall, G. E. (1987). Domestic violence and determination of visitation and custody in divorce. In D. Sonkin (Ed.), *Domestic violence on trial: Psychological and legal dimensions of family violence* (pp. 127–154). New York: Springer.

Williams, P. H. (1991). *The alchemy of race and rights*. Cambridge, MA: Harvard University Press.

5

FEMINIST ETHICS IN THE PRACTICE OF SCIENCE: THE CONTESTED MEMORY CONTROVERSY AS AN EXAMPLE

JENNIFER J. FREYD AND KATHRYN QUINA

Imagine the following situation: An influential academic psychologist, renowned for his empirical and theoretical contributions, is speaking at a scientific conference about his latest findings and ideas about the intricacies of his discipline, cognitive science. Not far into the presentation, this famous professor veers into the territory of the recovered memory debate. He states with great certainty that science shows that women with recovered memories of abuse are suffering false memories.

As an attendee at this conference, you are a bit perplexed; the proclamation is made with authority and in a context that endows whatever is said with credibility, yet there is little offered in the way of empirical evidence (or at least clearly relevant evidence) for the proclamation. What has just happened here? A person with the label "scientist" has invoked the mantle of science to assert something. But is this science?

The answer to this question can be informed by the feminist ethical thought of the past 3 decades. Ethical principles initially applied to the therapeutic setting can guide other forms of practice, including research and scientific thought. The feminist principles of therapy introduced in the early 1970s seemed quite radical at the time. Yet today many of the original ideas of feminist therapy are seen almost universally as "good" therapy. Similar revolutions in the practice of science were spurred on by early feminist critiques (e.g., Unger, 1983; Wittig, 1985). Today to a large extent, the practices recommended in these "radical" critiques are considered standard scientific and ethical principles (American Psychological Association [APA], 1992). Drawing from the ethical mandates of feminist therapy (e.g., Feminist Therapy Institute, 1990), we begin this review with three overarching tenets of an ethical and feminist science.

- The scientist has a responsibility to recognize and acknowledge her or his own biases.
- The scientist has a responsibility to act in the best interest of her or his participants.
- The scientist is not a god but an explorer, an interpreter of data, and a guide for future scientific knowledge acquisition.

At this point, a question arises that also applies to the therapeutic setting: Are the fundamentals of a feminist ethical science not just good scientific principles? The answer is, well, yes, to a large extent. But feminist ethics require an explicit statement of these principles and a systematic review of actual practices in light of these principles: bringing these ethical questions to the forefront, addressing them systematically, and making explicit decisions for action.

Beyond good practice, feminist ethics offer a more proactive approach. Laura Brown (1994) decried that in clinical practice, ethics has become dominated by rules to prevent lawsuits. Basing her work in part on the work of the Feminist Therapy Institute (1990), Brown discussed ethics as a statement of what clinicians should want to accomplish for their clients as opposed to proscriptions against very bad behavior. In this chapter, we take the same approach to the application of a feminist ethical science. Beyond proscriptions, we concur with others that a feminist ethical science raises questions about the values, interpretations, and intended uses of the science (Harding, 1993). Inherent to a feminist ethical science is a process whereby one constantly analyzes the research process and outcomes from a gendered and sociocultural perspective.

Some researchers may think explicitly about ethics in science only when appeasing their institution's human subjects committee. Yet the research process can be viewed as a series of decisions, from the conceptualization of the problem to empowerment of those who are affected by the use of the results (Quina & Kulberg, 1988). Feminist ethics can inform each of those decisions. Science would be far better if researchers examined the activity that goes into their scientific knowledge base, the use of that knowledge base, and the treatment of humans (and animals) along the way.

In this chapter, we take the position that current scientific work may shed significant insight on any given issue, even such a difficult-to-research area as delayed recall of childhood abuse. We discuss some of the ways that science has been misapplied and principles of good science have been violated, using examples from the debate over delayed recall of childhood abuse. We demonstrate how a feminist ethical perspective can inform this debate, regardless of the position one assumes with respect to the issue. We also suggest some guidelines that may be useful in minimizing further misapplications of science through careful applications of feminist ethical principles.

We do not, in this chapter, attempt to explain memory phenomena in detail (see Freyd, 1996) or to discuss therapeutic interventions with sexual abuse survivors (Gold & Brown, 1997; Pope & Brown, 1996). Nor do we go into great detail about specific studies (e.g., Brown, 1997; Pope, 1996). Instead, we focus on the ethical issues to which feminist scientists could and should be paying attention. Although we focus more on the misuse of science to support the false memory position, the popular press and much of academia have embraced or promoted the position that science supports premises of false memory proponents (see Beckett, 1996; Bowman & Mertz, 1996b; Pope, 1996, 1997; and Stanton, 1997). Of course, misuse in the other direction can and has occurred.

WHAT IS THE CONTESTED MEMORY CONTROVERSY?

The contested memory controversy is an intense debate within mental health fields, academia, and segments of current Western culture at large (for reviews, see Enns, McNeilly, Corkery, & Gilbert, 1995; Freyd, 1996, 1998; Pope, 1996; and Pope & Brown, 1996). Questions about disbelief and belief, passionate testimonials, and assertions of scientific authority saturate this conceptual landscape. At question is whether memories can accurately be recalled after a period of being unavailable for recall. On the one hand are individuals and groups, including scientists and clinicians, who find very plausible evidence that people sometimes forget and then accurately recall sexual abuse; on the other hand are individuals and groups, including scientists and clinicians, who assert that noncontinuous memories of childhood abuse are likely to be (or, according to some, are always) false.

Questions about the existence of a false memory syndrome are particularly troubling because one group of individuals has been able to create a label without scientific evidence and to apply it freely to women without ever meeting them—often merely from the word of a parent (see a discussion in Pope, 1996). We argue that from the outset, it is a mistake to give the power of voice to just one side of a debate. We also need to focus on the alleged perpetrator's memories, framing this as contested memories rather than presuming false memories.

Freyd (1996) provides a review of the literature and a potential resolution to this debate. Her review of the cognitive science and memory literature concludes the following about scientists' current state of knowledge.

- They should not assume, without more information, that a recovered memory of sexual abuse is true.
- They should not assume, without more information, that a recovered memory of sexual abuse is false.
- Essentially false memories exist, whether those memories are newly recovered or have been apparently continuously available.
- Essentially true memories exist, whether those memories are newly recovered or have been apparently continuously available.
- Most memories, whether recovered or continuously accessible, are a perplexing mixture of true and false.
- When an individual reports a recovered memory (or apparently continuously accessible memory), scientists do not yet know the probability that the memory is essentially true.
- When an individual denies an accusation of sexual abuse, scientists do not yet know the probability that the denial is essentially true.
- Given someone who did not experience parental sexual abuse, scientists do not yet know the probability that the person falsely "remembers" sexual abuse.
- Given someone who did experience parental sexual abuse, scientists do not yet know the probability that the memory becomes unavailable and then later available.

Given all this uncertainty about "truth," it is essential that each case of contested memory be considered on an individual basis. Sometimes particular information in a case can provide evidence that reduces the general uncertainty; other times uncertainty remains dominant even in an individual case.

The first author's (Freyd) research focuses primarily on the following questions: Does amnesia for child sexual abuse happen, and in particular, if so, why and how? How can someone forget an event as traumatic as sexual abuse in childhood? Betrayal trauma theory proposes that it is adaptive to forget certain kinds of betrayal—as in childhood sexual abuse by a trusted caregiver—and that this forgetting is understandable in terms of what is known about cognitive psychology (Freyd, 1996). This theory takes care to disentangle the motivations, mechanisms, and phenomena of memory disruptions in response to trauma from one another.

Memory repression is shown to exist, not for the reduction of suffering but because not knowing about abuse by a caregiver is often necessary for survival. From a logical analysis of developmental pressures and cognitive architecture, we can expect there to be cognitive information blockage under certain conditions, such as sexual abuse by a parent. This information blockage creates various types of betrayal blindness and traumatic amnesia. Betrayal trauma theory makes testable predictions about when forgetting abuse is most likely to occur. Freyd (1996; in press); Freyd, Martorello, Alvarado, Hayes, and Christman (1998); and DePrince and Freyd (1999) discussed preliminary empirical support for this theory and future research directions.

Individual Cases and Population Studies

One source of evidence for the assertion that people sometimes forget sexual abuse and recover them with some accuracy comes from individual cases, such as the case of Frank Fitzpatrick who recovered memories of childhood sexual abuse by Father Porter and the case of Ross Cheit who recovered memories of childhood sexual abuse by William Farmer (see Butler, 1996; Cheit, 1998; and Freyd, 1996). Ross Cheit has an extensive website archive of systematically corroborated recovered memories at www.brown.edu/departments/taubman_center/recovmem/archive.html.

Another source is current estimates based on systematic studies of various populations, which suggest that a sizable percentage of those who have been abused experienced some amnesia for the abuse. Table 5.1 shows results from three retrospective studies and one prospective study, which provide empirical evidence indicating forgetting abuse is a real (and not infrequent) phenomenon.

Evidence used to deny delayed recall of childhood abuse does not focus on the fact that recall is disrupted but instead on the accuracy of memories that appear to show up after a period in which the memory was not present. As with evidence in support of delayed recall, much of the data used to support the false memory position is anecdotal (e.g., Loftus & Ketcham, 1994; Pendergrast, 1996).

(Sometimes) Logical Arguments

Other authors have appealed to what appears to be a logical, but not empirical, form of argument. For example, Holmes (1990) has been often cited (by those who argue that recovered memories must be false) for his

Table 5.1
Empirically Determined Rates of Forgetting Sexual Abuse

Study	Participants	Reported rates for forgetting
Herman & Schatzow (1987)	53 women in short-term incest therapy groups	36% moderate memory loss, 26% severe memory loss
Feldman-Summers & Pope (1994)	79 psychologists reporting childhood sexual or physical abuse	40% forgot and recovered some or all of their abuse
Loftus et al. (1994)	52 substance abuse treatment clients	19% forgot and recovered their memory of abuse, 12% partially forgot
Williams (1994, 1995)	129 women seen during childhood in hospital emergency room for sexual abuse	10% forgot and recovered their memory of abuse, 38% did not recall abuse

claim that "despite 60 years of research[,]" there is at present "no controlled laboratory evidence supporting the concept of repression" (p. 96). But Holmes defined repression as the involuntary "selective forgetting of materials that cause the individual pain" (p. 86) and hinted that anxiety is a necessary motivation in his definition.

Separating the phenomena of forgetting and recall from the potential motivations and mechanisms for these phenomena can avoid this logical error. In a detailed analysis of Holmes's (1990) chapter, Gleaves (1996) concluded that Holmes's conclusions "do not allow one to make inferences about the reality of amnesia for trauma or subsequent recovery of memories" (p. 1). The misapplications of this article are extreme and obvious. Holmes was interested in a particular mechanism, and he postulated particular motivations for forgetting. He claimed that good experimental evidence was lacking for this particular mechanism. This is very different than claiming to find no evidence for a particular phenomenon. Exhibit 5.1 summarizes some of the separate conceptual issues that get tangled in this debate, issues that must be carefully disentangled to discuss the empirical data logically (also discussed in Freyd, 1996).

Empirical Evidence

Data generated by experimental methodologies are readily gathered for both malleability and stability of memory in nontraumatic laboratory situations. In support of the malleability side of the debate, there have been demonstrations that children can be pressured or led by parents, or other presumedly truthful adult sources, to make inaccurate claims (e.g., White, Leichtman, & Ceci, 1997), that adults can make errors in detailed memory

Exhibit 5.1
Separate Conceptual Issues in the Memory Controversy

Terminology	Repression, dissociation, dissociative amnesia, traumatic amnesia, and knowledge isolation
Observable phenomena	Experiencing a significant event but not consciously recollecting significant aspects of it, later recollecting the event
Proposed motivations	Avoidance of • pain • being overwhelmed • threats to self-perception • threats to assumptions of a meaningful world • information threatening a necessary attachment
Possible mechanisms	Selective attention, inhibition of consolidation after initial encoding, state-dependent learning, and inhibition of accessing information already well stored

for elaborate lists or scenes (Roediger & McDermott, 1995), and that adults can be pressured to believe that nontraumatic childhood events occurred when told that an older family member remembers those events (Loftus, 1997). As noted in critiques by Pope (1996) and Freyd (1998), authors of these studies too often have drawn the conclusion that if one can demonstrate that some cognitive mistakes can be made (in remembering a list of words) or that some people can be convinced that something happened to them as children that is untrue, then delayed memories are most likely false.

Experimental evidence is less readily found as a source of knowledge for the reality of traumatic amnesia and memory recovery. One reason is that experimental methodology is not as easily exploited in the study of traumatic memory as it is for "normal" memory; one cannot simply or ethically create many of the traumatic contexts hypothesized to be related to amnesia for trauma. Another reason is that it is easier (and more interesting for many scientists) to focus on "mistakes" in responses than on accuracies, even though researchers find important accuracies as well as errors (e.g., Pezdek, Finger, & Hodge, 1997; Pezdek & Roe, 1997). Although experimental evidence directly supporting forgetting and remembering real trauma is difficult to achieve, there is a solid empirical literature based on systematic, statistically evaluated data supporting the reality of both memory failure and recovery of traumatic material (Freyd, 1996).

Some people may have also underestimated the extent to which experimental results from studies of nontraumatic memory are at least as indicative of the plausibility of forgetting and later remembering abusive events because the results are indicative of the malleability of memory. Freyd (1996) offered a review of this research and its implications.

WHAT CAN A FEMINIST ETHICAL CRITIQUE
BRING TO THE CONTROVERSY?

As Ken Pope (1996) observed, "science, policy, and education suffer when the vigorous authoritative promotion of claims fails to meet vigorous critical examination" (p. 957). This concern echoes nearly 3 decades of feminist critiques of biases throughout the history of applications of science in psychology. In this section, we review several forms of inappropriate use of science in the controversy.

Truth, Falsity, and the Struggle for Authority

The fundamental disagreement is centered—or stuck—on the essential truth or falsity of recovered memories for childhood abuse. When the core issue is whether an alleged abuse happened and the abuse is contested by the alleged abuser, there arises a struggle for authority to define reality. Perhaps because the stakes are so very high, this struggle for authority has been at times vicious. It is a struggle seen over and over again in the history of raising awareness about and responding to sexual abuse in Western culture: An individual case becomes a struggle for authority in the media, scientific world, and popular culture.

An ethical concern inherent in this debate is problematic throughout science: attempting to boil a complex issue down to a simple "yes–no" or "true–false" dichotomy. In this simplistic view of the recovered memories debate, the true–false dichotomy leads to two red herrings. First, the debate sometimes looks like it is about whether people can and do sometimes forget (and later remember) abuse. But most people on both sides recognize that people can and do forget (and later remember) abuse (Freyd, 1996; Pope, 1996). Second, the debate is characterized as being about whether memory is sometimes essentially false. In fact, researchers on both sides have invoked the concept of memory distortion, and most also have invoked some notion of human suggestibility (see a review in Freyd, 1996). The debate is not about truth or falsity. Instead, the debate is about who has the authority to determine the truth about an individual's experience. As Freyd (1998) pointed out, the debate would more accurately be described as one between the truth of the parent's memory versus the truth of the child–adult's, between the authority of the person denying abusive behavior or the authority of the one remembering abuse. There is no evidence that parents' memories (or claims) are more accurate than their children's, whether continuous or discontinuous.

At times, the struggle for authority has deeply threatened the agency and personhood of adult survivors (see Bowman & Mertz, 1996a; and Brown,

1996). Poole, Lindsay, Memon, and Bull (1997) reflected that in their often-cited study of therapists' techniques (Poole, Lindsay, Memon, & Bull, 1995), they

> should have more scrupulously avoided language implying that the relationship we observed reflected an effect of therapy . . . [and] agree with some of Pope's [(1996)] arguments (e.g., that claims about false memories have sometimes been exaggerated and that exaggerated claims about false memories may have a chilling effect on victim advocacy and support). (p. 992)

Although there may be an urgent need to adjudicate certain individual cases of alleged abuse, for most scientists it would be better to suspend judgment on contested cases and to investigate and research the underlying phenomena. Whatever one learns about the issues in general in the domain of science, for any particular case of contested memories one must look at the individual case. The difference between examining cases individually versus posing scientific questions to ask about the issues in general has sometimes been lost in this debate.

Misrepresentations of Data and Results

Pope (1996) noted that many of the claims of an epidemic of false allegations are made without sufficient empirical support. Beyond serious questions about the extent of false remembering of abuse going on in the population at large (Pope, 1996), it is important to ask questions about the data presented to support claims in this controversy. For example, Salter (1992) reviewed over 100 references from a book authored by a false memories proponent and found extreme misapplications of research cited. Her efforts to achieve scientific accuracy were rewarded with a lawsuit, in which she (and independent science) ultimately triumphed, although at great personal expense (Salter, 1998).

One of the most egregious suggestions is that there is an epidemic of false memory syndrome. From its inception, the False Memory Syndrome Foundation has made media influence a priority, funneling public perceptions of the research literature through a specific value-laden filter (Stanton, 1997). Yet there is no research to date documenting either a set of symptoms making up such a syndrome or an epidemic of those symptoms, in spite of the widespread promulgation of this term for political uses. We need to ask the following: Do false denials happen? If one is going to name syndromes, one also needs to ask about a false denial syndrome, which work with abusers suggests (Salter, 1995).

Evidence from one domain has been used to make claims about another unrelated domain. As Dahlenberg (1996) and Freyd (1998) pointed out, there is no evidence that a memory that is not persistent (i.e., has been forgotten for some period of time) is any more or less true than one that has always been recalled. Yet the key empirical evidence cited as support for false memories consistently fails to separate these two dimensions of memory, claiming without support that noncontinuous memories are more or most likely to be false (Freyd, 1998). Likewise, memory research in laboratory settings has been used to make claims about real-life case studies— an issue addressed later in this chapter.

Unfortunately, to many people not intimately familiar with the empirical literature on trauma and memory and not acutely skeptical about claims to scientific authority, the contested memory debate is easily passed off as a war between therapists and scientists. The controversy is often described in ways that prejudice the issues, namely, applying labels such as "true believers" versus "skeptics" (terms that could be misapplied to either side, actually). Therapists are accused of believing their clients' accounts of recovered memories of abuse, no matter their implausibility, and of unwittingly or intentionally implanting those very stories. Some scientists, aware of the research on the malleability of nontraumatic memory and perhaps shocked by the large numbers of abuse stories, doubt the accuracy of delayed abuse allegations. Personal experiences and clinical case studies are pitted against data from laboratory studies. As a consequence, not only is this controversy intense, but it is also confusing.

The scientist-versus-therapist characterization of the debate has also been greatly exaggerated; this exaggeration is one of the many current entanglements standing in the way of progress. In fact, it may be fair to characterize most clinicians and most scientists (and most who use both labels) as holding positions that are moderated by an awareness of many evidential and epistemological ambiguities and uncertainties.

Perhaps most distressing from a compassion standpoint has been the misrepresentations of individuals who have recovered memories and of those who have been accused of perpetrating abuse. Jennifer Hoult (1998), a survivor who successfully sued her father, poignantly described misrepresentations of her and the facts of her case by those with a different agenda.

Conflicting Values in Researchers With Multiple Roles

It is common teaching in psychology that an empirical (and hence scientific) approach is essentially amoral and that motives, whether monetary or passionate, have no place in science (Quina & Kulberg, 1988). Nearly every undergraduate in the country is taught the scientific method, in which theoretical bias as well as moral and emotional issues are presumed to be disconnected from the researcher and her or his relationship with the participants (for a historical perspective, see Danziger, 1985). We go further and argue that objectivity has too often been equated with a lack of compassion or emotion and that having compassion or feelings is perceived as unscientific. Yet this disconnection virtually never occurs in the real world of science, particularly not in any arena that has meaning beyond the laboratory (and most hope their research will have some meaning!). Noddings (1988) in fact argued that including an ethic of care should be a primary concern of education, including education about research. Feminist critiques have long demonstrated how researchers have both reflected and directed the biases of their theoretical and political beliefs (Shields, 1975; Unger, 1983).

The recovered memories debate is no exception; societal, professional, personal, and moral issues are enmeshed in the scientific process. The debate began with intense beliefs on both sides of the issues, and these intense beliefs fueled some of the initial studies. Carried into courts, ethics committees, and legislatures, the debate has become infused with vast amounts of money. These funds may influence the process, just as the federal government's decision to fund a certain research priority influences the kind of research that is conducted. One must recognize the influence of one's own values—including power and authority—in the science one carries out and promotes. These values are often shaped by one's other roles, in which value-laden tactics are more acceptable.

Consider, for example, the concept of *objectivity*. Courtroom tactics include attempts to maintain an appearance of objectivity by applying general findings from research studies to individual cases, sometimes in ways that an objective scientist would consider absurd (e.g., arguing that an individual's experience of abuse did not happen because a participant in a laboratory misremembered a computer keystroke). The increasing use of expert witnesses in court cases compounds these problems. Unfortunately, with the increasing crossover or slippage among the various roles psychologists fill (see, e.g., Loftus & Rosenwald, 1993), particularly between the courtroom and research or practice, scientific journals are now being infiltrated with failures to recognize different roles and uses of data acceptable to each. One potential problem stems from the fact that psychologists serving as expert witnesses are often paid an hourly rate that far exceeds payment from other employment. Expert witnesses may find that they have a financial interest in the outcome of the research that they conduct insofar as their research findings influence their employability as expert witnesses. This creates a potential conflict of interest for the researcher who is also an expert witness. We advocate a standard disclosure statement for psychological researchers who anticipate a financial gain, or an appearance of significant financial gain, from the results they report.

"Scientists" or Scientific Data?

It is crucial to distinguish between the wisdom, tools, findings, and epistemological promise of science, on the one hand, and the very different issue of misuses of wisdom, tools, findings, and epistemology in the name of scientific authority, on the other hand. When anyone—especially a scientist—claims that science demonstrates X and that good scientists support his or her view, this is a claim of scientific authority. However, proclaiming scientific authority by virtue of specialized training in scientific methods is fundamentally different from the use of science to illuminate. What an authority claims may or may not in fact coincide with what science actually demonstrates or what scientists actually support.

Another outcome of the scientist–therapist version of the debate is a false belief that systematic data support those who take the false memory position, whereas only anecdote or intuitive impression support those who take the position that many recovered memories are essentially true. In reality, anecdotal evidence and intuition have played an essential role on both sides of this debate (see, e.g., the anecdotes that form the basis of the argument of Loftus & Ketcham, 1994, that repressed memories do not occur). Furthermore, qualitative reports are not always suspect, as is suggested by the science–anecdote distinction. Valuable data can be obtained from a presentation of case studies for which primary information is available to other researchers for scrutiny, whether offered by a person labeled as a "clinician" or as a "scientist."

Perhaps some have mistakenly assumed that experimental methodology conducted in a laboratory-based setting is the only sort of systematic or scientific data that can inform about memory or any other phenomenon (in which case, what does one make of astronomy or paleontology?). Even though experimentation can be valuable and informative, especially in revealing causal relationships, systematic observation and documentation have in fact formed the bulk of the knowledge base in the world and can be just as informative here. After all, most psychologists have never questioned the notion of *love*, even though we suspect that no study could satisfactorily define it operationally within the context of an experiment, attempts to manipulate it would not be acceptable, and no one could adequately experimentally demonstrate its existence.

Overgeneralizations From Laboratory Data

Perhaps most serious among the misapplications of science in this debate are the overgeneralizations from laboratory studies to clinical cases of trauma (see DePrince & Freyd, 1999; Freyd, 1996; Gleaves, 1996; Gleaves

& Freyd, 1997; and Pope, 1996, 1997). For example, Roediger and McDermott (1995) used a standard laboratory recall task to demonstrate that participants sometimes inaccurately insert associated but never-presented words as part of a long list. Yet they began their report of these data in the *Journal of Experimental Psychology: Learning, Memory, and Cognition* with these words: "False memories—either remembering events that never happened, or remembering them quite differently from the way they happened—have recently captured the attention of both psychologists and the public at large" (Roediger & McDermott, 1995, p. 803). The phenomenon of errors in recall of information exceeding the typical short-term memory store has been known for decades (Bransford & Franks, 1971) and is sometimes attributed to probability guessing in response to information beyond the short-term memory capacity (Holland, 1975). Similarly, it is old news that people make errors in recall of information from long-term memory. Whereas the gist of memories are maintained (as in Roediger & McDermott's findings), Deese (1959) demonstrated the intrusion of related words and Posner and Keele's (1968) classic experiments show that a never-present stimulus is considered presented so long as it is prototypical for a category in which members were presented, and Freyd (1987) demonstrated that object position may be misremembered in the direction of implied motion (and many additional similar findings). Yet Roediger and McDermott (1995) presented their laboratory results as "dramatic evidence of false memories" (p. 812) in such a way that some readers might well understand this to mean dramatic evidence for the concept of false memories of abuse. (For specific critiques of generalizations based on methods and stimuli, see the response commentary by Freyd & Gleaves, 1996.)

The laboratory definition of false memory also does not apply to most cases of contested memories, where one side argues that the memories are not just false in detail but also false in essence. Thus, if someone who was exposed as a child to anal rape and was forced to watch pornography of vaginal rape later incorrectly remembered she was vaginally raped, would one argue that her memory was false (analogous to the false memories in the Roediger and McDermott, 1995, experimental paradigm) or essentially true with false aspects?

Also in many laboratory studies of false memory such as Roediger and McDermott's (1995) experiment involving list learning, participants do not apparently experience their memories as recovered. Instead, the participants apparently experience their so-called false memories as continuously available. The results from these sorts of studies are thus arguably most applicable to memories experienced by people as continuous, not to memories that are experienced by people as newly recovered. A complication in this domain is that people may be incorrect in their assessments of how inaccessible or accessible given memories have been; that is, one may forget having previously remembered something, or one may believe that a new memory has been remembered before. This potential for metacognitive error is true in the laboratory and in real life. It is interesting and disturbing that a false memory in a study not apparently involving "recovered" memory may be readily applied to recovered memories for abuse. The equating of memory errors (or memory accuracy) with memory recovery (or memory persistence) is a persistent problem in the memory debate (Freyd, 1998).

Problems of application are also common when results of laboratory research are applied to individual cases of contested memories, such as the infamous Ingram case. In 1988, Ingram, a deputy sheriff in Olympia, Washington, confessed to sexually abusing his two daughters. Later, after extended and repeated questioning, Ingram claimed to remember committing increasingly bizarre and horrific crimes. Charges based on these later confessions (which have been criticized widely for being inappropriately obtained) were eventually dropped. Ingram pled guilty to the original charges and was sentenced to prison. He later recanted all of his confessions; the appeals courts then ruled that the initial confession of sexual abuse was properly obtained.

In a newspaper article about the Ingram case (Shannon, 1996), psychologist Elizabeth Loftus was quoted as saying "it is entirely possible to take individuals and create wholly false memories in their minds." The article reports that "Loftus said a scholarly journal this month reported on an experiment in which 90 percent of subjects would confess if you tell them someone else saw them do it." Loftus was apparently referring to the article by Kassin and Kiechel in the May 1996 issue of *Psychological Science*. Kassin and Kiechel reported a single experiment in which participants were accused of damaging a computer by pressing the wrong key during a typing task. Although all participants were innocent, some participants came to confess to this "crime" after they were given false incriminating information by a confederate. Reporting this finding in an article about Paul Ingram would seem to equate accidentally and fleetingly hitting the wrong key while typing (something all typists have done) with a father repeatedly and intentionally raping his daughter over several years. Making such a leap in a presumably scientific journal is particularly egregious (Gleaves & Freyd, 1997).

Even when a study does appear to demonstrate a real-life memory fallibility, there are problems with overgeneralization. Loftus (Loftus & Ketcham, 1994) demonstrated that a minority of participants could be convinced by a close family member (or an experimenter who had talked with their parent) that they had, as a child, once been temporarily lost in a shopping mall. These results have been used in several scientifically unjustified ways:

(a) generalizing from a mildly stressful but not uncommon experience (being lost in a large store) to a highly stressful and uncommon experience (being raped), despite evidence to suggest that more traumatic memories are resistant to implanting (Pezdek et al., 1997)

(b) assuming that the influence of a close family member who insists that they witnessed an event is equivalent to the influence of a therapist suggesting that unwitnessed events might have occurred

(c) presuming that influence only happens in one direction (remembering things that did not occur), even though it is just as plausible to assume that a similar application of pressure from a family member insisting that abuse never happened could lead to an equal level of influence

(d) using the parents as the informants on what did or did not happen during the childhood of a college student participant, which assumes that the parent is an objective authority on the reality of that person's childhood experiences, even though there is no evidence that parents' memories are any more accurate than their adult children's.

Perhaps most disturbing to the scientific community should be the giant misstep made when a finding that some false memories can be created is used to impeach a particular memory.

Finally, there are problems in overgeneralizations from data on one topic, namely, the distortion of memory content, to conclusions about a conceptually and empirically different topic, the recovery of memories once forgotten. Although fabricated memories and recovered memories are both real phenomena, many people tend to tangle the two sets of issues into a hopeless snarl, so that evidence in support of memory distortions and errors is used to invalidate a particular recovered memory, whereas evidence in support of memory tenacity is used to validate a particular recovered memory. Because we know that an essentially true recovered memory is possible and that an essentially false memory is also possible, then logically individually contested memories can only be adjudicated on an individual basis.

WHAT CAN FEMINIST ETHICAL SCIENCE OFFER BEYOND A SCIENTIFIC CRITIQUE?

Beyond the basic concerns that any scientist should have about the specific uses of data and their interpretations, there are several actions mandated by feminist ethics that could and should be applied here and to any similar situation.

1. *Demand logical and carefully crafted science*. Because the controversy involves disagreement about a complex reality, it is essential to attempt to separate the questions one is attempting to ask and answer. If one takes care to pose separate questions, one can find out which questions one in fact can already answer, which questions one cannot answer, and which questions carefully constructed research may allow one to answer. Do not attempt to decide whether a memory is true if deciding is not absolutely necessary. So instead of beginning from the question, Is this recovered memory true? or even Are most of these recovered memories true?, it would be a better investment for scientists to attempt to understand basic features of response to trauma, memory for trauma, and human vulnerability to memory distortion.

2. *Expose the gendered nature of this debate*. Gender is not at all incidental to the contesting of memories of abuse. It has been known for the better part of the past century that memory of a trauma can be unavailable to the male traumatized war or disaster survivor. McFarlane and van der Kolk (1996) noted that only after delayed memories were identified among female sexual abuse survivors (Herman & Schatzow, 1987) did the political forces muster to deny their existence.

   Throughout this debate, there are strong threads of antifeminism and sexism from those who assume those most vulnerable to implanting of memories are women, those who accuse feminists of creating a "child sexual abuse witchhunt," and those who regularly monitor and ridicule posts on feminist psychology email lists and their authors.

3. *Attend to power differentials*. Researchers need to be asking themselves over and over again the following question: What is the role of power and authority in what is being said and what is being believed? It is an ethical imperative, not just scientifically useful, to promote free discussion of these issues in any research. Attending to power differentials seems particularly important for researchers in this controversy. Laboratory scientists must attend to their power to define reality for others. It is the nature of child sexual abuse that those who allege abuse, even adult survivors, are invariably on average significantly less financially and socially powerful. Those who support them are often less powerful within the profession.

Free discussion must also include the freedom to criticize claims made by proponents—no matter how famous, influential, and powerful those proponents are in academic psychology. Abusive treatment of opponents, including such tactics as disruptive picketing, harassing legal actions, and ad homina–hominum smears (Calof, 1998; Salter, 1998), must be challenged. As Pope (1996) stated, "that which tends to disallow doubt and discredit anyone who disagrees is unlikely to foster the specific venture or promote public policies and clinical practices based on scientific principles" (p. 971).

4. *Demand accountability in uses of one's own and others' research.* Researchers must make an effort to untangle the appropriate from inappropriate applications of research results to this debate. Disturbingly, many scientists have failed to meet the obvious overgeneralizations of laboratory research by false memory proponents with timely discussion of "good" and "bad" scientific ethics. Experimental psychology has much to offer in the current debate about memories for childhood abuse. However, with their enormous cognitive authority to define reality for the rest of the population, laboratory scientists must be especially conservative when arguing that laboratory results on memory generalize to contested memories of abuse.

Misleading the lay public with this sort of generalization without challenge has serious consequences for the justice system, suggesting that confessions to felonies are easily coerced and that memories of being criminally victimized are easily suggested. Thus, not only are the goals of psychological science best served by accuracy and caution in generalizing from laboratory to real-life situations (which may differ on fundamental dimensions), such accuracy and caution may also affect real people and events in current society.

5. *Explore the role of culturally instituted oppressions.* It is difficult to keep private traumas that generally affect oppressed individuals (women and children) in the public light. The silencing that occurs can be insidious, including not only overt attack, failure to respond, and so on but also internalized silencing of the private horrors. This can lead researchers in this area to pathologize victims. A feminist stance requires vigilance to protect against such destructive forces as infantalizing victims (also see Armstrong, 1994). We also think it will become increasingly essential to conduct research on abuse perpetrators, not just victims, but this remains challenging for many reasons.

6. *Integrate a rational and scientific perspective with a moral and compassionate approach.* Researchers have long held that the claim to objectivity frees them of any responsibility to individuals, other than not harming them while in the research setting (e.g., see Fisher, chap. 6, this volume). Thus, when data from a laboratory study are applied in a courtroom to ridicule a survivor, for example, the detached researcher can shrug his or her shoulders and claim value freedom. However, a feminist ethical stance looks beyond the individual participants in a study and explores the uses of data by society (or by oneself). This does not mean that one should only publish "positive" work or that one should ignore contradictory data. Instead, it means that one should consider on whom and how one's data will have an impact. Extraordinary claims about the meaning or implications of one's data should never be made, and any speculation should be reviewed for its potential uses and impact.

7. *Accept responsibility for improving the lives of individuals and society through social action.* Data can be used for positive social change. Feminist ethics demand that one not remain isolated from one's roots as humans–women in society; instead, one should work in whatever role one chooses to improve the situation of all women. As a scientist, one has a particular kind of voice that can be heard in an influential way. One must put one's skills and training as a scientist—and the credibility that comes with being a responsible scientist—to good use. One must be the voice for those without a voice, whether through poverty, education, socioeconomic or social status, or victimization. One must create opportunities to share data and critiques with others in a scholarly, accurate, and responsible way. When harmful claims about an individual or group are made, every effort should be undertaken to respond and correct the misrepresentation. In addition, where possible, one should carry out good science oneself to explore the questions faced in the contested memory and other significant debates.

8. *Make self-care a priority.* When so much is at stake, it is hard for some researchers to balance personal lives and privacy needs with demands to research, reply, and react. For some, activism and empowering others is energizing; for others, it is essential to avoid these issues. One needs to recognize and appreciate these variations and respect one's own and others' styles while demanding only the highest standards from all.

CONCLUSIONS

We conclude with some guidelines for researchers and consumers of research that arise frequently in the contested memories debate. We believe these ethical guidelines need to be considered whenever one conducts or disseminates scientific research.

1. Examine individual cases individually versus posing scientific questions to ask about the issues in general.
2. Sort out the appropriate roles of objectivity, power, and authority in the laboratory, therapy room, popular media, courtroom, conference, and archival journal pages and disclose overlaps and potential gain from research published in the scientific literature.
3. Examine the research and the uses of the research for social and cultural context.
4. Embrace the extraordinary importance of doing careful, open-minded, thoughtful, and ethical science by:
   - posing scientific questions rationally, ethically, and clearly
   - avoiding exaggerations and overgeneralizations while retaining commitment, passion, and motivation for one's work
   - striving to be aware of biases and identifying them openly in one's work
   - striving to be aware of power and authority (and use it responsibly)
   - attending to the social context and the social implications of one's research, including who is framing the debate and the reasons for doing so
   - attending to the language and terms used
   - not using stigmatizing and terrorizing tactics in disagreements
   - trying not to succumb to efforts to stigmatize and terrorize
   - when possible, shining a light on stigmatizing and terrorizing tactics in an ethical and constructive way
   - challenging authoritarian claims to scientific truth when such claims are not actually supported by the scientific evidence
   - not colluding by replaying abusive power dynamics
   - taking responsibility to keep the research grounded in human experience (listening to people's diverse and unique testimony, making the research accessible)
   - helping create a political and cultural context for others to also do ethical, competent science
   - keeping an open heart and mind.

Freyd's (1996) conclusion sums up the hopefulness we share.

Survivors of childhood abuse and betrayal traumas have learned to be disconnected internally, so as to manage a minimal kind of external connection. But with adult freedom and responsibility comes the potential to break silence, to use voice and language to promote internal integration, deeper external connection, and social transformation. (p. 196)

REFERENCES

American Psychological Association. (1992). Ethical principles of psychologists and code of conduct. *American Psychologist, 47*, 1597–1613.

Armstrong, L. (1994). *Rocking the cradle of sexual politics: What happened when women said incest.* Reading, MA: Addison-Wesley.

Beckett, K. (1996). Culture and the politics of signification: The case of child sexual abuse. *Social Problems, 43*(1), 57–76.

Bowman, C. G., & Mertz, E. (1996a). A dangerous direction: Legal intervention in survivor therapy. *Harvard Law Review, 109*, 549–639.

Bowman, C. G., & Mertz, E. (1996b). What should the courts do about memories of sexual abuse? Towards a balanced approach. *The Judge's Journal, 35*(4), 7–17.

Bransford, J. D., & Franks, J. J. (1971). The abstraction of linguistic ideas. *Cognitive Psychology, 2*(4), 331–350.

Brown, L. S. (1994). *Subversive dialogues: Toward a theory of feminist therapy.* New York: Basic Books.

Brown, L. S. (1996, March). *Theory and feminist therapy: Where do we go from here?* Distinguished Publication Award address presented at the Association for Women in Psychology 21st annual conference, Portland, OR.

Brown, L. S. (1997). The private practice of subversion: Psychology as *tikkun olam. American Psychologist, 52*, 449–462.

Butler, K. (1996). The latest on recovered memory. *Family Therapy Networker, 20*(6), 36–37.

Calof, D. L. (1998). Notes from a practice under siege: Harassment, defamation, and intimidation in the name of science. *Ethics & Behavior, 8*(2), 161–180.

Cheit, R. E. (1998). Consider this, skeptics of recovered memory. *Ethics & Behavior, 8*(2), 141–160.

Dahlenberg, C. J. (1996). Accuracy, timing and circumstances of disclosure in therapy of recovered and continuous memories of abuse. *Journal of Psychiatry and Law, 24*, 229–275.

Danziger, K. (1985). The origins of the psychological experiment as a social institution. *American Psychologist, 40*, 133–140.

Deese, J. (1959). On the prediction of occurrence of particular verbal instructions in immediate recall. *Journal of Experimental Psychology, 58*, 17–22.

DePrince, A., & Freyd, J. J. (1999). Dissociative tendencies, attention, and memory. *Psychological Science, 5,* 449–452.

Enns, C. Z., McNeilly, C., Corkery, J., & Gilbert, M. (1995). The debate about delayed memories of child sexual abuse: A feminist perspective. *The Counseling Psychologist, 23,* 181–279.

Feldman-Summers, S., & Pope, K. S. (1994). The experience of "forgetting" childhood abuse: A national survey of psychologists. *Journal of Consulting and Clinical Psychology, 62,* 636–639.

Feminist Therapy Institute. (1990). Feminist Therapy Institute code of ethics. In H. Lerman & N. Porter (Eds.), *Feminist ethics in psychotherapy* (pp. 37–40). New York: Springer.

Freyd, J. J. (1987). Dynamic mental representations. *Psychological Review, 94,* 427–438.

Freyd, J. J. (1996). *Betrayal trauma: The logic of forgetting childhood abuse.* Cambridge, MA: Harvard University Press.

Freyd, J. J. (1998). Science in the memory debate. *Ethics & Behavior, 8*(2), 101–113.

Freyd, J. J. (in press). Memory for trauma: Separating the contributions of fear from betrayal. In J. R. Conte (Ed.), *Child sexual abuse: Knowns and unknowns—A volume in honor of Roland Summit.* Thousand Oaks, CA: Sage.

Freyd, J. J., & Gleaves, D. H. (1996). Remembering words not presented in lists: Implications for the recovered–false memory controversy? *Journal of Experimental Psychology: Learning, Memory, and Cognition, 22,* 811–813.

Freyd, J. J., Martorello, S. R., Alvarado, J. S., Hayes, A. E., & Christman, J. C. (1998). Cognitive environments and dissociative tendencies: Performance on the standard Stroop task for high versus low dissociators. *Applied Cognitive Psychology, 12,* S91–S103.

Gleaves, D. H. (1996). The evidence for "repression": An examination of Holmes (1990) and the implications for the recovered memory controversy. *Journal of Child Sexual Abuse, 5,* 1–19.

Gleaves, D. H., & Freyd, J. J. (1997). Questioning additional claims about the "false memory syndrome" epidemic [Commentary]. *American Psychologist, 52,* 993–994.

Gold, S. N., & Brown, L. S. (1997). Therapeutic responses to delayed recall: Beyond recovered memory. *Psychotherapy, 34*(2), 182–191.

Harding, S. (1993). Rethinking standpoint epistemology: What is "strong" objectivity? In L. Alcoff & E. Potter (Eds.), *Feminist epistemologies* (pp. 49–82). New York: Routledge.

Herman, J. L., & Schatzow, E. (1987). Recovery and verification of memories of childhood sexual trauma. *Psychoanalytic Psychology, 4*(1), 1–14.

Holland, M. F. (1975, November). A rational approach to the Bransford–Franks memory paradigm based on subjective probability estimates. *Dissertation Abstracts International, 36*(5B), 2497.

Holmes, D. S. (1990). The evidence for repression: An examination of sixty years of research. In J. L. Singer (Ed.), *Repression and dissociation: Implications for personality theory, psychopathology, and health* (pp. 85–102). Chicago: University of Chicago Press.

Hoult, J. (1998). Silencing the victim: The politics of discrediting child abuse survivors. *Ethics & Behavior, 8*(2), 125–140.

Kassin, S. M., & Kiechel, K. L. (1996). The social psychology of false confessions. *Psychological Science, 7,* 125–128.

Loftus, E. F. (1997). Memories for a past that never was. *Current Directions in Psychological Science, 6*(3), 60–65.

Loftus, E. F., & Ketcham, K. (1994). *The myth of repressed memory.* New York: St. Martin's Press.

Loftus, E. F., Polonsky, S., & Fullilove, M. T. (1994). Memories of childhood sexual abuse: Remembering and repressing. *Psychology of Women Quarterly, 18,* 67–84.

Loftus, E. F., & Rosenwald, L. (1993, November). Buried memories, shattered lives. *American Bar Association Journal,* pp. 70–73.

McFarlane, A., & van der Kolk, B. A. (1996). Conclusions and future directions. In B. A. van der Kolk, A. McFarlane, & A. L. Weisaeth (Eds.), *Traumatic stress: The effects of overwhelming experience on mind, body, and society* (pp. 559–575). New York: Guilford Press.

Noddings, N. (1988). An ethic of caring and its implications for instructional arrangements. *American Journal of Education, 96*(2), 215–230.

Pendergrast, M. (1996). *Victims of memory: Incest accusations and shattered lives* (2nd ed.). Hinesberg, VT: Upper Access.

Pezdek, K., Finger, K., & Hodge, D. (1997). Planting false childhood memories: The role of event plausibility. *Psychological Science, 8,* 437–441.

Pezdek, K., & Roe, C. (1997). The suggestibility of children's memory for being touched: Planting, erasing, and changing memories. *Law and Human Behavior, 21*(1), 95–106.

Poole, D. A., Lindsay, D. S., Memon, A., & Bull, R. (1995). Psychotherapy and the recovery of memories of childhood sexual abuse: U.S. and British practitioners' opinions, practices, and experiences. *Journal of Clinical and Consulting Psychology, 63,* 426–437.

Poole, D. A., Lindsay, D. S., Memon, A., & Bull, R. (1997). Did Pope (1996) read a different Poole, Lindsay, Memon, and Bull (1995)? *American Psychologist, 52,* 990–993.

Pope, K. S. (1996). Memory, abuse, and science: Questioning claims about the false memory syndrome epidemic. *American Psychologist, 51,* 957–974.

Pope, K. S. (1997). Science as careful questioning: Are claims of a false memory syndrome epidemic based on empirical evidence? *American Psychologist, 52,* 997–1006.

Pope, K. S., & Brown. L. S. (1996). *Recovered memories of abuse: Assessment, therapy, and forensics.* Washington, DC: American Psychological Association.

Posner, M. I., & Keele, S. W. (1968). On the genesis of abstract ideas. *Journal of Experimental Psychology, 77*, 353–363.

Quina, K., & Kulberg, J. (1988). The experimental psychology course. In P. Bronstein & K. Quina (Eds.), *Teaching a psychology of people* (pp. 69–79). Washington, DC: American Psychological Association.

Roediger, H. L., & McDermott, K. B. (1995). Creating false memories: Remembering words not presented in lists. *Journal of Experimental Psychology: Learning, Memory, and Cognition, 21*, 803–813.

Salter, A. (1992). *Accuracy of expert testimony in child sexual abuse cases: A case study of Ralph Underwager and Hollida Wakefield.* Alexandria, VA: National Center for Prosecution of Child Abuse, American Prosecutors Research Institute.

Salter, A. C. (1995). *Transforming trauma.* Thousand Oaks, CA: Sage.

Salter, A. C. (1998). Confessions of a whistle-blower; lessons learned. *Ethics & Behavior, 8*(2), 115–124.

Shannon, B. (1996, June 8). Ingram's son claims he was abused. *The Olympian*, p. A1.

Shields, S. A. (1975). Functionalism, Darwinism, and the psychology of women: A study in social myth. *American Psychologist, 30*, 739–754.

Stanton, M. (1997, July–August). U-turn on memory lane. *Columbia Journalism Review*, pp. 44–49.

Unger, R. K. (1983). Through the looking glass: No wonderland yet! (The reciprocal relationship between methodology and models of reality). *Psychology of Women Quarterly, 8*, 9–32.

White, T. L., Leichtman, M. D., & Ceci, S. J. (1997). The good, the bad, and the ugly: Accuracy, inaccuracy, and elaboration in preschoolers' reports about a past event. *Applied Cognitive Psychology, 11*, S37–S54.

Williams, L. M. (1994). Recall of childhood trauma: A prospective study of women's memories of child sexual abuse. *Journal of Consulting and Clinical Psychology, 62*, 1167–1176.

Williams, L. M. (1995). Recovered memories of abuse in women with documented child sexual victimization histories. *Journal of Traumatic Stress, 8*, 649–674.

Wittig, M. A. (1985). Metatheoretical dilemmas in the psychology of gender. *American Psychologist, 40*, 800–811.

6

RELATIONAL ETHICS IN PSYCHOLOGICAL RESEARCH: ONE FEMINIST'S JOURNEY

CELIA B. FISHER

When I was a child, I hoped to become a warrior in the scientific quest for knowledge. The word *warrior* with its battle-driven, masculine connotations was appropriate for my worldview at the time. I saw scientists as gallant and adventurous, logisticians engaged in a battle for truth, and logic and adventure as distinctly masculine. Coming of age as a developmental psychologist in the modern feminist revolution of the 1970s did not dampen my love for science, but it did alter my view of the ideal scientist. I came to believe that a researcher, armed with the weapons of hypothesis testing, randomization, quantification, experimental control, and replicability, could take an Amazonian stance against sexist and racist assumptions about human development by generating value-free knowledge.

I did not discover the limitations of my "enlightened reason" assumptions through scholarly pursuit of philosophical writings and considered reflection on the value of my own scientific findings. Instead, motherhood

Portions of this chapter originally appeared in "Relational Ethics and Research With Vulnerable Populations," by C. B. Fisher (pp. 29–49), in *Research Involving Persons With Mental Disorders That May Affect Decision-Making Capacity* (Vol. 2) [Commissioned papers], 1999, Rockville, MD: National Bioethics Advisory Commission. Copyright in the public domain.

is what stopped me dead in my "Donna" Quixote tracks. When I was testing the visual perception of infants in laboratory studies, I would think of my own baby son and wonder the following: Did group means based on infant visual gaze bring scientists any closer to understanding what infant eye movements meant to the baby they were observing? Did the experimental question warrant exposing these infants to even the mild discomforts of sitting in a strange infant seat, in a strange room, without their mothers? Would I, as a mother, consent to having my baby participate in these studies?

I first attempted to address my discomfort with a shift to more applied research questions and more qualitative analyses of children and adolescent narratives. However, as the years passed and I became the mother of two growing children, I constantly saw my son and daughter in the faces of those I interviewed. I wondered whether, despite parental permission and a nod of assent, my young research participants really wanted to be in these studies? Was the investigation I was conducting of sufficient import to warrant the time the children were kept away from classroom studies? Were the tasks or nature of the questions asked eliciting feelings or new ways of looking at oneself that needed adult guidance? Once again I asked myself, would I, as a mother, consent to having my children participate in these studies?

These experiences and other fortuitous professional circumstances drew me into the field of scientific ethics. I began to write and teach about ethical issues in psychological research and practice and adjudicate ethical complaints through service on state boards and professional ethics committees. Old habits die hard, and I approached my newfound cause with the same formalism with which I had first pursued scientific knowledge years earlier. I hoped that through an ethicist's armory of moral principles and moral frameworks, one could construct universal codes of ethics to protect the welfare and autonomy of research participants. Drawing on the universalist–impersonalist tradition (Kant, 1785/1959; Sidgwick, 1907/1981), I believed that one could develop a scientific ethic through the application of abstract moral principles presumably free of subjective bias.

The inadequacy of this approach slowly became apparent. Parenting for more than a decade sensitized me (to a degree my extensive knowledge of developmental theory and research on contextual influences could not) to how very differently individual children and adolescents react to controlled procedures and how much their perspectives can differ from those of well-meaning adults. I began to realize that applying seemingly universal abstract moral principles in the absence of the particular and the contextual might actually decrease the adequacy of moral procedures (see Walker, 1992).

I came to believe that investigators could not design ethical procedures that would adequately protect the rights and welfare of research participants without learning how the research participants themselves viewed ethical issues. In addition, the duty and privilege of caring for my children had become a way of being for me that I could no longer compartmentalize into family versus others. I cared about my research participants. Thanks to the writings of feminist scholars like Gilligan (1982) and Noddings (1984), I began to see my own need for caring as a legitimate means to identify and address ethical issues in psychological research. I realized that the best way to truly care for research participants is to understand their point of view, and the best way to understand their point of view is to ask them.

THE NEGLECT AND IMPORTANCE OF
PARTICIPANT PERSPECTIVES

Seeking guidance on how to engage research participants in ethics-in-science dialogue, I quickly learned that traditional approaches to ethics-in-science decision making offered no guideposts by which to engage prospective research participants in dialogue. Such approaches typically reflect the application of ethical frameworks that prize the moral reasoning of the scientist and that ignore or devalue scientist–participant dialogue.

For example, since the Nuremberg Code (1946), federal regulations (Title 45, 1991) and professional guidelines for research (American Psychological Association, 1992) have drawn on the act–utilitarian or consequentialist position (Mill, 1861/1957) to resolve situations in which protecting the rights and welfare of research participants potentially threatens the internal validity of an experiment (Beauchamp, Faden, Wallace, & Walters, 1992). According to this position, when a conflict between scientific rigor and participant welfare arises, investigators and their institutional review boards (IRBs) are expected to evaluate the ethicality of their research by calculating the potential risks to participants against the potential knowledge gains for society. In so doing, the investigator's obligation to her or his research participants may be superseded by her or his responsibility to produce reliable data that can provide future benefits to the society at large. With its focus on utility and the "greater good," act–utilitarianism does not recognize a scientist's special relationship and subsequent moral obligations to research participants (Carroll, Schneider, & Wesley, 1985). In the act–utilitarian stance, I could not find support for participant-oriented ethics in which the concerns of research participants were valued above the abstract and intangible benefits of science to society (Fisher, 1994, 1997).

The deontological perspective, with its emphasis on intrinsic human worth and absolute moral principles, also provides a traditional foundation for ethics-in-science decision making. According to this moral framework, research participants should never be treated as simply the means by which investigators can achieve scientific goals (Kant, 1785/1959). The Kantian tradition's inherent respect for the dignity of people would appear to encourage scientists to incorporate participant perspectives into their ethical decision making. In practice, however, I observed that the deontic focus on the universality of moral principles and its indifference to particular relations and particular people (Carroll et al., 1985) often led investigators and IRBs to believe that they could determine which research procedures are ethical without consulting members of the population under study (Fisher, 1994, 1997). Thus, like act–utilitarianism, deontology did not provide a moral compass to help me orient scientists to their obligations to participants in their research.

By contrast, feminist approaches to moral agency, particularly the work of those seeking to synthesize principle-based justice ethic and relationship-based care ethic, provide a means by which scientists can reflect on ways to approach what Veatch (1987) coined the "scientist–citizen dilemma": the need to reconcile the researcher's professional commitment to the production of scientific knowledge with her or his humanitarian commitment to participant welfare (Fisher & Brennan, 1992; Fisher & Rosendahl, 1990). The justice perspective emphasizes moral agency based on principles of mutual respect, beneficence, and fairness (Kohlberg, 1984). It stresses moral decision making based on impartiality and distance from the scientist's own interests and her or his connectedness to others. The ethic of care emphasizes the duty to perceive people in their own terms and to respond to their needs (Gilligan, 1982; Noddings, 1984). It stresses moral decision making based on attention to the interpersonal situation and a narrative of relationships that extends over time.

In recent years, there has been growing recognition in philosophical and scientific circles that a morality based on justice can and does coexist with a morality based on interpersonal obligations (Brabeck, 1989; Higgins, 1989; Killen, 1996; Smetana, Killen, & Turiel, 1991; Waithe, 1989; Walker, 1992). Feminist moral philosophy values the application of such principles as beneficence, respect for personhood, and justice as guides for moral solutions rather than ethical universals (Steiner, 1997). For example, a justice–care orientation recognizes that care can temper moral decisions based on an impersonal concept of justice (Gilligan, 1982; Seigfried, 1989), that ethical principles can mediate a scientist's understanding of participant perspectives without placing a priority on the principles themselves over the moral frameworks of others (see Walker, 1992), and that respecting people involves responding to them on the basis of their own self-conceptions (Dillon, 1992).

RELATIONAL ETHICS, PARTICIPANT PERSPECTIVES, AND COLEARNING

The justice–care perspective enabled me to articulate a relational ethics for human subjects research that envisions scientists conducting risk–benefit analysis and applying moral principles to ethical decisions as guided by their responsiveness to research participants and awareness of their own boundaries, competencies, and obligations (Fisher, 1997; Fisher & Fyrberg, 1994; Fisher, Higgins-D'Alessandro, Rau, Kuther, & Belanger, 1996; O'Sullivan & Fisher, 1997; Prilleltensky, 1997; Sugden, 1993). This, in turn, allowed my colleagues and me (see, e.g., Fisher & Fyrberg, 1994) to draw on the works of other scholars to identify several moral arguments for including participants' perspectives in ethics-in-science decision making (Farr & Seaver, 1975; Melton, Levine, Koocher, Rosenthal, & Thompson, 1988; Sullivan & Deiker, 1973; Veatch, 1987; Wilson & Donnerstein, 1976).

The first argument recognizes that limiting ethical judgments to the investigator's own moral compass and the opinions of IRB members from the scholarly community risks treating participants as "research material" rather than as moral agents with the right to judge the ethicality of investigative procedures in which they are asked to participate. The second argument emphasizes that failure to consider participants' points of view leads to a reliance on scientific inference or professional logic. This, in turn, can lead to the implementation of research procedures causing significant participant distress or the rejection of potentially worthwhile scientific procedures that participants would perceive as benign, worthwhile, or both. A final argument acknowledges that failure to appreciate the interpersonal and contextual nature of ethical decision making places limitations on a scientist's own growth as a moral agent. Thus, understanding the point of view, needs, and expectations of others can enhance a psychologist's own moral development (Noddings, 1984) through the better understanding of a reciprocal relationship between the participants' expectations and the scientists' obligations.

Feminist political and moral philosophies assume that people of all genders, cultural orientations, and socioeconomic backgrounds have equal potential as moral agents (Steiner, 1997). Accordingly, a relational ethic that reflects the values and merits the trust of research participants cannot be achieved simply through a scientist's moral reflections but must be derived through scientist–participant dialogue (Ricoeur, 1990; Widdershoven & Smits, 1996). This dialogue is conceptualized as a process of colearning in which both scientist and participant are viewed as moral partners in the construction of ethical procedures. A major assumption of relational ethics is that colearning enhances the moral development of scientists and participants through a better understanding of the reciprocal relationship between the participant's expectations and the researcher's obligations. Relational ethics also recognizes that for research to be socially valuable and valid, scientists and participants must collaborate as moral agents working to construct research goals and ethical procedures. Such collaboration reflects a process of mutual influencing to discover shared and unshared values through which fair and ethical procedures are derived.

PARTICIPANT PERSPECTIVES ON DECEPTION RESEARCH

My first venture into approaching ethics-in-science problems from a colearning perspective was motivated by a personal experience. When I was a college freshman, my dorm resident assistant (RA) asked me to be in one of her professor's experiments. At the laboratory, I was introduced to another student participant, who left after a few minutes of conversation. Minutes later the RA rushed into the room to tell me the other student had left the experiment because she did not like me. The RA asked if I would fill out the test forms anyway so that her professor would not be angry. Feeling deeply humiliated, I agreed to fill out the forms, which asked me to evaluate the student who had just rejected me. With a desire to repair my damaged image, I rated the absent student high on a likability scale.

As I handed in the questionnaire, I was told that the other student was a confederate and that I had actually been in a study to assess people's feelings of affiliation for individuals who reject them. I felt even more humiliated than before. If what the RA was telling me was true, I had revealed my vulnerabilities to her by looking upset and giving high ratings to a person who had rejected me. When asked if I felt better having been "dehoaxed," I lied and said "yes," and then I hurried away. Embarrassed, I could never again look the RA in the eye. Indeed, it was not until I entered graduate school and read about deception studies that I realized that during the dehoaxing, she had (probably!) been telling the truth. Needless to say, years later when I began to have an interest in ethics-in-science, I had a personal reason for assuming that deception studies should never be conducted. I was particularly annoyed at those who defended the use of deception by saying that data collected on participants' "positive" responses to dehoaxing was proof that no harm was done to deceived individuals.

Deception Research and Moral Ambiguity

Acceptability of deception research in social science is an example of the ambivalence surrounding the fiduciary responsibilities of investigators. Following the Nazi medical science atrocities, society no longer trusted scientists to conduct their work in the best interests of individual participants. Informed consent, rather than responsible scientific conduct, was seen as the primary means of protecting participant autonomy and welfare. Deception research turns this requirement on its head. With the application of an act–utilitarian perspective, it subjugates participant autonomy and welfare to the greater good of science and returns the sole responsibility of participant protection back to the investigator and IRB.

Those who believe that deception research may be morally acceptable have looked to the scientific value and validity of a deception study as moral justification. There is no ethical justification for conducting a study that fails in its ability to yield a formal relationship between data and conclusions, from which reliable information can be acquired (Freedman, 1987). Similarly, even if a study is well designed, any risks to participant autonomy or welfare cannot be justified if the hypotheses are trivial. The traditional methodological argument for the use of deception techniques is the following: By creating experimental situations that participants view as "real," scientists see deception sometimes as the only means of ensuring that interpretations of results can be validly applied to everyday life (Aronson & Carlsmith, 1968). In considering the value of a deception study, researchers and IRB members by virtue of their training and institutional positions may overestimate the validity and value of deception research. Consequently, participants may be more legitimate judges of both the experimental realism and social value of a study.

A second set of issues applied to the ethical evaluation of deception research is psychological discomfort in response to both experimental procedures and dehoaxing. The psychological harm caused by deception procedures can include invasion of privacy, stress and discomfort, loss of self-esteem, and negative reactions to "inflicted insight" gained by being induced to commit antisocial or immoral acts (Baumrind, 1985; Keith-Spiegel & Koocher, 1985). In the absence of any empirical data, investigators and IRBs may over- or underestimate participant reactions to deception procedures. This is especially true when participant reactions to dehoaxing are assessed by their response to an investigator who has just told them they were deceived.

A related ethical problem inherent in many deception studies is that participants are typically college students who are required to participate for introductory psychology course credit. The potentially coercive aspect of "subject pool" requirements may cause additional stressors, especially when students are asked to reveal their feelings about the study immediately following dehoaxing. Participant opinions regarding the potential risks of specific research procedures and the psychological costs of dehoaxing are thus an essential means of guarding against ethical decisions based solely on the investigator's assumptions regarding the potential harm posed by deception practices.

Participant Perspectives on Deception Research

The approval of deception research implies a conception of scientific responsibility that emphasizes a fiduciary obligation to produce scientifically valid knowledge for the benefit of society over an obligation to conduct honest interpersonal interactions with participants for the benefit of the individual. Should deception research be banned because it violates participant autonomy and the fiduciary responsibility of scientists to be honest (see Baumrind, 1985)? Are there some deception studies that are so important that society might be deprived of critical knowledge if scientists did not conduct them? Can solicitation of participant opinions shift the ethical task away from calculating the costs and benefits of a deception project to selecting only those deception procedures that participants themselves would consider valid, caring, and ethical?

If I believed that knowledge concerning participant perspectives is essential to good ethical decision making about deception research, how could I go about generating this knowledge? To engage individuals in a deception study for the purpose of eliciting their reactions is ethically problematic because it exposes people to what the investigator believes may be procedures that potentially violate their autonomy and welfare. To give participants open-ended questions concerning the ethics of deception is equally problematic because it asks individuals to provide spontaneous and decontextualized responses to moral questions that require informed deliberation.

Denise Fyrberg and I (Fisher & Fyrberg, 1994) decided to take an alternative course of action. We used a method that would be a learning experience for both participants and investigators. Individuals in our study would learn about how the scientific method is applied to psychological studies and about areas of current ethical concern in the use of deception practices. In turn, we would learn what participants thought about specific ethically relevant issues, their views on whether deception studies should be conducted, and the moral frameworks applied to their decisions.

We decided to engage introductory psychology students in this exploration because they represent the predominant participant population for deception research (Higbee, Millard, & Folkman, 1982; Sears, 1986). Following a description of the purpose, procedures, participants, results, and interpretation of one of three recently published deception studies, students (predominantly White, with equal numbers of men and women) were asked to answer questions from philosophical and scientific critiques and defenses of the use of deception in psychological research. We used a combination of qualitative measures (essay-type response) and quantitative measures (Likert-type scale responses) to guard against the potential biases in each.

Challenge of Participant Perspectives

When we started this study (Fisher & Fyrberg, 1994), I assumed that introductory psychology students would share my own rather negative feelings about deception research. I also thought that women more than men would be sensitive to issues of potential harm. In both instances, I was wrong. To my surprise, although the majority of introductory psychology students believed that both the deception experimental procedures and dehoaxing would lead to participant stress and discomfort, they also thought that the deception studies were scientifically valid and valuable, that deception manipulation was preferable to alternative methodologies, that the benefits to society outweighed the costs to individuals, and that each of the deception studies should have been conducted. In addition, content analysis of their ethical justifications for or against conducting the study indicated a predominantly act–utilitarian moral ideology, similar to the cost–benefit approach to deception research within federal and professional ethical guidelines.

This placed me in an ethical quandary. On the one hand, the data enhanced my appreciation for the scientific method. As personally biased as I was toward finding negative participant views about deception research, the use of objective methodology yielded information contrary to my expectations. On the other hand, I worried that the data we collected might be used to justify deception procedures use. In fact, a few years after the article on this study was published, I was horrified to read an article that misused our findings that introductory psychology students would not believe the experimenter during dehoaxing as a rationale for not including a dehoaxing component in deception research.

Description Is Not Prescription

In confronting these challenges, I recognized how naive I had been to assume that understanding participant perspectives would in itself clarify the ethical task for social scientists considering the use of deception research. Respondents in our study (Fisher & Fyrberg, 1994) displayed a contradictory mixture of faith in and skepticism about dehoaxing procedures. The majority believed that their peers would be embarrassed or annoyed to learn during dehoaxing that they had been deceived and would be concerned that their responses to dehoaxing itself would potentially jeopardize their course credit. In contrast, they expressed in their essays faith in dehoaxing as a means to alleviate harm caused by deception practices and cited dehoaxing as the ethical justification underlying their act–utilitarian rationales for considering deception practices ethical. We speculated that this mixture of confidence and distrust in dehoaxing procedures might reflect what Davis (1940) described as *youthful idealism*: the lack of social experience that enables young adults to maintain utopian ideals, despite apparent inconsistencies. If this is the case, then the ethical evaluation of deception research requires a consideration of both student idealism and the investigator's hard-earned adult realism.

This first venture into applying the relational model to empirical investigation of an ethical issue threw me into what Sidgwick (1907/1981) identified as the *fallacy of is to ought*: the temptation to equate the moral judgments that people actually make with the moral judgments they should make. I realized that empirical understanding of participant perspectives is not a panacea for solving ethical problems. Instead, the knowledge, training, and status that places scientists in a fiduciary relationship with participants obligates the scientists to take ultimate responsibility for the rights and welfare of their research participants. Thus, participant perspectives inform but do not substitute for ethical deliberation by individual scientists (Fisher & Fyrberg, 1994). I then recognized that scientists as moral agents must integrate their caring and understanding of participant perspectives with a realistic sense of their own competencies to take responsibility for ethical decisions (see Noddings, 1984).

REPORTING RESEARCH PARTICIPANTS AT RISK:
THE VOICE OF URBAN ADOLESCENTS

I next turned my empirical attention to an ethical problem that was haunting me as I delved into research on adolescent risk behaviors. Descriptive and explanatory studies exploring the development of children and adolescents can pose ethical problems for researchers because they have the potential to tap previously unidentified sources of psychopathology, abuse, or delinquent behaviors (Fisher, 1993, 1994; Fisher & Rosendahl, 1990). During the course of such data collection, adolescent participants may reveal information indicating suicidal ideation, engagement in health-compromising behaviors, involvement in illegal or harmful behaviors, or life in abusive circumstances. Does the research psychologist have a moral duty to help a research participant if a problem is revealed during the course of research? Does this moral obligation override the duty to protect participant confidentiality?

Many discussions and ethical guidelines have been generated around the need to protect participant privacy through the maintenance of confidentiality. Intricate procedures for keeping data sheets free of identifying information and for keeping records secure have been developed. However, the idealization of confidentiality in human subjects research represents a false dichotomy between protection of participant autonomy and welfare.

The scientific community has been reluctant to assist teenagers with problems uncovered during the course of research because the following situations are present: (a) a healthy skepticism that inferences from measures designed to evaluate differences between groups may not have diagnostic validity for individual participants, (b) awareness that disclosing information can sometimes create harmful consequences for the participant if adults react to information with punitive measures, and (c) concern that helping a research participant may threaten the internal validity of an experiment or jeopardize the trust and participation of others in the research (Fisher, 1993; Fisher & Brennan, 1992; Fisher, Higgins-D'Alessandro, et al., 1996; Fisher, Hoagwood, & Jensen, 1996). Applying the rule–utilitarian framework to when a conflict emerges between participant welfare and scientific rigor, investigators often see the production of well-controlled data that can benefit society as superseding their duty to facilitate or procure services for individual participants (Fisher, 1993; Fisher & Brennan, 1992).

Adolescent Perspectives on Reporting and Referring

An additional untested assumption underlying scientists' reluctance to assist adolescents who have indicated potential problems during the course of research is the belief that adolescents place the highest moral value on autonomy and would feel betrayed by an investigator who disclosed confidential information to protect them. Blind faith in this assumption has prevented scientists from asking two critical questions. (a) What moral role does an adolescent research participant expect of an investigator? (b) What are the consequences of failing to fulfill this role?

Ann Higgins-D'Alessandro, Jean Marie Rau, Tara Kuther, Sue Belanger, and I (Fisher, Higgins-D'Alessandro, et al., 1996) asked these questions of predominantly Hispanic 7th-, 9th-, and 11th-grade female and male students attending a public school in a low-income urban neighborhood. The students gave opinions concerning three ethical strategies an investigator could follow if during the course of research an adolescent participant indicated that she or he were in danger or engaged in a high-risk behavior. The investigator could (a) keep the information confidential, (b) talk to the teenager and assist her or him in finding a referral source, or (c) tell a parent or other concerned adult. To avoid imposing our own evaluations of risk severity, we asked the adolescents to rate their perceptions of how problematic they considered each of the following 12 behaviors: use of alcohol, use of illegal drugs, use of cigarettes, physical abuse, sexual abuse, suicidal ideation, sexually transmitted diseases, truancy, vandalism, theft, violence, and shyness.

Influencing Participants' Lives

> Those of us who study lives are aware that we influence the lives we examine—perhaps very little, perhaps a great deal. (Agronick & Helson, 1996, p. 80)

Not surprisingly, adolescents of all ages viewed self-referrals most favorably because it reflected a concern with both participant autonomy and welfare. However, probably the most important contribution of this research was the finding that the adolescents viewed the maintenance of confidentiality negatively, especially in situations in which an investigator learned that a research participant was a victim of or engaged in behaviors adolescents themselves perceive as a serious problem (Fisher, Higgins-D'Alessandro, et al., 1996).

This finding confirms what had caused me such initial concern about confidentiality in adolescent risk research: Even when adolescent participants were promised confidentiality under traditional informed-consent procedures, they expected to be helped when they told an adult interviewer that they were a victim of violence or were involved in a high-risk behavior. From adolescents' reports, it followed that an investigator's failure to help an adolescent, rather than having no impact, may have had a long-lasting negative impact on how an adolescent interpreted the significance of his or her own risk behaviors and the fiduciary responsibility of adults. Adolescents may interpret the scientist's lack of action as an indication that their problem is unimportant, that no services are available, or that knowledgeable adults cannot be depended on to help children in need (Fisher, 1993, 1994; Fisher, Higgins-D'Alessandro, et al., 1996)

The data also underscore the value of what I learned from our (Fisher & Fyrberg, 1994) college students' opinions about deception research: Participant opinions must assist but not replace a psychologist's duty to apply her or his own moral compass to ethical decisions. For example, although rated as a serious problem, most adolescents in our study (Fisher, Higgins-D'Alessandro, et al., 1996) did not believe an investigator should report sexually transmitted diseases to concerned adults. Whereas providing adolescents with a referral to a health clinic may respect their autonomy, given the life-threatening nature of some of these diseases, an investigator must evaluate the risk to participant autonomy against the risk to a minor's health if the problem remains unreported.

Placing what I learned about adolescents' concerns about confidentiality within the framework of my knowledge as a psychologist about risk outcomes, I arrived at a set of guidelines for confidentiality and disclosure decisions for adolescent risk research that act as a foundation for my work at Fordham University. These guidelines call for the researcher to

(a) consider the expectations of prospective adolescents and their guardians

(b) identify her or his fiduciary responsibility to design studies that produce valid and reliable data and protect the rights and welfare of research participants

(c) clarify her or his ability to accurately assess individual risk

(d) identify resources that can best serve the interests of adolescent participants in need of referral or direct intervention

(e) based on the above determine an appropriate confidentiality policy

(f) during informed consent share with participants and their guardians the policy that the investigator will follow.

POWER AND PARTNERSHIP

The fiduciary responsibility that obligates the scientist to take final moral responsibility for the ethical procedures selected for his or her research also underscores the power asymmetry inherent in research. The scientist–participant relationship is not equal because the scientist has directive power that the participant does not and because the hypothesis may not be known to the participant. Most prerogatives lie with the researcher.

A scientist has the prerogative to select who will be recruited for her or his research, the question under investigation, whether to ask a person to extend her or his participation in a treatment study, and how research will be interpreted and disseminated. The participant has the prerogative to decline research participation and withdraw once consent has been granted but does not usually have the right to demand additional scientific assessments of treatment efficacy or determine how and where research findings will be disseminated after a study is completed. The participant's responsibility is to apply his or her best efforts to follow the experimental protocol during the study. The scientist's responsibility is to protect the participant's autonomy and welfare and to maintain the scientific and ethical integrity of the study before, during, and after experimentation.

When working with vulnerable and marginalized individuals, the responsible scientist needs to ensure that power differentials are not a product of the participant's special circumstance. Context-derived power asymmetries can occur when guardian consent is given higher priority than participant assent simply because of an individual's legal, psychological, or social status. Power asymmetries are also magnified when the experimental arrangement itself increases participant dependency. This can occur, for example, when an individual who is inexperienced in challenging authority freely assents to participation, but he or she is not aware of his or her right to withdraw participation or does not know the actions he or she could take to withdraw. Potentially destructive power asymmetries also emerge when science is used as a tool of subordination to legitimize oppressive policies (Freyd & Quina, chap. 5, this volume; Prilleltensky, 1997).

Those who seek greater symmetry in power relationships emphasize that each party must derive something out of the relationship and be able to exercise discretionary control over the resources prized by the other (Goodin, 1985). However, these resources must be used to enhance, not compromise, the ethical and scientific integrity of experimentation. Relational ethics recognizes that both scientists and participants can misuse their influence: Scientists can use their status and control of resources to coerce participant compliance in research procedures that the participant may view as harmful, unjust, or unworthy. Participants, or their community representatives, can exploit the science establishment's dependency on their cooperation to coerce investigator compliance in research practices that compromise scientific validity.

Although power relationships between scientist and participant may not be truly symmetrical, they can be complementary and noncoercive. Such complementarity derives from trust that each party will work to understand and respect the value orientations of the other. Relational ethics views an action as unethical if it violates the moral values of either the scientist or participant. If colearning discourse reveals that mutual accommodation cannot take place, the investigator must be willing to abandon a particular research plan. The argument is that to truly accept a relational model, one must value the moral claims of both investigators and research participants. Scientific procedures gain moral legitimacy only if they are the product of solutions that do not require compromises that would coerce, exploit, or deprecate the values of either party. In a relationally based approach, ethics-in-science decision making is based on respect and mutual accommodation between scientist and participant, not compromise and coercion.

CONCLUSION: THE SCIENTIST AS MORAL PARTICIPANT

In my journey toward a relational ethic for science, feminist philosophy has provided a conceptual foundation for my commitment to construct ethical procedures that reflect the interpersonal nature and obligations inherent in the scientist–participant relationship. Feminist writings challenge the traditional universalistic and principle orientation of ethics-in-science decision making to include the importance of intersubjectivity, particularity, and context; they also move scientists toward a reinterpretation of their own moral agency (see Smith, 1985; and Walker, 1992). The feminist perspective enables them to integrate their rational and relational caring selves in ways that enhance their ability to engage research participants as partners in creating experimental procedures reflecting both scientific and interpersonal integrity (Grossman et al., 1997).

A relational perspective serves as a guide for moral discourse, which can move science toward an orientation of the good life lived with others in social conditions that are just (Widdershoven & Smits, 1996). It pushes scientists to envision ethics as a process that draws on investigators' human responsiveness to those who participate in their research and the scientists' awareness of their own boundaries, competencies, and obligations. If becoming a moral agent is the critical moral task for all individuals (Smith, 1985), then for me recognizing that morality is embedded in the investigator–participant connection is the essential moral activity of science (Fisher, 1997).

REFERENCES

Agronick, G., & Helson, R. (1996). Who benefits from an examined life? Correlates of influence attributed to participation in a longitudinal study. In R. Josselson (Ed.), *Ethics and process in the narrative study of lives* (pp. 80–93). Thousand Oaks, CA: Sage.

American Psychological Association. (1992). Ethical principles of psychologists and code of conduct. *American Psychologist, 47,* 1597–1611.

Aronson, E., & Carlsmith, J. M. (1968). Experimentation in social psychology. In G. Lindzey & E. Aronson (Eds.), *The handbook of social psychology* (Vol. 2, pp. 1–79). Reading, MA: Addison-Wesley.

Baumrind, D. (1985). Research using intentional deception: Ethical issues revisited. *American Psychologist, 40,* 165–174.

Beauchamp, T. L., Faden, R. R., Wallace, R. J., & Walters, L. (1992). *Ethical issues in social science research.* Baltimore: Johns Hopkins University Press.

Brabeck, M. M. (1989). Introduction: Who cares? In M. M. Brabeck (Ed.), *Who cares? Theory, research, and educational implications of the ethic of care* (pp. xi–xviii). New York: Praeger.

Carroll, M. A., Schneider, H. G., & Wesley, G. R. (1985). *Ethics in the practice of psychology.* Englewood Cliffs, NJ: Prentice Hall.

Davis, K. (1940). The sociology of parent–youth conflict. *American Sociological Review, 1,* 523–537.

Dillon, R. (1992). Care and respect. In E. B. Cole & S. Coultrap-McQuin (Eds.), *Explorations in feminist ethics* (pp. 69–81). Bloomington: Indiana University Press.

Farr, J. L., & Seaver, W. B. (1975). Stress and discomfort in psychological research: Subject perceptions of experimental procedures. *American Psychologist, 30,* 770–773.

Fisher, C. B. (1993). Integrating science and ethics in research with high-risk children and youth. *SRCD Social Policy Report, 7*(4), 1–27.

Fisher, C. B. (1994). Reporting and referring research participants: Ethical challenges for investigators studying children and youth. *Ethics & Behavior, 4,* 87–95.

Fisher, C. B. (1997). A relational perspective on ethics-in-science decision-making for research with vulnerable populations. *IRB: A Review of Human Subjects Research, 19*(5), 1–4.

Fisher, C. B. (1999). Relational ethics and research with vulnerable populations. In *Research involving persons with mental disorders that may affect decision-making capacity* (Vol. 2, pp. 29–49) [Commissioned papers]. Rockville, MD: National Bioethics Advisory Commission.

Fisher, C. B., & Brennan, M. (1992). Application and ethics in developmental psychology. In D. L. Featherman, R. M. Lerner, & M. Perlmutter (Eds.), *Life-span development and behavior* (pp. 189–219). Hillsdale, NJ: Erlbaum.

Fisher, C. B., & Fyrberg, D. (1994). Participant partners: College students weigh the costs and benefits of deceptive research. *American Psychologist, 49,* 417–427.

Fisher, C. B., Higgins-D'Alessandro, A., Rau, M. B., Kuther, T., & Belanger, S. (1996). Referring and reporting research participants at-risk: Views from urban adolescents. *Child Development, 67,* 2086–2100.

Fisher, C. B., Hoagwood, K., & Jensen, P. S. (1996). Casebook on ethical issues in research with children and adolescents with mental disorders. In K. Hoagwood, P. S. Jensen, & C. B. Fisher (Eds.), *Ethical issues in mental health research with children and adolescents* (pp. 135–238). Mahwah, NJ: Erlbaum.

Fisher, C. B., & Rosendahl, S. A. (1990). Psychological risks and remedies of research participation. In C. B. Fisher & W. W. Tryon (Eds.), *Ethics in applied developmental psychology: Emerging issues in an emerging field* (pp. 43–60). Norwood, NJ: Ablex.

Freedman, B. (1987). Scientific value and validity as ethical requirements for research: A proposed explication. *IRB: A Review of Human Subjects Research, 9*(6), 7–10.

Gilligan, C. (1982). *In a different voice.* Cambridge, MA: Harvard University Press.

Goodin, R. E. (1985). *Protecting the vulnerable.* Chicago: University of Chicago Press.

Grossman, F. K., Gilbert, L. A., Genero, N. P., Hawes, S. E., Hyde, J. S., & Marecek, J. (With Johnson, L.). (1997). Feminist research: Practice and problems. In J. Worell & N. G. Johnson (Eds.), *Shaping the future of feminist psychology: Education, research, and practice* (pp. 73–91). Washington, DC: American Psychological Association.

Higbee, K. L., Millard, R. J., & Folkman, J. R. (1982). Social psychology research during the 1970's: Predominance of experimentation and college students. *Personality and Social Psychology Bulletin, 8,* 180–183.

Higgins, A. (1989). The just community educational program: The development of moral role-taking as the expression of justice and care. In M. M. Brabeck (Ed.), *Who cares? Theory, research, and educational implications of the ethic of care* (pp. 197–215). New York: Praeger.

Kant, I. (1959). *Foundations of the metaphysics of morals.* Indianapolis, IN: Bobbs-Merrill. (Original work published 1785)

Keith-Spiegel, P., & Koocher, G. P. (1985). *Ethics in psychology.* New York: Random House.

Killen, M. (1996). Justice and care: Dichotomies or coexistence? *Journal for a Just and Caring Education, 2,* 42–58.

Kohlberg, L. (1984). *Essays on moral development. Vol. W: The psychology of moral development.* San Francisco: Harper & Row.

Melton, G. B., Levine, R. J., Koocher, G. P., Rosenthal, R., & Thompson, W. C. (1988). Community consultation in socially sensitive research: Lessons from clinical trials of treatments for AIDS. *American Psychologist, 43,* 573–581.

Mill, J. S. (1957). *Utilitarianism.* New York: Bobbs-Merrill. (Original work published 1861)

Noddings, N. (1984). *Caring: A feminine approach to ethics and moral education.* Berkeley: University of California Press.

Nuremberg Code. (1946). *Journal of the American Medical Association, 132,* 1090.

O'Sullivan, C., & Fisher, C. B. (1997). The effect of confidentiality and reporting procedures on parent–child agreement to participate in adolescent risk research. *Applied Developmental Science, 1,* 185–197.

Prilleltensky, I. (1997). Values, assumptions, and practices: Assessing the moral implications of psychological discourse and action. *American Psychologist, 52,* 517–535.

Ricoeur, P. (1990). *The self as other.* Paris, France: Editions du Seuil.

Sears, D. O. (1986). College sophomores in the laboratory: Influences of a narrow data base on social psychology's view of human nature. *Journal of Personality and Social Psychology, 51,* 515–540.

Seigfried, C. H. (1989). Pragmatism, feminism, and sensitivity to context. In M. M. Brabeck (Ed.), *Who cares? Theory, research, and educational implications of the ethic of care* (pp. 63–83). New York: Praeger.

Sidgwick, H. (1981). *The methods of ethics.* Indianapolis, IN: Hackett. (Original work published in 1907)

Smetana, J. G., Killen, M., & Turiel, E. (1991). Children's reasoning about interpersonal and moral conflicts. *Child Development, 62*(3), 629–644.

Smith, R. L. (1985). Feminism and the moral subject. In B. H. Andolsen, C. E. Gudorf, & M. D. Pellauer (Eds.), *Women's consciousness, women's conscience* (pp. 235–250). Minneapolis, MN: Winston Press.

Steiner, L. (1997). A feminist schema for analysis of ethical dilemmas. In F. L. Casmir (Ed.), *Ethics in intercultural and international communication* (pp. 59–87). Mahwah, NJ: Erlbaum.

Sugden, R. (1993). The contractarian enterprise. In D. Gauthier & R. Sugden (Eds.), *Rationality, justice and the social contract: Themes from morals by agreement* (pp. 1–23). Ann Arbor: University of Michigan Press.

Sullivan, D. S., & Deiker, T. E. (1973). Subject–experimenter perceptions of ethical issues in human research. *American Psychologist, 28*, 587–591.

Title 45 Public Welfare, Pt. 46, C.F.R., Protection of Human Subjects. (1991, August). Department of Health and Human Services.

Veatch, R. M. (1987). *The patient as partner*. Bloomington: Indiana University Press.

Waithe, M. E. (1989). Twenty-three hundred years of women philosophers: Toward a gender undifferentiated moral theory. In M. M. Brabeck (Ed.), *Who cares? Theory, research, and educational implications of the ethic of care* (pp. 3–18). New York: Praeger.

Walker, M. W. (1992). Moral understandings: Alternative "epistemology" for a feminist ethic. In E. B. Cole & S. Coultrap-McQuin (Eds.), *Explorations in feminist ethics* (pp. 165–175). Bloomington: Indiana University Press.

Widdershoven, G. A. M., & Smits, M. (1996). Ethics and narrative. In R. Josselson (Ed.), *Ethics and process in the narrative study of lives* (Vol. 4, pp. 274–287). Thousand Oaks, CA: Sage.

Wilson, D. W., & Donnerstein, W. (1976). Legal and ethical aspects of non-reactive social psychological research: An excursion into the public mind. *American Psychologist, 31*, 765–773.

7

FEMINIST CYBERETHICS

KATHRYN QUINA AND DAVID L. MILLER

In the past decade, a quiet revolution has taken place in the way most people use their computers. This change occurred as computer users stopped using their machines solely for computation and started using them for communication. The communication infrastructure of on-line services and the Internet coupled with increasing ease-of-use have made email and websites commonplace. The rapid growth of computer-mediated communication (CMC) has made a cyberspace address as expected as a telephone number. Just as social communication in real time has been a key issue for feminist activism for the past 3 decades, social cybercommunication now is in dire need of similar attention.

Feminists, ourselves included, are poised at an important point in this revolution. They must cope with a new medium, new possibilities, and new challenges. *Cyberspace*, the popular term for that electronic screen-to-screen network now stretched over the world, is full of both promise and challenges for feminists. Whether they spend their on-line time in chat rooms, "surf the net," design websites, just write to their friends and family, or have not yet become "wired," they must confront some basic ethical issues if they

This chapter is based on a paper presented at the 104th Annual Convention of the American Psychological Association, Toronto, Ontario, Canada, on August 11, 1996.

are to leap forward in step with—or better yet, to help create—this evolving culture.

In this chapter, we look at the cultural and ethical structures of cyberspace and explore what feminist cyberethics could look like. We first address the current status and then theoretical issues: How may the environment of cyberspace shape feminist culture, and how may feminist ethics, in turn, shape the culture of cyberspace? How can "cyber" extend one's thinking about feminist ethics, and what can feminists do to extend current thinking about cyberethics? There is of course much overlap among these domains, but there are also some meaningful differences. Later, we identify four challenges for a feminist ethical cyberspace and offer potential solutions.

GENDER IN CYBERSPACE

Gender is certainly a relevant dimension to CMC. Cyberspace was designed by defense industry engineers for other defense industry engineers—few of them women and none of them openly feminist (Rheingold, 1993). Virtually every corner of cyberspace is dominated by the male voice (Taylor, Kramarae, & Ebben, 1993). In several ways, the computer culture resembles the academic and psychotherapy worlds that spawned the feminist movement 3 decades ago. Even the language shows that there is a hierarchy and who is expected to be in charge: Open public lists are moderated by owners, and websites are managed by masters. Behavior on-line is not always civil, and "flame wars" are a frequent occurrence (see Lea, O'Shea, Fung, & Spears, 1992). Emotional nuances are expressed in exclamation points, capitalized words, and "emoticons"—[: - (or ; -)]—their use may also reveal gender differences (Sudweeks, McLaughlin, & Rafaeli, 1998).

Several important discussions of gender and computers have taken place (e.g., Kramarae & Taylor, 1993; Matheson, 1991, 1992). There are many women's voices available on the Internet and the World Wide Web, including valuable feminist resources (see Exhibit 7.1). There are safe spaces reserved fiercely by women for women, by survivors for survivors, and other affinity groups. Yet sadly it is easy to document the dearth of women. Not a single woman appeared in a recent survey of the highest paid CEOs of high-tech corporations ("Top CEOs," 1996). Women account for fewer than 3% of the tenured faculty in academic departments of computer science and engineering (Cottrell, 1992; Quina, Cotter, & Romenesko, 1998). Currently, three times as many men earn degrees in computer science than do women, and the National Science Foundation reports that this gap is growing (Kantrowitz, 1994).

Exhibit 7.1
Helpful Feminist Resources

- Network services: East Coast Hang Out (ECHO), an on-line network service run by women, and Women's Wire (San Francisco, CA), a network service with 90% women subscribers, where "flaming" is not allowed and there is no such thing as a dumb question. See Broadhurst's (1995) *The Woman's Guide to Online Services* for other listings.

- Websites that link to other sites (e.g., www.feminist.org, http://www.library.wisc.edu/libraries/WomensStudies/fcmain.htm, http://www.mills.edu/ACAD_INFO/MCS/SPERTUS/Gender/gender.html), to mailing lists and newsgroups (www-unix.umbc.edu/~korenman/wmst/ forums.html), and to papers of interest (http://www.ascusc.org/jcmc/) and social issues in computing (http://www.aaas.org/spp/dspp/shr/cushrid.htm; all retrieved on July 13, 1999).

- Public lists: the Psychology of Women Resource List (POWR-L), cosponsored by American Psychological Association Division 35 and the Association for Women in Psychology (to subscribe, send a message with your name to listserv@uriacc.uri.edu: for example, "Subscribe POWR-L Sally Smith") and for the Women's Studies list ("Subscribe WMST-L Sally Smith").

- Extensive bibliographies on women and information technology can be found in Shade (1993) and Taylor et al. (1993). A more general bibliography is available from ProjectH (http://www.arch.su.edu.au/~fay/projecth/about.html). Also see regular features in *Feminist Collections: A Quarterly of Women's Studies Resources* (retrieved July 13, 1999 from the World Wide Web: http://www.library.wisc.edu/libraries/WomensStudes/fcmain.htm) and in "Sexuality and Cyberspace," a special issue of *Women and Performance* (retrieved July 13, 1999 from the World Wide Web: http://www.echonyc.com/ ~women/Issue17/index.html).

Linguistic patterns in CMC follow patterns observed during in-person conversation. Selfe and Meyer (1991) examined conversation patterns in a self-selected academic environment and found that even there, men dominated conversations and initiated more disagreements than women; women asked more questions (although there were no gender differences in "polite" speech). Even without facial cues when the gender of the "other" is provided, computer-based communications include stereotypical expectations and perceptions of the receiver, just as in other attribution research (e.g., Quina, Wingard, & Bates, 1987). Cheris Kramarae and Jeanie Taylor (1993) raised a concern that "in almost any open network, men monopolize the talk. . . . Even open networks where the topic is women's issues are, we have found, overrun by men" (p. 55). In 1993, Gladys We reported that men posted 83% and 78% of the messages on two unmoderated feminist Usenet groups, alt.feminism and soc.women, although Leslie Shade (1993) cited another such count that suggested that men's posts were usually merely cross-posts from other lists. We should take heart from the fact that in the past few years the numbers of women on-line have increased dramatically, and on some lists (e.g., WMST-L, POWR-L), women clearly dominate.

Maluso (1997) described differences in the behaviors of men and women in LambdaMOO, an on-line virtual world estimated to be 70% men and 80% college educated, with an age range from early teens to late 70s. In her study, male-, female-, and no gender-identified posters requested various types of assistance, from how to exit to how to end harassment. She found no differences in the rate of men's and women's responses to nongendered requests, but in gendered requests, men were much less likely to help other men. Women were more likely to respond to the harassment request than men, and both responded to harassment more often than to other kinds of requests. Overall, responses to requests were more helpful when the poster's gender was known. More of this sort of research is beginning to identify interesting implications for understanding on-line behavior, in general, and gendered responding, in particular. Sudweeks et al.'s (1998) book of studies of an on-line community, ProjectH (www.arch.usyd.edu.au), devotes considerable attention to gender issues.

EXAPTATION OF FEMINIST ETHICS TO CYBERSPACE

Numerous discussions of ethical and related issues for cybercommunication have arisen as a result of the cyberspace social revolution. By 1994, ProjectH collected over 300 references, and the number continues to grow with the medium. These ethical discussions include efforts to establish legal codes ("net-law," e.g., Rose, 1995), discussions of ethical problems (e.g., the December 1995 issue of *Communications of the* ACM; Kallman & Grillo, 1993; Spinello, 1995, 1997), handbooks of acceptable use policies ("netiquette") for on-line conduct (e.g., McLaughlin, Osborne, & Smith, 1995; Shea, 1994), and volumes of technical discussions. Ainspan (1994) provided an on-line bibliography of over 200 articles on organizational uses and abuses of computers, including such important workplace issues as on-line monitoring of employee productivity and conversations (e.g., Aiello, 1993).

There is a small but fascinating literature on the social psychology–anthropology of CMC, including contributions from feminist scholars (e.g., Cherny & Weise, 1996; Haraway, 1991), which extends feminist ethical theory into CMC. A key assumption of this literature is that CMC is a social (and socially mediated) set of acts. Rheingold (1993) discussed the development of what he referred to as communities, which exist independently of physical space but fulfill many of the same functions as physical communities. There is disagreement about whether a group of people communicating on-line should be called a community; and if so, how strong it is, how different it is from physically structured communities, and how idealized both the real and the virtual versions of community are (see, e.g., a critique by Jones, 1995). Nevertheless, anyone who has grown to know others through an electronic connection, such as a list or a "chat group," would argue that the experience is social and that over time, it feels like a community has developed. Furthermore, these cybercommunities are clearly socially constructed (Chayko, 1993). If feminists are to be truly effective in cyberspace, then they must take charge of this social construction wherever possible.

Over the past 3 decades, feminists have formulated important ethical principles, originally with therapy and subsequently in other domains of practice (Brabeck & Brown, 1997; Feminist Therapy Institute, 1990). They have successfully altered much of society's thinking about the gendered nature of discourse, need for equity, horrors of abuse, accountability each of them has for themselves and for the future, and need to infuse everyday life as well as larger society with activism for positive social change.

For this chapter, we take the perspective, adapted from Laura Brown (1994), that ethics are more than rules for preventing lawsuits, the "thou shalt nots" that persuade most users to follow the letter of the law. Guided by Brown's (1994) view that a satisfactory outcome of ethical feminist therapy "rarely find[s] the client's world intact in its pretherapy form, because the social and political connections drawn by feminist interpretations often lead to changes in more than a person's self-esteem" (p. 37), we envision a cybersociety that is antidominating in its goals, empowering in its interactions, multicultural in its scope, and transformational in every act. This transformation enhances one's awareness of the dominant forces that impinge on oneself and others with whom one is connected. As a consequence, one may be compelled to face a life of struggles to subvert oppression (Brown, 1994). However, from a feminist perspective, it will not be a life of discomfort because the struggle will be from a position of inner strength and empowerment. We thus approach CMC when driven by feminist ethics as a transformative (and subversive) dialogue.

Ellen Balka (1995), a feminist community organizer and a CMC systems designer, pointed out the difficulties in bringing feminist organizations onto the "information superhighway." The collectivist, nonhierarchical philosophies so carefully worked out (more or less successfully) by usually all-volunteer feminist organizations may be antithetical to the introduction of computer systems, a process that involves authority and expertise, economic investments, and enormous amounts of time. These observations are well taken. However, once the technology is in place, we believe that the same decades of feminist community building, replete with collective organizing experience and the development of ethical decision-making strategies, have now placed feminists in a prime position for forming and transforming CMC. This serendipitous preadaptation of their methods to a new evolving need—

what Gould and Vrba (1982) have termed "exaptation" in the paleobiological literature—could grant feminist communities a central place on the construction site of cyberspace.

How could the feminist (r)evolution be exapted to the new structures created by CMC and vice versa? Much of our answer lies in the ethics—and the skills that make an ethical practice possible—developed by contemporary feminist thinkers (e.g., Brown, 1994; Chin, 1993; Lerman & Porter, 1990). Some potential connections for an idealistic exaptation model are found in Exhibit 7.2.

In discussing feminist cyberethics, we must view CMC as a source of power, a political enterprise, and a place for potential evolution and revolution (inspired by such futurist authors as Bornstein, 1994; Haraway, 1991; McCorduck, 1996; and Turkle, 1995). The technology and the number of regular CMC users have reached "critical mass" for a real (or virtual) community. As with any community, there are many possible cultural institutions and social values. Steven Jones (1995) critiqued as naive the view that CMC is free of the social structures of other communication: "Just because the spaces . . . are electronic[,] it is not the case that they are democratic, egalitarian, or accessible, and it is not the case that we can

Exhibit 7.2
Exaptation of Feminism to Cybercommunities

Ethical Feminist Community	Effective Cybercommunity
Is experienced in creating and responding to social change	Is flexible and adaptive to the rapid change in technology (1 Internet year = 2 or 3 calendar months)
Continually self-reflects in the context of practice, culture, and theory	Monitors individual and group process
Is nonhierarchical and collectivist, fighting dominance in all its forms	Is cooperative
Welcomes open process; giving voice is one form of empowering	Is open; secrecy is a disadvantage in CMC (Jones, 1995)
Requires a passionate commitment to a shared vision	Is made up of individuals committed to a common goal and social identity (Spears & Lea, 1992)
Uses modes of analysis sensitive to politics, power plays, themes and dissociations, dominations and silences, texts and subtexts	Appreciates interpersonal–social cues and nuances in the absence of face-to-face cues
Moves beyond multiple groups to explore meanings of inclusion and diversity and to embrace and celebrate multiculturalism	Moves beyond multiple subcommunities to involve people from different cultures

forego asking in particular about substance and dominance" (p. 23). Feminist theory offers an approach for analyzing gender and power relations within that space and for guiding one to a feminist consciousness that "leads one to be responsible to self and others, attend to one's own and collective well-being, is un-numbing and re-integrating of all experiences and leads to social transformation" (Chin, 1993, p. 11).

The troubling question is Who determines the future? Branscomb (1993, in Jones, 1995) pointed out that the critical question is not What are the laws or the technologies? but Who will determine the laws and the technologies through which people can interact in cyberspace? Yet numbers have never daunted a feminist's spirit. It could be argued that it is precisely because women are a minority, an outside voice, that ethical issues can be so clearly recognized. Feminists have argued that people in subordinate positions can see the whole picture more clearly, can adapt to different roles, and can subvert power structures (e.g., Miller, 1986). In cyberspace, this power may even be strengthened as their voices spread more widely and are just as "loud" as men's. Sproull and Kiesler (1991) suggested that in larger organizations, CMC serves well those who ordinarily are powerless in the formal hierarchy because their voices may be heard by a wider audience.

Feminists can find CMC a very effective medium for disseminating feminist ethical thinking. Research demonstrates that far from being an isolating, depersonalizing experience, communication through a screen to an unseen other can actually enhance thoughtfulness (e.g., Matheson, 1992). Fears that CMC will sway the ill-formed opinions of zoned-out "cyberaddicts" are not borne out by data. Instead, it seems that in experimental decision-making situations, readers comprehend and respond to the logic of the written word, not the emotional content. Furthermore, laboratory experiments show that self-reflection is actually greater in CMC than face-to-face conditions (Spears & Lea, 1992). A critical thinking model for CMC should not be difficult to achieve: Feminist scientists and practitioners have demanded logic and critical thinking throughout history, of both themselves and others (e.g., Caplan & Caplan, 1999; Unger, 1996; see also Freyd & Quina, chap. 5, this volume).

CHALLENGE FOR A FEMINIST CYBERSPACE

How do feminists imagine themselves and their collective future? What will it take to make their imagined future a reality? With these questions in mind, we begin a long, ongoing process with a brief foray into cyberspace issues that demand feminist ethical attention: access, accountability, abuse, and activism. These four closely resemble the guidelines for feminist ethics adopted by the Feminist Therapy Institute (see Lerman & Porter, 1990) and suggest again and again that feminist real space should have much to do with feminist cyberspace.

Access

A steadfast goal of feminist ethics has been to give voice to women and legitimacy to their needs. Feminist teachers struggle with ways to give voice; feminist publications encourage many voices to join in; feminist organizations urge everyone to have their say; feminists hope to be global. But always in the real world, there are limitations on time and space, and travel is expensive. What greater empowerment can one envision than the unlimited time and space of the Internet? What kind of voice might be raised by millions of people on-line?

The feminist movement began over demands of access: to the vote, to protection from harm, to the workplace. Access allows one to confront and change from within institutions, to construct the future actively. How appropriate, then, that this core principle of women's (and human) rights is now a core principle of ethics in cyberspace.

Patti Whaley of Amnesty International began a keynote address to a human rights conference in 1995 with the following words: "My mom has a Compuserve account." We already know the power of numbers in politics, the intellectual power of networks to inform feminist psychology, and the empowerment that comes from sharing pain in the healing process. CMC offers feminists an opportunity for all these kinds of power; it can bring people (even daughters and mothers!) together quickly and inexpensively across wide-ranging spaces.

Some have raised concern that limited access to CMC has created new hierarchies, with the same people still in control and with a new set of barriers (Ross, in Jones, 1995). As technology expands into visual technology (CUSeeMe), for example, the gap between those who have access and those who do not has the potential to widen even more. Balka (1993) identified access to CMC (as well as its underlying technology) as a key issue for feminist organizing in the future; feminists must extend that concern to people in less privileged situations.

What about access for poor women? The relative cost of computer hardware and software has continued to decline over time, as have the commercial rates of Internet service providers. "Free" access has increased as more educational and nonprofit organizations are connected. As a consequence, discussion groups and websites have grown exponentially. But although academic and professional feminists put email addresses on their business cards and demand the same of their congresspeople, they represent a small fraction of the population. As Whaley (1995) suggested, to limit one's concern to one's mother's access falls short of the goals of human rights. Reid (1991) pointed out that if one looks at the larger picture, computer users are actually quite similar to each other, socially and economically, and are quite different from the millions of unwired people. About half of the U.S. Internet users have incomes greater than $50,000 (Reilly Research, 1996).

The RAND Corporation recently issued a report called "Universal Access to E-Mail," which recommends, among other things, that the United States provide email to every citizen and encourage multiple access points, civic participation, and responsiveness from government to increased democratic participation (Anderson, Bikson, Law, & Mitchell, 1995). In 1996, President Clinton and Vice President Gore extolled the virtues for children's development through access to the Internet and announced various election-year programs to put computers in every classroom (although some question how many of those computers actually reached underprivileged—or any—schools).

This privilege of access becomes even more shocking when we consider the global picture. Most of the world's citizens do not have access to a telephone, particularly in noncoastal Africa, and even if lines were available, there would not be sufficient electricity to power computers, fiber optic telephone lines to connect them, or satellites conveniently waiting to transmit messages. Several countries, most visibly China, have taken drastic steps to prohibit international communication by its citizens. This trend is spreading throughout various undemocratic regimes. Even if technological and political gaps were overcome, most Internet communications remain solidly based on the English language, although at least one author believes that simultaneous and instant translation programs will be built into future systems (Oudet, 1997).

Several groups' access must be increased. The first group is recalcitrant women of the more privileged classes, those potential feminist voices who are digitally homeless not because they are in poverty but because they have not become comfortable with the cyberworld. These women need help learning how to become connected, eliminate phobias, and the like through training, technical support, user groups, and so forth. Social science researchers need to look beyond hardware to the cognitive, social, and other human factors that could promote better access (D. L. Miller, 1997). All users should demand that technology producers and marketers create products that are "user friendly" and that arrive with instructions that any consumer could understand. Once wired, people need to become purveyors of their knowledge to expand the power of others who are less privileged.

The second group consists of those living in poverty or with restricted means. These people might benefit from the model of an expansion from the private car to public transit. Public schools and libraries must continue their missions of providing access to all. In addition, feminists can identify or create shared resources, perhaps with institutions already in place. Feminists can carry messages on behalf of nonwired organizations to and from the wired public (the "message in a bottle" approach). Nonprofit and social organizations should become wired, and they should share their access with their clients. For example, how would access to the World Wide Web change the knowledge and perspective of a woman staying at a local shelter or women dropping by during the day who are thinking about leaving their abusive partners but are not yet ready to do so? Feminists who reach responsible levels in high-tech and computer firms need to consider donating equipment and providing after-hours assistance with training for access. After these women become wired, feminists should help them develop the skills to accompany the technology.

An example of this kind of empowerment comes from Santa Monica (CA), where a citywide network was established and free computer terminals were placed in public spaces such as the library (Collins-Jarvis, 1993; Varley, 1991). Among the constituents using the terminals were homeless people. They began dialogues with home-dwelling people who would otherwise have had no contact with them. These discussions led to significant improvements in services that were designed by the homeless people themselves (e.g., a safe place to shower and change connected with a job bank). Katharina Echt (1997) introduced older men and women to computers with an interactive compact disk training module and found that even those who had never used a computer were able to make use of ElderNet, a network set up for their use. The editors of *Consumer Reports* recently observed that disabled individuals reported their computer access to the outside world was invaluable to their emotional health, both because it gave them access not available to them physically and because people with rare disorders could find others with similar challenges on-line ("Finding medical help online," 1997).

In considering access, we must not overlook those with different abilities. One of the marvels of computer technology is that auditory output allows instantaneous "reading" without vision. HTML, the software most often used for building websites, has previously been friendly to programs that provide flexible searching and scanning for visually impaired users. But will excitement over "cool pictures" mean that graphics-intensive websites will be less accessible (Raman, 1997)?

Access concerns do not stop with getting fingers onto keyboards. After getting on-line, there is still much access work to be done. How can feminists connect in cyberspace? How can they send out and receive the important signals amongst ever-increasing noise? Feminist websites and lists must be easily located through most search engines and should contain links to other feminist sites. Links must appear in mainstream cyberspace, including hotlinks in many places not specifically concerned with women or feminist practice (e.g., workplace, environment, news, entertainment). A number of feminists, ourselves included, have begun to include feminist website addresses in their signature files, which go out onto their personal emails. Authors in a special section of the March 1997 *Scientific American* (The Internet: Fulfilling the Promise) suggested creative ways to bring greater order to the chaos caused by the increase in usage (e.g., from 130 websites in June 1993 to over 230,000 three years later; Lynch, 1997).

Cyberspace also holds data on which researchers increasingly rely rather than going to libraries and seeking out historical documents. But what gets translated into digital form is also political: Who funds the process? Who decides what is important enough to be made available on a mass scale (Lesk, 1997)? We need to transfer the American heritage into digital form and place the classic works into easily retrievable files, along with pictures and copies of important documents from the Women's Movement's history. Current discussions should be archived just as carefully as feminists now wish they had archived activities of feminist organizations from the "early years." Kahle's (1997) report on his effort to archive websites offers a glimpse into the travails of this mostly unfunded task.

Cyberspace by its very nature is multicultural and multinational—or perhaps acultural and anational. The possibilities for social action on a worldwide scale are indeed boundless. Whaley (1995) described one of the first examples of how this works: the extraordinary and instantaneous information flow to and from the Beijing Fourth World Conference on Women (and how she shared her excitement with her mother!). For access to and from the rest of the world, feminists need to reframe their thinking. It is a good idea to donate cast-off computer hardware to those who cannot access or afford them, but feminists need to go further. They must see cyberspace not as in competition with food, health care, and human rights but as a facilitator for the delivery of these essential goods and services. They must lobby wherever possible for free and affordable access to technology and, after that is obtained, to information (because some countries such as China still deny opportunities to communicate freely, although the wires are in place).

Accountability

Feminist ethics demands accountability of every individual for her or his own actions, guided by principles of beneficence and respect (Brabeck & Brown, 1997; Lerman & Porter, 1990). Ethical feminists must demand accountability from others and from themselves. Although they cannot control others' deception, they can learn ways to evaluate information to reduce its devastating impact. In addition, they certainly are able to evaluate their own potentially deceptive actions. One does not have to be untruthful to be deceptive; one can mislead, misguide, or misspeak to others. CMC is particularly adaptive to this sort of deception because one can choose words carefully and communicate them without nonverbal cues, such as demeanor.

Feminists need to evaluate their on-line communications as carefully as they would evaluate behaviors in other settings, such as teaching a class or speaking with a client in therapy. Laura Brown's (1994) ethical feminist practitioner continually inspects her own motives to explore whether she is acting–speaking out of her own needs (e.g., to be liked) or those of her client (e.g., to find her voice). In CMC, feminists can be misguided or guided by the same choice of motives. For example, someone may post frequent messages for a variety of reasons: to provide information useful to other readers, to enjoy praise from others, to achieve a sense of control, or just to feel like the most active member of a community. Only the first of these fits comfortably within a feminist ethic.

The immediacy of cybercommunication is a seductive experience. Ideas can swirl around quickly and simultaneously be shared with thousands of others. People can discuss issues without regard to gender, color, size, hair length, age, or abilities (as the success of homeless people in Santa Monica demonstrated)—all voices sound the same in cyberspace. Individuals can participate in the modern version of Victorian letter writing: romances blossom, friendships form and deepen as relationships transcend time and space, morning breath, and fuzzy old bathrobes. In spite of reduction to words and symbols, emotions are expressed and communication can be intensely personal (Reid, 1991). Many people find themselves surprised at how open and self-revealing they become in CMC. (Perhaps this is the thinking behind therapy, where the therapist assumes a role as a "stranger," or the religious confessional, where the speaker is prevented from viewing the listener while presumably sharing her or his deepest secrets.) In fact, this experience is so comfortable that some are hoping that on-line visual displays do not quickly catch on.

However, when one loses bodily–facial information, one also loses the ability to confirm one's correspondent's identity, so one's communication may not be as honest or complete as one had hoped. The phenomenon of men posing as women or girls in "chat rooms" has been mentioned briefly by several authors, who described it as adolescent male experimentation (regardless of the age of the experimenter; see Sagan, 1995, for a disturbing self-portrait). Although age does enter into the picture, the phenomenon may be more revealing. Turkle (1995) described the "Internet self" as a collection of multiple, changeable identities, a phenomenon with extraordinary implications for communications (or more appropriately, simulations?). Interviews with men who met others on-line sometimes reveal their amazement—and dismay—at the immediate attention they received from other men when they signed on with a female name (e.g., Reid, 1991). Bornstein (1994) described the experience of women who go on-line as men: "There's this wonder . . . 'they really do have this power!' As soon as men cop to the idea that women are learning this, they're gonna be more frightened" (quoted in Thomas, 1995, p. 116). Then there is the reaction of the deceived. Lindsey van Gelder (1983) described the horror and betrayal felt by a group of women who had become deeply intimate in conversations with an able-bodied middle-aged male psychiatrist who led them on for several months in the character of a disabled woman. Under current systems, there is often no way to avoid being deceived by others. Few systems use real names, instead relying on the individual to supply a "handle," which may then change as often as the user wishes.

The spontaneity of CMC and one's tendency to send immediately without rereading often allows carelessly worded comments. Intentional and nonintential meanings can lead to hurt feelings and terrible confrontations. Instances of quasilibelous attributions about others, inappropriate personal attacks, and self-righteous claims of entitlement occur even among feminists. Even though the message exchange seems fleeting, any post to a public list, and some private posts, become part of a permanent record, which is usually impossible to expunge. Several authors have discussed the widely observed CMC phenomenon of disinhibition or *flaming*: saying things one would never say in person (Spears & Lea, 1992). Feminists must challenge themselves to critique their linguistic styles and practices on-line as they do in their personal and professional worlds.

Another challenge is the problem of authority and expertise. Feminists have worked hard to give authority to women's voices, regardless of training or societal power. Cyberspace offers that voice, unfiltered by the media, editors, or people who would disagree. But by the same token, anyone can claim expertise, provide false information, or give inappropriate advice in astonishingly convincing ways. Without credentialing of the authors or peer review of the information they are providing, cyberauthority can be quite dangerous. The challenge is to promote authentic information without losing authentic voices, to provide a nonexclusive yet safe space.

Privacy and confidentiality also are not well protected in cyberspace, even in individual conversations. System monitors "peek" into ongoing conversations; occasionally private messages are accidentally sent to whole lists. Posts on lists, even closed nonpublic lists, are always subject to being forwarded and distributed widely. Most servers do nightly backups of data, thereby preserving information for future access by others. In a recent experience of one of the authors (Quina), a student using her family computer to read what was supposed to be a confidential class email list discovered her father had read various messages and was sending out angry mail to the posters (including the teacher!). Even though she had signed on with the intention of being confidential, the email program used by the university allows anyone access to messages that are not immediately deleted. Although this was a relatively minor situation, for protection of client and personal confidentiality, private information should be shared only over the most secure of connections and should never be left overnight on a large system.

One must also consider the impact of even the best-intentioned communications. In cyberspace, the distribution of one's ideas is not orderly; rather, it is like wildfire, spreading rapidly, widely, and unpredictably. What is said in one place may be spread to unanticipated routes with unpleasant outcomes. For example, a well-meaning request for a therapist referral gives some brief information about the client. The request is cross-posted to another list, and on and on, until a few contacts later the client receives a copy of the original post. Such standard feminist ethical practices as confidentiality are even more critical on-line, where thousands of people may ultimately read the message (including, perhaps, an abusive spouse).

Abuse

As in the real world, feminism gained its strongest foothold and has made some of its strongest gains in the identification and response to abuse, whether emotional or physical, public or domestic. Now feminists are faced with similar kinds of behaviors but in a new medium, and the demand for new laws to curb abuse and for creative ways to intervene early or to prevent the abuse can and should be addressed by feminists.

Abuses on the Internet have ranged from verbal threats and assaults by intimates to "stalking" by complete unknowns. Sometimes acts of aggression are public: hostile charges leveled at list subscribers with dissenting agendas and requests for "dirt" on folks who will be competitors (see also chap. 11, this volume, on hate crimes). Occasionally, there are serious threats. Antigay activists have used subscriber lists from a gay men–lesbians network to track down individual members and reveal their identities in the real world. Most lists are set up as open lists, and several sites archive all posts; thus, any subscriber remains vulnerable to abuse in the future as well. In a landmark decision,[1] a federal jury in Portland, Oregon, recently awarded $107 million in damages to a group of doctors who performed abor-

---

[1] *Planned Parenthood of the Columbia/Willamette, Inc.; Portland Feminist Women's Health Center; Robert Crist, MD; Warren M. Hern, MD; Elizabeth Newhall, MD; James Newhall, MD; and Karen Sweigert, MD, individually and on behalf of all persons similiarly situated v. American Coalition of Life Activists; Advocates for Life Ministries; Michael Bray; Andrew Burnett, David Crane, Timothy Paul Dreste, Michael Dodds, Joseph L. Foreman; Charles Roy McMillan; Stephen P. Mears; Monica Migliorino Miller; Bruce Evan Murch; Catherine Ramey; Dawn Marie Stover; Donald Treshman; and Charles Wysong* (1999, February 2), Civil No. 95-1671-JO.

tions, some of whom had been seriously injured, who sued over an Internet website that listed detailed personal information about them and others (Sanchez, 1999). The case is still under appeal, but the precedent demonstrates a struggle between those who claim First Amendment rights to publish and those who see specific danger in focusing anger against specific individuals.

Emotional abuse can also happen in cyberspace, which is not always a welcoming world. Some women who have entered chat rooms (open areas for immediate conversation) have described hostile, unfriendly, sexist (including violent) messages (often attributed to teenage boys), which often lead to women leaving the list (Kantrowitz, 1994; Wittig, in Varley, 1991). Subscription services and some lists attempt to reduce this kind of hostility by unsubscribing anyone who posts offensive material, but they can only do so after an offensive message has been posted. Unfortunately, the individual can often resubscribe under another alias or system.

Legal protection from abuse is a complex issue. In some ways, protection is enhanced ironically because CMC often travels across state lines (even when talking to someone within your state). Thus, federal authorities may become involved in cases of illegal activity and have done so in several cases involving child pornography or specific threats to harm an individual sexually. But there are no simple solutions to protecting users on-line. Some private services have installed "filters" that limit access to any website that contains certain words deemed offensive (hence the banning of a support group for women with breast cancer, an act quickly reversed by the embarrassed corporation). The 1996 Federal Telecommunications Act claimed protection was a goal when it limited some speech, but its approach was far too political (including an overturned effort to prohibit discussions of abortion).

Responsibility for abuse is often diffused. For example, in 1995 four Cornell University freshmen wrote a list of "75 reasons why women should be seen and not heard," which included such items as "can't cry rape." They sent the list to about 20 others, who then forwarded the list to a few others; before long, thousands of angry emails poured in to the Cornell administration office, including a threat to bomb the computer center. As none of the original recipients of the email complained, the following question arose: Who is guilty of harassment, the author or the sender? Feminists posted the list to various feminist lists; were they guilty of harassment? Was the threat of physical violence to the university in line with the original offense? According to an announcement distributed through email by Cornell University officials, ultimately the four young men apologized publicly, took a sensitivity course, and did community service, even though there were no legal grounds for harassment charges. Perhaps ultimately the best response was a list of "75 reasons why angry Cornell women (your worst nightmare) are exercising their freedom of speech," a compendium of statistics on women's lives of abuse, poverty, and discrimination that was distributed to many of the same lists.

One challenge is to make a safer cyberspace and to develop effective ways to cope with cyberabuses of all sorts, while maintaining free speech rights. For now, the rules of cyberspace remain indeterminate. When attacks and assaults happen in cyberspace, rarely is action taken because the action to take is not clear.

But there is another issue raised by cyberabuse. The media has grabbed onto the relatively small number of dangerous acts on-line and has greatly exaggerated others. For example, "A Rape in Cyberspace" that received headlines in the *Village Voice* (Dibbell, 1993) was never characterized as a rape by the target of the attack (Maluso, 1997). Therein lies the danger of widespread media attention to abuse: Women will believe cyberspace is yet another dangerous space and will avoid it. As Maluso (1997) pointed out,

> the Internet has sometimes been represented as a wild and woolly place dominated by dangerous and somewhat gonzo young men who either ignore or harass the few women who dare to enter their electronic domain. From the popular media, we learn that you can be raped in cyberspace . . . that online pedophiles are stalking your children. The message inherent in this widely repeated portrayal of cyberspace is that the Internet is not a place for women, children, or the faint of heart.

Many have heard women express such fears, just as they fear going out alone at night or even going out to seek employment in nontraditional careers. It seems the media is creating another potential chapter for Faludi's (1991) next revision of *Backlash*.

Activism

The feminist principle perhaps most dear to many feminists' hearts and most demanding of their time and courage is activism, whether it is changing the world or (his) changing the diaper. In 1999 as the Association for Women in Psychology celebrated 30 years of feminist social activism, feminists found that they must expand their consciousness as well as their behavior for their activism to succeed.

We see two spheres for cyberspace activism: one within cyberspace that affects the structure of cyberspace and the other using cyberspace to create change in the real world. In cyberspace, feminists must work to realize the opportunities to create an agent of social change. They should educate themselves about and support public policy to increase access (see www.fcc. gov for information and action). Shapiro (1997) pointed out that a nationwide commitment to access made it possible for 87% of U.S. households with annual incomes under $10,000 to have a telephone, which today is not a convenience but a lifeline. Traditionally, such access for poor people to telephone service was paid for by mandatory contributions from the telephone companies themselves. Shapiro suggested making a similar demand on Internet service providers.

The possibilities are here for dominance and disempowerment of people on a global scale. Feminists must pay greater attention to the people directly harmed by corporate greed (ironically including many high-tech companies). Multinational technology manufacturing plants that use dangerous chemicals in making everybody's beloved machines often move to impoverished countries to avoid the environmental and safety regulations that would be required in the United States. Global communications have enabled corporations to move from country to country, seeking lower worker minimum ages and wage scales and avoiding regulatory oversight. Activists can use that same technology to pursue exploiters wherever they hide. They must work together with those outside their dissolving national boundaries.

The second sphere is the use of technology to conduct real-world activism. For at least one antifeminist group, cybertechnology is their "high-tech armament." Goldberg (1996) reported on the sophisticated antiabortion activism by the Christian Coalition at the 1996 Republican National Convention in San Diego, California: "They have a 'war room.' They have 'rapid response capability.' They have 102 crack infantry whips. And best of all, leaders of the Christian Coalition say, they have the technological weapons . . . to give them tactical superiority" (p. A24). With wireless digital phones, delegates on the floor could connect with one another, to pagers, faxes, and the Internet, which resulted in an instantaneous flooding of messages to any politician who appeared to be veering "off course." Feminists can learn the same tricks with better language and better goals.

Feminists must use cyberspace actively as an instrument of empowerment, both individually and globally. At an immediate level, universities are exploring forms of distance learning in hopes of reaching new populations. A special issue of *Feminist Collections: A Quarterly of Women's Studies Resources* was recently devoted to information technology and women's studies. In that issue, several authors considered the implications of increased technology and cybervoices in the feminist classroom. Mary Zahm (1997) teaches a "Towards Self Understanding" course and one of us (Quina) teaches "The Female Experience" course almost entirely on-line. Our experience to date concurs with others who have used this format that some students have reported that it is an opportunity to "find their voice," a space in which to speak freely. It is indeed the case that women (especially women with children) are among the first to sign up to accommodate their already overbooked schedules.[2] Such courses have a great deal of potential because they can reach out to others across many physical miles and allow instructors to teach globally while typing locally.

As part of that activism, feminists must teach critical thinking on-line, helping their students become more astute in separating the good from the bad, the relevant from the irrelevant. Feminist teachers have described class assignments that involve on-line searches on a topic and then evaluated the "hits" against criteria more commonly applied to print journalism and research. Evaluating electronic sources of knowledge is a skill to be taught to clients, students, and employees, as relevant as teaching the difference between types of print or other media sources.

Feminists must themselves become more vigilant against doing harm. Activists can also disempower and disenfranchise those whom they seek to help. Just as therapists can forget their role and become their client's voice, feminists can forget to listen and speak too hastily for the voiceless. This is not a new issue; it has been long debated that one cannot presume to know the problems of other cultures or how best to solve them. Because there is not yet an international language—or a fully international community—on the Internet (unless they speak English), one whose activism occurs solely through CMC may be particularly dangerous. One may harm the opportunity for collective action if one violates cultural norms; one may harm individuals if one carelessly sends inflammatory messages to repressive countries that may place the recipient at risk. Thus, one cannot let CMC replace one's responsibility to become informed about those whom one wishes to help when one crosses cultural lines.

Whaley (1995) presented a list of ways one can turn a website, network, or email account into an activist project with a minimum of special effort. For example, a key complaint of feminist scholars has been the lack of voice. On-line activism is relatively inexpensive, and one can reach a wide audience. What gets published is no longer limited to what is marketable, whether because it is nonmainstream (e.g., 'zines like *Riot Grrls*) or too esoteric to sell many copies (e.g., some scholarly debates). Now people can reach wider audiences through a variety of on-line methods from email to videoconferencing. Without much more sophistication (but more memory), one can set up a website with messages that "mentor" sight unseen—one's stories might help others. Those who design conferences, offer courses, and work with community agencies need to take advantage of these new methods to bring feminist thinkers into "direct" contact with their students. The same can be done with government officials and members of other cultures—all are as near as the closest computer.

---

[2] For syllabi and more information, contact Quina.

Whaley (1995) made an important distinction that we must consider: the difference between "browsing" and "activism." It is easy to press a few buttons to forward a message, not too difficult to type out a quick protest message and send it electronically to the distribution list of a government official, and not too difficult to create a webpage for one's organization to "get the word out." It requires more effort to make the world change (for starters, one has to get out of that comfortable old fuzzy bathrobe and brush those teeth). Perhaps the ultimate challenge is to find the best way to use this amazing new tool for promoting, supporting, and sustaining activism that ultimately still achieves the old-fashioned in-your-face real-world change.

CONCLUDING COMMENTS

Centuries of fighting dominance have certainly earned feminists useful skills for nonhierarchical community building. The experience of entering and changing old organizations has helped feminists develop the ability to analyze them and to find creative strategies to operate within and without. They understand a range of subversive dialogues (Brown, 1994) and can adapt them to new situations. Feminist modes of analysis, designed to identify the structures and meanings of one's gender, culture, and social environment serve them well here.

In cyberspace, communities require a vision that transcends specific media or technologies. Certainly, feminists have demonstrated the ability to have a dream and to pursue it steadily. The existence of a strong feminist ethical vision that looks beyond simple "rules" will help maintain a feminist presence through media explosions, births and deaths of networks, corporate monopolies, and a vast array of new communities—much as the spider who weaves her web systematically will always be at home, even when parts are torn away or when she spins a new one.

The feminist movement has always found heart and soul in the act of consciousness raising, which relies heavily on self-reflection, self-aware-ness, and voice giving. Our messages can indeed be exapted to the cyber medium. But we must guard against the tendency to feel that it is all too large, too overwhelming. Thus, in closing, we offer a few suggestions:

1. Get on-line or help someone else get on-line.
2. Use your on-line voice responsibly, and demand the same of others in your cybercommunities.
3. Work toward creative responses to empower those with less power and to halt the abuse of women and minorities on- and off-line.
4. Use all of your voices for a better real world.

REFERENCES

Aiello, J. R. (1993). Computer-based work monitoring: Electronic surveillance and its effects. *Journal of Applied Social Psychology, 23*(7), 499–507.

Ainspan, N. D. (1994). Organizational justice and computers in the workplace. *Journal of Computer-Mediated Communication* [On-line journal]. Retrieved July 13, 1999 from the World Wide Web: http://www.ascusc.org/jcmc

Anderson, R. H., Bikson, T. K., Law, S. A., & Mitchell, B. M. (1995). *Universal access to e-mail: Feasibility and societal implications* [On-line report]. Santa Monica, CA: RAND. Retrieved July 13, 1999 from the World Wide Web: http://www.rand.org/publications/MR/MR650/

Balka, E. (1993, February). Women's access to on-line discussions about feminism. *Electronic Journal of Communications/La Revuwe Electronique de Communication, 3*(1). Retrieved July 19, 1999 from the World Wide Web: http://www.eff.org/pub/Net_culture/Gender_issues

Balka, E. (1995, August). *Viewing the world through a gendered lens.* Paper presented at the Universal Access Workshop, Burnaby, British Columbia, Canada. Retrieved July 13, 1999 from the World Wide Web: http://www.fis.utoronto.ca/research/iprp/ua/gender/balka.html

Bornstein, K. (1994). *Gender outlaw: On men, women and the rest of us.* New York: Routledge.

Brabeck, M., & Brown, L. (With Christian, L., Espin, O., Hare-Mustin, R., Kaplan, A., Kaschak, E., Miller, D., Phillips, E., Ferns, T., & Van Ormer, A.). (1997). Feminist theory and psychological practice. In J. Worell & N. Johnson (Eds.), *Shaping the future of feminist psychology: Education, research, and practice* (pp. 15–35). Washington, DC: American Psychological Association.

Broadhurst, J. (1995). *The woman's guide to online services.* New York: McGraw-Hill.

Brown, L. S. (1994). *Subversive dialogues: Toward a theory of feminist therapy.* New York: Basic Books.

Caplan, P. J., & Caplan, J. B. (1999). *Thinking critically about research on sex and gender* (2nd ed.). Reading, MA: Addison Wesley.

Chayko, M. (1993). What is real in the age of virtual reality? *Symbolic Interaction, 16*(2), 171–181.

Cherny, L., & Weise, E. R. (1996). *Wired women: Gender and new realities in cyberspace.* Seattle, WA: Seal Press.

Chin, J. L. (Ed.). (1993). *Proceedings of the National Conference on Education and Training in Feminist Practice.* Boston, MA: Boston College. (Available from the Women's Programs Office, American Psychological Association, Washington, DC)

Collins-Jarvis, L. (1993). Gender representation in an electronic city hall: Female adoption of Santa Monica's PEN system. *Journal of Broadcasting and Electronic Media, 37*(1), 49–65.

Cottrell, J. (1992, November). "I'm a stranger here myself": A consideration of women in computing. *Association for Computing Machinery*, pp. 71–76. Retrieved July 13, 1999 from the World Wide Web: http://www.eff.org/pub/Net_culture/Gender_issues

Dibbell, J. (1993, December 21). A rape in cyberspace. *Village Voice*, pp. 36–42.

Echt, K. (1997, April). *Bringing seniors online: Research in effective training models for older newbies*. Paper presented at the annual meeting of the Eastern Psychological Association, Washington, DC.

Faludi, S. (1991). *Backlash: The undeclared war against American women*. New York: Anchor Books.

Feminist Therapy Institute. (1990). Feminist Therapy Institute code of ethics. In H. Lerman & N. Porter (Eds.), *Feminist ethics in psychotherapy* (pp. 37–40). New York: Springer.

Finding medical help online. (1997, February). *Consumer Reports*, 62(2), 27–29.

Goldberg, C. (1996, August 9). In abortion war, high-tech arms. *New York Times National*, p. A24.

Gould, S. J., & Vrba, E. S. (1982). Exaptation—A missing term in the science of form. *Paleobiology*, 8(1), 4–5.

Haraway, D. J. (1991). *Simians, cyborgs, and women: The reinvention of nature*. New York: Routledge.

Jones, S. G. (Ed.). (1995). *CyberSociety: Computer-mediated communication and community*. Thousand Oaks, CA: Sage.

Kahle, B. (1997). Preserving the Internet. *Scientific American*, 276(3), 82–83.

Kallman, E. A., & Grillo, J. P. (1993). *Ethical decision making and information technology*. New York: Mitchell McGraw-Hill.

Kantrowitz, B. (1994, May 16). Men, women, & computers. *Newsweek*, pp. 48–54.

Kramarae, C., & Taylor, H. J. (1993). Women and men on electronic networks: A conversation or a monologue? In H. J. Taylor, C. Kramarae, & M. Ebben (Eds.), *Women, information technology, and scholarship* (pp. 52–61). Urbana, IL: Center for Advanced Study.

Lea, M., O'Shea, T., Fung, P., & Spears, R. (1992). "Flaming" in computer-mediated communication: Observations, explanations, implications. In M. Lea (Ed.), *Contexts of computer-mediated communication* (pp. 89–110). New York: Harvester Wheatsheaf.

Lerman, H., & Porter, N. (Eds.). (1990). *Feminist ethics in psychotherapy*. New York: Springer.

Lesk, M. (1997). Going digital. *Scientific American*, 276(3), 58–60.

Lynch, C. (1997). Searching the Internet. *Scientific American*, 276(3), 52–56.

Maluso, D. (1997, March). *Gender and helping in cyberspace: The welcome wagon on the electronic frontier*. Paper presented at the annual meeting of the Association for Women in Psychology, Pittsburgh, PA.

Matheson, K. (1991). Social cues in computer-mediated negotiations: Gender makes a difference. *Computers in Human Behavior, 7,* 137–145.

Matheson, K. (1992). Women and computer technology: Computing for herself. In M. Lea (Ed.), *Contexts of computer-mediated communication* (pp. 66–88). New York: Harvester Wheatsheaf.

McCorduck, P. (1996). *The futures of women: Scenarios for the 21st century.* Reading, MA: Addison Wesley.

McLaughlin, M. L., Osborne, K. K., & Smith, C. B. (1995). Standards of conduct on Usenet. In S. G. Jones (Ed.), *CyberSociety: Computer-mediated communication and community* (pp. 90–111). Thousand Oaks, CA: Sage.

Miller, D. L. (1997, April). *Cyberspace: Extending access beyond psychology.* Presented at the annual meeting of the Eastern Psychological Association, Washington, DC.

Miller, J. B. (1986). *Toward a new psychology of women* (2nd ed.). Boston: Beacon Press.

Oudet, B. (1997). Multilingualism on the net. *Scientific American, 276*(3), 77–78.

Quina, K., Cotter, M., & Romenesko, K. (1998). Breaking the (plexi-)glass ceiling in higher education. In L. Collins, J. Chrisler, & K. Quina (Eds.), *Arming Athena: Career strategies for women in academe* (pp. 215–238). Thousand Oaks, CA: Sage.

Quina, K., Wingard, J. A., & Bates, H. G. (1987). Language style and gender stereotypes in person perception. *Psychology of Women Quarterly, 11*(1), 111–122.

Raman, T. V. (1997). Netsurfing without a monitor. *Scientific American, 276*(3), 55–56.

Reid, E. M. (1991). *Electropolis: Communication and community on Internet relay chat.* Unpublished honour's thesis, University of Melbourne, Melbourne, Australia. Retrieved July 13, 1999 from the World Wide Web: http://www.crl.com./emr/

Reilly Research. (1996, November 25). Internet users by annual income. *Interactive Week, 3*(27), 42.

Rheingold, H. (1993). *The virtual community.* New York: HarperCollins.

Rose, L. (1995). *Netlaw: Your rights in the online world.* Berkeley, CA: Osborne McGraw-Hill.

Sagan, D. (1995, January). Sex, lies, and cyberspace. *Wired, 3.01,* 78–84.

Sanchez, R. (1999, February 3). Antiabortion web site loses lawsuit. *The Washington Post,* p. A1.

Selfe, C. L., & Meyer, P. R. (1991). Testing claims for on-line conferences. *Written Communications, 8*(2), 163–192.

Shade, L. R. (1993, August). *Gender issues in computer networking.* Paper presented at Community Networking: The International Free-Net Conference, Ottawa, Ontario, Canada. Retrieved July 13, 1999 from the World Wide Web: http://www.eff.org/pub/Net_culture/Gender_issues

Shapiro, A. L. (1997, January 6). Total access (Editorial). *The Nation, 264*(1), 5–6.

Shea, V. (1994). *Netiquette.* San Francisco: Albion Books.

Spears, R., & Lea, M. (1992). Social influence and the influence of the "social" in computer-mediated communication. In M. Lea (Ed.), *Contexts of computer-mediated communication* (pp. 30–65). New York: Harvester Wheatsheaf.

Spinello, R. (1995). *Ethical aspects of information technology.* New York: Prentice Hall.

Spinello, R. (1997). *Case studies in information and computer ethics.* New York: Prentice Hall.

Sproull, L., & Kiesler, S. (1991). *Connections: New ways of working in the networked organization.* Cambridge, MA: MIT Press.

Sudweeks, F., McLaughlin, M., & Rafaeli, S. (Eds.). (1998). *Network and netplay.* Cambridge, MA: MIT Press.

Taylor, H. J., Kramarae, C., & Ebben, M. (Eds.). (1993). *Women, information, technology, scholarship.* Urbana, IL: Center for Advanced Study.

Telecommunications Act of 1996, Pub. LA. No. 104-104, 110 Stat. 56.

Thomas, T. (1995). Puttin' on the titz: An entr'acte with Kate Bornstein. *Mondo 2000, 13,* 115–117.

Top CEOs by total compensation. (1996, November 25). *Interactive Week, 3*(27), 28.

Turkle, S. (1995). *Identity in the age of the Internet.* New York: Simon & Schuster.

Unger, R. K. (1996). Using the master's tools: Epistemology and empiricism. In S. Wilkinson (Ed.), *Feminist social psychologies: International perspectives* (pp. 165–181). Bristol, PA: Open University Press.

van Gelder, L. (1983, October). The strange case of the electronic lover. *Ms.,* pp. 94–103, 117, 123–124.

Varley, P. (1991, November–December). Electronic democracy. *Technology Review,* pp. 43–51.

We, G. (1993). *Cross-gender communication in cyberspace* [Unpublished paper, Department of Communication, Simon Fraser University, Burnaby, British Columbia, Canada]. Retrieved July 13, 1999 from the World Wide Web: http://www.eff.org/pub/Net_culture/Gender_issues

Whaley, P. (1995, November). *Potential contributions of information technologies to human rights.* From the Canadian–U.S. Human Rights Information Documentation Network Conference, College Park, MD. [Available in *Women-and-Performance, 17:* Sexuality and Cyberspace]. Retrieved July 13, 1999 from the World Wide Web: http://www.echonyc.com/~women/Issue17/public-whaley.html and http://www.shr.aaas.org/CUSHRID/1995/panel1.htm

Zahm, M. (1997, April). *Teaching psychology on-line.* Paper presented at the annual meeting of the Eastern Psychological Association, Washington, DC.

8

TEACHING AS TRANSFORMATION: RESOLVING ETHICAL DILEMMAS IN FEMINIST PEDAGOGY

JUDITH WORELL AND DANIELLE R. OAKLEY

Questions about ethical issues in academia are seldom asked and rarely debated (Blevins-Knabe, 1992; Keith-Spiegel, Wittig, Perkins, Balogh, & Whitely, 1993). Historically, college and university regulations have mandated certain classroom procedures to protect student rights, but these standards are generally limited to provision of appropriate course information, equitable testing and grading practices, and ethical behavior in research projects. More recently, concerns about equity in education have led to the introduction of explicit sexual harassment policies into most faculty codes (Paludi, 1990; Paludi & Barickman, 1991) as well as into the Ethical Standards of the American Psychological Association's (APA) Ethical Principles of Psychologists and Code of Conduct (1992). Psychologists are also aware of additional ethical constraints on their academic behavior with respect to issues of instructional competency and dual relationships with students (APA, 1992).

Advocates of feminist pedagogy do not distance themselves from such academic and professional concerns. They take a bold step forward, however, in asserting the primacy of feminist principles and strategies, the mandate to raise student consciousness regarding a range of societal injustices, and the challenge of encouraging activism to promote social change (Forrest & Rosenberg, 1997; Hughes, 1995; Kimmel & Worell, 1997; Morley & Walsh, 1995). In doing so, they are confronted with the dialectic between established and revisionist beliefs about knowledge, epistemology, and the proper role of the teacher. These conflicts are considered here in the light of feminist ethics.

The ethics of feminist pedagogy raise many questions for faculty members and students in the feminist classroom. In this chapter, we consider a sample of these questions from the standpoint of both teachers and students. The reader is invited to confront the ethical issues raised in the dilemmas presented here and to grapple with the solutions that respect both the participants and the fundamental principles of feminist pedagogy.

The ethical dilemmas that feminist teachers face frequently originate from their efforts to implement feminist principles within traditional academic constraints. Although responsibility for instructional planning and strategies rests primarily with the faculty, students in a feminist teaching environment are encouraged to become partners in the collaborative goal of mutual growth and learning (Friedman, 1985; LaFrance, 1988). The perspective of students in such classrooms vis-à-vis the professor is certainly relevant and equally valid. We acknowledge the separate positions of faculty and students by including responses from both groups to a set of ethical dilemmas in feminist pedagogy.

In this chapter, we highlight four aspects of the teaching process that may introduce ethical dilemmas for the feminist teacher: confronting inequalities in power and authority (e.g., Aisenberg & Harrington, 1988; Apple, 1982; Brunner, 1992; Heald, 1989; Morgan, 1987), honoring all voices and uncovering silences (e.g., Hoffman, 1985; Schrewsbury, 1987), defining the boundaries of faculty–student relationships (e.g., Blevins-Knabe, 1992; Glaser & Thorpe, 1986; Pope, Levensen, & Shover, 1979), and promoting student activism toward the goal of social justice (e.g., Stake, Roades, Rose, Ellis, & West, 1994). For each of these concerns, an array of ethical issues arises. We consider these issues within the context of a decision-making approach to ethical dilemmas, in which all possible answers become the object of scrutiny and debate. To place these examples within the context of a feminist process, we consider first some of the elements of ethical decision making.

ELEMENTS OF ETHICAL DECISION MAKING

All ethical considerations engage evaluative aspects of judgment and choice, including the emotional, intuitive, and rational processes of arriving at conclusions. Kitchener's (1984) rational–intuitive approach includes five commonly held ethical principles that can be applied to academic concerns.

Autonomy ensures both faculty and students the rights of personal privacy and independent choice and encourages dialogue and the free expression of ideas. *Nonmaleficence* mandates the professor to do no harm by neglecting, abusing, or exploiting students and colleagues. *Beneficence* promotes the welfare of others through the teacher's responsibility to foster student learning and development. *Justice* promotes fairness and equity among students and colleagues. *Fidelity* creates an atmosphere of honesty and trust and honors commitments to students and colleagues.

Keith-Spiegel et al. (1993) added three principles to this list with respect to the ethics of teaching: *Dignity* accords respect for diversity and extends dignity to others in the academic community, *caring* shows compassion and concern for all within the academic community, and *excellence* involves doing one's best and "taking pride in one's work" (p. xiii).

Decision-making dilemmas typically arise when two or more ethical principles conflict and cannot be respected simultaneously. For example, a teacher wishes to encourage and to promote free expression of ideas in the classroom but is disturbed when blatant sexist or racist opinions are voiced. Here, the principle of autonomy clearly conflicts with the principles of nonmalfeasance and dignity.

Although ethical principles offer ideals toward which to strive, their articulation within concrete situations frequently becomes clouded by differences in interpretation. Perceptions of "harm" or "welfare of others" may be construed very differently by the participants, depending on the situational context and the perspectives of the decision maker. For example, the student who expresses sexist or racist opinions in the classroom may believe fervently in these ideas, yet these opinions may evoke feelings of personal outrage or shame in other students. Across situational contexts, students, faculty, and research participants may view ethical dimensions very differently. Nevertheless, these broadly based principles serve as useful criteria in implementing a feminist model of ethical decision making.

MODELS OF ETHICAL DECISION MAKING

The traditional approach to decision making is based on the assumption of reasoned choice. A traditional decision-making model typically includes at least five basic steps: (1) gathering information to identify the ethical issues involved; (2) identifying the stakeholders to determine whose concerns are at risk; (3) brainstorming or considering all possible solutions; (4) applying a cost–benefit analysis to each possible solution; and (5) choosing a solution and evaluating the outcomes of the action taken (Ajzen, 1996). In most models, consultation becomes part of the process. Consultation may assist the decision maker at different points of the process in arriving at a solution that is satisfactory to all parties involved. In what respects can we consider the rational components of ethical decision making to be consistent with feminist ethics?

The introduction of the principles of feminist ethics into the decision-making model merges a system of values and priorities with the decision process. The principles of feminist ethics are rooted in the concern that the subordinate position of women in most societal structures has resulted in disadvantages that have accrued across time, communities, situations, and interpersonal transactions (Morgan, 1996a; Robb, 1987). Feminist theories differ on the origins and roots of this subordination and may attend differentially to the choice of ethical situations that demand priority (Jaggar & Rothenberg, 1984). Across feminist theories, however, respect and honoring of the personal, subjective, and lived experiences of women are primary. In the process of ethical decision making, then, it is essential to consider particular feminist values and principles as well as personal and emotional contributions of the decision maker.

In a recent articulation of feminist decision making in psychotherapy, Hill, Glaser, and Harden (1995) offered a model that integrates the cognitive, intuitive, and personal into a multidimensional framework; they began with the following question: "How does who I am affect this process?" (p. 28). A primary awareness is that of one's commitment to feminist principles and values. Within this context, the decision maker proceeds to self-inquiry, with further questions at each step: Do I feel uncomfortable in applying my feminist values here? What are my student's feelings about the situation? Would I want to be treated this way? How am I using my power? Similar questions may confront the decision maker who strives to meet a criterion of integrating rational, emotional, and feminist considerations. Although Hill et al.'s (1995) model was developed in the context of a therapeutic relationship, its structure is clearly applicable to ethical issues within academic settings.

ETHICAL DIMENSIONS OF FEMINIST PEDAGOGY

Feminist pedagogy is aimed at uncovering, confronting, and transforming the connections among gender, knowledge, and power within academia. Across the literature on feminist pedagogy, a central matrix of principles and associated strategies was identified by Kimmel and Worell (1997). In applying feminist principles to practice, these authors articulated 14 princi-

Exhibit 8.1
Fourteen Principles of Feminist Pedagogy

1. Acknowledge differentials in power, privilege, and oppression.
2. Acknowledge the power inherent in the teaching role—empower students.
3. Encourage, value, and hear all voices—foster respect.
4. Recognize and accommodate differences in learning styles.
5. Integrate cognition, feelings, and experiences into all learning.
6. Connect personal experience with social–political reality.
7. Engage teacher and students in a mutual learning process.
8. Increase knowledge of and sensitivity to diverse cultural realities.
9. Model acceptance of legitimate authority and expertise.
10. Include multiple sources of knowledge.
11. Connect learning to social change.
12. Connect learning to self-awareness and personal growth.
13. Reclaim women's histories and cultures.
14. Transform the discipline.

Note. From "Preaching What We Practice: Principles and Strategies of Feminist Pedagogy" (Appendix, pp. 148–154), by E. Kimmel and J. Worell (With J. Daniluk, M. A. Gawalek, K. Lerner, G. Stahley, and S. Kahoe), in J. Worell and N. G. Johnson (Eds.), *Shaping the Future of Feminist Psychology: Education, Research, and Practice,* 1997, Washington, DC: American Psychological Association. Adapted with permission.

ples of feminist pedagogy and cross-matched them with 28 specific strategies to implement these principles. The 14 principles are summarized in Exhibit 8.1. Over the course of time, ethical dilemmas may be precipitated by a commitment to any or all of these principles as individuals translate their meanings and intentions into classroom and academic practices. Such dilemmas arise when two or more feminist teaching principles conflict or when they clash with the broader range of ethical ideals, such as those discussed by Kitchener (1984) and Keith-Spiegel et al. (1993).

ETHICAL DILEMMAS

Ethical dilemmas can be presented as questions for which the answers require a process of sensitive thought and decision making. In this section, we consider four major questions that reflect the possible dilemmas raised by the adherence to principles of feminist pedagogy. First, how can feminist teachers ensure that principles of equality prevail within a setting defined in terms of hierarchy and authority? How can they acknowledge the power inherent in the academic role and yet still empower their students? Second, how do feminist teachers negotiate the principle of "all voices are honored, valued, and heard" with discordant views that support sexism, racism, or homophobia? Third, how can feminist teachers engage their students in a mutual teaching–learning process that embodies meaningful, caring, and productive interactions yet maintain ethical boundaries between themselves and their students? Fourth, what are the ethical implications of introducing the politics of activism and social change into the traditional academic institution? As a corollary of this dilemma, What are the implications for student awareness and personal development of "coming out" as a feminist?

We now consider these questions from the perspective of the feminist pedagogy principles, as identified by Kimmel and Worell (1997). We selected four principles that may precipitate an ethical dilemma for the teacher who attempts to activate them in practice. For each principle, we then provide an example of an ethical dilemma confronting a teacher who implemented that principle. To embrace the perspectives of both faculty and students, we include two responses with each dilemma, one response from the point of view of an identified feminist university faculty member and the other from the perspective of a feminist-identified graduate student.[1] Consider how the two positions coordinate or contrast. You may or may not agree with these solutions to the proposed dilemmas, as they reflect the outcomes of individual decisions. Our challenge to the reader is to develop your own response to each dilemma, using a feminist-modified decision-making approach and any of the ethical principles discussed in this chapter. If possible, share your perspective with a colleague and compare your solutions.

Acknowledge Power—Empower Students (Principle 2 in Exhibit 8.1)

By definition and historical precedent, the role of the teacher has been entrusted with authority and power. Kathryn Morgan (1996b) pointed out the multiple ways in which power is invested in the position of the faculty. *Expert* power is represented by the level of the teacher's training and experience. *Informational* power reflects the teacher's professional scholarship and advanced knowledge of the discipline. *Legitimate* power rests on the teacher's

---

[1]The dilemma situations presented were all true events. The responses to the four dilemmas were provided by four feminist female faculty members (over the age of 35) who teach in the College of Education at the University of Kentucky. The four student respondents (ages mid-20s to mid-40s) were enrolled in a graduate program in counseling psychology. Three of the four were teaching assistants as well, and their responses may reflect the dual perspectives of both student and teacher. All respondents were White, of diverse religious–ethnic identities, and probably middle class, given their educational and professional attainment. Each volunteer respondent was given one dilemma and the instructions provided in the appendix, which included a decision-making model provided by Hill et al. (1995), and the 14 feminist pedagogy principles outlined in Exhibit 8.1. No other formal ethical principles were provided, so that respondents presumably relied on their personal knowledge and experiences. Respondents were assured that their names would not be used with their responses, and some responses were edited to conserve space. We wish to recognize and express our deep gratitude to the following individuals who gave generously of their time, effort, and incisive insight to assist us in illuminating the process of ethical feminist decision making: Kim Gorman, Dawn Johnson, Sandra Medley, Maude O'Neill, Pam Remer, Susan Scollay, and Karen Tice. Judith Worell was also one of the faculty respondents.

position as a professor assigned to instruct and to advise a group of students. *Reward and coercion* power naturally accompany the position of professor, who is able to make assignments and determine grades. Insofar as students can relate to the teacher as a member of their own in-group, *referent* power may also exist.

For a woman in a traditionally subordinate location in academia, holding a position that signifies power and authority presents a basic paradox and many potential dilemmas (Heald, 1989). On the one hand, it seems important for the feminist to take ownership of the sources of faculty power and to use them legitimately in the service of faculty–student mutual learning and personal growth (Principles 7 and 9). In using legitimate authority, the feminist teacher is free to introduce new content into the curriculum, to open up the classroom to personal feelings and the sharing of lived experiences (Principle 5), and to encourage students to view their world through the fresh lens of gender. The feminist teacher may even wish to use this legitimate power to relinquish authority to the students, thereby deciding in an alternative manner how the teaching–learning process will proceed (Principle 9). The feminist teacher seems then to be caught in the web of the academic structure to manage this power by keeping it, sharing it, or abandoning it.

On the other hand, as feminist teachers ourselves, we strive to meet the goal of reducing status differentials among faculty and students, with the aim of empowering students through their own sense of competence, self-efficacy, and personal authority (Principle 1). Negotiating these competing demands reveals the complexity of common classroom dilemmas. Consider the situation depicted in Dilemma A.

> *Dilemma A:* In your Gender in Education class, you have 2 male and 29 female students. You have structured the classroom so that the students are seated in a circle facing one another, and you encourage open discussion and dialogue. You notice that both men initiate discussion and talk in almost every class session. Only a few of the women speak up. After a few sessions, you begin to bypass the men and to recognize women who raise their hands in an effort to encourage women's participation. One of the men writes you an angry note and accuses you of female favoritism and antimale bias. He has not attended class now for 2 weeks.

Faculty Respondent A

"I am sensitive to both the continuing concern with empowering the women students by facilitating their participation as well as recognizing the legitimate right of the men to be heard. How can I balance these two? And how can I bring back the disengaged student, who I suspect is nursing his feelings of anger, as well as experiencing some discomfort and guilt about his actions and his disclosure to me? [Because] the other students have no awareness of his stance unless he has revealed his position to them outside of class, I assume my responsibility is to engage him somehow in productive and supportive dialogue. Here, I have to balance the benefits and costs of contacting him outside of class. Perhaps he will escalate his hostility and we will have an unpleasant encounter in which he may increase his feelings of alienation. In this event, the outcome will be counterproductive to my goals. Perhaps he really does want to resolve his feelings and will welcome my intervention at a personal level. What happens if I leave him alone to resolve his issues independently?

I resolve this dilemma by determining that it is to his benefit to air his concerns openly in a safe environment. I decide to call him and invite him to my office to discuss his concerns. I assure him [that] there is no penalty or punishment, only an honest dialogue in which we can each voice our perspectives. As I lift the telephone to call him, I hope that I have made the right decision. I recognize that my resolution of this dilemma again 'engages' my power and authority, but I justify it as a move in the direction of enhancing student development."

Student Respondent A

"There are two prongs to this problem. I am troubled by the fact that the [man] left the classroom and I am troubled by the fact that many of the women do not feel comfortable enough in the classroom to speak out. I am most aware of the classroom setting and how the traditional setting has some impact on this situation. I mean two things by that awareness: (1) traditional classrooms and classroom learning has been directed at the large group process (speaking and teaching to a large group), and (2) educators have tended to encourage more responses from males than females. As such, I believe that the protagonist is a product of the traditional classroom and has been very accustomed to having his voice heard and to being encouraged to participate. He is also the product of a sexist society that asserts that women do not have a voice and should not be heard. He is impacted in two ways: He does not respect the views of his female classmates, and he does not respect his professor, if she is female. Likewise, the women in the classroom are accustomed to being devalued and not having their voices heard. A situation has been created in which they may not respect themselves or what they have to say.

The issue of power is also very evident in this situation. That is, the [men], although few in number, have a certain amount of power given to them by a sexist society. The professor also has some power that is given by the institution. The problematic nature of power in this situation is that the professor is trying to decrease the power differential while also using power to determine who gets to speak in class.

The situation [to be resolved] with the male student is difficult since he has left and not returned. I would want to discuss the issue with him and the reasoning behind my actions. Brainstorming may be beneficial to find other ways that his views can be expressed without taking time away from others in class. I definitely would not want this to be his last experience with these issues.

I am now left with what to do with the class. Since they have not been particularly anxious to speak out in a large group, I would encourage small group discussions and would absent myself from the room. I would also use a collaborative problem-solving approach with the class in order to create an environment that is conducive to open discussion. I think this solution would work in equating voices and giving opportunities for all views to be heard."

Encourage, Value, and Hear All Voices (Principle 3 in Exhibit 8.1)

In traditional academic settings, women are frequently self-silenced or without a voice (Hoffman, 1985; Maher, 1985). Women's reluctance or failure to speak in group and public settings reflects a myriad of intersecting circumstances. From a socialization perspective, assertiveness and public self-promotion are not encouraged for women. From a self-esteem position in the context of male-entrenched academia, many women believe that they have little importance to contribute. Within most disciplines, women's contributions and history have been absent from the curriculum (Bleier, 1988; Crawford & Marecek, 1989), which results in a "womanless" scholarship. Consequently, women may feel less connected to the content and "objective thrust" of the established class conduct. For many traditional classrooms, the primary style of pedagogy is a standup-professor lecture, so that student questions and contributions are held to a minimum. In these settings, students who disagree or wish to add to the dialogue need to be assertive and persistent—qualities that many women have learned to suppress in themselves, particularly in public settings.

In the feminist classroom, efforts are directed toward opening up the structure, content, and process to encourage an inclusive learning community. In such an atmosphere, women should feel freer to initiate and to express their views, and honest dialogue is encouraged. For some, however, residues may persist from a lifetime of silencing, whereby additional strategies may be required to encourage women students to assert their authority in the classroom through asking questions, offering opinions, and sharing personal experiences. Self-silencing occurs in particular for minority women surrounded by members of the majority or dominant group (Ginorio, Gutierrez, Cauce, & Acosta, 1995; Spelman, 1985). Self-silencing is also found in mixed-sex classrooms where more dominant or outspoken male students tend to monopolize the floor. In such circumstances, an ethical dilemma may arise in terms of how to acknowledge the views of the more outspoken members yet to empower and to give voice to the more silent members.

Suppose we now add to this scenario the occurrence of inflammatory statements, in which one or more individuals express racist, sexist, or homophobic beliefs? Although dominant groups have been noted to avoid expressing their biased "isms" in public (Spelman, 1985), some classroom discussions may provide the catalyst for such viewpoints to emerge. How does the feminist teacher deal with negatively biased statements that reflect a dominant and oppressive position in relation to race, religion, gender, or sexuality? (Principle 8). How does one negotiate the principle of "honoring all voices" with the competing principle of "sensitivity to diverse realities"? These conflicting demands are portrayed in Dilemma B.

> *Dilemma B*: During a class discussion on parenting issues, the psychological impact of a lesbian couple adopting a child is brought up by one of the students. After what seems to be an honest debate of the issues, an often silent woman in the back of the classroom raises her hand. When invited to speak, she states that children need the love of a "natural couple," not the "sick twisted parenting of two selfish women" who will inevitably destroy the child's sense of what is right and wrong. You realize that a lesbian parent is sitting in your classroom, and you recall that several of your students have revealed in confidential writing assignments that they live with a lesbian partner.

Faculty Respondent B

"As a feminist teacher, I strive to establish a climate of mutual respect among all participants that does not oppress anyone based on sex, sexual orientation, race, ethnicity, religion, age, or handicap. I believe that to accomplish this goal, students and faculty must own their opinions and values and recognize the difference between facts and values. I also emphasize cognitive and affective learning in my classes. At the beginning of each class I would have discussed these values with the class and would have worked collaboratively with the students to create such a climate.

I imagine that when the 'silent woman' speaks, I would feel uncomfortable immediately. I would trust these feelings as a signal of a problem needing attention . . .[;] she is not owning her statements, is not differentiating between facts and opinions, and is oppressing a particular group. . . . I know that these statements are wounding the lesbian students in the class. I also understand that she is espousing a position which is probably a result of her socialization in our mainstream culture. My dilemma is that if I confront the student, she may return to her silence[;] and if I do not confront, I have violated my feminist principles and my commitment to diversity. Further, I am aware that many of my students are feminists-in-progress who look to me to role-model feminist behaviors and use of feminist process.

I can identify the following alternatives: (a) Say nothing and let the class handle the problem; (b) actively listen to the student, ask her to own her statement and cite the source of her information; (c) respond to the student by giving research-based information about lesbian motherhood and its impact on children; (d) confront her about her 'labeling,' comment that her views reflect ones often put forth by society, and challenge her to look at how she learned them; (e) speak my inner dialogue out loud (self-involve) to the class; and/or (f) actively listen to the student and then invite her to 'role reverse' into being a lesbian mother and 'hear' what she just said.

Choosing among the alternatives is difficult[,] and I am aware that I might choose differently depending on the particular class group. I would begin by . . . asking her to restate her comment as an 'I' statement. I would point out how her comments reflect mainstream views of homosexuality[,] and I would educate the class about research findings on lesbian mothers and their children. (As a feminist teacher, I would have located this informa-tion prior to presenting a class on parenting.) I might then form groups of four students who each would be responsible for locating one research article related to lesbian mental health or lesbian motherhood to summarize orally in the next class. These presentations would then be followed by a discussion of the myths perpetuated by our society and of the impact of these myths on lesbian and gay individuals.

With the exception of alternative 'a[,]' which puts too much compli-cated responsibility on the students, I like most of the alternatives I have generated. Without more details on the nature of this class or group, I am satisfied with the alternative I have chosen because it relies on research, challenges societally perpetuated myths, and addresses the affective impact of oppression."

Student Respondent B

"My view of the situation is that all students have the right to voice their opinions in my class whether I agree with them or not. However, I do not want to send the message that derogatory comments are acceptable in my classroom by ignoring the comment. My experience with teaching has shown me that when a very strong statement is made about a controver-sial issue, there is almost always intense debate from the students. Students will challenge one another and[,] in the process, educate one another. At that point, I often serve as a moderator. In this situation, I view the comment made by 'the often silent woman' as derogatory. However, I am also cognizant of the issue of cultural context. This woman did not develop her beliefs in a vacuum. I am also excited, however, that she is participating in class, which appears to be unusual.

I might respond by giving the class members positive reinforcement for actively participating. I might say to the class that I want people to express their viewpoints and that I value what everyone has to say. I might acknowledge that homosexuality and lesbian parenting are controversial issues for many people. I would talk about our United States culture in particular and how many factions of this culture are opposed to homosexuality for different reasons. I would also recognize that many people in our United States culture advocate for the rights of homosexual individuals. I might engage the class in a discussion in which they are to identify the cultural aspects that influence peoples' adverse and supportive beliefs about homosexuality. I would encourage 'the often silent woman' to continue discussing her viewpoint. I would also encourage the other class members to respond to the 'silent woman's' statements. I would take care to remind people that one of my expectations for this class is that we support our arguments without labeling or putting down any individuals or groups of people. I would own that it is important to me that people share their viewpoints in a respectful and nonhurtful way.

I then might assign a homework task to find research that supports their viewpoint on homosexuality or lesbian parenting. I would also bring in articles that have examined the effects of lesbian parenting and homosexuality in general to the next class meeting."

Engage Teacher and Students in a Mutual Learning Process (Principle 7 in Exhibit 8.1)

In traditional academic practice, learning is assumed to be directed from faculty to student: The teacher is the knower, and the student is the learner. The role of faculty power and authority remains relatively unchallenged, and the goal is the factual transmission of knowledge. Feminist pedagogy assumes that both teacher and student are involved in a mutual learning enterprise, in which each has knowledge and expertise that can be shared. Although the teacher accepts authority as an expert in the academic subject, student expertise and experience are acknowledged, with the goal of student growth and development.

For both pedagogical positions, relationships other than direct classroom instruction may emerge. In such relationships, the teacher may become a mentor and role model, a supervisor or collaborator in research, an employer on a paid project, or a friend with whom to spend extracurricular social time. As the faculty–student relationship moves further away from direct academic structures, issues surrounding dual relationships may arise. In a dual or overlapping relationship, the faculty member interacts with the student in multiple roles that extend beyond the functions circumscribed by the professional academic role. For the feminist in academia, the reciprocal sharing of knowledge and authority presents the opportunity for expanded interaction at a collegial level. In addition, the imperative to facilitate students' personal growth and self-awareness is likely to introduce the personal experiences of both faculty and students. The felt obligation to mentor and to encourage one's students enlarges the arena within which such interactions may occur. Aside from the absolute ethical imperative to avoid relationships of a sexual nature (APA, 1992), feminist faculty who wish to mentor and to support their students may find themselves in questionable or compromising situations that are less clearly unethical.

To what extent do overlapping faculty–student relationships present the occasion for an ethical dilemma? Among the criteria suggested by Belinda Blevins-Knabe (1992) for determining whether a particular relationship presents an "ethical risk" (p. 151) are the following: Does this relationship compromise the designated role of the professor? Is the student being exploited for the gain or personal agenda of the professor? Can the student realistically choose to participate in this relationship? Finally, "is the professor's behavior interfering with the professional roles of other faculty?" (p. 155). (Principles 1, 2, 4, 5, and 12 in Exhibit 8.1 may all be applicable.) To this list we would add the following: Is this relationship interfering with the rights and opportunities provided or available to other students? Each of these questions raises a number of issues that one must confront when determining whether a particular overlapping relationship presents an ethical dilemma. Consider the following situation.

> Dilemma C: One day in the student lounge you overhear a conversation between a faculty member and a student who are both members of the same ethnic minority. The details of a picnic for the upcoming weekend are outlined, and the student ends the conversation by offering to drive and pick up the faculty member. This is not the first time you have been aware of their social plans that involve evening or weekend activities together. You know that this faculty member is dedicated to mentoring students from her ethnic group and has always professed an ethical stance on matters of interacting with students. Several days later, the faculty member announces that she nominated the student for a prestigious award. Only one student from the department may be nominated, and many students in the department are both eligible and qualified.

Faculty Respondent C

"The situation holds several dilemmas for me. Among them are the following: I am concerned about student/faculty socializing because the power differential between roles makes a balanced and equitable relationship impossible, no matter what the faculty member professes. Taking an ethical stance on matters of interacting with students is only part of the issue, and it does not address the realities, perceptions, understandings, or concerns of the student(s) at all; I am unsure whether to interject myself into the situation, and if I were to do so, how best to do it, for there may well be cultural mores at work about which I know nothing.

Nevertheless, I would probably talk with the faculty member to ensure that she has thought about the situation from the student's perspective and that she is cognizant of and sensitive to issues of relative power and authority. I might speak to the student involved as well. If my faculty colleague put forth the student's name for consideration as the departmental nominee for the award, I would be pleased and would look forward to hearing her presentation of the case. If she singlehandedly usurped the departmental prerogative of selecting its nominee for that award, I would be less than pleased and would definitely speak with her about the need to respect the rights of other faculty in the process of selecting the departmental representative."

Student Respondent C

"As a White graduate student, my immediate reaction to this scenario is an immense feeling of being 'stuck.' On the one hand, I see the importance of developing mentoring relationships between ethnic minority students and faculty. On the other hand, I see a possible dual-relationship problem with the resulting favoritism. Indeed, I realize that I may be one of the students overlooked for this nomination. Therefore, I must question the biases and motives behind any decision to act.

I am also aware of the power differentials between students and faculty, and I feel some apprehension in confronting the situation. However, I realize that in this case the department faculty may not be aware of the extent of the relationship between this student and a faculty member. Therefore, my decision would be to consult my faculty advisor.

I realize that all students may not feel comfortable discussing this issue with their advisor. However, as a feminist, with a feminist mentor who respects my input, I would feel comfortable in addressing this issue with her. Additionally, my advisor and I would collaboratively inspect the situation to determine if there is indeed a dual-relationship problem and possible solutions to the problem. If the student and faculty member are confronted, I predict some tension and defensiveness. However, I cannot decide whether to confront the student and faculty member without knowing all the factors that are important here. I believe that making an informed and collaborative decision with my faculty advisor is the best possible solution given the circumstances."

Connect Learning to Social Change (Principle 11 in Exhibit 8.1)

One of the more controversial themes of feminist pedagogy is encompassed by the two principles of "transforming the discipline" and "advocating for activism and social change." The mandate to effect revisions in the multiple ways that society subordinates and oppresses women of all backgrounds has been at the heart of the Women's Movement and remains as its cornerstone (Carabillo, Meuli, & Csida, 1993). Although these principles are interpreted and articulated in many ways, the extent to which they enter into requirements for class participation may well present an underlying conflict between faculty and individual students.

For the feminist teacher, the choice of "coming out" as a feminist to the class remains one of personal decision and may have demonstrable consequences on student growth and personal identity. Regardless of whether faculty feminist identity becomes explicit for students or stays contained within the curriculum and teaching process, we know that course content related to gender and women's issues will affect student attitudes and behavior (Bargad & Hyde, 1991; Stake et al., 1994; Worell, Stilwell, Oakley, & Robinson, in press). In each of these recent studies, students exposed to courses in women's studies or sociocultural gender arrangements scored higher than others on measures of feminist identity and intentions to become active in the service of women and other social issues related to gender justice and equity.

To what extent will academia tolerate the intrusion of personal values into the teaching–learning process? Have feminist teachers used their power to impose their political agenda on captive students in unethical ways? Feminist writers have pointed out that all academic disciplines introduce values, some more explicitly than others (Gentry, 1989; Unger, 1989). The revolution in feminist pedagogy has been to make these values explicit and to link values to the process and outcomes of education (Beck, 1983). What dilemmas might this position present? (Principles 2, 3, and 7 may all be relevant here.) How would you resolve the situation in Dilemma D?

> *Dilemma D:* In confidence, a male student states that he is uncomfortable in one of your colleague's classes. The student reports that on the first day of the class, the professor announced her support for the feminist movement and encouraged all students to become involved. The student does not feel comfortable in the classroom because to him it is an arena for "male bashing." He must complete the class to graduate but refuses

to complete the class project that requires him to analyze an institutional policy that is sexist.

Faculty Respondent D

"My most immediate response would be to advise the student to go to his professor and deal directly with the problem. Issues such as this must be dealt with first hand, not by students trying to garner support for their positions behind the backs of their professors. I am somewhat uncomfortable with the professor's behavior in advising the students to take a certain political stance. In my opinion, feminist teaching involves helping students to think for themselves critically about social policies, social structures, their own life stories and how these are similar to and different from others' and how to draw out the implications of these different forms of analysis for making informed decisions. Thinking about sexism is not male bashing. The student has no right to refuse to do an assignment that requires examining sexist policies. Whether such an experience leads him into embracing a feminist position is, of course, something altogether different and his own choice.

I would also encourage the teacher to create a classroom atmosphere that allows 'free space' for the students to explore their differences of perspectives, values, and emotions. I would also suggest that humor goes a long way in facilitating such a climate. On the first meeting of my women's studies class, I bring a baseball bat to class and say to the students, 'OK, now for male bashing 101.' My point is that the class will not be about 'male bashing' and that thinking about and learning about sexism is not that. I try from the beginning to reduce students' fears about what to expect in the course."

Student Respondent D

"If I knew my colleague well enough to know that she was sensitive to the issue of 'male bashing,' I would encourage the student to complete the requirement and to talk with his professor about his concerns. I might suggest that he use the course to which he objects as the subject of his class project. Since the student approached me in confidence, I would not feel free to discuss my concerns with my colleague. I might ask his permission to discuss his concerns with my colleague while attempting to safeguard his identity. But if he refused this request and I had no knowledge of my colleague's level of functioning or had concerns about it, I would inform the student of his right to take his complaint to the head of the department. If I heard more than one or two students express similar concerns, I would approach my colleague after the students had completed their courses, and express my concerns without divulging any identifying information. I believe that most professors who are well intentioned would take critical feedback very respectfully. If this did not occur, I would consider taking my concerns to the head of the department, after informing my colleague of my concern and intention."

SUMMARY AND CONCLUSIONS

In this chapter, we addressed some of the ethical implications of being a feminist teacher within the traditional academic structures. The feminist professor is frequently confronted with situations in which the realities of traditional academic expectations must be negotiated within the values and principles of a feminist position. To the extent that these values may bring the faculty member into conflict with either students or other faculty, ethical dilemmas can arise. Such dilemmas can also be generated by a conflict between two values or principles jointly held by the individual.

We saw that the implementation of any of a dozen feminist teaching principles may produce conflict among them. In such instances, it is helpful and instructive to use a model of decision making that facilitates thoughtful solutions that consider both the situation and the personal experiences of the decision maker. To illuminate this process, we presented four ethical dilemmas to a sample of feminist faculty and graduate students and asked them to respond from their personal perspectives. In several instances, the responses of student and faculty to a specific dilemma overlapped in terms of gender analysis and proposed solutions. However, a sufficient diversity of concerns and solutions suggests that when ethical dilemmas arise within academic settings, the views of all participants in the ethical context should be considered. When student and faculty views are not in agreement, the ethical issues become engaged with feminist values about how to acknowledge and manage power while empowering the student.

The diverse perspectives of our respondents clearly suggest that an ethical dilemma may result in more than one ethical solution. Although some similarities may be detected across the four pairs of solutions, there were also idiosyncratic responses, such as taking a baseball bat to class to illustrate an idea. These varied solutions to real problematic situations provide encouraging evidence that there are many paths to achieving ethical behavior in feminist pedagogy. From our small sample of students' and faculty's solutions to ethical dilemmas in the context of teaching, we were gratified and particularly impressed with their sensitive and creative approaches to difficult situations. Each response generated suggests that a grounded understanding of feminist principles can provide the framework for examining difficult ethical dilemmas and resolving them in ways that are fair, equitable, and true to one's feminist values.

REFERENCES

Aisenberg, H., & Harrington, M. (1988). *Women of academe: Outsiders in the sacred grove*. Amherst: University of Massachusetts Press.

Ajzen, I. (1996). The social psychology of decision making. In E. T. Higgins & A. W. Kruglanski (Eds.), *Social psychology: Handbook of basic principles* (pp. 297–328). New York: Guilford.

American Psychological Association. (1992). Ethical principles of psychologists and code of conduct. *American Psychologist, 47,* 1597–1611.

Apple, M. W. (1982). *Education and power*. Boston: Routledge & Kegan Paul.

Bargad, A., & Hyde, J. S. (1991). Women's studies: A study of feminist identity development. *Psychology of Women Quarterly, 15,* 181–201.

Beck, E. T. (1983). Self-disclosure and the commitment to social change. *Women's Studies International Forum, 6,* 159–163.

Bleier, R. (1988). *Feminist approaches to science*. New York: Pergamon.

Blevins-Knabe, B. (1992). The ethics of dual relationships in higher education. *Ethics & Behavior, 2,* 151–163.

Brunner, D. D. (1992). Dislocating boundaries in our classrooms. *The Feminist Teacher, 6,* 18–24.

Carabillo, T., Meuli, J., & Csida, J. B. (1993). *Feminist chronicles: 1953–1993*. Los Angeles, CA: Women's Graphics.

Crawford, M., & Marecek, J. (1989). Psychology reconstructs the female: 1968–1988. *Psychology of Women Quarterly, 19,* 147–167.

Forrest, L., & Rosenberg, F. (1997). A review of the feminist pedagogy literature: The neglected child of feminist psychology. *Applied and Preventative Psychology, 6,* 179–192.

Friedman, S. S. (1985). Authority in the feminist classroom: A contradiction in terms? In M. Culley & C. Portuges (Eds.), *Gendered subjects: The dynamics of feminist teaching* (pp. 203–208). Boston: Routledge & Kegan Paul.

Gentry, M. (1989). Feminist perspectives on gender and thought: Paradox and potential. In M. Crawford & M. Gentry (Eds.), *Gender and thought: Psychological perspectives* (pp. 1–16). New York: Springer-Verlag.

Ginorio, A. G., Gutierrez, L., Cauce, A. M., & Acosta, M. (1995). Psychological issues for Latinas. In H. Landrine (Ed.), *Bringing cultural diversity to feminist psychology: Theory, research, and practice* (pp. 241–264). Washington, DC: American Psychological Association.

Glaser, R. D., & Thorpe, J. S. (1986). Unethical intimacy: A survey of sexual contact and advances between psychology educators and female graduate students. *American Psychologist, 41,* 43–51.

Heald, S. (1989). The madwomen in the attic: Feminist teaching in the margins. *Resources for Feminist Research, 18,* 22–26.

Hill, M., Glaser, K., & Harden, J. (1995). A feminist model for ethical decision-making. In E. J. Rave & C. C. Larsen (Eds.), *Ethical decision making in therapy: Feminist perspectives* (pp. 18–37). New York: Guilford.

Hoffman, N. J. (1985). Breaking silences: Life in the feminist classroom. In M. Culley & C. Portuges (Eds.), *Gendered subjects: The dynamics of feminist teaching* (pp. 147–154). New York: Routledge & Kegan Paul.

Hughes, K. P. (1995). Feminist pedagogy and feminist epistemology: An overview. *International Journal of Lifelong Education, 14*, 214–230.

Jaggar, A. M., & Rothenberg, P. S. (1984). *Feminist frameworks: Alternative accounts of the relations between women and men.* New York: McGraw-Hill.

Keith-Spiegel, P., Wittig, A. F., Perkins, D. V., Balogh, D. W., & Whitely, B. E. (1993). *Ethics of teaching: A casebook.* Muncie, IN: Ball State University, Office of Teaching Resources.

Kimmel, E., & Worell, J. (With Daniluk, J., Gawalek, M. A., Lerner, K., Stahley, G., & Kahoe, S.). (1997). Preaching what we practice: Principles and strategies of feminist pedagogy. In J. Worell & N. Johnson (Eds.), *Shaping the future of feminist psychology: Education, research, and practice* (pp. 121–153). Washington, DC: American Psychological Association.

Kitchener, K. S. (1984). Intuition, critical evaluation, and ethical principles: The foundation for ethical decisions in counseling psychology. *The Counseling Psychologist, 12*, 43–55.

LaFrance, M. (1988). Feminism as practical theory: Transforming the teaching of social psychology. *Contemporary Social Psychology, 13*, 63–71.

Maher, F. (1985). Classroom pedagogy and the new scholarship on women. In M. Culley & C. Portuges (Eds.), *Gendered subjects: The dynamics of feminist teaching* (pp. 29–48). Boston: Routledge & Kegan Paul.

Morgan, K. P. (1987). The perils and paradoxes of feminist pedagogy. *Resources for Feminist Research, 16*, 49–52.

Morgan, K. P. (1996a). Describing the emperor's new clothes: Three myths of educational (in-)equity. In A. Diller, B. Houston, K. P. Morgan, & M. Ayim (Eds.), *The gender question in education: Theory, pedagogy, and politics* (pp. 105–122). Boulder, CO: Westview Press.

Morgan, K. P. (1996b). The perils and paradoxes of the bearded mothers. In A. Diller, B. Houston, K. P. Morgan, & M. Ayim (Eds.), *The gender question in education: Theory, pedagogy, and politics* (pp. 124–134). Boulder, CO: Westview Press.

Morley, L., & Walsh, V. (Eds.). (1995). *Feminist academics: Creative agents for change.* London: Taylor & Francis.

Paludi, M. A. (Ed.). (1990). *Ivory power: Sexual harassment on campus.* Albany: State University of New York Press.

Paludi, M. A., & Barickman, R. B. (1991). *Academic and workplace sexual harassment: A resource manual.* Albany: State University of New York Press.

Pope, K. S., Levensen, H., & Shover, L. R. (1979). Sexual intimacy in psychology training: Results and implications of a national survey. *American Psychologist, 34*, 62–89.

Robb, C. (1987). A framework for feminist ethics. In B. H. Andolsen, C. E. Guldorf, & M. D. Pellauer (Eds.), *Women's consciousness, women's conscience* (pp. 211–234). New York: Harper & Row.

Schrewsbury, C. M. (1987). What is feminist pedagogy? *Women's Studies Quarterly, 15*, 6–13.

Spelman, E. V. (1985). Combating the marginalization of Black women in the classroom. In M. Culley & C. Portuges (Eds.), *Gendered subjects: The dynamics of feminist teaching* (pp. 240–244). Boston: Routledge & Kegan Paul.

Stake, J. E., Roades, L., Rose, S., Ellis, E., & West, C. (1994). The women's studies experience: Impetus for feminist activism. *Psychology of Women Quarterly, 18*, 403–412.

Unger, R. K. (1989). Sex, gender, and epistemology. In M. Crawford & M. Gentry (Eds.), *Gender and thought: Psychological perspectives* (pp. 17–35). New York: Springer-Verlag.

Worell, J., Stilwell, D., Oakley, D., & Robinson, D. (in press). Educating about women and gender: Cognitive, personal, and professional outcomes. *Psychology of Women Quarterly*.

APPENDIX:
Responding to Ethical Dilemmas

We are writing a chapter on ethics in feminist pedagogy for a book on feminist ethics to be published by the American Psychological Association. We are inviting you to become an active participant in providing your response to an ethical situation that might confront faculty and students in academia.

In the course of teaching and learning, situations arise that may provide an ethical dilemma in terms of the actions to take. Either way that you solve the problem seems to violate one or more of your ethical principles or values. For feminist teachers or students, ethical dilemmas may involve their culturally based ethical constraints as well as their feminist beliefs and values.

For the dilemma presented here, how would you, as a feminist in academia, resolve the situation? What action would you take or do you believe should be taken? We would like you to write a short paragraph describing your reaction to the situation and your solution if the situation had confronted you. To help you in this process, we included two documents: (a) an outline of a feminist decision-making model and (b) a brief list of 14 principles of feminist pedagogy. You may use any, or none, of these materials in arriving at your solution, should you choose to do so.

In your paragraph, you may wish to include

(1) your view of the situation
(2) your feelings or beliefs about the protagonists
(3) your "best fit" solution to the dilemma presented
(4) your anticipation of the outcomes of your solution, both in terms of yourself and others.

Your participation in this exercise will provide a valuable contribution to the dialogue on feminist ethics in pedagogy and will assist others as they struggle with similar dilemmas. You may choose to sign your name to the response or to remain anonymous.

9

ETHICAL ISSUES IN USING SELF-DISCLOSURE IN FEMINIST THERAPY

JAMES R. MAHALIK, E. ALICE VAN ORMER, AND NICOLE L. SIMI

Awareness and analysis of power in society, power in relationships, and the connection between the two are fundamental to feminism. This focus on power is central to understanding societal structures that disenfranchise women. It also serves as a foundation for applying feminist principles to areas ranging from educational policy to psychotherapy. When applying a feminist framework to psychotherapy, for example, practitioners emphasize how power inequities in women's lives contribute to women's presenting issues. As a result of such consciousness, feminist psychotherapists work to modify the traditional practice of psychotherapy and to remove, as much as possible, the same power inequities in the therapeutic setting that oppress women in society at large.

This priority of addressing how power structures affect people's lives is a central theme of feminism (Worell, 1996). Therefore, an ethical feminist perspective must involve a proactive stance, self-reflection of values and biases, careful attention to context, and analysis of oppressive power dynamics (Lerman & Porter, 1990). The Feminist Therapy Institute Code of Ethics provides guidelines for considering the complexities inherent to ethical issues. Addressing self-disclosure, the code offers the following guideline:

> A feminist therapist discloses information to the client that facilitates the therapeutic process. The therapist is responsible for using self-

disclosure with purpose and discretion in the interests of the client. (Lerman & Porter, 1990, p. 39)

In this chapter, we intend our discussion of therapist self-disclosure to more concretely highlight this general guideline about the ethical use of therapist self-disclosure involved with the practice of feminist psychotherapy. First, we define therapist self-disclosure and discuss why it is a particularly salient technique of feminist therapy to analyze. Next, we discuss the role of self-disclosure in feminist therapy by summarizing recent research findings that compare feminist therapists with other therapists on therapist self-disclosure (Simi & Mahalik, 1997). Finally, we examine the importance of taking the clinical context into account when evaluating the use of self-disclosure and discuss three guidelines for ethical approaches for the use of self-disclosure in feminist therapy that emerged from the clinicians studied.

DEFINITION OF SELF-DISCLOSURE

Existing definitions of therapist self-disclosure range from the inclusive, "a process by which the self is revealed" (Stricker, 1990, p. 277), to the more specific, "verbal behavior through which therapists consciously and purposely communicate ordinarily private information about themselves to their patients" (Simon, 1990, p. 208). Because much of the discussion of therapist self-disclosure is focused on intentional verbal self-disclosure that occurs within the therapy hour, we follow Simon's definition and limit our discussion to therapists' intentional, verbal self-disclosure about domains that in many other forms of psychotherapy are considered private. The content of self-disclosure can include theoretical orientation, political beliefs, socioeconomic background, sexual orientation, reactions toward clients, and personal values and biases.

We wish to acknowledge, however, the multiple, complex ways that therapist self-disclosure occurs. The use of self-disclosure should be recast from the dichotomy of whether to self-disclose or not to a continuum of degrees of self-disclosure. Recognizing a continuum acknowledges that there is always information about the therapist being provided to the client. That is, revealing the therapist's self is inevitable when clients observe a therapist's age, gender, ethnicity, race, and physical challenges in addition to how a therapist decorates his or her office, dresses, sets fees, chooses settings in which to practice, and is involved in public activities (e.g., forensic work, political activism). Additionally, seeing self-disclosure on a continuum serves to highlight the dangers of underdisclosing and overdisclosing because to date most of the literature focuses on the latter while ignoring the former.

SELF-DISCLOSURE IN FEMINIST THERAPY

Although self-disclosure is only one technique in a feminist practitioner's therapeutic repertoire, it is a useful intervention to illustrate issues related to a feminist ethic in therapy for three reasons. First, grounded in feminist values, the literature discusses what content and rationale for self-disclosure are consistent with feminist principles and makes recommendations about the use of self-disclosure in feminist therapy. This is a rich source of scholarship and should be relied on to help guide practice.

Second, although principles or guidelines for feminist psychotherapy are essential to an ethical framework, practitioners must struggle with the application of those abstract frameworks to specific situations. By analyzing a situationally specific human interaction such as a therapist's self-disclosure in feminist therapy, we may be able to identify ethical principles grounded in clinical events that are applicable to a broad array of therapeutic issues.

Third, the results of a recent survey identify unique content and rationales for feminist therapists using self-disclosure (Simi & Mahalik, 1997). This empirical evidence for actual differences between feminist therapists and other therapists concerning self-disclosure allows for a more specific examination of the ethical issues of self-disclosure in feminist therapy. Most compelling was qualitative data from Simi and Mahalik's practitioner respondents who raised some contextual issues related to power in using self-disclosure in feminist therapy. As such, the importance of addressing the contextual dimension of self-disclosure is necessary to reflect on and discuss.

ROLE OF SELF-DISCLOSURE IN FEMINIST THERAPY

Feminist approaches to psychotherapy have supported the use of appropriate therapist self-disclosure since their beginnings in the early 1970s (Wyche et al., 1997). This is a result of the early consciousness-raising groups that were intended to be egalitarian and when the sharing of personal experiences led to increased political awareness of women's oppression. Principles of egalitarianism and connections made between the personal and political were carried over into fledgling models of feminist psychotherapy. Self-disclosure, as a technique, became one way to attend to both of these principles. Although feminist approaches to psychotherapy have evolved over the past 2 decades, therapist self-disclosure has remained one of the unique attributes of feminist therapy.

The use of self-disclosure is thought to serve several therapeutic goals from a feminist perspective (Brown & Walker, 1990; Enns, 1993; Lerman & Porter, 1990). Most broadly, self-disclosure may serve as a vehicle for transmitting feminist values and promoting social transformation at the individual level by nurturing the development of feminist consciousness (Brabeck & Brown, 1997). This occurs through a number of specific goals, including equalizing (as much as is possible) the power differential between client and therapist (Brown, 1991; Brown & Walker, 1990; Enns, 1993; Greenspan, 1986). Therapist self-disclosure may also facilitate clients' growth in psychotherapy (Brown & Walker, 1990; Lerman & Porter, 1990; Russell, 1986). Some believe that self-disclosure fosters a sense of solidarity with the client (Brown, 1991; Brown & Walker, 1990; Greenspan, 1986; Russell, 1986), helps clients view their own situations with less shame (Greenspan, 1986), and encourages feelings of liberation (Brown & Walker, 1990). Consistent with APA's Ethical Standards in the Ethical Principles of Psychologists and Code of Conduct (1992) regarding the rights of clients and the responsibilities of therapists (Hare-Mustin, Marecek, Kaplan, & Liss-Levinson, 1979), feminist therapists suggest that therapist self-disclosure of lifestyle, background, and beliefs, such as theoretical orientation, political and religious ideals, sexual orientation, other values, and socioeconomic background, is considered important for clients to make informed decisions about working with a therapist and possibly to choose a therapist who can serve as a role model for them. Finally, feminist clinicians' use of self-disclosure is in part an attempt to incorporate the use of the self into therapy and to acknowledge the importance of the real relationship between client and therapist.

Research on self-disclosure by traditional therapists focuses on reasons why therapists self-disclose to clients (Mathews, 1988, 1989; Simon, 1988) and what they disclose (Anderson & Mandell, 1989; Berg-Cross, 1984; Robitschek & McCarthy, 1991). Traditional therapists in these studies have reported self-disclosing to promote feelings of universality and provide reality testing (Mathews, 1988) and to decrease rigidity with clients and increase client disclosure (Mathews, 1989). In addition, a clinician's theoretical orientation (i.e., eclectic, humanistic, and existential counselors disclosed more), therapist self-awareness (i.e., high disclosers had fewer hours of personal therapy), and the therapy relationship (i.e., high disclosers emphasized the "realness" of the relationship) affected the decision to self-disclose (Simon, 1988). Reasons traditional therapists reported for not self-disclosing included believing that it removed the focus from the client, was not helpful, and interfered with the transference (Mathews, 1988, 1989).

Results from studies examining the content of therapist self-disclosure reported that therapists, at large, most often disclosed their training experience and counseling style (Berg-Cross, 1984; Robitschek & McCarthy, 1991) as well as their personality, personal history, and current relationships (Anderson & Mandell, 1989). Among the topics least often disclosed in all the studies were sexual experience and beliefs, financial status, and political affiliation. Although content areas of disclosure by therapists also show great variability, from demographic information and professional training to more personal information, therapists with traditional training generally avoid self-disclosing on the topics of sex, money, and politics.

In contrast, feminist scholars suggest that appropriate content for therapist self-disclosure includes the therapist's beliefs and lifestyle (Brown & Walker, 1990; Hare-Mustin et al., 1979), religious and class background (Brown & Walker, 1990), sexual orientation (Brown & Walker, 1990; Rochlin, 1982), political beliefs (Brown & Walker, 1990), and feelings toward the client including angry feelings (Greenspan, 1986). By disclosing these content areas, some feminist scholars believe clients are provided with adequate information to make informed decisions about working with a particular therapist (i.e., APA Ethics Code) and have an opportunity to choose a therapist who can serve as a role model (Brown & Walker, 1990; Gilbert, 1980).

EXAMINATION OF DIFFERENCES BETWEEN FEMINIST AND TRADITIONAL THERAPISTS' USE OF SELF-DISCLOSURE

In research examining therapist self-disclosure, Simi and Mahalik (1997) developed the Feminist Self-Disclosure Inventory to assess therapists' endorsement of principles related to self-disclosure in feminist therapy. They surveyed feminist and traditional psychotherapists (i.e., psychoanalytic–dynamic, cognitive–behavioral, family, humanistic) about therapist self-disclosure. This was done because although there was evidence that practitioners from different theoretical orientations use self-disclosure differently from each other (Brunink & Schroeder, 1979; Dies, 1973; Mathews, 1988, 1989; Simon, 1988), there was no research that examined whether feminist therapists actually use self-disclosure differently from other therapists, despite the well-articulated discussion of this topic by feminist scholars.

Using factor analysis, Simi and Mahalik (1997) identified five factors in their inventory: the content of self-disclosure (i.e., therapist background), rationale for disclosure (i.e., promotes liberatory feelings, promotes egalitarianism, and empowers the client), and availability to self-disclose (therapist availability). They found that the three groups of therapists surveyed were different from each other on overall self-reported endorsement of feminist principles related to self-disclosure. Specifically, feminist therapists, more so than psychoanalytic–dynamic therapists and "other" therapists (i.e., cognitive–behavioral, family, and humanistic), agreed with self-disclosing background information, self-disclosing as a means of promoting egalitarianism in the therapy relationship, and making themselves available for client requests of self-disclosure. Feminist therapists and the other therapists were significantly more likely than psychoanalytic–dynamic therapists to self-disclose to promote liberatory feelings and to minimize the power differential between the therapist and client.

Finally, analysis of the individual items within the factors revealed that feminist therapists were more likely than the other two groups to support the use of self-disclosure to promote a more egalitarian relationship with the client and to provide better opportunities for the client to choose a therapist to serve as a role model. With regard to content, feminist therapists were more likely to self-disclose their religious background, political beliefs, and sexual orientation than were the other groups.

These results support those of researchers who believe self-disclosure is an important distinguishing technique of feminist therapy (Brown, 1991; Brown & Walker, 1990; Greenspan, 1986) and that of other research in which feminist identity was found to be related to feminist therapy behaviors (Juntunen, Atkinson, Reyes, & Gutierrez, 1994). It is important to note that feminists reported being forthcoming about their values in light of the evidence that some feminist therapists experienced pressure to conceal their values in the current political backlash against feminism (Marecek & Kravetz, 1996).

IMPORTANCE OF CONTEXT FOR SELF-DISCLOSURE

The above results that feminist therapists differed from nonfeminist therapists in their use of self-disclosure raise some issues in counseling and therapy related to the context of self-disclosure (Simi & Mahalik, 1997). For example, the item that most differentiated feminist therapists from the other therapists was "I disclose my sexual orientation to clients in verbal or written form." Evidence suggests that disclosure of sexual orientation may have beneficial impact on therapeutic outcome in some contexts. Specifically, earlier researchers found positive therapeutic outcomes related to client–therapist similarity of sexual orientation when the client and therapist were mutually disclosive (Liljestrand, Gerling, & Saliba, 1978) and that gay men and lesbians preferred gay male or lesbian counselors (McDermott, Tyndall, & Lichtenberg, 1989).

Findings that therapist self-disclosure is appreciated by clients and is beneficial to the counseling process run counter to the traditional literature that focuses on the dangers of overdisclosing. The feminist perspective may help to bring a more balanced understanding of the role of self-disclosure by highlighting the ethical issues of underdisclosing. This includes clients' lacking salient information (e.g., sexual orientation) needed to make informed decisions about working with a particular therapist.

However, qualitative responses from Simi and Mahalik's (1997) feminist participants reminds us that their pencil-and-paper questionnaire did not assess the context in which the self-disclosure took place. Assessing the context is critical to judging the overall impact on the relationship and client outcome. For example, disclosure of the therapist's sexual orientation might be helpful for one client in establishing trust and building the therapeutic alliance. For another client, such disclosure might make the relationship feel unsafe. Because context is affected by power dynamics between client and therapist, the therapist's decision to disclose to a given client about sexual orientation should be carefully evaluated in the context of a number of issues.

Simi and Mahalik's (1997) survey respondents identified three such issues. First, they were interested in how self-disclosure affected the balance of power. They reported that they might use self-disclosure to lessen the hierarchy of power in the therapeutic relationship. However, they were concerned that self-disclosure might change the nature of the relationship with the client, resulting in dual relationships or confused boundaries. Their concern was whether the therapist's needs might compete with the needs of the client through either "emotional reversal" (Hill, 1990), where the client becomes the nurturer, or the therapist's disclosing to the client who already has difficulty maintaining boundaries.

In accordance with good therapeutic work and as specified in the Feminist Therapy Institute's Code of Ethics (Lerman & Porter, 1990), therapists must be accountable for preventing unnecessary confusion for the client and keeping the client's needs paramount when using self-disclosure (Biaggio & Greene, 1995). Such guidelines specify that therapists must preserve the relationship for the benefit of the client (Biaggio & Greene, 1995) and take care of their own personal and professional needs outside the therapeutic relationship (Adleman & Barrett, 1990).

The need for the therapist's self-care is important for both the welfare of the client and the therapist. Therapists, who are people drawn to helping others, are sometimes at risk for discounting the importance of their own needs in the interest of helping others. Paradoxically, when therapists focus exclusively on the needs of others and neglect good care of themselves, they tend to be more vulnerable to confusing boundaries in therapy. As such, we strongly encourage therapist self-care or, for feminist therapists, to engage in what the members of the Theory Group at the National Conference on Education and Training in Feminist Practice called "response-ability" (Brabeck & Brown, 1997; Noddings, 1984). That is, therapists need to have "the ability to respond to one's own self as well as others" (Brabeck & Brown, 1997, p. 15).

The second issue Simi and Mahalik's (1997) respondents noted was self-disclosing to act as a role model for the client. Many of the feminist respondents saw this as a vital function of their role as therapists. Some, however, were concerned that clients might perceive the therapist's own resolution of a particular issue as the only way or the one the therapist thinks is best, regardless of the client's unique situation. Therapists must consider whether a particular client views the therapist's words as gospel and forecloses other possible perspectives, options, or solutions. This highlights the importance of considering the client's social, emotional, cognitive, and developmental level of functioning in predicting the effect of a more powerful other's self-disclosure.

In considering the dynamics of power in the therapeutic relationship, one needs to consider how therapist self-disclosure might potentially undermine the voices of clients who invariably occupy less powerful positions than their therapists. A tenet of feminist theory of psychological practice is the "authoriz[ation of] the experience of the oppressed in their own voices" (Brabeck & Brown, 1997, p. 32). An important consideration when disclosing to the client is whether the therapist is privileging her or his own experience over her or his client's when she or he chooses to self-disclose.

An irony that Marecek and Kravetz (1996) identified is that although feminist therapists value free choice and self-determination for women and view the therapist's role as validating and honoring the client's values, feminist therapists also ascribe and promote values specific to a feminist vision that are not value neutral. For example, in self-disclosing their stand against societal forms of oppression, feminist therapists encourage clients to be concerned about social injustice and to be politically active. By being cognizant of the potential tension between honoring the client's values and working within a feminist values framework, clinicians may help preserve the client's voice and her or his potential for exercising power in the therapeutic relationship. Indeed, one of the strengths of a feminist therapist is her or his willingness and perceived responsibility to be self-reflective regarding the therapist's values. Self-disclosure of the therapist's feminist orientation early in the therapeutic process enables clients to make informed choices about with whom to work. Failure to disclose feminist values, or any other set of values, robs clients of this choice.

The third concern that Simi and Mahalik's (1997) respondents raised was that self-disclosure was most helpful to clients when it was a conscious decision on the part of the therapist in which the therapist had an explicit clinical rationale based on an assessment of the client's needs. They indicated this by comments such as "it should be calculated to be helpful" and "it must be thought through." In developing this clinical rationale, the therapist needs to consider the broad context of interpersonal events and experiences related to the therapeutic relationship and the client's needs.

Impulsive self-disclosure, no matter how benign the impulse, carries the risk of violating the client because the specific effect on the therapeutic relationship is not thought through or assessed (Brown, 1994). Brown (1994) wrote that "it is important for us, as feminist therapists, to ask ourselves how we have arrived at the decision to engage in a certain behavior, and whether or not our actions are impulsive rather than understood" (p. 35).

In his work involving eclectic models, Dryden (1986) specified a number of questions clinicians need to answer in explicating their clinical decision making. Some of these questions are relevant to Simi and Mahalik's (1997) discussion of self-disclosure in feminist therapy. These include the following: (a) How do practitioners establish and maintain effective alliances with clients? (b) What important ways do clients differ from one another? and (c) How do therapeutic processes change over time?

Ethical feminist clinicians seeking to understand their self-disclosure might be well served by asking themselves the following questions: How would self-disclosure help form or maintain my therapeutic alliance with this client? What unique experiences has this client had that are different from others' (and mine) that I need to respect when using self-disclosure? How does where the client and I are in the therapeutic work affect the client's experience of my self-disclosure? Clinicians who ask such questions tend to increase their awareness and understanding of how they arrived at the decision to disclose.

These "how often, what content, by whom, and when" questions (Krumboltz, 1966) help to bring conscious clinical decision making to the use of self-disclosure with clients and help therapists use techniques that are the best match in the context of the therapeutic relationship, uniqueness of the client, and the status of work with the client. Thus, clinicians who are aware of how they arrive at a clinical decision are in a better position to exercise power ethically and responsibly by making self-disclosure a helpful part of the clinical treatment rather than something done impulsively.

ASPIRATIONAL ETHICS

In discussing the issues that Simi and Mahalik's (1997) respondents raised and making suggestions for guiding clinical practice, we intend to follow Mills's suggestion of focusing on "aspirational ethics" versus "basement level ethics" (David Mills, personal communication, March 1996). That is, Mills saw much of psychologists' energy invested in delineating what not to do and specifying what constituted unethical behavior. Similarly, feminist scholars have criticized traditional thinking about ethics by mental health professionals for its lack of grounding in a conceptual framework, resulting in ponderously detailed, reactionary lists of "thou shalt nots," which reduce complex ethical issues into dichotomous "good–bad," "right–wrong" ones (Lerman & Porter, 1990; Rave & Larsen, 1995). As an alternative mindset, Mills encouraged psychologists to consider aspirational ethics. In this frame of reference, ethical decision making becomes focused on what behavior to encourage, or aspire to, in being an ethical professional. In this fashion, the intention of Simi and Mahalik's article was to identify issues and suggest professional behaviors that therapists might aspire to when seeking to preserve clients' power when therapists self-disclose.

Although we recognize the danger that broad guidelines may be converted into hard and fast rules that are unhelpful to feminist practitioners (Brown, 1994), the articulation of guidelines to consider when making decisions about self-disclosure can serve to stimulate an ongoing dialogue and inform future research. Such guidelines can also help clarify potential confusion for feminist practitioners.

We advocate practitioners to aspire to (a) preserve the therapeutic relationship for the client, (b) exercise self-care, (c) preserve the client's voice in the therapeutic interaction, and (d) develop explicit clinical rationales for interventions. We see these aspirational guidelines as a useful starting point to help preserve the client's power when her or his therapist uses self-disclosure. Also such aspirational guidelines should apply broadly to feminist therapy, not only to the use of self-disclosure. For example, in facilitating the expression of client anger (Gilbert, 1980), clinicians would benefit by (a) addressing their own anger around issues their clients raise, (b) recognizing each clients' voice of anger as unique, and (c) having an explicit rationale for why facilitating the expression of anger is clinically beneficial to a given client at a particular time.

CONCLUSION

In this chapter, we focused on one very specific technique of feminist psychotherapy. However, we see the discussion of self-disclosure as particularly useful for developing feminist practice, given the well-articulated rationale for its use in feminist therapy, the fact that it shows clinical issues with other aspects of feminist practice, and the rather scant empirical evidence we have regarding self-disclosure's impact on clients. Continued discussion about self-disclosure and other techniques used in feminist therapy will strengthen feminist practice and help train ethically conscious feminist practitioners. We view our discussion as part of the continuing discourse of feminists who focus on self-reflection of values and biases, pay careful attention to context, and analyze oppressive power dynamics (Lerman & Porter, 1990).

REFERENCES

Adleman, J., & Barrett, S. E. (1990). Overlapping relationships: Importance of the feminist ethical perspective. In H. Lerman & N. Porter (Eds.), *Feminist ethics in psychotherapy* (pp. 87–91). New York: Springer.

American Psychological Association. (1992). Ethical principles of psychologists and code of conduct. *American Psychologist, 47,* 1597–1611.

Anderson, S. C., & Mandell, D. L. (1989, May). The use of self-disclosure by professional social workers. *Social Casework: The Journal of Contemporary Social Work, 70,* 259–267.

Berg-Cross, L. (1984). Therapist self-disclosure to clients in psychotherapy. *Psychotherapy in Private Practice, 2,* 57–64.

Biaggio, M., & Greene, B. (1995). Overlapping/dual relationships. In E. J. Rave & C. C. Larsen (Eds.), *Ethical decision making in therapy: Feminist perspectives* (pp. 91–123). New York: Guilford Press.

Brabeck, M., & Brown, L. (With Christian, L., Espin, O., Hare-Mustin, R., Kaplan, A., Kaschak, E., Miller, D., Phillips, E., Ferns, T., & Van Ormer, A.). (1997). Feminist theory and psychological practice. In J. Worell & N. Johnson (Eds.), *Shaping the future of feminist psychology: Education, research, and practice* (pp. 15–35). Washington, DC: American Psychological Association.

Brown, L. S. (1991). Ethical issues in feminist therapy: Selected topics. *Psychology of Women Quarterly, 15,* 323–336.

Brown, L. S. (1994). Boundaries in feminist therapy: A conceptual formulation. *Women and Therapy, 15*(1), 29–38.

Brown, L. S., & Walker, L. E. A. (1990). Feminist therapy perspectives on self-disclosure. In G. Stricker & M. Fisher (Eds.), *Self-disclosure in the therapeutic relationship* (pp. 135–154). New York: Plenum Press.

Brunink, S. A., & Schroeder, H. E. (1979). Verbal therapeutic behavior of expert psychoanalytically oriented, gestalt, and behavior therapists. *Journal of Consulting and Clinical Psychology, 47,* 567–574.

Dies, R. R. (1973). Group therapist self-disclosure: Development and validation of a scale. *Journal of Consulting and Clinical Psychology, 41,* 97–103.

Dryden, W. (1986). Eclectic psychotherapy: A critique of leading approaches. In J. C. Norcross (Ed.), *Handbook of eclectic psychotherapy* (pp. 353–378). New York: Brunner/Mazel.

Enns, C. Z. (1993). Twenty years of feminist counseling: From naming biases to implementing multifaceted practice. *The Counseling Psychologist, 21,* 3–87.

Gilbert, L. (1980). Feminist therapy. In A. E. Brodsky & R. T. Hare-Mustin (Eds.), *Women and psychotherapy: An assessment of research and practice* (pp. 245–265). New York: Guilford Press.

Greenspan, M. (1986). Should therapists be personal? Self-disclosure and therapeutic distance in feminist therapy. *Women and Therapy, 5,* 5–17.

Hare-Mustin, R. T., Marecek, J., Kaplan, A. G., & Liss-Levinson, N. (1979). Rights of clients, responsibilities of therapists. *American Psychologist, 34,* 3–16.

Hill, M. (1990). On creating a theory of feminist therapy. In L. S. Brown & M. P. P. Root (Eds.), *Diversity and complexity in feminist therapy* (pp. 53–66). New York: Haworth Press.

Juntunen, C. L., Atkinson, D. R., Reyes, C., & Gutierrez, M. (1994). Feminist identity and feminist therapy behaviors of women psychotherapists. *Psychotherapy, 31,* 327–333.

Krumboltz, J. D. (1966). Promoting adaptive behavior. In J. D. Krumboltz (Ed.), *Revolution in counseling* (pp. 3–26). Boston: Houghton-Mifflin.

Lerman, H., & Porter, N. (Eds.). (1990). *Feminist ethics in psychotherapy.* New York: Springer.

Liljestrand, P., Gerling, E., & Saliba, P. A. (1978). The effects of social sex-role stereotypes and sexual orientation on psychotherapeutic outcomes. *Journal of Homosexuality, 3,* 361–372.

Marecek, J., & Kravetz, D. (1996, August). *A room of one's own: Power and agency in feminist therapy.* Paper presented at the 104th Annual Convention of the American Psychological Association, Toronto, Ontario, Canada.

Mathews, B. (1988). The role of therapist self-disclosure in psychotherapy: A survey of therapists. *American Journal of Psychotherapy, 42,* 521–531.

Mathews, B. (1989). The use of therapist self-disclosure and its potential impact on the therapeutic process. *Journal of Human Behavior and Learning, 6,* 25–29.

McDermott, D., Tyndall, L., & Lichtenberg, J. (1989). Factors related to counselor preference among gays and lesbians. *Journal of Counseling and Development, 68,* 31–35.

Noddings, N. (1984). *Caring: A feminine approach to ethics and moral education.* Berkeley: University of California Press.

Rave, E. J., & Larsen, C. (Eds.). (1995). *Ethical decision making in therapy: Feminist perspectives.* New York: Guilford Press.

Robitschek, C. G., & McCarthy, P. R. (1991). Prevalence of counselor self-reference in the therapeutic dyad. *Journal of Counseling and Development, 69,* 218–221.

Rochlin, M. (1982). Sexual orientation of the therapist and therapeutic effectiveness with gay clients. *Journal of Homosexuality, 7,* 19–35.

Russell, M. (1986). Teaching feminist counseling skills: An evaluation. *Counselor Education and Supervision, 25,* 320–331.

Simi, N., & Mahalik, J. R. (1997). Comparison of feminist versus psychoanalytic/dynamic and other therapists on self-disclosure. *Psychology of Women Quarterly, 21,* 465–483.

Simon, J. C. (1988). Criteria for therapist self-disclosure. *American Journal of Psychotherapy, 42,* 404–415.

Simon, J. C. (1990). Criteria for therapist self-disclosure. In G. Stricker & M. Fisher (Eds.), *Self-disclosure in the therapeutic relationship* (pp. 207–225). New York: Plenum Press.

Stricker, G. (1990). Self-disclosure and psychotherapy. In G. Stricker & M. Fisher (Eds.), *Self-disclosure in the therapeutic relationship* (pp. 277–289). New York: Plenum Press.

Worell, J. (1996). Opening doors to feminist research. *Psychology of Women Quarterly, 20,* 469–485.

Wyche, K. F., & Rice, J. K. (With Cantor, D., Claster, B., Fodor, I., Gregory, C., Hassinger, J., Keita, G. P., Lerman, H., Rawlings, E., Rocchio, L., Rosewater, L. B., Silverstein, L., & Walker, L.). (1997). Feminist therapy: From dialogue to tenets. In J. Worell & N. Johnson (Eds.), *Shaping the future of feminist psychology: Education, research, and practice* (pp. 57–71). Washington, DC: American Psychological Association.

10

THE INTEGRATION OF FEMINISM AND MULTICULTURALISM: ETHICAL DILEMMAS AT THE BORDER

ELIZABETH E. SPARKS AND AILEEN H. PARK

Silence

Too many women in too many countries speak the same language of silence.
My grandmother was always silent—always aggrieved—only her husband had
the cosmic right (or so it was said) to speak and be heard.
They say it is different now (after all, I am always vocal and my grandmother thinks
I talk too much).
But sometimes, I wonder.
When a woman gives her love, as most do generously—it is accepted.
When a woman shares her thoughts, as some do, graciously—it is allowed.
When a woman fights for power, as all women would like to, quietly or
loudly, it is questioned.
And yet, there must be freedom—if we are to speak.
And yes, there must be power—if we are to be heard.
And when we have both (freedom and power), let us not be misunderstood.
We seek only to give words to those who cannot speak (too many women in
too many countries). I seek only to forget the sorrows of
my grandmother's silence.[1]

---

[1] Anasuya Sengupta: Lady Sri Ram College, read by Hillary Rodham Clinton to reporters during her
visit to India (Naresh & Surendran, 1996).

This chapter is an exploration of the complexities involved in the integration of feminism and multiculturalism. Our goal is to describe one aspect of the journey that feminist practitioners embark on when working with first-generation immigrant and refugee women of Color in the United States who are strongly identified with cultural norms and values that support hierarchical gender relationships. We label this component of feminist practice as a "borderland." Its boundaries are defined by the conflicts that can occur when assumptions that underlie feminist principles of practice are inconsistent with clients' cultural values and norms. The feminist practitioner is challenged at these times to determine an appropriate course of action, and the decision-making process that ensues often involves ethical considerations. This is particularly problematic in situations where a client's cultural context supports the oppression and subordination of women. The borderland is a complex entity, and an analysis of its parameters could be undertaken from many different perspectives. We choose to focus our discussion on practice and to explore instances where practitioners' commitment to feminist principles and the clients' adherence to cultural values and norms pose ethical dilemmas.

Entering this borderland is not unique to feminist practitioners and could occur in treatment conducted from most theoretical perspectives with this population of women. However, feminist practitioners may enter this borderland more frequently because of their firm commitment to engage in political–social activism in situations where cultural norms and practices are oppressive to women. The crux of the ethical dilemma for feminist practitioners who find themselves in the borderland is to determine the "right" direction to take in the treatment process, while remaining respectful of the clients' cultural beliefs and norms. In their efforts to meet both of these important tenets of feminist practice, feminist practitioners may find themselves having to reason through ethical considerations. We provide two clinical vignettes to illustrate the parameters of the borderland and highlight cultural issues that contribute to the complexity of the treatment process. We conclude our chapter by suggesting landmarks that can serve as navigational guides through this borderland to help feminist practitioners arrive at a place of mutuality and shared therapeutic goals with clients.

Our interest in this issue stems from years of scholarship in the areas of feminism and multiculturalism and our lived experiences as women psychologists of Color. I (Sparks) am an African American practitioner and academician who has worked with ethnic–minority women for over 20 years. I have taught a course in multicultural counseling for the last 6 years. I began to formulate the notion of a borderland when my students repeatedly questioned the applicability of feminist principles to practice with women who come from cultures that support traditional, hierarchical gender roles and the subordination of women. As we continued to discuss this issue, my students and I became aware of the complexities involved in integrating principles of feminism and multiculturalism and the ethical questions that can arise in this work. I (Park) am a Korean American doctoral student whose clinical training and research focuses on both feminist and multicultural theories of practice. I, like Sparks, have often encountered a borderland when struggling to integrate a social justice ethic, initially inspired for me by feminism, with an ethic of nonjudgmental cultural empathy, first evoked for me by multiculturalism.

DEFINITIONS OF TERMS

Throughout this chapter, we use the terms *feminism* and *multiculturalism* to represent two similar, yet distinct, theoretical orientations. Both terms have multiple definitions and have undergone numerous revisions since their initial articulations. These revisions were prompted by an increasing awareness of the significant ways in which racism, culture, class, and sexual orientation influence the lives of women. In this chapter, we try to use the most recent articulations of these two perspectives. However, the nature of our thesis requires that we make some generalizations concerning the ways in which feminists and multiculturalists conceptualize clinical problems and the nature of their work with clients. When making such generalizations, there is always a risk of ignoring and minimizing some aspects of these theories. We try to remain conscious of this and hope that the definitions we provide make our perspective clear.

The definition of feminism that we use characterizes it as both a political movement and a theoretical orientation that advocates for social and political equality of the sexes. There is no one feminist theory; however, certain assumptions are consistent across the various theories of feminist practice. Feminist theory of practice primarily addresses issues of gender and power. An important goal of feminist practice is to enhance women's perceptions of their reality by including an understanding of the oppression they experience within the patriarchal society and to facilitate the creation of feminist consciousness (Chin, 1994; Worell & Johnson, 1997).

Multiculturalism is defined as a philosophy that affords the development of flexibility and diversity of orientations to life and for the development of pluralistic identities (Ramirez, 1983). This orientation calls for an increased awareness of the influence of culture on lived experiences and dictates that mental health practitioners provide services that are culturally sensitive to clients' values and cultural traditions. Cervantes and Cervantes (1993) articulated several premises inherent in a multicultural perspective: (a) While anchored within a particular cultural mindset, one continuously examines and questions one's own ethnocentrism as well as any held stereotypes or assumptions regarding the behavior of individuals from other cultures; (b) intelligence, problem-solving skills, and coping abilities are equally distributed within all cultural groups; (c) psychological reality is not fixed in time and space because culture is a dynamic, continuous entity; (d) ethnic–minority groups create innovative lives, enhancing coping styles and strategies to maintain a viable identity in an oppressive social structure; (e) it is appropriate for individuals to be bicultural–multicultural; and (f) cultural diversity is just that—diversity—both within and between ethnic groups.

Feminism and multiculturalism as theoretical perspectives have evolved over the last 2 decades. Both grew out of a sense of dissatisfaction with the ways in which traditional theories of psychology incorporated the lived experiences of women and people of Color. Feminist and multicultural writers have mounted well-documented critiques of the ethnocentric and sexist nature of most of this traditional scholarship (Chesler, 1972; Chodorow, 1978; Espin & Gawalek, 1992; King, 1989; J. B. Miller, 1976; Sue, Ivey, & Pedersen, 1996; Sue & Sue, 1990). They have chided traditional theorists for their lack of attention to the roles that gender, oppression, and culture play in psychological development and functioning. Feminism is primarily concerned with the oppression of women within society, whereas multiculturalism focuses on the impact of oppression and racism on ethnic–minority groups (both men and women) within the United States. The lived experiences of individuals are the foundation of both feminism and multiculturalism, and there is a high value placed on the authority of personal experiences. For both women and people of Color in the United States, discrimination and economic disadvantage characterize these experiences (Sherwin, 1992; Sue & Sue, 1990). The resulting oppression is understood by both feminists and multiculturalists to be embedded within the social fabric of this country. Both call for an end to the existing status quo and believe that political action and social reform are necessary to end the subordination and discrimination of all individuals (Pellauer, 1985; Sherwin, 1992; Sue & Sue, 1990).

There are extensive debates in the literature regarding the differential emphasis placed on the various "isms" by feminist and multicultural theorists (hooks, 1981; Lorde, 1984; Sampson, 1993; Spelman, 1988). In this chapter, we avoid rehashing these debates. We choose instead to ground our thesis in the belief that both feminist and multicultural practitioners are attempting to understand the lives of individuals through a sociopolitical lens that recognizes the complex interaction of race, ethnicity, culture, sexual orientation, and gender. A borderland does exist at the intersection of feminism and multiculturalism, and feminist practitioners who find themselves within this territory are required to decide on an appropriate course of action. As Brabeck and Ting (chap. 1, this volume) state, "feminist ethical theories provide unique lenses for determining what one ought to do and deciding on a course of action in the face of competing ethical principles" (p. 18). By discussing the parameters of the borderland and exploring the ethical considerations inherent in this component of the treatment process, we hope to contribute to the discourse in both the feminist and multicultural literature concerning psychotherapy with immigrant and refugee women of Color whose indigenous cultures support traditional, hierarchical gender relationships.

UNDERLYING ASSUMPTIONS

In reviewing some of the basic assumptions that underlie feminism and multiculturalism, we found that both orientations highlight the significance of culture in the development of theory and practice. Brabeck and Ting (Introduction, this volume) suggest that feminist theory of practice is based on a set of tenets that recognizes the significance of human diversity and culture (including ethnicity, sexual orientation, able-bodiness, religion, and language). A number of these tenets are consistent with the viewpoints expressed in multiculturalism. For example, one of the tenets states that

> feminist theory of feminist practice embraces human diversity as a requirement and foundation for practice. Diversity ... not only is a goal in its own right but also is necessary for feminist theory to be complete and reflective of the total range of human experience. (p. 5)

A second tenet states the following.

> Feminist practitioners expand the parameters of conceptions of identity or personhood. Feminist theorists and practitioners seek models of human growth and development that describe a variety of ways that people have a sense of identities and multiple subjectivities. (p. 5)

Both of these tenets are consistent with the philosophy and perspectives contained in multiculturalism. Yet some have argued that the discourse within feminism concerning race and culture is problematic. As Cervantes and Cervantes (1993) stated, "a tension exists between culture and feminism that goes beyond male domination of women. Women are influenced by their ethnicity and cultural heritage and they bring their perspective to their understanding of women's rights within their own cultural boundaries" (p. 167). Friedman (1995) suggested that the discourse on race within feminism needs to be expanded. In her analysis of the narratives of race in feminist discourse, she identified three scripts that she believes reflect binary thinking: denial, accusation, and confession. She argued that these three scripts lead to much of the frustration that occurs when feminists attempt to talk about race and ethnicity.

Friedman recommended (1995) moving beyond such binary modes of thinking and suggested a fourth narrative that she terms "relational positionality." This perspective reflects the narratives produced by women and men of different racial and ethnic standpoints where identity is situationally constructed and defined. Identities are thought to be fluid states, shifting with a changing context, and dependent on their points of reference. For example, an African American woman may be a "woman of Color" when compared with European Americans but is "African American" in relation to other women of Color and is a "middle-class, college-educated woman" when compared with other African American women. Freedman's position is that such a perspective opens the door for dialogue, affiliations, alliances, and coalitions across racial and ethnic boundaries and can move the feminist discourse on race to a more comprehensive level.

The notion of relational positionality in feminist discourse is similar to the ways that multicultural theorists describe the richness and complexity of culturally diverse populations. Multicultural theories not only highlight the similarities among ethnic minority groups due to the effects of racism and oppression, they also celebrate the uniqueness of cultural experiences and identify within-group variability created by gender, social class, and acculturation status (Pedersen, Draguns, Lonner, & Trimble, 1989; Sue et al., 1996; Sue & Sue, 1990). Experiences based on such factors as ethnicity, social class, culture, gender, immigration status, and acculturation are acknowledged in multicultural theories to highlight the heterogeneity that occurs both between and within racial–ethnic groups. As with feminist theories, there are many different theories of multicultural practice. We choose to use the metatheory of multicultural counseling and therapy (MCT), developed by Sue et al. (1996), for our discussion to illustrate some of the similarities between feminism and multiculturalism. MCT Proposition 3 states that

> cultural identity development is a major determinant of counselor and client attitudes toward the self, others of the same group, others of a different group, and [others of] the dominant group. These attitudes, which may be manifested in affective and behavioral dimensions, are strongly influenced not only by cultural variables but also by the dynamics of dominant–subordinate relationships among culturally different groups. (Sue et al., 1996, p. 17)

The first feminist tenet, discussed earlier, reflects a similar sentiment and speaks to the centrality of cultural diversity and the role of oppression in understanding women's experiences. The importance of self-reflection for practitioners is also addressed in both perspectives. Similarly, both acknowledge the politicized nature of practice and work to bring about social transformation and heightened consciousness about issues of power and privilege.

Thus, feminism and multiculturalism have similar underlying principles that endorse the significance of race and culture in the lives of individuals. They share the belief that practitioners must attain a level of self-awareness and sufficient knowledge about their own and other cultural groups to work effectively with clients. They also give credence to lived experiences and strive to respect clients' cultural values and norms. Finally, both perspectives recognize the influence that power dimensions and dynamics have on inter-group and within-group relationships.

PARAMETERS OF THE BORDERLAND

In light of the similarities between the underlying assumptions, tenets, and principles of feminism and multiculturalism, it may be difficult to imagine how feminist practitioners find themselves facing ethical considerations during the treatment process with immigrant and refugee women of Color. How is it possible for self-aware, culturally informed, and sensitive feminist practitioners to reach a point in the treatment process where they are unsure of how to resolve conflicts encountered when their clients' cultural values and norms are very different from their own or when the approach to treatment informed by feminist principles of practice may be in conflict with the clients' wishes for a resolution to the problems they are facing? To answer this question, we need to examine some of the principles that form the foundation of feminist ethics.

According to the theory of morality proposed by Beauchamp and Childress (1983), a moral conclusion about a particular action is based on the rules at work within that cultural context that dictate which actions should (or should not) be done because they are right (or wrong). These rules reflect principles that serve as the foundation or source of justification for the decisions. Ethical theories are, in turn, developed to explain these rules and principles. All theories of feminist ethics begin with the historical and contemporary experiences and roles of women in the U.S. cultural context (Robb, 1985). Within this framework, in making ethical decisions one must take into account all of the relevant data, determine the sufficiency of the data for women's lives, and give weight to the data depending on the extent to which it affects women's lived experiences. Feminist ethics were developed from the explicitly political perspective of Western feminism and reflect a concern for the equality of women within a patriarchal system. There is diversity among feminist perspectives reflected in feminist ethical theories; however, a key factor in all of the theories is an analysis of the roots of oppression (Robb, 1985). Feminist ethicists generally agree that the appropriate starting point for ethical reflection is to attend to the concrete situations and fabric of women's lives. The oppression of women is seen as morally and politically unacceptable, and there is a commitment to the feminist agenda to eliminate the subordination of women and other oppressed people in all of its manifestations. Hence, feminist ethics involve more than recognition of women's actual experiences and moral practices; they incorporate a critique of the specific practices that constitute women's oppression (Sherwin, 1992).

In many ways, feminist ethics have been shaped by American notions of individualism and autonomy (Brabeck, 1996). The term *individualism* is defined as a social pattern generated and reflected by people who view themselves as loosely linked individuals, independent of collectives; are primarily motivated by their own preferences, needs, rights, and the contracts they established with others; give priority to their personal goals over the goals of others; and emphasize rational analyses of the advantages and disadvantages to associating with others (Triandis, 1995). This individualism leads to a certain tension between the individual and the group and supports an understanding of social obligations that protect individual rights and personal liberties.

Multiculturalists have criticized this individualistic orientation for its incompatibility to the values of most, if not all, oppressed communities of Color in the United States. Many ethnic–minority individuals, particularly those who are less acculturated, place a high value on a collectivist orientation. *Collectivism* is defined as a social pattern consisting of closely linked individuals who see themselves as part of one or more collectives (family, tribe, country); are primarily motivated by norms of, and duties imposed by, those collectives; are willing to give priority to the goals of these collectives over their own personal goals; and emphasize their connectedness to members of these collectives (Triandis, 1995). In collectivist cultures, the self is perceived as interdependent (vs. independent and autonomous), and there are culturally prescribed roles and responsibilities to others and the community.

Extensive anthropological and psychological evidence exists documenting marked culturally based differences in the views of self held among individuals from the United States as contrasted with those from most non-Western cultures (Cheng, 1990; Heelas & Lock, 1981; Markus & Kitayama, 1991; B. Miller, 1995; Shweder & Bourne, 1982; Triandis, 1989, 1995). Women, as well as men, in collectivist cultures are embedded in a web of interpersonal relationships that carry many socially prescribed duties and responsibilities that are not only structurally supported by the culture but also contribute to their identity and sense of self. When individuals from these cultures immigrate to the United States, they bring with them the values and norms of their indigenous cultures. As they continue to reside in the United States, some changes in attitude and beliefs do occur as a result of acculturation. However, the extent to which individuals adopt the prevailing U.S. values and customs differs.

One way of interpreting the impact of individualism and collectivism on the interactions and behaviors of individuals in society is expressed by Joan G. Miller (1994). She argued that the type of interpersonal moral code emphasized in the U.S. cultural context can be considered individually centered, where interpersonal commitments are viewed as matters of personal decision making and responsibilities to others are weighed against one's responsibilities to oneself. This is contrasted with the type of interpersonal moral code found in collectivist cultures where interpersonal responsibilities are mandatory and based simultaneously on one's position in the social whole and on one's nature. There are no sharp distinctions drawn between the self and the role, and emphasis is placed on interpersonal interdependence.

In cultures that adopt this latter moral code, interpersonal responsibilities are treated as matters for social regulation. Interpersonal interdependence and paternalism are usually emphasized, with attention directed to the requirements of the social whole and the processes of interdependence. Although individual happiness does not appear to be a goal per se, J. G. Miller (1994) believes that the system tends to be experienced neither as oppressing the individual nor as requiring that individual needs be subordinated to the requirements of the social order. Instead, individuals tend to view themselves as realizing their own essential natures and attaining spiritual merit through the meeting of their social role and status expectations. Miller concluded that collectivist cultures seem to maintain duty-based views of interpersonal responsibilities, as contrasted with the individually oriented views of individualist cultures such as the United States.

These differences in moral codes and expectations for interpersonal behaviors found in individualist and collectivist cultures contribute to the complexities experienced by feminist practitioners in their work with recent immigrant and refugee women of Color in the United States. This is a particularly problematic situation when the clients' cultural values and norms reflect collectivism and a rigid adherence to hierarchical gender roles. Not all women who come from such cultures totally endorse these values and norms; however, they may still find it difficult to act in ways that are in opposition to these beliefs.

For feminist practitioners, working with clients who ascribe to these cultural beliefs can become confusing when they must figure out ways to incorporate political awareness and social activism into their work with women who are being oppressed by their indigenous cultural beliefs and practices. As Elshtain (1991) wrote, "all feminisms share an explicit political urge—to reform or to remake the world in line with a deeply held conviction that women have been the victims of faulty and exploitative social institutions" (p. 128). Feminist practitioners enter the metaphorical borderland when they must decide how to act in situations where a woman's or man's adherence to cultural norms and values is jeopardizing her or his psychological or physical well-being. If a clinical decision is made to support the client's wish to adhere to her or his indigenous cultural beliefs, practitioners may feel that they are violating feminist principles by not actively addressing the oppression sanctioned within the client's culture. However, if practitioners decide to confront and challenge the client's cultural values and norms, practitioners may feel that this also constitutes a violation of feminist principles because they are not supporting the woman's values and beliefs.

We present two clinical vignettes to further illustrate the complexities involved in navigating through this borderland. In both vignettes, the client is a victim of domestic violence. This particular clinical issue was selected because we feel it is one of the most complicated situations faced by feminist practitioners working with women of Color who have immigrated from collectivist, patriarchal cultural contexts. It is also one where there is a high probability that feminist practitioners may find themselves in the borderland.

Vignette 1: M. L. N.

M. L. N. is a 35-year-old Vietnamese refugee who immigrated to the United States 3 years ago with her husband and their four children (ages 5, 7, 10, and 14 years old). The N. family left Vietnam in 1990 and lived in a refugee camp for 2 years prior to their relocation to the United States. Their flight from Vietnam and experiences in the refugee camp were characterized by extreme hardships and exposure to violence. The family was resettled in a small, Midwestern farming community where they are currently living in a low-income, ethnically diverse neighborhood.

In Vietnam, Mr. N. worked as an independent businessman and had been financially successful. Although he was not bilingual before entering the United States, he developed some English language ability over the years as a result of his business dealings with Americans. Since the family's arrival in the United States, Mr. N. has worked in a Vietnamese restaurant. He has hopes of starting his own business within the next 5 years. Mrs. N. had been a homemaker before coming to the United States. She recently sought employment to contribute to the family income and currently is working as a teacher's aide in a day care center that serves the Vietnamese community. She has begun taking English as a Second Language classes at a local church to improve her English skills.

The school guidance counselor referred the N. family for psychological services because their oldest son, L., was having difficulties in school. He was sad, angry, and not completing his schoolwork. L. was reluctant to talk with the school counselor about his behavior; the counselor felt that it would be helpful to refer the whole family to the local community mental health clinic where they could receive treatment from a counselor who was knowledgeable of Vietnamese culture.

The initial contact was only with Mr. N., who expressed his frustration with L. because of his refusal to do his schoolwork and his "disrespectful" attitude at home. Follow-up sessions were held with Mrs. N. and L. (Mr. N. was unavailable for sessions because of his work schedule). After three sessions, L. acknowledged being angry because of his father's physical abuse of his mother. Mrs. N. was subsequently seen individually by a therapist; in exploring Mrs. N.'s response to the domestic violence, the therapist discovered that Mrs. N. did not like being battered but was willing to tolerate the violence for the sake of her children and family.

Vignette 2: M. L.

M. L. is a 30-year-old Mexican woman who immigrated to the United States 5 years ago with her husband and their three children (ages 4, 7, and 12 years old). The L. family left their rural community in central Mexico in search of more economic opportunities in the United States. The family had been extremely poor when living in Mexico and hoped to find a better life for themselves. The family now lives in a low-income, predominantly Latino urban community in Houston, Texas. Mr. and Mrs. L. are illegal immigrants and must cope with a constant fear of detection. They have been able to find employment; however, both are working in jobs (gardener and domestic) that have little security. Although neither is bilingual, Mr. and Mrs. L. have limited English skills as a result of having family members, who were long-term U.S. residents, make frequent visits through the years to the extended family home in Mexico. It was this family network in the United States that assisted the couple in immigrating from Mexico.

The L. family came to the attention of the local community mental health facility because of developmental delays exhibited by the two youngest children. Both were experiencing language and learning problems in school, and there were concerns about the resources available within the home to meet the children's special needs. The entire family attended the initial sessions at the clinic; with a great deal of support and assurance from the therapist that they would not be reported to the U.S. Immigration and Naturalization Service because of their undocumented status, the family began to actively engage in the treatment process.

After approximately 4 months of treatment, Mr. L. requested a session for himself and his wife (without the children). During this session, he disclosed that they were having some difficulties that were causing him concern. He reported needing to yell at his wife often and, at times, hitting her to make her conform to his expectations. Mr. L. was not comfortable with this behavior, and he hoped that the therapist could help his wife understand his wishes better, so he would not need to hit her so often. During this interview, Mrs. L. was silent, did not maintain eye contact with the therapist, and appeared to be ashamed.

NAVIGATING THROUGH THE BORDERLAND

As we begin this section on navigating through the borderland, it is important to point out that there is no one "right" way to work through experiences in the treatment process with immigrant and refugee women of Color. Our suggestions should be taken only as a guide, with points for consideration that can be used to help feminist practitioners who are culturally different from their clients locate landmarks to help their clients move through this phase of the treatment process. We also want to reiterate that we do not support or condone violence against women, regardless of the cultural context. We suggest that putting the experience of domestic violence within a cultural context will help practitioners engage more authentically with their clients and provide a way for them to sort through complex ethical considerations.

Landmark 1: Understanding the Cultural Context

The feminist practitioner working with immigrant and refugee women of Color who adhere to traditional, patriarchal cultural values and norms must contend with two distinct realities. First, violence against women is oppressive and intolerable, regardless of a woman's cultural and social background. Second, the cultural context surrounding the violence must be understood and taken into account to determine how best to restore harmony and safety within the family. Thus, the first landmark in navigating through the borderland is for the feminist practitioner to gain a comprehensive understanding of the cultural perspectives regarding power dynamics, gender relationships, and wife battering that the couple has brought with them to the United States. In the case of Mrs. N., the practitioner would need to obtain a thorough understanding of Vietnamese cultural attitudes toward authority, submission of women, rules regarding family relationships, and the moral codes that govern behaviors (Ho, 1990; Pressman, 1994). It is also important to understand the sanctions (both formal and informal) applied in cases of wife battering and in the use of sanctuary for abused wives (Brown, 1992).

Some generalizations can be drawn from the literature about Vietnamese culture; however, it is important to keep in mind that every culture is heterogeneous and not all individuals adhere to these values and normative behaviors. Given this qualification, the literature suggests that Vietnamese culture values collectivism over individualism. The family is viewed as more important than the individual, and its needs take precedence over individual needs (Ho, 1990; Root, Ho, & Sue, 1986). The culture also supports male dominance over women. The power structure within the family is such that a high value is placed on respecting authority figures, and gender roles and relationships are clearly defined (Cervantes & Cervantes, 1993). Despite some within-culture variability among families, gender roles in Vietnamese culture are rigidly prescribed, with the wife responsible for internal family affairs and the husband responsible for negotiations and contacts with the outside world. For women, suffering and perseverance are valued virtues, with the ability to do so in silence seen as fundamental to the building of a strong character (Kim, Okamura, Ozawa, & Forrest, 1981).

In a study of ethnic differences in attitudes toward battering in four populations of Southeast Asian refugees in the United States, Ho (1990) found that both Vietnamese women and men reported more tolerance of physical violence. She also found that Vietnamese men described a more overt sense of ownership of their wives and that their domination was more overt. She cited examples of male prerogative condoned within the culture, such as intolerance of wives refusing sexual overtures and expectations that wives would tolerate their husbands' extramarital sexual activity. Wife battering is seen as a form of discipline and is thought to be justifiable because of a firm belief that the entire social fabric would unravel if such wifely behaviors as disobedience and insubordination were allowed (Ho, 1990).

The moral codes for interpersonal relationships in many collectivist cultures, such as in Vietnam, also influence society's response to domestic violence. Within these cultures, wife battering may be seen as either a personal–moral concern (where the behavior is governed by an objective obligation but not legitimately regulated) or a matter of personal choice (a behavior that is neither governed by an objective obligation nor legitimately regulated). In such societies, there is no context to support institutional involvement in domestic violence. This can result in a battered woman being ostracized by her family and community if she decides to publicly disclose the abuse. As Naresh and Surendran (1996) stated, "sadly enough, a wife can suffer through a beating, a threat, or a rape while a mother-in-law looks the other way, a sister-in-law smiles, a mother doesn't accept her daughter, or a friend chooses to ignore" (p. 3). In the case of many Southeast Asian women, Ho (1990) suggested that

> seeking outside help and leaving home would not only cause [them] to
> break away from their traditional expectations to persevere, keep peace
> and care for the home and husband under any circumstances, it also
> would cause shame and loss of face for the entire family. (p. 143)

For some women, this may prove to be a powerful deterrent to acknowledging the abuse and could inhibit active participation in efforts to ensure their safety (e.g., securing restraining orders or entering a shelter).

As with many battered women, one of the greatest issues that immigrant and refugee women of Color must overcome is denial. First-generation immigrant women may have an even harder time coming forth and seeking help because of a sense of shame, concern for the family reputation, spouse's job status, and feelings of betrayal of the family. They also typically lack information on the resources available to them in the United States. Given this situation, the batterer may be extremely convincing in shifting responsibility for the violence from himself to the victim. Divorce is still a social taboo in the Southeast Asian immigrant community and is often unthinkable for many women. On the basis of this cultural acceptance of domestic violence combined with cultural expectations and gender socialization, immigrant and refugee women may not perceive themselves as victims.

A feminist practitioner working with Mrs. L. would also need to undergo a similar process of becoming familiar with the family's indigenous culture. As with all cultural–ethnic groups, there is significant variability across families and the generalizations made in the literature pertaining to Mexican American culture do not preclude individual–family differences. Given this qualification, the literature suggests that for low-income rural and semirural Mexican immigrant families, the nuclear family is embedded in an extended family network. Both a high degree of cohesion and of hierarchical organization are normal, and patterns of interaction are characterized by generational interdependence and loyalty to the family of origin (Falicov, 1982).

Traditional views about family life and Roman Catholicism exert important influences on many Mexicans' attitudes toward marriage and divorce. Although there are some changes occurring in these views as a result of increasing urbanization, traditional gender roles continue to be prescribed as the public norm. In most traditional Mexican American marriages, there is outward compliance with the cultural ideal of male dominance and female submission. This, however, may not be the case in private. Some Mexican American families include husbands who are domineering and patriarchal in public but are submissive and dependent on their wives for major decisions or follow a more egalitarian power structure (Hawkes & Taylor, 1975; Penalosa, 1968). Couples seem to find their own balance of power and control, which may change over time or in different contexts (Falicov,

1982). Within traditional cultural beliefs, it is expected that there will be a certain formality in the relationship between spouses. For many couples, no deep intimacy or intense conflict is expected. Respect, consideration, and curtailment of anger or hostility are highly valued, and the individual is able to gain respect as a result of his or her ability to perform his or her designated role appropriately (Cervantes & Cervantes, 1993; Falicov, 1982).

When domestic violence does occur within a Mexican American immigrant family, research suggests that wives appear to be bound by a norm of "loyalty to motherhood" that contributes to their remaining silent. Mexican American women marry at a younger age, have larger families, and stay in relationships longer than Anglo and African American battered women (Gondolf, Fisher, & McFerron, 1988). Some research suggests that Mexican American women tend to be more tolerant of the abuse and to identify fewer types of behaviors as abuse. However, any generalizations about ethnic–cultural influence on domestic violence must be weighed with caution because of the existence of intra-ethnic differences based on the degree of acculturation, generation since immigration, religiosity, and available social supports (Keefe, 1982).

Another issue that practitioners should incorporate into their understanding of the cultural context surrounding immigrant and refugee families is immigration status. Research suggests that immigrant women constitute a large portion of those who are battered (Bradshaw, 1993; Mederos, 1998). The process of migration and acculturation produces a transitional crisis in the family. Cultural dislocation, language limitations, limited economic and support resources, and acculturative stress can have a negative impact on a family's functioning. During the immigration process, not only must individual family members adapt to the cultural transition, but also the family unit itself may be reconstructed. New patterns of interaction emerge, and often the rules that define roles, boundaries, and hierarchies within the family begin to shift.

There is often an accompanying concern over immigration laws, and immigrant women may be unfamiliar with the legal protections that exist for those who are battered and married to non-U.S. citizens or nonpermanent residents. Mederos (1998) noted that women of Color who are undocumented immigrants are subject to additional sources of pressure by spouses, such as threats of being deported by the U.S. Immigration and Naturalization Service if they make their plight public. These women may have more difficulty accessing resources or may be unaware of legal remedies that exist through the judicial system. They may also be more reluctant to pursue help through this system because undocumented immigrant men who batter face deportation when they are prosecuted and convicted of domestic violence.

Landmark 2: Awareness of Oppressive Forces in U.S. Cultural Context

The second landmark pertains to the importance of acknowledging the negative effect that oppressive forces in the U.S. cultural context (e.g., racism and gender–racial stereotyping) have on people of Color (Ridley, 1995; Sue & Sue, 1990; Tyler, Brome, & Williams, 1991). Feminist practitioners must remain mindful of these conditions and incorporate this awareness into their understanding of the clients' lived experiences. For example, Asian American women are subjected to conflicting gender stereotypes that characterize them as exotic, shy, submissive, demure, erotic, and eager to please, on the one hand, or wily, manipulative, inscrutable, and untrustworthy, on the other hand (Bradshaw, 1993). Women of Color are damaged by such images because they obscure individuality, can prevent the expression of aspirations and dreams, and interfere with opportunities for self-actualization.

At initial contact with outside authority figures, many immigrant and refugee women may appear to be accepting of abusive situations and may be reluctant to disclose and use self-protective measures to control the violence. Mederos (1998) suggested that

> advocates need to understand that battered women of color are not more passive or more paralyzed by cultural prescriptions (than are Anglo battered women). Instead, they may be actively protecting their family and their community from outsiders who do not share their values. (p. 4)

Feminist practitioners must remember that despite their efforts to avoid establishing hierarchical relationships with clients, they may be initially seen as "outside, authority figures" by immigrant and refugee women of Color. When this occurs, it requires a conscious awareness of the power dynamics inherent in the therapeutic dyad and careful attention to the establishment of trust.

Landmark 3: Enhancing Self-Awareness

The third landmark to consider when navigating through the borderland is self-awareness. Akamatsu (1998) wrote that all therapists, regardless of their racial–ethnic heritage, "must view themselves as cultured, ethnic, racial beings and move beyond a one-sided description of 'them' and toward a recursive dialogue, in which one's own culture and professional assumptions are also called into self-awareness and questioned" (p. 134). It is important for feminist practitioners to critically assess their own values and beliefs about the roles of women in society and within the family, the ways in which power should be handled in marital relationships, and the power dynamics that exist within the therapeutic dyad. Much has been written in the multicultural literature about the importance of developing self-awareness when working with clients whose cultural experiences are different from one's own (e.g., see Pedersen, 1997; and Sue, Arrendondo, & McDavis, 1992). Feminist practitioners can use this information to enhance their own self-awareness.

Feminist practitioners should also remain aware of the possibility that there can be tension between a family's cultural values and norms and feminist principles of practice. Friedman's (1995) conceptualization of relational positionalities highlights the need for practitioners to be consciously aware of their own values, norms, and positionality vis-à-vis the client. For example, a European American therapist working with a refugee client like Mrs. N. faces a complex interplay of how American Vietnamese political, economic, and social relations over time are reflected in the dynamics of the treatment relationship. An awareness of the altering positionalities that occur with regard to such issues as race, gender, third-world versus first-world status, and the like would certainly need to be addressed, as would dominant–subordinate dynamics that can be present (even if not discussed or acknowledged) within the therapeutic dyad. Maintaining such an awareness will assist feminist practitioners in finding ways of intervening that are respectful and sensitive to the client's cultural values and norms. As Cervantes and Cervantes (1993) suggested,

> feminism, both as a political movement and as a theoretical orientation, has advocated for the equality of the sexes, which is often in direct conflict with cultural values. . . . Multiculturalism advocates respect for patterns of behavior and consciousness within cultural diversity. Feminism honors the integrity and freedom of the woman regarding free choice, equal opportunity and equal distribution of power in relationships. The essence of preventing domestic violence must involve both perspectives in the assessment, treating and healing processes. (pp. 164, 168)

Landmark 4: Flexibility in Determining Solutions

Throughout our discussion, we focused on the aspects of culture that condone male dominance and that give permission for men to be violent and for women to tolerate such violence. However, as Mederos (1998) pointed out, "the reality is that all cultures have elements—values and traditions—that are protective against the use of violence and that offenders can use to shape a nonabusive identity" (p. 6). As one considers ways to help battered women who have immigrated from cultures that condone the subordination of women, one must keep in mind that not all women from these cultures accept being beaten. Many struggle to find ways to fight back and to resist the silencing forces of others' reactions to the violence as well as their own guilt and shame (Lykes, Brabeck, Ferns, & Radan, 1993). Research of women living in their indigenous cultures suggests that some women find personal strength through sustaining relationships with ancestors and in their own spirituality (Ofei-Aboagye, 1994). Other women challenge male authority and demand a voice in such domestic affairs as choosing a mate or deciding how to distribute family resources. These women fight back when they perceive that they are being treated unfairly and are willing to risk ill treatment in their efforts to maintain control over their lives (Counts, 1992).

Similar to the Women's Movement in the United States, activists in many parts of the world are challenging cultural traditions that subordinate women and are working to end domestic violence and other culturally sanctioned practices (e.g., female circumcision) that subject women to extreme forms of victimization and abuse. This work is done in ways that reflect an understanding of the cultural influences on gender identity, interpersonal relationships, morality, and gender roles. Feminist practitioners in the United States can learn from this work and should be able to adapt some of the perspectives and approaches of these feminist activists to their own work with immigrant and refugee women. However, we must remember that within the U.S. cultural context, immigrant and refugee women of Color are not only influenced by the cultural values and traditions from their indigenous cultures but also negatively affected by acculturative stress and oppressive forces within the U.S. context.

Another point for consideration is that feminist practitioners should try to remain flexible about the remedies they offer to women. Ho (1990) suggested that for Asian American battered women, therapists could consider asking older people in their community to provide support for these women and to act as respected, hierarchical figures that reinforce an end to the violence. She also suggested using the guilt and shame that comes from public exposure to help inhibit future abuse. Bradshaw (1993) made a similar suggestion by highlighting the use of community, family, and social pressures to aid the intervention process. Cervantes and Cervantes (1993) suggested reinforcing cultural skills that may impede domestic violence, such as attempting to reestablish the respect between couples, which is a valued cultural norm for Mexican American (and other Latino) families. Mederos (1998) called attention to the need for changes in the way in which services are provided for immigrant and refugee women. He noted that the restraining orders and shelters that are the essential protective options for battered women in the United States may not meet the needs for immigrant and refugee women of Color. He suggested establishing forms of probation that monitor men who stay with their families or who have contact with their families following violent incidents. These are only a few examples from the literature to illustrate the ways in which services can be adapted to be more responsive to a woman's cultural context. As feminist practitioners navigate through the borderland, maintaining a commitment to such flexibility will enhance treatment planning.

CONCLUSION

The incorporation of multicultural principles into feminist practice has become the expected standard of care; as feminist practitioners accept this challenge, there may be times when they are called on to reexamine some of their principles in an effort to determine the most appropriate course of action. At these times, the treatment direction may not be clearly defined, and it will be necessary for practitioners to undergo an ethical reasoning process to maintain mutuality within the therapeutic dyad. In this chapter, we identified four issues, which we called landmarks, that can help guide practitioners through this process. It is our hope that the description of the borderland and the suggested guide will contribute to the continuing discourse on the integration of multiculturalism and feminism, particularly as it relates to psychotherapy with first-generation immigrant and refugee women of Color.

REFERENCES

Akamatsu, N. (1998). The talking oppression blues: Including the experience of power/powerlessness in the teaching of cultural sensitivity. In M. McGoldrick (Ed.), *Revisioning family therapy: Race, culture, and gender in clinical practice* (pp. 129–143). New York: Guilford Press.

Beauchamp, T. L., & Childress, J. F. (1983). *Principles of biomedical ethics* (2nd ed.). New York: Oxford University Press.

Brabeck, M. (1996). The moral self, values, and circles of belonging. In K. F. Wyche & F. J. Crosby (Eds.), *Women's ethnicities: Journeys through psychology* (pp. 145–165). Boulder, CO: Westview Press.

Brabeck, M., & Ting, K. (1997, February). *The challenge of feminist ethics for feminist research.* Paper presented at the Midwinter Conference of APA Division 35, Seattle, WA.

Bradshaw, C. K. (1993). Asian and Asian-American women: Historical and political considerations in psychotherapy. In L. Comas-Diaz & B. Greene (Eds.), *Women of Color: Integrating ethnic and gender identities in psychotherapy* (pp. 72–113). New York: Guilford Press.

Brown, J. (1992). Introduction: Definitions, assumptions, themes and issues. In D. A. Counts, J. K. Brown, & J. C. Campbell (Eds.), *Sanctions and sanctuary:*

Cultural perspectives on the beating of wives (pp. 1–18). Boulder, CO: Westview Press.

Cervantes, N. N., & Cervantes, J. M. (1993). A multicultural perspective in the treatment of domestic violence. In M. Hansen & M. Harway (Eds.), *Battering and family therapy: A feminist perspective* (pp. 156–174). Newbury Park, CA: Sage.

Cheng, S. K. (1990). Understanding the culture and behavior of East Asians— A Confucian perspective. *Australian and New Zealand Journal of Psychiatry*, 24, 510–515.

Chesler, P. (1972). *Women and madness*. New York: Doubleday.

Chin, J. L. (Ed.). (1994). *Proceedings of the National Conference on Education and Training in Feminist Practice*. Washington, DC: American Psychological Association, Office of Women's Affairs.

Chodorow, N. (1978). *The reproduction of mothering: Psychoanalysis and the sociology of gender*. Berkeley: University of California Press.

Counts, D. A. (1992). All men do it: Wife-beating in Kaliai, Papua New Guinea. In D. A. Counts, J. K. Brown, & J. C. Campbell (Eds.), *Sanctions and sanctuary: Cultural perspectives on the beating of wives* (pp. 63–76). Boulder, CO: Westview Press.

Elshtain, J. B. (1991). Ethics in the Women's Movement. *Annuals of the American Academy, 515*, 126–139.

Espin, O. M., & Gawalek, M. A. (1992). Women's diversity: Ethnicity, race, class, and gender in theories of feminist psychology. In L. S. Brown & M. Ballou (Eds.), *Personality and psychopathology: Feminist reappraisals* (pp. 88–107). New York: Guilford Press.

Falicov, C. J. (1982). Mexican families. In M. McGoldrick, J. K. Pearce, & J. Giordano (Eds.), *Ethnicity and family therapy* (pp. 134–163). New York: Guilford Press.

Friedman, S. S. (1995). Beyond White and other: Relationality and narratives of race in feminist discourse. *Signs: Journal of Women in Culture and Society*, 21(1), 1–49.

Gondolf, E. W., Fisher, E., & McFerron, R. (1988). Racial differences among shelter residents: A comparison of Anglo, Black and Hispanic battered. *Journal of Family Violence, 3*, 39–51.

Hawkes, G., & Taylor, M. (1975). Power structure in Mexican and Mexican American farm labor families. *Journal of Marriage and the Family, 31*, 807–811.

Heelas, P., & Lock, A. (1981). *Indigenous psychologies: The anthropology of the self*. London: Academic Press.

Ho, C. K. (1990). An analysis of domestic violence in Asian American communities: A multicultural approach to counseling. In L. S. Brown & M. P. Root (Eds.), *Diversity and complexity in feminist therapy* (pp. 129–150). New York: Haworth Press.

hooks, b. (1981). *Ain't I a woman: Black women and feminism*. Boston: South End Press.

Keefe, S. (1982). Help-seeking behavior among foreign-born and native-born Mexican Americans. *Social Science and Medicine, 16,* 1467–1472.

Kim, B. C., Okamura, A. I., Ozawa, N., & Forrest, V. (1981). *Women in shadows*. LaJolla, CA: National Committee Concerned With Asian Wives of U.S. Servicemen.

King, D. K. (1989). Multiple jeopardy, multiple consciousness: The context of a Black feminist ideology. In M. R. Malson, J. F. O'Barr, S. Westphal-Wihl, & M. Wyer (Eds.), *Feminist theory in practice and process* (pp. 75–105). Chicago: University of Chicago Press.

Lorde, A. (1984). *Sister outsider: Essays and speeches*. Oakland, CA: Crossing Press.

Lykes, M. B., Brabeck, M. M., Ferns, T., & Radan, A. (1993). Human rights and mental health among Latin American women in situations of state-sponsored violence. *Psychology of Women Quarterly, 17,* 525–544.

Markus, H., & Kitayama, S. (1991). Culture and the self: Implications for cognition, emotion, and motivation. *Psychological Review, 98,* 224–253.

Mederos, F. (1998). *Domestic violence and culture: Moving toward more sophisticated encounters*. Unpublished manuscript, Boston, MA.

Miller, B. (1995). Cultural psychology: Bridging disciplinary boundaries in understanding the cultural grounding of self. In P. K. Bock (Ed.), *Handbook of psychological anthropology* (pp. 85–102). Westport, CT: Greenwood.

Miller, J. B. (1976). *Toward a new psychology of women*. Boston: Beacon Press.

Miller, J. G. (1994). Cultural diversity in the morality of caring: Individually oriented versus duty-based interpersonal moral codes. *Cross-Cultural Research, 28*(1), 3–39.

Naresh, H., & Surendran, A. (1996). *Silence: Domestic violence* [Poem]. Retrieved March 5, 1999 from the World Wide Web: http://www.columbia.edu/cu/zamana/sangarn/fall96/Silence.html

Ofei-Aboagye, R. O. (1994). Altering the strands of the fabric: A preliminary look at domestic violence in Ghana. *Signs, 19*(4), 924–938.

Pedersen, P. B. (1997). *Culture-centered counseling interventions: Striving for accuracy*. Thousand Oaks, CA: Sage.

Pedersen, P. B., Draguns, J. G., Lonner, W. J., & Trimble, J. E. (Eds.). (1989). *Counseling across cultures* (3rd ed.). Honolulu: University of Hawaii Press.

Pellauer, M. D. (1985). Moral callousness and moral sensitivity: Violence against women. In B. H. Andolsen, C. E. Gudorf, & M. D. Pellauer (Eds.), *Women's consciousness, women's conscience: A reader in feminist ethics* (pp. 33–50). New York: Winston Press.

Penalosa, P. (1968). Mexican family roles. *Journal of Marriage and the Family, 30,* 680–689.

Pressman, B. (1994). Violence against women: Ramifications of gender, class, and race inequality. In M. P. Mirkin (Ed.), *Women in context: Toward a feminist reconstruction of psychotherapy* (pp. 352–389). New York: Guilford Press.

Ramirez, M., III. (1983). *Psychology of the Americas*. New York: Pergamon.

Ridley, C. R. (1995). *Overcoming unintentional racism in counseling and therapy*. Thousand Oaks, CA: Sage.

Robb, C. S. (1985). A framework for feminist ethics. In B. H. Andolsen, C. E. Gudorf, & M. D. Pellauer (Eds.), *Women's consciousness, women's conscience: A reader in feminist ethics* (pp. 211–234). New York: Winston Press.

Root, M. P., Ho, C. K., & Sue, S. (1986). Issues in the training of counselors for Asian Americans. In H. P. Letley & P. B. Pedersen (Eds.), *Cross-cultural training for mental health professionals* (pp. 199–209). Springfield, IL: Charles C Thomas.

Sampson, E. E. (1993). *Celebrating the other: A dialogic account of human nature*. Boulder, CO: Westview Press.

Sherwin, S. (1992). *No longer patient: Feminist ethics and health care*. Philadelphia, PA: Temple University Press.

Shweder, R. A., & Bourne, E. J. (1982). Does the concept of the person vary cross-culturally? In A. J. Marsella & G. M. White (Eds.), *Cultural conceptions of mental health and therapy* (pp. 97–137). London: Reidel.

Spelman, E. (1988). *Inessential woman: Problems of exclusion in feminist thought*. Boston: Beacon Press.

Sue, D. W., Arrendondo, P., & McDavis, R. J. (1992). Multicultural competencies/standards: A pressing need. *Journal of Counseling and Development, 70*(4), 477–486.

Sue, D. W., Ivey, A. E., & Pedersen, P. B. (1996). *A theory of multicultural counseling and therapy*. Boston: Brooks/Cole.

Sue, D. W., & Sue, D. (1990). *Counseling the culturally different: Theory and practice*. New York: Wiley.

Triandis, H. C. (1989). The self and social behavior in differing cultural contexts. *Psychological Review, 96*, 508–520.

Triandis, H. C. (1995). *Individualism and collectivism*. Boulder, CO: Westview Press.

Tyler, F. B., Brome, D. R., & Williams, J. E. (1991). *Ethnic validity, ecology, and psychotherapy: A psychosocial competence model*. New York: Plenum Press.

Worell, J., & Johnson, N. G. (Eds.). (1997). *Shaping the future of feminist psychology: Education, research, and practice*. Washington, DC: American Psychological Association.

11

HATE SPEECH OR FREEDOM OF EXPRESSION? BALANCING AUTONOMY AND FEMINIST ETHICS IN A PLURALISTIC SOCIETY

MELBA J. T. VASQUEZ AND CYNTHIA DE LAS FUENTES

Psychology has a heritage of promoting social responsibility. The Ethical Principles of Psychologists and Code of Conduct of the American Psychological Association (APA, 1992) state, in part, that psychologists "apply and make public their knowledge of psychology in order to contribute to human welfare . . . to mitigate the causes of human suffering" (p. 1600). The Ethics Code further tells psychologists, ourselves included, that they should "encourage the development of law and social policy that serve the interests of their patients and clients and the public" (p. 1600).

As leaders in promoting social responsibility within the profession of psychology and in society in general, feminist psychologists have long been concerned with advocating for oppressed groups. For example, Brabeck and Brown (1997) described how feminist practice focuses on the development of strategies and interventions to deal with the practical and political problems, such as marginalization, discrimination, and violence, which women and other oppressed groups face. Indeed, these authors identified the development of a feminist consciousness in support of social and political transformation as central to feminist practice (Brabeck & Ting, chap. 1, this volume).

225

In this chapter, we examine hate speech and verbal violence from the perspectives of feminist and psychological ethics. Our goal is to acknowledge the value of autonomy and free speech in this society, while providing a feminist conceptual rationale for developing codes and other strategies to prohibit and discourage hate speech. We address the impact of hate speech and verbal violence, describe the prevalence and future predictions of hate speech and hate crimes, and explore the feminist dilemma and paradox of balancing freedom of speech with the need for strategies to prohibit hate speech, both from ethical and legal perspectives. Paradigms for ethical decision making, including conceptions from Kitchener's (1984) theory of ethical decision making and Meara, Schmidt, and Day's (1996) virtue ethics in decision making, are applied to increase understanding and the capacity for decision making for the dilemma of balancing freedom of speech with protections against harm in an increasingly pluralistic society.

IMPACT OF HATE SPEECH AND VERBAL VIOLENCE

Hate speech is defined, for our purposes, as offensive verbal statements that communicate loathing, dislike, and animosity directed toward someone solely on the basis of the attacker's perception of the victim's group affiliation. For example, ethnic and racial minorities, Jews, lesbians and gay men, and women have typically been targets of hate speech.

Hate Speech and Physical Violence

One of the consequences of hate speech, or "hate talk" as some refer to the behavior, is violence, such as that tracked by the Southern Poverty Law Center, an organization that combats hate, intolerance, and discrimination. White supremacist movements and other "hate groups" use the Internet, radio talk shows, and newsletters to promote their philosophies, which sometimes lead to violence on the part of their listeners. Hate speech, which can be proven to result in behavioral violence, has been successfully fought in the courts. For example, the Southern Poverty Law Center has won judgments against such hate groups as the Christian Knights of the Ku Klux Klan. Its state leader, Horace King, South Carolina's Grand Dragon, and four other Klansmen were tried for promoting the burning of Black churches. The defense spoke of Horace King as an old man merely exercising his right to free speech. But jurors determined that he was a "hate monger" whose words led to the destruction of Black churches (Southern Poverty Law Center, 1998a, p. 2).

Across the country, concern over the potential solicitation of murder motivated a federal civil suit by Planned Parenthood and several doctors in Portland, Oregon, against militant abortion opponents for their website, which simulated blood dripping from fetus parts. The website listed the names of dozens of doctors and clinic workers around the country who provide abortions. The information included photographs, home addresses, license plate numbers, and the names of the doctors' spouses and children. The site also listed doctors who had been fatally shot with a line drawn through their names and showed wounded doctors' names in gray (Verhovek, 1999). The defendants cited free speech and argued that most of the information could be found in telephone directories. However, Judge Robert E. Jones of the U.S. District Court turned down requests to dismiss the case outright, in effect ruling that the website was not automatically protected free speech. The federal jury in Portland, Oregon, ruled that in the context of nationwide violence against abortion doctors and clinics, the lists were illegal threats of violence against the doctors and clinic operators who had sued. The jury ordered the antiabortion activists to pay $107 million in damages for their roles in launching and promoting wanted-style posters and the Nuremberg Files listings. The Atlanta-based Internet service provider, MindSpring Enterprises, stopped service to Neil Horsley and his Christian Gallery site that included the listings (McMahon, 1999).

Emotional Impact of Hate Speech

Hate speech can also be debasing and offensive to members of oppressed groups. This verbal violence may have a negative impact on identity development and the well-being of individual members of these oppressed groups (Daniel, 1994; Sanchez & Vasquez Nuttall, 1995) and may result in the victims experiencing various effects of trauma and the psychological sequelae associated with such experiences (Root, 1992). Various universities have enacted faculty and student speech codes over the last 2 decades because of concern about the effects of offensive and harassing speech. Such codes have always been controversial and have more recently been under attack (Zuckoff, 1998). The dilemma is the difficulty in determining the difference between irritating speech protected by the First Amendment and atrocious speech, for example, where a faculty member makes the environment hostile because of a student's race, color, gender, sexual orientation, and so forth. At the University of Wisconsin, some questions centered on whether a farm science professor should be punished for using a *Playboy* centerfold to illustrate different cuts of meat or whether a history professor could use a racial epithet when describing the slave trade.

The impact of hate speech and other forms of racism, sexism, ageism, and homophobia has not been consistently conceptualized as traumatic. Daniel (1994) challenged the exclusion of racism and political, cultural, and economic oppression as psychological trauma in Judith Lewis Herman's

(1992) classic *Trauma and Recovery*. Daniel suggested that race and ethnicity are highly associated with the existence of trauma in the lives of people of Color; she expressed alarm that a classic book on trauma would ignore the existence of such a large segment of the U.S. population. Exposure to experiences and events that threaten psychological safety for people of Color can result in what Wyatt (1989) named the "terrorism of racism," which sometimes causes debilitating emotional effects through continuous exposure to injustices.

Root (1992) provided a feminist reconstruction of trauma theory and suggested three categories of traumatic impact: direct, indirect, and insidious. Direct traumas include natural disasters, certain forms of maliciously perpetrated violence, war experiences, sexual abuse, emotional abuse, and other forms of interpersonal violence. Examples of direct trauma include destruction of cultural communities, for example, the internment of Japanese Americans and removal of Native Americans and Native Hawaiians from their homelands (Root, 1992). Indirect trauma includes being vicariously traumatized by the witnessing or learning of the trauma sustained by another with whom one identifies in some significant way.

Root (1992) suggested that women might be more likely than men to experience indirect trauma during the course of a lifetime. Because of women's less privileged position in U.S. society, they are mutually interdependent with others and are more likely to feel threatened or even wounded when someone with whom they feel connected is hurt. Others (e.g., McGrath, Keita, Strickland, & Russo, 1990) have noted that victimization and trauma in interpersonal relationships are listed as major risk factors related to the incidence of depression in women. Women experience depression at twice the rate men do. The gender difference in depression rates holds for White, Black, and Hispanic women and persists when income level, education, and occupation are controlled (McGrath et al., 1990).

According to Root (1992), hate crimes are increasingly directed toward racial and ethnic minorities, gay men, and lesbians. Exposure to acts of verbal violence increases these groups' vulnerability to indirect trauma. As Root (1992) explained, insidious trauma is an experience of trauma usually associated

> with the social status of an individual being devalued because a characteristic intrinsic to their identity is different from what is valued by those in power, for example, gender, color, sexual orientation, physical ability. As a result, it is often present throughout a lifetime and may start at birth. (p. 240)

The impact of insidious trauma shapes a worldview rather than shatters assumptions about the world; over time, it may result in a picture of symptomatology similar to that of direct or indirect trauma, including anxiety, depression, paranoia or heightened sensitivity, irritability, anger or hostility, and substance abuse (Root, 1992).

Preliminary results of the most comprehensive research project on middle age indicate that discrimination may not necessarily affect success but may affect mental health (Azar, 1996, p. 26). The MacArthur Foundation Research Network on Successful Middle Age Development started an interdisciplinary research project to identify the major biomedical, psychological, and social factors that permit some people to become fit, psychologically healthy, and socially responsible adults. One third of the respondents in a comprehensive survey, which included a nationally representative sample of 7,240 men and women ages 25 to 74, indicated that they had been discriminated against at least once because of their race, ethnicity, gender, age, or physical appearance. The most common basis for discrimination was gender; women reported many more discriminatory experiences than did men. Race was the next most common reason for discrimination, followed by age and weight. Most respondents reported that whereas they might have had to work harder for their success than others, they felt that they had accomplished just as much as they would have otherwise. However, people who reported discrimination experienced much higher rates of anxiety and depression.

In summary, hate speech, which is often a form of racism, sexism, homophobia, ageism, anti-Semitism, classism, or other forms of oppression, is experienced as difficult and traumatic and may result in various symptoms, such as anxiety and depression. Hate speech, which many believe has dramatically increased in recent times (Root, 1992; Rowan, 1996; Southern Poverty Law Center, 1998a, 1998b), is a form of oppression that can be experienced as trauma (direct, indirect, or insidious) by members of targeted groups. The impact of insidious trauma, with its ensuing symptoms, affects an individual's capacity to cope and destroys feelings of safety and security. Even resilient survivors can be permanently affected in their ability to trust and must expend energy to deal with intermittent anxiety and depression, among other difficulties.

PREVALENCE AND FUTURE PREDICTIONS OF HATE SPEECH AND HATE CRIMES

The future of the United States will be shaped in part by the nation's increasing racial, ethnic, and cultural diversity and by society's response to that increasing diversity. In 1995, people of Color constituted 26.4% of the nation's population. Soon after the Year 2050, this group is predicted to approach the majority of the United States. More specifically, the U.S. Bureau of the Census (1995) reported that in 1995, the U.S. population by race and ethnicity was as follows: Blacks, 12.0%; Hispanics, 10.2%; Asian Americans, 3.5%; American Indians, 0.7%; and Whites, 73.6%. In the Year 2050, the U.S. population by race and ethnicity is predicted to be as follows: Hispanics, 22.5%; Blacks, 14.4%; Asian Americans, 9.7%; American Indians, 0.9%; and Whites, 52.5% (U.S. Bureau of the Census, 1995, Table 19).

Changing demographics challenge the identity of a society. In society, the concepts of *group identity, oppression,* and *empowerment* of oppressed groups, such as people of Color, women, gay men and lesbians, and people with disabilities, have in the last 3 decades altered the consciousness of the United States by directing attention to the ways in which policies and practices have discriminated against groups in the workplace, public schools, and communities (Trickett, Watts, & Birman, 1994). In society and psychology, the challenge of diversity is to develop ways of thinking that can illuminate the notion of diversity as a positive phenomenon. However, it is difficult to do so if the issues have been perceived and dealt with in part by fear, guilt, and obligation as well as by political, legal, and social pressures and a sense of fairness and equity. Mixed motives to affirm diversity mean that struggles will prevail for scarce resources, conflicts over perceived access to education and jobs will persist, and competition for whose values will prevail in one's society or community will continue (Sue, 1994; Trickett et al., 1994).

Evidence shows that increased human diversity may increase political polarization. Personal and cultural values are challenged by diversity. Violence, prejudice, and discrimination based on diversity are common in all parts of the world (Sue, 1994). Rowan (1996), a well-known political commentator, believes that in the United States, there is a rise in hate crimes, including hate speech. He pointed to the burning of Black churches, Black Muslims preaching against Jews, and Neo-Nazis in the U.S. military as evidence of an approaching crisis. There is also evidence that U.S. society is, at best, compassion weary, tired of attempting to address the complexities involved in seeking gender and ethnic minority parity and equality. Passage of Proposition 209 in California in November 1996, which dismantled the state's Affirmative Action plan, and the anti-immigration laws passed at the national level in 1996 are evidence of lowered commitment to supporting strategies to promote equity and possibly evidence of rising tensions in society.

There is also disturbing evidence of a backlash against the minimal progress that women have made at work, in politics, and in their own minds. Faludi (1991) suggested that the antifeminist backlash has been set off by women's small advances rather than their achievement of full equality. She suggested that leaders of backlash movements use the fear of change as a threat before major change has occurred to create a backlash. Rowan (1996) similarly challenged leaders in academia, media, and government who intentionally or unintentionally fan the flames of racial and ethnic hatred. He suggested that the signs of a coming race war are everywhere.

A Federal Bureau of Investigation (FBI) report, summarized through the Associated Press by Sniffen (1996), indicates that more than three out of every five hate crimes reported in 1995 were motivated by race or ethnicity. Race was the motivation in 60.8% of 7,947 hate crimes reported for 1995, and 61.9% of race motives were directed at Blacks. Religious bias was the second most frequent motivation (16.1%), with Jews the most frequent target (82.9% of 1,058 instances). Sexual orientation motivated 12.8% of the total crimes (1,019 instances). Ethnicity and national origin motivated 10.2% of the total (814 crimes), and Hispanics were targets of 63.4% of these crimes. Intimidation was the most frequently reported hate crime, accounting for 41.0% of the total. Destruction and vandalism of property accounted for 23.0% of the offenses, assault for 18.0%, and aggravated assault 13.0%. In 1994, the FBI reported a total of 5,852 hate crimes, but statistics from 1995 cannot be compared with the previous year's totals because the number of voluntary reports from police agencies have grown substantially from 7,200 agencies serving 58% of the U.S. population to 9,500 police agencies serving 75% of the U.S. population.

ETIOLOGY OF HATE SPEECH AND OTHER FORMS OF INJUSTICE: MORAL EXCLUSION

Social psychologists often attempt to investigate the complexities of human behavior, including those behaviors that are harmful and exploitative (Staub, 1989). Opotow (1990), for example, suggested that moral exclusion provides an explanation for the ability of human beings to harm or exploit others, from forms of discrimination to genocide.

> Moral exclusion occurs when individuals or groups are perceived as outside the boundary in which moral values, rules, and considerations of fairness apply. Those who are morally excluded are perceived as nonentities, expendable, or undeserving. Consequently, harming or exploiting them appears to be appropriate, acceptable, or just. (Opotow, 1990, p. 1)

One's personal position on various social issues (immigration policies, abortion, civil rights for lesbians and gay men, affirmative action) depends on whom one includes or excludes from one's moral boundaries. Social order, conflict, and unconnectedness are all factors identified by Opotow (1990) as evidence of moral exclusion. Contemporary society appears to be increasing its moral exclusion. Hate speech is likely one of the behavioral consequences of that process.

THE DILEMMA

In a discussion of paradoxes inherent to feminist theory building, Brabeck and Brown (1997) talked about the fact that whereas feminist theory empowers individuals, it is not without evaluation, discrimination, or judgment. It embraces diversity but is not relativistic. The relativistic view that all opinions are of equal merit would not allow the judgment that torture, rape, hate speech, or other gross acts that harm individuals are always wrong, regardless of context. One of the examples that Brabeck and Brown (1997) provided is particularly relevant. That is, feminist theory tries to break the silencing of women's voices but, at other times, advocates silencing some voices to privilege the marginalized or to prevent damage to someone. Thus, feminist theory establishes moral standards "by which we authorize some voices and privilege some experiences and knowledge claims" (Brabeck & Brown, 1997, p. 22).

One of the goals of feminist practice is the social transformation toward the development of feminist consciousness (Brabeck & Brown, 1997), which is based on Lerner's (1993) definition of feminist consciousness:

> the awareness of women that they belong to a subordinate group; that they have suffered wrongs as a group; that their condition of subordination is not natural, but is societally determined; that they must join with other women to remedy these wrongs; and finally, that they must and can provide an alternate vision of societal organization in which women as well as men will enjoy autonomy and self-determination. (p. 14)

This feminist consciousness is inherent to the position that speech codes and other strategies to manage hate speech are important to develop and maintain. Knowing that the second-class position of women and other groups is societally determined and that hate speech is partly an expression of that second-class determination would lead one to manage atrocious speech, which makes environments hostile for those groups. The value of developing rules, standards, and codes that monitor hate speech are reflective of a community's moral sentiment and consciousness of the wrongness of subordination of any group. Feminist consciousness provides the argument to those who propose that speech codes violate free speech and create a hostile environment for White men. That is, the destruction that results from hate speech is partly based on the fact that it is directed toward groups that have been treated in a subordinate position in society to begin with. White men with middle- and upper-class backgrounds are members of the privileged group in U.S. society. Feminists attend to hierarchies of power and dominance. As such, hate speech is a behavioral extension of oppressive power and dominance.

Barbara Jordan—an orator, former congressional representative, and an advocate of ethical behavior and justice—taught political ethics and values at the University of Texas at Austin for 15 years before she died in January 1996. She was a strong proponent of the individual development of principles and ethical standards, which she believed led to maximizing hope and fostering a sense of community. She believed that individuals in society had a responsibility and imperative to define what is right and to do it (Boyd, 1994). However, defining what is right is often the biggest challenge of that imperative. Policy making and decision making in the arena of balancing hate speech with the freedom of expression is an ongoing problem for those in positions to make such decisions. Hate speech poses both legal and ethical dilemmas and raises particular issues for feminist psychologists. Although feminist theory advocates the empowerment and expression of women's voices, the theory also advocates silencing some voices to equalize power, privilege marginalized people, or prevent damage to someone.

THE DILEMMA FROM A LEGAL PERSPECTIVE

Public policy and legal dilemmas arise when ordinances in communities and codes of conducts in universities are developed. Typically, the First Amendment of the U.S. Constitution, which guarantees freedom of expression as long as it does not violate the rights of others, is used to argue against proposed ordinances or policies aimed at limiting hate speech (Jones, 1994). The 14th Amendment, which guarantees equal protection under the law regardless of race, is often the basis for various civil rights initiatives, such as the prohibition of hate speech and other hate crimes. The obvious legal and ethical conflicts that emerge when protecting oppressed groups against various forms of demeaning and verbally violent forms of expression are interpreted as impinging on an individual's right to freedom of expression under the First Amendment.

Feminists and multiculturalists who renounce hate speech are not advocates of censorship; they are working toward the elimination of those attitudes, beliefs, and behaviors designed to buttress the oppression, marginalization, and disempowerment of traditionally disenfranchised groups of people. Parallel arguments have been made in regard to attempts to pass antipornography ordinances in communities. In an interview and discussion about censorship in regard to pornography, Dworkin, French, Ramos, and Shange (1994) described how "in legal terms censorship has always meant prior restraint: you pass a law that stops something from being made or being done" (p. 37). An antipornography ordinance, however, "is a civil law that allows somebody to bring a lawsuit after they've been injured on very specific grounds" (p. 37). Thus, they argued that definitions of civil rights must be expanded to include the concept of *prior restraint* aimed at protecting the well-being of all individuals.

How can controls related to hate speech and racial harassment be established without inhibiting the free expression of thoughts, ideas, and opinions? The Forum, a section of the journal *Ethics & Behavior,* at times presents fictionalized case vignettes that embody complex ethical dilemmas with professional or public policy overtones (Jones, 1994; Laird, 1994; von Hippel, 1994). A case vignette was presented of a university student who yelled apparent racial slurs at a group of African American women students because he was angry about the noise they were making while he was trying to study. Various respondents to the case vignette offered comments, illustrating the legal issues affecting hate speech policies.

Proponents of campus policies governing racial harassment, such as hate speech, have argued that codes of conduct are necessary to provide students with a proper educational environment and to protect those students' constitutional guarantees (Laird, 1994). Laird noted that the arguments to provide a nonhostile environment for students to live and study comes partly from universities' attempts to guarantee equal educational opportunities under the contractual obligation from *Brown v. Board of Education.* However, Laird reviewed several judicial cases that challenged campus policies covering racial harassment, citing *John Doe v. University of Michigan* (1989) in which the jury struck down a state policy covering racial harassment as being "too broad, too vague, and a violation of the First Amendment protection of free speech" (p. 391). This *Doe* case also stated that the university had "the right to regulate the reasonable time, place and manner of their educational procedures" (p. 391).

That decision has led colleges and universities to draft what they deem to be narrower, more specific policies, despite the fact that such regulations may not restrict hate speech. In *Stacy v. Williams* (1969), the court clearly indicated that colleges "cannot restrict speech simply because they find the views expressed by any group to be 'abhorrent'" (Laird, 1994, p. 392). In *Sweezy v. New Hampshire* (1957), the court affirmed school faculties' rights to hold and voice unpopular opinions, arguing that universities should be a place where students and professors pursue ideas free from watchful eyes of paternalistic administrators. Laird's summary suggests that court rulings seem to be in agreement that universities have the authority to control student conduct, particularly toward the goal of providing an environment conducive to education, but the court seems ready to reject arguments that university students need further regulation of speech.

Jones (1994) argued that the First Amendment right is not absolute. He provided examples of speech that are not protected by the First Amendment, including speech that disseminates an official secret, defames or libels someone, is obscene, creates a hostile workplace, is "patently offensive" and directed at a captive audience, is "fighting words," violates trademarks or plagiarizes another's words, or creates a harmful impact, like shouting "fire" in a crowded theater. (p. 396)

Indeed, the Southern Poverty Law Center has successfully won judgments against hate groups by establishing that violence, including the burning of Black churches, is a consequence of hate speech. Hate speech, which can be proven to result in behavioral violence, has been successfully fought in the courts (Southern Poverty Law Center, 1998a).

The 14th Amendment guarantees equal protection of the laws, regardless of race or condition of prior servitude. This is the basis for the interpretation that harassment, which creates a hostile public workplace or educational environment, should not be allowed. However, Jones (1994) eschewed the fact that the "courts have issued several rulings and in general have not followed this interpretation with respect to specific statutes developed by institutions or local jurisdictions" (p. 396). Jones challenged the claim that the First Amendment "comes from our Constitutional heart—the individual is supreme. Thus the First bullies the Fourteenth [Amendment] in courts of law" (p. 396). The focus, he argued, should not be on the perpetrator's action but on the experience of those who are the target of the violation. He suggested that psychologists should focus on ethical and moral obligations involved in creating a humane society. Jones further asserted that the responsibility to implement the ethical and moral intent of the 14th Amendment rests on all U.S. citizens.

THE DILEMMA FROM AN ETHICAL PERSPECTIVE

The role of psychology in helping to resolve social conflicts is an important but neglected one (Kendler, 1993); ethics in psychology are defined almost exclusively in terms of obligations toward individual clients or research participants (Prilleltensky & Walsh-Bowers, 1993). The role of psychology, in general, and APA, in particular, in implementing the moral and ethical intent of the 14th Amendment is an important issue in psychology. Kendler (1993) suggested that "psychology can assist society in settling ethical disputes by revealing the empirical consequences of different policy choices, thus allowing society to make informed decisions as to which competing social policies to adopt" (p. 1052). His position was viewed as a clear challenge to APA's activism in the social policy arena (Pellegrin & Frueh, 1994). He claimed, for example, that it is not for psychologists to judge or take sides in moral conflicts by demonstrating that one social policy is good and the other is bad. As an example, Kendler (1993) illustrated that if a study revealed that bilingual education for Hispanic children showed stronger ethnic identification but inferior academic performance, such findings would not logically generate support for either bilingual or monolingual English education. That is, psychology cannot judge the relative moral value of enhancing ethnic identification compared with improving academic performance. (p. 1047)

Although psychology, as a behavioral science, is unable to validate moral principles because of the fallacy of inferring ethical imperatives from empirical data, behavioral data can nevertheless assist society's members in choosing among competing social policies by revealing their empirical consequences (Kendler, 1993). Kendler (1993) suggested, for example, that rather than take a stand regarding abortion, psychologists should evaluate abortion policies in terms of social consequences, provide relevant information about the psychological consequences of different abortion policies, and allow "democratic procedures combined with psychological information [to] help moderate or resolve the ethical conduct" (p. 1051).

Prilleltensky (1994b) suggested that although empirical data can help make moral decisions, a set of values, derived from moral philosophy, should inform psychologists' conception of human welfare. He suggested, in fact, that it is impossible for a social scientist to extricate oneself from the social reality one wishes to examine. Many have suggested that various aspects of psychological research, including the terminology chosen to define the subject matter, are socially constructed and very much linked to the interests and values of the researcher (Kvale, 1992; Prilleltensky, 1994a; Riger, 1992). Prilleltensky (1994b) recommended that "if we are really serious about serving the public, the public should know what are our individual and collective biases" (p. 967). Prilleltensky's (1994b) concern was partly that Kendler's (1993) recommendation (to assist society in settling ethical disputes by revealing the empirical consequences of different policy choices, thus allowing society to make informed decisions as to which competing social policies to adopt) would not ensure that research results would be used in a socially and ethically responsible manner. Furthermore, Prilleltensky (1994b) wrote that "hiding behind a veneer of scientism will do little to produce a sound social ethics for psychology" (p. 967).

Stroud (1994) suggested that attempting to separate Aristotelian scientific heritage, which separates science, ethics, and application from each other, leads to difficulty for psychologists in deciding the degree to which moral judgments may or may not be a part of their professional expertise. Stroud believes that science, ethics, and practice are not inherently disparate enterprises and that if science, ethics, and practice were integrated, psychologists could become more informed moral participants.

We contend that careful analysis of psychological knowledge combined with the methods available for feminist consciousness in ethical decision making renders feminist psychologists, ourselves included, able to take stands and make recommendations regarding social policy, including against such contentious dilemmas as hate speech and freedom of expression. An analysis of the methods available for resolving those dilemmas is presented next.

A QUESTION OF ETHICS

Ethical Decision Making

According to the APA Ethics Code, "if neither law nor the Ethics Code resolves an issue, psychologists should consider other professional materials and the *dictates of their own conscience,* as well as seek consultation with others within the field when this is practical" (p. 1598, emphasis added). It is, thus, the matter of conscience and its phenomenological nature that may create a variance in moral and ethical behavior when individuals seek resolution of a dilemma. Whereas APA's Ethics Code gives psychologists the latitude to make decisions within the context of their own beliefs and circumstances, the dilemmas of ethics and morality are confounded when the implementation of one set of ethics jeopardizes another set. Herein lies the opportunity for feminist consciousness to inform moral choices.

As an illustration, imagine you are a feminist psychologist opposed to the oppression of women and people of Color. Imagine too that you highly regard American values of autonomy and freedom of expression. Now imagine you are walking down the street and witness a White man yelling racist and sexist epitaphs at a woman of Color. Feminists judge some acts as immoral because they violate tenets of feminist consciousness (e.g., listening to the voices of marginalized and oppressed groups), even though the practitioner of these behaviors is exercising a "right" as an autonomous individual enjoying the constitutionally protected freedom of expression. What do you do? Should you intervene, thus nullifying the rights of these two individuals to decide about their own lives?

An examination of ethics may enhance one's ability to understand the tension between autonomy and feminist consciousness in ethical decision making when balancing one's protection from hate speech and freedom of speech. This examination takes into consideration ethical principles and ethical orientations as well as feminist and societal values. As this study of ethics illustrates, the tenets of feminist theory, as described in Brabeck and Brown (1997), are intricately woven into this discussion of hate speech.

Principles of Ethics

Kitchener's (1984) two-level theory of ethical decision making conceptualizes the process of ethical justification underlying decision making in terms of two qualitatively different stages of ethical reasoning: the intuitive level and the critical–evaluative level. The intuitive level is an "ordinary moral sense," which results from living and being in relation with other humans. Included in this level is moral development, socialization, and life experiences. Kitchener argued that this is the basis of what people intuitively feel is right or wrong.

Virtue ethics, firmly established in a community's wisdom and moral sense, also informs the process of decision making (Meara et al., 1996) at the "intuitive level" (see Kitchener, chap. 2, this volume). The distinguishing characteristics of virtue ethics involve the identification of the motivation, emotion, character, ideals, and moral habits of an individual who functions within the traditions and practices of a culture, group, or community (Meara et al., 1996; Meara & Day, chap. 12, this volume). Therefore, that which is virtuous is determined within a context. Virtue ethics focus on the character of the individual rather than on the solution of particular ethical dilemmas. As Kitchener (1996) stated,

> there are too many occasions when someone knows what is the right or principled thing to do but fails to act on those principles because of what we might consider to be a character flaw or acts out of principle but with little compassion or kindness for the person affected by his or her actions. (p. 92)

Virtue ethics focus on the individual's character development (Jordan & Meara, 1990), which, as asserted here, provide the basis of Kitchener's (1984) "ordinary moral sense."

An individual using hate speech does not practice acontextually. As members of a feminist community, we evaluate this individual's motivations to perpetuate the disempowerment of an oppressed group, the anger and hatred with which the speech is conveyed, and the environment in which the individual is practicing (Tenet 8, Brabeck & Brown, 1997, p. 32; also see chap. 1, this volume). Theoretically, if the community is supportive of the behavior, the hate speech may not be considered immoral to those members of that community. An individual in a Ku Klux Klan meeting may not see him- or herself engaging in hate speech, but when that individual changes contexts, that same speech may be considered highly objectionable.

If the individual from a Ku Klux Klan community were to become a history professor, for example, and used the word *nigger* in teaching about slaves, what kind of faculty code should be developed to prevent that? The University of Wisconsin (Zuckoff, 1998) struggled with just such a case and determined that if directed repeatedly at an individual or even made in passing remarks to a class, there could be no good educational reason for such an epithet in that context and discipline was appropriate. However, if a professor assigned readings on race that used the same epithet and the professor used the word in class discussions of the book, that would be protected speech.

Thus, if the intuitive level is not sufficient to make a moral judgment about what is right or wrong, Kitchener's (1984) critical–evaluative level is invoked. The critical–evaluative level consists of rules (i.e., laws, professional codes, and institutional policies), principles (i.e., autonomy, nonmalefi-cence, beneficence, justice, and fidelity; Beauchamp & Childress, 1979), and ethical theories or ideologies. The ethical principles proposed by Beau-champs and Childress are discussed in Kitchener's chapter (2, this volume). Kitchener (1984) argued that the principles are "*prima facie* valid (i.e., moral principles are neither absolute nor relative, but they are always ethically relevant and can be overturned only when there are stronger ethical obliga-tions)" (p. 52, emphasis in original). These principles, justice, fidelity, be-neficence, and nonmaleficence, then, form the foundations of the critical evaluation level of Kitchener's model of ethical reasoning in the context of psychology.

The principle of autonomy contains two elemental tenets: the concept of free will and respect for others as autonomous agents. Implied in the tenets is the ability of rational, discriminating thought. There are, however, two limitations to this principle of autonomy. The first is the observance of others' rights to autonomy in the exercise of one's own autonomy. This includes the prohibition against harming others or infringing on their rights. The second limitation involves the capacity of the individual to engage in competent, rational thought.

The principle of autonomy has been used in arguments supporting the right of individuals to exercise their constitutional freedom of expression, regardless of the potential damage it may inflict on others. In their vigilance to relieve themselves of the problems of colonialism by a distant crown, the originators of the U.S. Constitution decided that dire harm would befall U.S. citizens if restrictions were placed on the ability to freely express one's beliefs. Unfortunately, as it is practiced today, freedom of expression has, at times, been vulgarized and abused by many to perpetuate a climate of hostility, oppression, and marginalization against traditionally disempowered groups, such as with hate speech, often perpetrated by individuals or "hate groups," and hate talk, such as that communicated through the Internet, radio, and newsletters. The Southern Poverty Law Center (1998b), for example, described the rise of the National Alliance, a group headed by William Pierce, author of the *Turner Diaries*, who is thought to have strongly influenced Timothy McVeigh, convicted in the Oklahoma City bombing.

Pierce has used the Internet, newsletters (e.g., *Free Speech*), and radio to espouse White supremacy, antigovernment violence, and a war won by Whites and has recruited members of the military.

Individualistic libertarians (e.g., Barry, 1987) have argued that spontaneous individual activity maximizes social well-being more effectively than could any deliberate, rationalistic plan (Naveson, 1988). In a moral sense, therefore, libertarians have argued that any attempt to restrict an individual's autonomy by coercive activity destroys the "separateness" and identity of each person and makes him or her a means to be used for the ends of a social or collective entity. The general conviction of libertarianism is that laws and morality should be limited to enforcing the equal right of each individual to pursue his or her own interest. However, from a feminist perspective, groups of people who have been traditionally disempowered and disenfranchised from mainstream society have not "counted" in the short history of democracy. The patriarchal system, which has benefited White men of the middle and upper classes, has been the definition maker of what is harmful and to whom. Illegal immigration is harmful—to whom? Affirmative action is harmful—to whom? Equal pay for equal work is harmful—to whom? Providing insurance benefits to all employees is harmful—to whom?

An ethical dilemma of paternalism arises in attempts to balance the virtue of nonmaleficence and beneficence with autonomy (Kitchener, 1984; chap. 2, this volume). What does a feminist psychologist do when ethical ideologies about rights to autonomy and freedom of expression conflict with feminist consciousness? If paternalism is a system under which people in positions of power control the beliefs and behaviors of traditionally disempowered groups of people, then feminist consciousness helps her or him address this conflict by enjoining her or him to "be response-able to self and others, attend to one's own and collective well-being . . . lead[ing] to social transformation" (Tenet 2, Brabeck & Brown, 1997, p. 32; see also Brabeck & Ting, chap. 1, this volume). A feminist consciousness means that one is aware that women, people of Color, gays and lesbians, individuals with disabilities, and older people hold a position of subordination, given the social construction, and that one has a responsibility to alter the consciousness of society by directing attention to the ways in which policies and practices (or the lack of them) continue to oppress. For example, given that the objectification of women's bodies contributes to the oppression of women, is it just that a *Playboy* centerfold as a "teaching" tool to distinguish cuts of meat should be used by an agriculture professor?

Ethical feminists must also work to change the values inherent in a construction of society unjustly based on power and dominance. As Sue (1994) suggested, the culprit is not White men. The world would not necessarily be better if the dominant group were women or Latino. Instead, feminist ethicists need to work to change how people think about human beings, and the diversity inherent in being human should be appreciated. Likewise, Martín-Baró, Aron, and Corne (1994) suggested that in situations of state-sponsored violence, all people are potential targets of violence; that is, all live with the possibility of death. If the United States continues to ignore the destruction of hate speech, then any person from any oppressed group will daily potentially be subjected to a hostile environment. Feminist ethicists insist that the environment must be changed through changes in policies and practices that address how one thinks about human beings.

As discussed in Brabeck and Ting's chapter (1), feminists are committed to eliminating the subordination of women and all oppressed people. A feminist approach to ethics asks questions about power (i.e., domination and subordination) before it asks questions about good and evil or care and justice (Tong, 1993) because it sees power as intricately connected to these concepts. Feminist ethicists have argued that if people are not each other's equals in reality as well as in theory, any approach to ethics is bound to fail because people who oppress cannot treat those whom they oppress with the same respect and consideration with which they treat their peers (Tong, 1993). A feminist approach to ethics enjoins people, particularly women, to collectively resist and overcome oppressive forces (e.g., sexism, racism, and classism) under patriarchy (Jaggar, 1992). Therefore, feminist ethics is more than simply a state of mind; it is a commitment to action. As Brabeck and Brown (1997) stated, "persons are viewed as capable of acting (response-able) to effect change, and each person is viewed as responsible for participating in the process of change" (p. 32, Tenet 8; also see Brabeck & Ting, chap. 1, this volume).

AN APPLICATION OF VIRTUE ETHICS, PRINCIPLE ETHICS, AND FEMINIST ETHICAL CONSCIOUSNESS

Meara et al. (1996) described how virtues are similar to ideals or aspirations because they are traits of character assigned merit in a context. That is, what is considered virtuous is determined within a context. In the case of hate speech, we could conclude that a morally exclusive community is destructive because it promotes discrimination and oppression. The "right to exclude" is partly based on the concept of *autonomy*, an ethical principle based on Western European thought.

In 1996, top executives of Texaco were caught speaking in derogatory ways about Black employees who had filed a discrimination lawsuit. The exclusive community of Texaco top executives had created a boundary in which "others" were perceived as nonentities, expendable, and undeserving. This scandal shows that no one is immune from the backlash of racism and discrimination. Indeed, Texaco became painfully aware of the cost of cultural insensitivity and racism; the CEO rushed to control the damaged image by settling for amounts that Texaco had previously not expected. In addition, the U.S. Armed Forces, with the image of "Tail Hook" still lingering in the minds of many, struggle with a scandal that goes beyond sexual harassment to the apparent systematic abuse and rape of women in training camps. The objectification of women for one's pleasure is another example of how human beings in positions of power determine that they may harm or exploit others. If women are psychologically morally excluded from one's group, then it does not matter if they are objectified, even if they have technically joined the ranks of the Armed Forces.

The ethical principle of autonomy allows hate groups to espouse their hatred of various groups so long as they are not bombing, robbing, raping, or impinging on the rights of others as autonomous agents. The virtues of respectfulness and benevolence; the ethical principles of nonmaleficence, beneficence, and justice; and the ethical orientation of feminism, however, all encompass much more than respect for autonomy.

Virtue ethics calls on individuals to aspire toward ideals and to develop virtues or traits of character that enable the individuals to achieve these ideals. Groups or individuals that espouse hatred toward oppressed groups or groups that are different are not being virtuous. The feminist ethical principles of the avoidance of harm, promotion of human welfare, and moral inclusiveness of the principle of justice all require that the group change their beliefs and behaviors. Feminist ethicists decry the actions of such groups and individuals as being abusive of their power as privileged members of a pluralistic society. Utilitarian ethicists might be concerned that the violence, which may come from the hateful expressions of this group, is creating more harm than good in society. At the same time, utilitarians are concerned that limitations on a group's rights to association and freedom of expression impose undue limits on society in general (Sidgwick, 1893/1969).

Feminist ethics expand the understanding of community and responsibility (Tenet 8, Brabeck & Brown, 1997) and emphasize inclusion (Tenet 5, Brabeck & Brown, 1997). Moral inclusion refers to relationships in which individuals are relatively equal, the potential for reciprocity exists, and all parties are entitled to fair processes and a share of community resources. Assuming these parameters, clearly engaging in hate speech or other such behaviors in the United States' pluralistic society should not occur. However, a narrow conception of one's moral community results when one constricts the scope of situations in which considerations of justice govern one's conduct. The extension of one's moral community is thus fundamental to the psychology of justice (Opotow, 1990).

Cook (1990) reviewed data from four studies of cooperative, equal-status, interracial contact that showed increases in favorable beliefs about and liking for Blacks by formerly prejudiced Whites. Oliner and Oliner (1988) examined variables involved between those who helped Jews survive Nazi Germany's Holocaust and those who did nothing. Those who offered a helping hand, usually at great risk to themselves, were more empathic and more caring and had a much greater sense of responsibility to others. These attitudes were developed partially by living among people who were different from themselves and seeing them as human beings. Thus, it seems that contact in a context that allows for cooperation, equal status, and diversity allows for more openness, flexibility, empathy, caring, and an increased sense of responsibility.

A CALL TO ACTION

Despite his alarming prediction of a coming race war, Rowan (1996) portended hope by suggesting various courses of action, including increased community involvement and greater support for education. Psychologists must add to these strategies of change by committing to an ethic of care through beneficence, nonmaleficence, and justice (Kitchener, 1984) and by embracing human diversity (Tenet 5, Brabeck & Brown, 1997). Whether psychologists act as individuals or as a profession largely depends on whether they are able to conceptualize the responsibility to act as "virtuous agents." A *virtuous agent*, according to Meara et al. (1996), is one whose moral community extends to include out-groups. The virtuous agent

> (a) is motivated to do what is good, (b) possesses vision and discernment, (c) realizes the role of affect or emotion in assessing or judging proper conduct, (d) has a high degree of self-understanding and awareness, and perhaps most importantly, (e) is connected with and understands the mores of his or her community and the importance of community in moral decision making, policy setting and character development and is alert to the legitimacy of client diversity in these respects. (pp. 28–29)

The virtuous agent, according to Meara et al., is motivated to do what is right in accordance with high ethical standards or ideals. In addition, principle ethics can advise one about what is morally justified.

As feminist ethicists, we are informed by both virtues and principles as well as tenets of feminist consciousness and the values inherent in the ability to understand the direct and indirect influences of systems, institutions, cultures, and circumstances on people's lives. Feminist psychologists have focused on solutions to practical problems and have confronted the pain of marginality as it is imposed on the lives of women, ethnic and racial minorities, older people, differently abled people, religious minorities, and gay men and lesbians through discrimination, violence, and oppression.

These foci speak to a passion in feminist ethics and psychology and point to a commitment to the public interest. This commitment means that feminist and multicultural psychologists should and must be at the forefront in promoting public policy and other strategies to diffuse tensions and build trust (Tenets 1, 2, & 8, Brabeck & Brown, 1997; Brabeck & Ting, chap. 1, this volume).

Because research (Cook, 1990; Oliner & Oliner, 1988) shows that a particular kind of contact results in a broadening of the moral community, the role of psychology, especially feminist and multicultural psychologies, comes to the fore. As ethicists, we have the skill to facilitate this contact and effect a broadening of the boundaries of moral inclusion in American society. As psychologists, we have the mandate to use our knowledge to bring about individual, familial, communal, educational, institutional, legal, and societal change from the intimacy of the therapy room to the socio-political discourse of public policy making.

CONCLUSION

Feminist ethics expand psychologists' understanding of the destructive nature of hate speech beyond virtues and principles to include a feminist consciousness that mandates action. They have the power to address the expansion of moral inclusiveness beyond college campuses and mental health settings. The need for faculty and student speech codes, cross-cultural sensitivity, and antiracist and antisexist training are apparent in all sectors of society. The racism and discriminatory actions of Texaco executives in 1996 illustrates that no one is immune from the backlash of racism and discrimination. In addition, the U.S. Armed Forces struggle with a situation of apparent systematic abuse and rape of women in training camps. Clearly, as feminist psychologists, we have a role to play in offering cross-cultural and gender awareness training by becoming more visible, vocal, and available for consultations to organizations and institutions in our attempts to affect societal transformation.

REFERENCES

American Psychological Association. (1992). Ethical principles of psychologists and code of conduct. *American Psychologist, 47,* 1597–1613.

Azar, B. (1996, November). Project explores landscape of midlife. *The APA Monitor,* p. 26.

Barry, N. P. (1987). *On classical liberalism and libertarianism.* New York: St. Martin's Press.

Beauchamp, T. L., & Childress, J. F. (1979). *Principles of biomedical ethics*. New York: Oxford University Press.

Boyd, D. (1994, March 2). Jordan challenges students' ethical views [Report of lecture "Ethical dilemmas in leadership," delivered by Barbara Jordan on March 1, 1994]. *The Daily Texan* [University of Texas at Austin], p. 2.

Brabeck, M., & Brown, L. (With Christian, L., Espin, O., Hare-Mustin, R., Kaplan, A., Kaschak, E., Miller, D., Phillips, E., Ferns, T., & Van Ormer, A.). (1997). Feminist theory and psychological practice. In J. Worell & N. Johnson (Eds.), *Shaping the future of feminist psychology: Education, research, and practice* (pp. 15–35). Washington, DC: American Psychological Association.

Cook, S. W. (1990). Toward a psychology of improving justice: Research on extending the equality principle to victims of social injustice. *Journal of Social Issues, 45*, 147–162.

Daniel, J. H. (1994). Exclusion and emphasis reframed as a matter of ethics. *Ethics & Behavior, 4*, 229–235.

Dworkin, A., French, M., Ramos, N., & Shange, N. (1994). Where do we stand on pornography? [Interview conducted by M. A. Gillespie]. *Ms., 4*, 32–41.

Faludi, S. (1991). *Backlash: The undeclared war against American women*. New York: Crown.

Herman, J. L. (1992). *Trauma and recovery*. New York: Basic Books.

Jaggar, A. M. (1992). Feminist ethics. In L. Becker & C. Becker (Eds.), *Encyclopedia of ethics* (pp. 361–370). New York: Garland.

John Doe v. University of Michigan, 721 F.Supp. 852 (E.D. Mich. 1989).

Jones, J. J. (1994). A perpetrator-less crime? *Ethics & Behavior, 4*, 395–397.

Jordan, A. E., & Meara, N. M. (1990). Ethics and the professional practice of psychologists. *Professional Psychology: Research and Practice, 21*, 107–114.

Kvale, S. (Ed.). (1992). *Psychology and postmodernism*. London: Sage.

Kendler, H. H. (1993). Psychology and the ethics of social policy. *American Psychologist, 48*, 1046–1053.

Kitchener, K. S. (1984). Intuition, critical evaluation, and ethical principles: The foundation for ethical decisions in counseling psychology. *The Counseling Psychologist, 12*, 43–55.

Kitchener, K. S. (1996). There is more to ethics than principles. *The Counseling Psychologist, 24*, 92–97.

Lerner, G. (1993). *The creation of feminist consciousness*. New York: Oxford University Press.

Laird, M. (1994). Political correctness [Commentary]. *Ethics & Behavior, 4*, 390–394.

Martín-Baró, I., Aron, A., & Corne, S. (Eds.). (1994). *Writings for a liberation psychology*. Cambridge, MA: Harvard University Press.

McGrath, E., Keita, G. P., Strickland, B. R., & Russo, N. (Eds.). (1990). *Women and depression: Risk factors and treatment issues*. Washington, DC: American Psychological Association.

McMahon, P. (1999, February 8). Anti-abortion site kicked off web. *USA Today*, p. A1.

Meara, N. M., Schmidt, L. D., & Day, J. D. (1996). Principles and virtues: A foundation for ethical decisions, policies, and character. *The Counseling Psychologist, 24*, 4–77.

Naveson, J. (1988). *The libertarian idea*. Philadelphia, PA: Temple University Press.

Oliner, S. B., & Oliner, P. (1988). *The altruistic personality: Rescuers of Jews in Nazi Germany*. New York: Free Press.

Opotow, S. (1990). Moral exclusion and injustice: An introduction. *Journal of Social Issues, 46*, 1–20.

Pellegrin, K. L., & Frueh, B. C. (1994). Why psychologists don't think like philosophers. *American Psychologist, 49*, 970–971.

Prilleltensky, I. (1994a). *The morals and politics of psychology: Psychological discourse and the status quo*. Albany: State University of New York Press.

Prilleltensky, I. (1994b). Psychology and social ethics. *American Psychologist, 49*, 966–967.

Prilleltensky, I., & Walsh-Bowers, R. (1993). Psychology and the moral imperative. *Journal of Theoretical and Philosophical Psychology, 13*, 90–102.

Riger, S. (1992). Epistemological debates, feminist voices: Science, social values, and the study of women. *American Psychologist, 47*, 730–740.

Root, M. P. P. (1992). Reconstructing the impact of trauma on personality. In L. S. Brown & M. Ballou (Eds.), *Personality and psychopathology: Feminist reappraisals* (pp. 229–265). New York: Guilford Press.

Rowan, C. T. (1996). *The coming race war in America: A wake-up call*. Boston: Little, Brown.

Sanchez, W., & Vasquez Nuttall, E. (1995). It's about time! *Ethics & Behavior, 5*, 355–357.

Sidgwick, H. (1969). *The methods of ethics* [Excerpt]. In W. T. Jones, F. Sontag, M. O. Beckner, & R. J. Fogelin (Eds.), *Approaches to ethics: Representative selections from classical times to present* (2nd ed., pp. 390–401). New York: McGraw-Hill. (Original work published 1893)

Sniffen, M. J. (1996, November 4). FBI: Most hate crimes racist. *Associated Press Wire Report*. (Also available from the FBI Hate Crime Page: "Hate Crime—1995." Retrieved July 29, 1999 from the World Wide Web: http://www.fbi.gov// homepage.html)

Southern Poverty Law Center. (1998a, December 31). *Jury hits Klan with $37 million verdict* [Report]. Retrieved January 17, 1999 from the World Wide Web: http:// www.splcenter.org/legalaction/la-1.html

Southern Poverty Law Center. (1998b, December 31). *The rise of the National Alliance* [Report]. Retrieved January 19, 1999 from the World Wide Web: http://www.splcenter.org/intelligence project/alliance.html

Stacy v. Williams, 306 F.Supp. 963 (1969).

Staub, E. (1989). *The roots of evil: Origins of genocide and other group violence.* Cambridge, England: Cambridge University Press.

Stroud, W. L., Jr. (1994). Dewey's integrated logic of science, ethics, and practice. *American Psychologist, 49,* 968–970.

Sue, S. (1994). Introduction. In E. J. Trickett, R. J. Watts, & D. Birman (Eds.), *Human diversity: Perspectives on people in context* (pp. 1–4). San Francisco: Jossey-Bass.

Sweezy v. New Hampshire, 354 U.S. 234, 355 U.S. 852 (1957).

Tong, R. (1993). *Feminine and feminist ethics.* Belmont, CA: Wadsworth.

Trickett, E. J., Watts, R. J., & Birman, D. (1994). Toward an overarching framework for diversity. In E. J. Trickett, R. J. Watts, & D. Birman (Eds.), *Human diversity: Perspectives on people in context* (pp. 7–26). San Francisco: Jossey-Bass.

U.S. Bureau of the Census. (1995). *Statistical abstract of the United States, 1995.* Washington, DC: U.S. Government Printing Office.

Verhovek, S. H. (1999, January 13). Anti-abortion site on web has ignited free speech debate. *The New York Times,* p. 1.

von Hippel, W. (1994). A social psychological perspective. *Ethics & Behavior, 4,* 397–399.

Wyatt, G. (1989, August). *The terrorism of racism.* Invited address at the 97th Annual Convention of the American Psychological Association, New Orleans, LA.

Zuckoff, M. (1998, October 21). A new word on speech codes: One school that led the way is rethinking its rules. *Boston Globe,* p. A1.

12

EPILOGUE: FEMINIST VISIONS AND VIRTUES OF ETHICAL PSYCHOLOGICAL PRACTICE

NAOMI M. MEARA AND JEANNE D. DAY

Since the Boulder Conference (Raimy, 1950) and arguably before (Napoli, 1981), major initiatives within psychology in this country have been focused on transforming the discipline from an exclusively academic endeavor to an academic undertaking inextricably connected to a valued service profession. In many quarters, there have been efforts to shape this profession so that one of its distinctive qualities is the availability of psychological expertise to less privileged or marginal members of society. Many feminist psychologists have been leaders in this latter endeavor.

A major goal has been to integrate systematically the "science and practice" of psychology based on an ideal, often referred to as the "Boulder model" or "scientist–practitioner model" (Raimy, 1950). A significant part of these initiatives involves continuing attempts to define what is meant by *ethical psychological practice*. These attempts encompass many empirical and theoretical perspectives, countless theoretical and political disagreements, and numerous well-developed and fragmented ideologies. They are marked by paradox; some might even say confusion. These paradoxes include attempts at inclusiveness and "giving psychology away," contrasted with fears of losing professional autonomy and thus ever-increasing credential requirements or insistence on being a health service in the midst of serious arguments with the medical profession. For the first 60 years of its existence, the American Psychological Association (APA) had no ethics code, although the possibilities of developing one were discussed. During psychology's transformation into a profession, however, APA has produced an initial version and nine revisions of the Ethical Principles of Psychologists and Code of Conduct (current name; APA, 1953, 1958, 1963, 1968, 1977, 1979, 1981b, 1990, 1992). APA has also produced numerous other statements with respect to the ethical treatment of clients, students, research participants, and special groups, such as women and racial–ethnic minorities (APA, 1975, 1981a, 1982, 1991; Fitzgerald & Nutt, 1986; "Principles Concerning the Counseling," 1979).

Statements about ethics related to psychological practice have also been developed in organizations other than APA (e.g., American Association for Marriage and Family Therapy, 1991; American Counseling Association, 1995; American Medical Association, 1980; Council of Medical Specialty Societies, 1998; and Feminist Therapy Institute, 1990). Besides the increasing professionalism of psychological services, another major stimulus to ensure ethical psychological practice has been the U.S. Federal Government's establishment of institutional review boards (IRBs; U.S. Department of Health, Education, and Welfare, 1971). The creation of IRBs, required for all institutions that conduct research with humans and receive federal monies, is partially in response to the Nazi medical experimentation atrocities uncovered at the Nuremberg trials. They were also established because of concern about certain medical research conducted in this country. A notorious example of such research is the infamous Tuskegee Syphilis Study, where for almost 40 years, African American "control" group human subjects were neither given known treatments for the disease nor informed that effective treatment existed (Jones, 1993; Thomas & Quinn, 1991). The proliferation of these ethical documents and the creation of clear outside review procedures to protect research participants leave little doubt that all facets of professional psychological practice are essentially ethical or moral endeavors that are the concern of professionals and the general public.

For the past quarter of the 20th century, feminist thought has been an important aspect of the science and practice of psychology. It has inspired efforts to promote ethical professional behavior, transformations of the status quo, social justice, and other virtues of civilized societies, where all individuals are treated with equal respect. Feminist thought has added several dimensions to the conversations and struggles related to the development of ethical psychological practice. These contributions include consciousness raising with respect to difference and discrimination. For example, feminist thought has revealed that women who responded to societal premises or policies with nonstereotypical attitudes or behaviors were often erroneously labeled "psychologically deviant."

Feminist scholars have also brought to awareness and analyzed the influence of role, status, and power in shaping intellectual, social, and moral perspectives. They have legitimized experiential knowledge as one method of psychological inquiry and as a foundation of ethical feminist practice and policy making. Finally, feminist thinking has reinforced the view that individual differences (e.g., distinctive moral voices) are more salient than abstract universals (e.g., "idyllic" justice as the quintessential standard of morality) in determining coherent ethical policies and practices of everyday life. As feminist scholarship has developed, its contributions have become more explicit and systematized (e.g., Worell & Johnson, 1997). This volume contributes to that explicitness by examining feminist ethics in relation to psychological practice. As such, it adds needed and welcome voices to the conversations about ethical psychological practice and the virtues, relationships, and understandings necessary to sustain and enhance such practice. It also provides a platform for conversing about and constructing a vision of practice that is not reactive but instead builds on progressive feminist tenets and virtues that can inform the highest aspirations of the profession.

Our purpose in this epilogue is to participate in and comment on these conversations. Our only major assumption is that conversations that aim to help one understand ethical psychological practice are conversations about morality. Furthermore, like all conversations about morality, they are (and from our perspective, need to be) open-ended conversations. With very few (if any) exceptions, ethicists cannot settle for all time, cultures, or circumstances all that is moral or ethical. So it is also with ethical psychological practice from a feminist perspective. As Brabeck and Ting (chap. 1, this volume) point out, however, as feminist ethicists, we must meet the challenge of postmodern pluralistic thought and, thus, cannot define as ethical a stance that embraces total relativism. We need to find consensus or common ground between the opposing values of acceptance of difference and intolerance of atrocity. As Vasquez (1996) pointed out, "abusive behavior is destructive to everyone" (p. 101). Whereas feminists do not speak with one voice, common ground is to be sought after and forged among their different voices across various conversations. These feminist voices and dialogues clearly have influenced the psychological community and the larger society over the past 25 years. They are now poised to make an even larger impact in defining relevant ethics for feminists, psychological professions, and society.

In the spirit of hoping to forge consensus while respecting differences, we comment on the current status of conversations that define ethical psychological practice. In particular, we focus on the significance of the contributions that the feminist scholars of this volume make to contemporary thinking about these ongoing dialogues. Briefly, we see these contributions as cogently and coherently presenting an extended definition of ethical psychological practice. The authors make explicit the perspectives that feminist ethics bring to an informed definition of practice and suggest characteristic virtues. Finally, we suggest that this volume provides guidelines that can transcend context and lead to the development of a more self-determined rather than reactive vision of the profession.

CHARACTERIZING ETHICAL PSYCHOLOGICAL PRACTICE

Over the past 50 years, the definition of *psychological practice* has become increasingly narrow. During that time, professional psychology has become almost exclusively a health service profession, whose services could be reimbursed by private and public insurance, thus putting psychological services on par with medical reimbursement plans. As employers (who pay for most of the health care for working people under 65) wished to contain costs, it became difficult for psychologists to collect insurance monies for treating clients who did not carry specific *Diagnostic and Statistical Manual of Mental Disorders* (DSM; American Psychiatric Association, 1994) diagnoses. Thus, psychological practice became synonymous with "remedial therapy" as directed toward alleviating mental illness.

An irony in the pattern of these events is that many of them occurred in the 1970s when the latest wave of feminism was beginning to take root in North American psychology. One of the many things these feminists (e.g., Tennov, 1976) were concerned about was the conclusion, often enunciated by psychoanalytic therapists, that women who were discontent with their roles or status should be categorized as "mentally ill," "inadequate," or "at fault." It seems fitting, therefore, that one of the goals of this volume is to expand (or, as we would argue, reinstate) a broader definition of practice or applied psychology. Whether from philosophical convictions or economic pressures from managed care (which has narrowed practice even further from the perspective of what one can treat, how one must treat it, and for how long), there are movements afoot elsewhere in the profession to do the same. Feminists, however, are not new to this endeavor. Had their earlier voices been given more credence, the profession might not have arrived at such a narrow view of psychological practice. Since the 1970s, feminist psychologists have pushed against the proscribed boundaries of psychological practice. They have challenged theoretical orientations that see women as weak. They have argued against rigid power arrangements in therapy that view women as passive recipients of assistance rather than as competent collaborators in the design and direction of the therapeutic work.

Among other strategies, feminism emphasizes collaboration, support groups, self-help, and political action toward social justice.

Feminists have also pushed the boundaries of psychological research, for example, advancing the premise that far from being totally objective, those who profess the "dust bowl objectivity" of logical positivism are unaware of or not concerned with its subjectivity. Another form of practice relates to the public policy arena, specifically to the changes feminists have advocated in the workplace and employers' handlings of issues related to child care. Feminists' work in these areas has resulted in greater societal understanding of the complexities involved in ensuring quality day care, equity in treatment and pay, and procedures for redressing more subtle forms of discrimination. Such subtle discrimination has included lawmakers' lack of attention to the widespread problem of unpaid child support. It includes "detouring" women into less desirable positions (e.g., a cashier rather than a produce manager in a supermarket or the "mommy track" rather than the partner track in a prestigious law firm). Feminists have also spent untold practice hours challenging other even more subtle forms of discrimination. Such forms include defining suitable career options for women (e.g., nursing, teaching) that keep with society's view of roles "proper to the female character" (e.g., helper, caretaker, service provider). Despite all the efforts by feminist psychologists and others to effect change in these arenas over the past 25 years, there are still problems that appropriate psychological expertise could alleviate.

Clearly, then, the traditional view of psychological practice should be more inclusive and closer to the work pioneered by feminists and others interested in prevention and policy (e.g., Albee, 1998). Feminists need to envision psychological practice as the application of knowledge, attitudes, and skills to a variety of events and issues in daily living. We do not mean to diminish the importance or necessity of earning a livelihood or of being synchronous with societal pressures on the profession. We do believe, however, that feminist practitioners need to be less concerned with what is medical or reimbursable and more affirmative of what is empirically sound and practically effective to deal with the concerns of everyday life. This volume challenges professional psychologists to be less reactionary to external pressures and more self-directed in envisioning practice. The authors develop a more comprehensive construct of practice that includes not only feminist theory, research, instruction, and an expanded view of traditional psychological services but also the intellectual and ethical perspectives that anchor and inform these phenomena.

The term *psychological practice* (vs. dental, educational, medical, or legal) as part of this expanded concept may deserve some comment. In some sense, at least for psychologists, it is difficult to separate psychological practice from other types of professional practice. Many might correctly argue that there are aspects of most contemporary professions that are psychological. Leaving the definition of practice per se aside for a moment, we consider psychological practice best conceptualized as the application of psychological principles and techniques to effect a psychological or other positive difference (e.g., educational, medical). Examples would be using psychological research to create a cooperative classroom or to assist parents in creating environments where children feel safe and can develop their talents. This definition does not preclude a combination of approaches (e.g., psychological and educational) to effect a psychological and an educational goal. It could also include psychological consultation to enhance psychological effects or benefits from educational, medical, or other professional interventions. The authors of the chapters in this volume who examine ethical issues in arenas other than therapy provide examples of psychological practice, just as do those authors who examine issues and ethics in therapy. In some cases, the ethical concerns may be the same (e.g., power, racial–ethnic sensitivity, justice); it is only the application or setting that varies.

The ethical aspects of psychological practice are developing. For example, as professions in the United States received pressure to become more democratic (or as the public's perceptions of the legitimacy of professional authority declined), the mores of ethical practice changed. Aspects of business also had to be accommodated to ethical practice. As therapy became fee-for-service (and many other aspects of practice did not), business aspects of professional psychology became more salient and the ethical codes themselves became more concentrated on issues related to therapy and issues of market share. The current Ethics Code (APA, 1992) is much more detailed than earlier codes in regard to specific responsibilities to clients (e.g., therapeutic contracts). As Koocher (1994) noted, one of the distinguishing features of the current code is its detail with respect to business issues. He, and others, also discussed its more legal tone, which seems more directed to matters of liability than to a "document that reflects our moral integrity and our primary mission for promoting human welfare" (Bersoff, 1994, p. 386).

Changes in the profession are also reflected in subtle language changes initiated by professional organizations. For example, now clients or patients are often known as consumers, and professionals are often designated as providers. Ironically, issues of enhanced client–professional collaboration are coupled with word changes that seem to connote a one-dimensional relationship and a demotion of status for both parties, with an accompanying decline in respect and perhaps respectfulness. Jennings, Callahan, and Wolf (1987) characterized the tensions that these changes have created as conflicts of the professional versus the entrepreneur or the language of ethics versus the logic of commerce. Balancing these conflicts has become a major focus in the development of ethical psychological practice. Excessive commercialism of professional expertise is anathema to the feminist agenda and the values that support it.

Finally, concurrent with these events, psychologists, policy makers, and ordinary citizens have committed to actions that ensure that class, race, ethnicity, and gender are emphasized in defining ethical psychological practice. Serious considerations of these issues have called into question psychologists' prior conceptualizations. At the 1969 APA Annual Convention (in Washington, DC), members of the newly formed Black Students Psychological Association (BSPA) asked to be heard. They rose from the audience as George Miller was being introduced to give the presidential address. BSPA members asked that their group be permitted to present a list of demands the following day at the Council of Representatives of the APA meeting. Miller agreed, and the council meeting became a forum where this group presented its concerns and ideas related to discrimination and the lack of opportunity throughout psychology for Blacks (Simpkins & Raphael, 1970; Williams, 1970). It took a serious political act to bring to the attention of established psychology that it needed to be more inclusive. The council discussed the issues for over 6 hours and, over the course of the next year, began to address them (McKeachie, 1971).

Similar events, at least in tone, occurred at the 1970 APA Annual Convention (in Miami Beach, FL). Women met in consciousness-raising groups to formulate issues of concern with respect to women. These issues included the status of research, in particular, the problem of generalizing to women research findings that were taken from studies that included mainly male research participants. Other issues included the treatment of women professionals in various psychological work settings and within organized psychology. They raised serious concerns about theoretical, societal, and individual biases in therapies for women. At this convention, representatives from the Association of Women in Psychology brought several of these issues to the attention of the Council of Representatives of the APA. The council acknowledged that the profession had ignored women's issues for too long and affirmed its commitment to ending discrimination and facilitating women's potential (McKeachie, 1971).

From these modest beginnings, a feminist presence quickly developed within APA with the establishment of Division 35 at the 1973 Annual Convention (in Montreal, Quebec, Canada), effective January 1, 1974 (McKeachie, 1974), and the first issue of *Psychology of Women Quarterly* in 1976 (Babladelis, 1976). Feminist presence quickly expanded to include scholarship, course development, policy issues, and effective leadership of feminists within the organization and throughout the profession where feminists work: universities, governmental agencies, health clinics, and community and state organizations. Their voices in these arenas and venues have changed the conversation in psychology and in society. As diverse voices of gender, race, ethnicity, and class within psychology attempted to become equal partners in the conversations with established psychology, it became apparent that the issues they raised and the causes they sponsored were ethical as well as political, empirical, and theoretical.

In this context of expanded and more fully developed feminist thought, this timely volume, *Practicing Feminist Ethics in Psychology*, enters conversations characterizing ethical psychological practice. The book is both a response to the flow of events to date and a challenge to advance such conversations by explicitly articulating what feminist ethics is about. We are challenged by the authors in this volume to advance the conversation not only by returning to a more expanded definition of practice but also by raising and making explicit important ethical issues embedded in this expanded definition that need thoughtful reflection, if not immediate action.

The agenda of a feminist moral vision that seeks to create, as this volume does, "social justice noise" (McIntyre, chap. 3, this volume; also see Grant & Zozakiewicz, 1995), is complicated. A pivotal contribution of these chapters, however, is the explicit presentation of characteristics or virtues of feminist ethics. These authors take a stand, and their explicit characterization provides a coherent statement that can be used as a basis for research, scholarly argument, and professional action. This volume places feminism clearly within the ethical or moral realm. We leave aside for the moment the complication that not all psychologists are committed to a feminist moral vision; neither do all feminists similarly interpret what a feminist moral vision is or might become. For the moment, we also bracket the notion that some believe that moral considerations are separate from the "doing of science." We assume that all serious academic theory and science and their applications have moral implications. The more explicit scientists, practitioners, and theoreticians can be about their vision or agenda, the more they are able to be prescient about both the intellectual and ethical consequences of pursuing particular paths or assumptions.

FEMINIST ETHICS OF PSYCHOLOGICAL PRACTICE AND VIRTUE ETHICS

The contributions of this volume provide a framework for not only defining and advancing the concepts of feminist ethics but also providing examples of how feminist ethics can and need to be realized in the professional activities of psychologists. In addition, the volume provides a platform for explicitly linking feminist and virtue ethics and, thus, the potential to further the agenda of those concerned about the ethical components of ethical psychological practice.

Since the early 1980s, there has been a revival of scholarship related to virtue ethics and, in particular, the application of virtue ethics to normative professional ethics (Dykstra, 1981; Hauerwas, 1981; MacIntyre, 1984; May, 1984). A major impetus for this revival was a concern that principle ethics, which focus on resolving dilemmas, provide an incomplete account of what it means to be ethical. Virtue ethics focus on the character of agents or actors and address the question "Who shall I be?" rather than "What should I do?" An underlying assumption of a virtue ethics perspective is that "historically formed character . . . [or] character development . . . provides the basis for professional judgment" (Jordan & Meara, 1990, p. 107).

Some commentators (Drane, 1994; Meara, Schmidt, & Day, 1996) have indicated that virtues relate not only to individuals but also to professions or philosophies. Virtues are contextualized or community specific. Thus, both feminist and virtue ethicists are explicit about the influence of context. From a professional perspective, virtues that are valued depend on the goals of the profession. For example, Drane asserted that the primary goal or task of the profession of medicine is to heal. He argued, therefore, that the primary virtue of physicians and the medical profession is compassion. The Council of Medical Specialty Societies (1998) maintains that the "practice of medicine is rooted in a convenant of trust among patients, physicians and society" (p. 2). Thus, the core values and principles that the council puts forth are relational and focus on the responsibilities of physicians to be clinically competent and to maintain relational trust through such virtues as honesty, compassion, dignity, and respect for individual autonomy. Meara et al. (1996) proposed that the primary goals of professional psychologists are to be competent and to provide for the common good. Within that context, they suggested that the public would be well served if the profession of psychology and the professionals within it are characterized and distinguished by virtues of prudence, integrity, benevolence, and respectfulness.

Punzo and Meara (1993), and others (e.g., Frankena, 1973; Pojman, 1990), distinguished between self-regarding and other-regarding virtues. *Self-regarding virtues* primarily benefit the agents who possess them and are viewed as marks of inner character strength. Frankena (1973) described them as "dispositions that are most conducive to one's own good or welfare" (p. 64). *Other-regarding virtues* are directed toward the welfare of others or provide for the good of the community in general. These two types of virtues interact to form the character of a person. Thus, in the Meara et al. (1996) conceptualization of the profession of psychology, prudence and integrity are self-regarding virtues and respectfulness and benevolence are other-regarding virtues. They submitted as well that "prudence and integrity are most closely related to the goal of competence and that respectfulness and benevolence further the goals of developing a psychology sensitive to multiculturalism and providing for the common good" (p. 47). We suggest here that understanding the character of a profession, such as psychology, or a philosophical perspective, such as feminism, can be enhanced by being explicit about professional or social goals and the moral traditions of the community that the philosophy or profession hopes to serve. We also suggest that such understanding is further clarified by knowing the relative emphases that a profession or perspective places on self-regarding and other-regarding virtues and, within each of these types, what virtues are valued.

Virtue ethics have their detractors. Several criticisms of this approach deserve careful analysis because the profession continues to determine the nature of and place for virtue ethics in ethical psychological practice. Virtues that are community specific may promote ethnocentric atrocities, even as serious as those committed by Adolf Hitler (Miller, 1991). Others (e.g., Ibrahim, 1996) are quite concerned that in a pluralistic culture, one must not continue to derive morality from an individualistic Western perspective. Ibrahim (1996) believes rather that as psychologists we

> need to develop strategies to arrive at a set of virtues or principles to guide our profession that addresses diversity in the United States . . . [and] . . . in proposing ethical guidelines for an international, cross-cultural context. (p. 78)

Although in a much less extreme fashion, Bersoff (1996) registered the same concern as Miller did, finding the reliance on community values problematic, worrying that communities with virtues that are antithetical to freedom of choice or that stigmatize the less powerful would prevail or oppressively set societal agendas. He also believes that a profession's ethics depend on "consensual decision-making about the integrity of the profession, not the singular vagaries of a psychologist's character" (p. 89). Finally, Bersoff, and others (e.g., Kitchener, 1996), also raised concerns about the possibilities of teaching virtues to adult students in professional training. Other authors (e.g., Jordan & Meara, 1991; Meara et al., 1996) have raised similar cautions about the dangers of virtue ethics, particularly within insular communities that can easily become oblivious to alternatives because they are blinded by the perspectives they advocate. An antidote to narrowly entrenched self-serving positions is to systematically and continually reassess motives, perspectives, and virtues that one encourages and, more important-ly, to remain open to exploring and adopting virtues other than one's own.

The authors of the chapters in this volume discuss and either implicitly or explicitly propose virtues inherent in feminist perspectives on aspects of psychological practice. In addition, the parameters and themes of feminist ethics put forth respond to some of the criticisms of virtue ethics (particularly those related to multiculturalism) and have the potential to expand the conversation about virtues beyond individualistic Western ethnocentrism.

All communities, including Western ones, have implicit or explicit virtues, ideals, or aspirations. The feminist virtues implied or specified in these chapters speak to many of the legitimate concerns raised by those who see ethical dangers in a virtue ethics perspective.

Expansion of the Feminist Critique

As noted above, one of the contributions of this volume and its predecessor (Worell & Johnson, 1997) is the explicit statement that feminists are obliged to expand the feminist critiques of cultural discrimination against women to a critique of all discrimination based on category. The chapters in this volume make clear that this moral obligation is the same whether the category is gender, race, ethnicity, class, sexual orientation, age, disability, or other. We add (see Sanders, 1994) that the point of such an expanded critique is not an assimilation of a minority by a majority but an authentic exchange, in that some of each's viewpoints and perspectives deserve to be and will be adopted by all. Thus, setting ethical standards, articulating aspirations, and developing virtues are ongoing collaborative processes.

In following the suggestions of Sparks and Park (chap. 10) and McIntyre (chap. 3, both in this volume) about developing a feminist theory that is more sensitive to diversity, we suggest that as feminists we need to concretely review the experiences of women of Color (and other women of less privilege), not only during the wave of feminism that resulted in women securing the vote but also their experiences of the "new" feminism. The feminist or women's "liberation" movement from the early 1970s forward has greatly benefited White upper middle-class women and has enabled them and their daughters to have greater financial freedom, more choices in general, and many more opportunities for occupational and professional success.

Women of Color, however, typically have not considered themselves included in this latest wave of feminism. Many of these women have always had to work, often well below their ability level and often in the homes of upper-class White women. Many of these White women were seeking liberation from household responsibilities. They were able to achieve this liberation because women of Color and other less affluent women were available to do their work. Usually, less affluent women were available for this work because, for whatever reason (most often discrimination), educational and vocational opportunities commensurate with their capabilities were not open to them. In the initial wave of the feminist revival in the 1970s, there was not a clear recognition of the burdens carried by these relatively powerless citizens, much less any explicit advocacy by feminists or others to lessen or remove them. Not questioning the context that made such success possible, some women gained a slightly better and more powerful place in U.S. society's hierarchical structure at the expense of others. In expanding the cultural critique, those of us who are White middle-class feminists must own our part in perpetuating the classism and racism inherent in the structure that has accompanied our "liberation" over the last quarter of a century. Several authors in this volume lead us toward such ownership. These chapters, which expand this critique, present several virtues to consider and evaluate. A primary one is the other-regarding virtue of respectfulness.

Expansion of Analyses of Power and Context

As one looks at formal policies of affirmative action in the United States, one is again struck by the fact that these initiatives arguably have benefited middle- or upper-class White women more than any other group. This fact, in yet another way, bestows on this group (White upper middle-class women) increasingly more power than women of Color or others (women or men) of lesser opportunities. In this country, White women have traditionally had less power, influence, and opportunity than White men have. As White women have gained more (i.e., not to say equal) parity with White men, they have widened the power difference between themselves and women of Color and others (e.g., women in lower status occupations), whom they regard as "sisters." There could be risks for White middle- and upper-class women to bond more closely with women of Color and to commit to and act for and, more significantly, *with* them in broader professional and societal contexts. One risk, of course, is with respect to their relationships and understandings with White male intimates and colleagues and with White men in general. For the integrity of the feminist critique, however, it seems that there is a risk or set of risks that as feminists we are obligated to embrace. Feminists are hesitant to describe power as a "zero sum game." However, in the present individualized, competitive, nonfeminist structure within which most of the Western world functions, power relationships are so constructed. In the short term, then, a more inclusive feminism is likely to have more integrity and less power. Such a profile, however, could enhance the credibility and trustworthiness of feminist social action goals.

Therefore, one complication in charting a feminist moral vision relates to how to understand the issue of power from multiple perspectives when one is so ingrained with a Western perspective. Perhaps in the early 1970s, feminist thought and actions focused on developing cultural critiques, moral aspirations, and social action policies from the perspective of the less powerful. Such a position may have provided a unique perspective. Now, as feminists develop more inclusive feminist ethics, we must consider that whereas we have not achieved equality, we have achieved greater power (partly at the expense of the less powerful); however, with such power comes an altered perspective. As raised earlier, part of that perspective can be anxiety or fear of losing what achievements (in particular, individual achievements) we now have. In this climate, it seems no accident that many young women do not want to be called feminists. Because of what has been gained for them by older feminists, there is much greater potential for loss. Some feminists (younger or older) may feel caught because in sharing their newfound power with the less powerful, they fear losing favor, ground, or personal power to those (e.g., White men) from whom they "took" the power in the first place. Collaboration and shared power are strong tenets of feminism and reflect the virtues of benevolence, compassion, and respectfulness among others. Such beliefs, however, are easier to sustain from outside the power structure than from within it. Until we address this conundrum, feminist ethicists will have great difficulty developing ethical psychological practice from a feminist perspective.

If feminist ethicists are to address these issues adequately, we need to break free of conventional views of power and context. Instead of adapting to the rules of the dominant power structure (or learning them better or being clever in circumventing them), we need to transcend the current context and change awareness about and understandings of power. Several authors approach this challenge. For example, several authors in this volume (Brown, chap. 4; Fisher, chap. 6; Freyd & Quina, chap. 5; Kitchener, chap. 2; McIntyre, chap. 3; Quina & Miller, chap. 7; Sparks & Park, chap. 10; Vasquez & de las Fuentes, chap. 11) encourage readers to reframe "traditional objective context," stressing the importance of experiential knowledge and, in particular, women's experiences in developing and articulating competent and ethical science, instruction, and practice. In addition, all of the chapter authors explicitly or implicitly call for an expansion of commitment and action directed toward social justice. For instance, Worell and Oakley (chap. 8, this volume; also see Kimmel & Worell, 1997) view feminist pedagogy as a means of social transformation and suggest that instruction marked by integrity with or fidelity to feminist principles of dignity, competence, collaboration, and respect presents unique ethical challenges.

Virtue Ethics Expand the Feminist Dialogue

Feminist ethics as presented here speak to some of the criticisms or concerns raised about virtue ethics, but the conversations between these two traditions need not be a one-way street. Virtue ethics can add some perspective on the vexing problems in feminist thought. As Brabeck and Ting (chap. 1, this volume) note, there have been arguments about special virtues or separate ways of knowing for women and men. Categorizing certain helping virtues as intrinsic to women can put them at a disadvantage. Virtue ethics in collaboration with feminist ethics cut through the issue of masculine or feminine traits. The virtues discussed here are feminist virtues; that is, they are characteristics (e.g., integrity, respectfulness, commitment to self-care, and social justice) essential for both women and men in furthering feminist aspirations toward equality. The depictions of practice in this volume make clear that feminist virtues are relevant to the activities described (e.g., cross-cultural research, forensic testimony). They are also relevant to furthering the goals of feminism, but they are not intended to be descriptions of the "nature of women and men."

In addition to leading one from the quandary of female and male traits, virtue ethics guide the rapprochement with feminism with their distinction between self-regarding and other-regarding virtues. The virtuous professional needs both. There has been a temptation for some commentators to expect women to display primarily other-regarding virtues, but competent ethical psychological practice requires self-regarding virtues as well. Such practice requires a certain competence, integrity, commitment, and good judgment on the part of the professional as well as respectfulness and compassion toward those one is trying to help (e.g., students or clients) or collaborate with (e.g., research participants or other professionals). Mahalik, Van Ormer, and Simi (chap. 9, this volume) talk about the importance of self-care (a self-regarding virtue) in providing for both the welfare of the client (an other-regarding basis for virtue) and the therapist. Whereas the virtues belong to individuals (and it is hoped would eventually mark the profession), they cannot be characterized accurately as masculine or feminine; nor can ethical psychological practice be conceptualized adequately without a balance of self-regarding and other-regarding virtues.

Virtue ethics can inform feminist ethics by promoting self-regarding professional virtues that are consonant with the feminist mission (e.g., self-care and integrity). Feminist ethics speak to some of the criticisms of virtue ethics by stressing inclusiveness, valuing the virtues of diverse communities, and stressing the other-regarding virtues (e.g., respectfulness). Neither virtue ethics nor feminist ethics have fared as well in psychology as feminists would hope. Both suffer from an individualized, competitive perspective that perhaps (for different reasons) judges them more harshly than they deserve. Feminists are judged harshly because they legitimize personal experience and call for social transformation. Applied virtue ethicists are similarly judged because they are seen as promoting a specialized personal (read Westernized) morality in professional life. In short, both are often judged as being too proscriptive. Merging their contributions to each other may enable feminists to create a new context in which to situate ethical psychological practice. Such a context could provide fertile soil for developing aspirations of competence, character, and advocacy for different visions of the common good. Visions that encompass a balance of self-regarding and other-regarding virtues and truly value the experience of others can make social justice much more probable. Perhaps together, these two perspectives can provide different visions on which to build social and community structures. Feminist visions could motivate aspirational or forward thinking conceptualizations that transcend strategies, which simply continue to react to oppressive societal structures.

In some respects, we have just begun to articulate an ethical psychological practice that embodies feminist virtues. In other respects, feminist psychologists, ethicists, and others committed to this goal have an honored history that has made possible these chapters' important contributions to the conversation. However, as noted above, even if participants in this conversation about ethics are committed to achieving the ethical feminist psychological practice envisioned by these authors, cultural pluralism poses complications to realizing that commitment. As noted throughout this volume, feminism that developed in the United States is not a unitary perspective. Not all feminists accept some of its most basic concepts. Many psychologists and individuals who are not feminists are resistant to feminist voices. In addition, the dominant U.S. culture, as Western, masculine, competitive, and individualized as it might be, does not share a unitary perspective either. This makes goal setting and strategy development, aimed at transcending current boundaries and transforming contemporary culture, exceedingly complex. It also means that feminist ethics must be more than a reaction to patriarchy and other forms of discrimination. To ensure ethical psychological practice and a societal ambiance hospitable to the tenets and virtues of feminism, feminists must articulate our perspectives based on our vision and aspirations for the future, not on our reactions to the past.

Finally and perhaps most significantly, integrity of the feminist mission with respect to the treatment of women often conflicts with one of its cardinal tenets: respect for individual, interpersonal, and cultural differences. This last complication relates directly to the point of how to determine what, if any, part of one's moral agenda is negotiable. The question simply put is this: How much right (or conversely, how much obligation) does any group (or individual) have to advocate for (or impose on) those not in the group the specific rules, procedures, principles, or virtues related to its central beliefs? To explain one's moral vision to those who do not share it is a formidable task. To insist on it poses an extremely difficult or "thorny" issue. For example, Payton (1994) commented that in her judgment, the current APA Ethics Code (APA, 1992) does not insist enough on its agenda. She believes that the Ethics Code makes too great a distinction between what is ethically acceptable in a psychologist's professional life versus her or his personal life.

Many believe that professors must insist on some values, such as racial tolerance. Others (e.g., Bernstein, 1994) have deemed such a stance as unreflective "political correctness" and often as an infringement on one's

First Amendment right to free speech. Others still (e.g., MacKinnon, 1993) have advocated that certain types of speech constitute pornography and that by definition pornography degrades women and should be unlawful. Vasquez and de las Fuentes (chap. 11, this volume) speak eloquently about hate speech as a quintessential example of the dilemma between respecting autonomy and upholding the feminist virtues of respectfulness and inclusiveness while honoring the feminist call to social justice and elimination of marginality. They explain how the "right to exclude" based in a Western competitive context is anathema not only to feminist tradition but also to the ideal of virtuous agents whose ethical obligation it is to extend their moral communities beyond ethnocentric boundaries.

SUMMARY AND FUTURE CHALLENGES FOR ETHICAL FEMINIST PRACTICE

The difficulties posed by these issues (lack of unitary perspective within and without feminism, the formation of a coherent vision that embraces diversity but possesses integrity) notwithstanding, we believe that this volume adds unique conceptualizations of feminist ethics and thus enhances conversations that strive to define and deliver ethical psychological practice. Collectively, these authors create a vision and a context for ethical psychological practice. That vision is guided by an appreciation of diversity and the other-regarding virtues of respectfulness and social justice as building blocks toward a common good. They call for competence and the self-regarding virtues of good judgment and integrity in developing this context. They also list other virtues to guide us, such as self-care, compassion, and courage. They promote social action directed toward improving the lives of girls, women, and all those who may be or that may believe themselves to be at the margins of society. To constantly define, refine, and evaluate this practice, they suggest an inclusive dialogue that relies on lived experiences of diverse people and the continued development and critical examination of research, other forms of scholarship, policy evaluation, and practice knowledge. They urge for a continued examination of the relationships between their enlarged views of psychological practice and lived experiences. Finally, each chapter author encourages expansion of feminist commitment to and actions toward social justice.

The authors of this volume present expanded analyses of power that go well beyond the conventional rhetoric because they extend such analyses to nonconventional arenas, such as cyberspace and forensic psychology. They demonstrate that to transcend hierarchical structure means acknowledging that White middle-class feminists were often reacting to their lack of power from a position of privilege. In chapter after chapter, authors reiterate the theme that inclusiveness means not only accepting diversity but also adopting as their own the virtues and sensitivities of those who differ from them. To value difference, as feminists we must learn what it has to offer to our profession, to society, and to us as individuals.

These themes and their attendant virtues do not solve the realities of modern pluralism and the other challenges confronting feminism and ethical psychological practice. The authors do, however, construct their moral vision with such problems in mind and suggest ways of dealing with them. They offer up the self-regarding virtues of critical care and the other-regarding virtues of respectfulness and social justice. They do not contradict virtues suggested by others, such as prudence, integrity, benevolence, and trust. They challenge all of us to envision possibilities that are not wedded to current contexts. They summon us to construct a more self-determined moral vision based on the ideals and virtues we believe should prevail in a milieu that fosters excellence, integrity, and compassion in feminist ethical psychological practice.

REFERENCES

Albee, G. W. (1998). Fifty years of clinical psychology: Selling our soul to the devil. *Applied and Preventive Psychology, 7,* 189–194.

American Association for Marriage and Family Therapy. (1991). *AAMFT code of ethics.* Washington, DC: Author.

American Counseling Association. (1995). *Code of ethics and standards of practice.* Alexandria, VA: Author.

American Medical Association. (1980). *Principles of medical ethics.* Chicago: Author.

American Psychiatric Association. (1994). *Diagnostic and statistical manual of mental disorders* (4th ed.). Washington, DC: Author.

American Psychological Association. (1953). *Ethical standards of psychologists.* Washington, DC: Author.

American Psychological Association. (1958). Standards of ethical behavior for psychologists. *American Psychologist, 13,* 268–271.

American Psychological Association. (1963). Ethical standards of psychologists. *American Psychologist, 18,* 56–60.

American Psychological Association. (1968). Ethical standards of psychologists. *American Psychologist, 23,* 357–361.

American Psychological Association. (1975). Report of the task force on sex bias and sex role stereotyping in psychotherapeutic practice. *American Psychologist, 30,* 1169–1175.

American Psychological Association. (1977, March). Ethical standards of psychologists. *The APA Monitor,* pp. 22–23.

American Psychological Association. (1979). *Ethical standards of psychologists*. Washington, DC: Author.

American Psychological Association. (1981a). Committee on professional standards. Specialty guidelines for the delivery of services. *American Psychologist, 36*, 639–681.

American Psychological Association. (1981b). Ethical principles of psychologists. *American Psychologist, 36*, 633–638.

American Psychological Association. (1982). *Ethical principles in the conduct of research with human participants* (rev. ed.). Washington, DC: Author.

American Psychological Association. (1990). Ethical principles of psychologists [Amended June 2, 1989]. *American Psychologist, 45*, 390–395.

American Psychological Association. (1991). *Guidelines for providers of psychological services to ethnic, linguistic, and culturally diverse populations*. Washington, DC: Author.

American Psychological Association. (1992). Ethical principles of psychologists and code of conduct. *American Psychologist, 47*, 1597–1611.

Babladelis, G. (Ed.). (1976). Editorial. *Psychology of Women Quarterly, 1*, 3–4.

Bersoff, D. N. (1994). Explicit ambiguity: The 1992 Ethics Code as an oxymoron. *Professional Psychology: Research and Practice, 25*, 382–387.

Bersoff, D. N. (1996). The virtue of principle ethics. *The Counseling Psychologist, 24*, 86–91.

Bernstein, R. (1994). *The dictatorship of virtue*. New York: Alfred A. Knopf.

Council of Medical Specialty Societies. (1998, April). *Consensus statement on the ethic of medicine*. Lake Bluff, IL: Author. Retrieved July 23, 1999 from the World Wide Web: http://www.cmss.org

Drane, J. F. (1994). Character and the moral life: A virtue approach to biomedical ethics. In E. R. Dubose, R. P. Hamel, & L. J. O'Connell (Eds.), *A matter of principles? Ferment in U.S. bioethics* (pp. 284–309). Valley Forge, PA: Trinity Press.

Dykstra, C. (1981). *Vision and character: A Christian educator's alternative to Kohlberg*. New York: Paulist Press.

Feminist Therapy Institute. (1990). Feminist Therapy Institute code of ethics. In H. Lerman & N. Porter (Eds.), *Feminist ethics in psychotherapy* (pp. 37–40). New York: Springer.

Fitzgerald, L. F., & Nutt, R. (1986). The Division 17 principles concerning the counseling/psychotherapy of women: Rationale and implementation. *The Counseling Psychologist, 14*, 180–216.

Frankena, W. K. (1973). *Ethics* (2nd ed.). Englewood Cliffs, NJ: Prentice Hall.

Grant, C. A., & Zozakiewicz, C. A. (1995). Student teachers, cooperating teachers, and supervisors: Interpreting the multicultural silences of student teaching. In J. Larkin & C. E. Sleeter (Eds.), *Developing multicultural teacher education curricula* (pp. 259–278). Albany: State University of New York Press.

Hauerwas, S. (1981). *A community of character*. Notre Dame, IN: University of Notre Dame Press.

Ibrahim, F. A. (1996). A multicultural perspective on principle and virtue ethics. *The Counseling Psychologist, 24*, 78–85.

Jennings, B., Callahan, D., & Wolf, S. M. (1987). *The professions: Public interest and common good* [Report supplement]. New York: Hastings Center.

Jones, J. H. (1993). *Bad blood: The Tuskegee syphilis experiment* (rev. ed.). New York: Free Press.

Jordan, A. E., & Meara, N. M. (1990). Ethics and the professional practice of psychologists: The roles of virtues and principles. *Professional Psychology: Research and Practice, 21*, 107–114.

Jordan, A. E., & Meara, N. M. (1991). The role of virtues and principles in moral collapse. *Professional Psychology: Research and Practice, 22*, 107–109.

Kimmel, E., & Worell, J. (With Daniluk, J., Gawalek, M. A., Lerner, K., Stahley, G., & Kahoe, S.). (1997). Preaching what we practice: Principles and strategies of feminist pedagogy. In J. Worell & N. G. Johnson (Eds.), *Shaping the future of feminist psychology: Education, research, and practice* (pp. 121–153). Washington, DC: American Psychological Association.

Kitchener, K. S. (1996). There is more to ethics than principles. *The Counseling Psychologist, 24*, 92–97.

Koocher, G. P. (1994). The commerce of professional psychology and the new ethics code. *Professional Psychology: Research and Practice, 25*, 355–361.

MacIntyre, A. (1984). *After virtue*. Notre Dame, IN: University of Notre Dame Press.

MacKinnon, C. A. (1993). *Only words*. Cambridge, MA: Harvard University Press.

May, W. F. (1984). The virtues in a professional setting. *Soundings, 67*, 245–266.

McKeachie, W. J. (1971). Proceedings of the American Psychological Association, incorporated, for the year 1970. *American Psychologist, 26*, 22–49.

McKeachie, W. J. (1974). Proceedings of the American Psychological Association, Incorporated, for the year 1973. *American Psychologist, 29*, 381–413.

Meara, N. M., Schmidt, L. D., & Day, J. D. (1996). Principles and virtues: A foundation for ethical decisions, policies, and character. *The Counseling Psychologist, 24*, 4–77.

Miller, D. J. (1991). The necessity of principles in virtue ethics. *Professional Psychology: Research and Practice, 22*, 107.

Napoli, D. S. (1981). *Architects of adjustment: The history of the psychological profession in the United States*. Port Washington, NY: Kennikat Press.

Payton, C. (1994). Implications of the 1992 ethics code for diverse groups. *Professional Psychology: Research and Practice, 25*, 317–320.

Pojman, L. P. (1990). *Ethics: Discovering right and wrong*. Belmont, CA: Wadsworth.

Principles concerning the counseling and therapy of women. (1979). *The Counseling Psychologist, 8*, 21.

Punzo, V. A., & Meara, N. M. (1993). The virtues of a personal morality. *Journal of Theoretical and Philosophical Psychology, 13*, 25–39.

Raimy, V. C. (Ed.). (1950). *Training in clinical psychology*. Englewood Cliffs, NJ: Prentice Hall.

Sanders, C. J. (1994). European-American ethos and principlism: An African-American challenge. In E. R. Dubose, R. P. Hamel, & L. J. O'Connell (Eds.), *A matter of principles? Ferment in U.S. bioethics* (pp. 148–163). Valley Forge, PA: Trinity Press.

Simpkins, G., & Raphael, P. (1970). Black students and the challenge of change. *American Psychologist, 25*, 22–26.

Tennov, D. (1976). *Psychotherapy: The hazardous cure*. New York: Doubleday.

Thomas, S. B., & Quinn, S. C. (1991). The Tuskegee Syphilis Study, 1932–1972: Implications for HIV education and AIDS risk education programs in the Black community. *American Journal of Public Health, 81*, 1498–1505.

U.S. Department of Health, Education, and Welfare. (1971). *The institutional guide to DHEW policy on protection of human subjects*. Washington, DC: U.S. Government Printing Office.

Vasquez, M. J. T. (1996). Will virtue ethics improve ethical conduct in multicultural settings and interactions? *The Counseling Psychologist, 24*, 98–104.

Williams, R. L. (1970). Report to the APA Council of Representatives. *American Psychologist, 25*, 27–28.

Worell, J., & Johnson, N. G. (Eds.). (1997). *Shaping the future of feminist psychology: Education, research, and practice*. Washington, DC: American Psychological Association.

AUTHOR INDEX

Numbers in italics refer to listings in reference sections.

Finger, K., 107, *122*
Fisher, C. B., 6, 9, 13, 118, 125, 127–
    129, 132–136, 139, *139–141*, 261
Fisher, E., 217, *222*
Fitzgerald, L., 96, 99, 250, 266
Flax, J., 19, 27, *33*
Fodor, I., *201*
Folkman, J. R., 132, *140*
Forrest, L., 168, *184*
Forrest, V., 215, *223*
Fox, E. L., 8, *15*
Frankena, W. K., 46, *53*, 257, *266*
Frankenberg, R., 57, *72*
Franks, J. J., 113, *120*
Freedman, B., 131, *140*
French, M., 233, *245*
Freyd, J. J., 6, 8, 13, 84, 99, 101, 103–
    110, 112–114, 120, *121*, 138,
    149, 261
Friedman, S. S., 168, *184*, 207, 208, 219,
    222
Frueh, B. C., 235, *246*
Frye, M., 8, *15*, 23, *33*
Fullilove, M. T., *122*
Fung, P., 144, *163*
Fyrberg, D., 129, 132–134, 136, *140*

Gawalek, M. A., 171, *185*, 206, *222*, *267*
Genero, N. P., *140*
Gentry, M., 181, *184*
Gerling, E., 194, *200*
Gilbert, L., *140*, 193, 198, *199*
Gilbert, M., 103, *121*
Gilligan, C., 20, 21, 23, 30, *33*, 50, *53*,
    127, 128, *140*
Ginorio, A. G., 176, *184*
Glaser, K., 40, *53*, 170, *185*
Glaser, R. D., 168, *184*
Gleaves, D. H., 106, 112–114, *121*
Gold, S. N., 103, *121*
Goldberg, C., 159, *163*
Goldberger, N. R., 21, *32*
Gondolf, E. W., 217, *222*
Goodin, R. E., 138, *140*
Gore, J., 70, *72*
Gould, S. J., 148, *163*
Grant, C. A., 14, *15*, 58, *72*, 256, *266*
Greene, B., 11, *15*, 195, *199*
Greenspan, M., 192–194, *199*
Gregory, C., *201*
Griffin, C., 55, *72*

Griffith, J., *15*
Grillo, J. P., 146, *163*
Grisso, T., 75, 76, 98, *99*
Grossman, F. K., 139, *140*
Gudorf, C. E., 3, *14*, 18, *32*, 56, *71*
Gutierrez, L., 176, *184*
Gutierrez, M., 194, *200*

Haas, L. J., 44, *53*
Hacker, A., 59, 60, *72*
Haraway, D. J., 146, 148, *163*
Harden, J., 40, *53*, 170, *185*
Harding, S., 8, *15*, 29, *33*, 49, *53*, 102,
    121
Hare-Mustin, R., 5, *14*, 22, *32*, *33*, 52,
    71, 92, *99*, 162, 192, 193, *199*,
    200, *245*
Harrington, M., 168, *184*
Harris, C., 56, *72*
Hartsock, N., 27, *33*
Hassinger, J., *201*
Hauerwas, S., 257, *267*
Hawes, S. E., *140*
Hawkes, G., 216, *222*
Hawkesworth, M., 29, *33*
Hayes, A. E., 105, *121*
Heald, S., 168, 173, *184*
Heelas, P., 210, *222*
Hegel, G. W. F., 27, *33*
Held, V., *15*, 22, *33*
Helms, J. E., 55, 57, *72*
Helson, R., 136, *139*
Herman, J. L., 106, 116, *121*, 227, *245*
Higbee, K. L., 132, *140*
Higgins, A., 128, *140*
Higgins-D'Alessandro, A., 129, 135, 136,
    140
Hill, M., 40, 44–46, *53*, 170, 172, *185*,
    195, *200*
Hinderly, H. H., *15*
Hintikka, M. B., 8, *15*, 29, *33*
Ho, C. K., 214–216, 220, *222*, *224*
Hoagland, S. L., 20, 25, *33*, *34*, 40, 41,
    45, 51, *53*, 83, *99*
Hoagwood, K., 135, *140*
Hodge, D., 107, *122*
Hoffman, N. J., 168, 175, *185*
Holland, M. F., 113, *121*
Holmes, D. S., 105, 106, *122*
hooks, b., 11, *15*, 26, *34*, 56, 59, *72*,
    206, *223*

Hoult, J., 110, *122*
Houston, B., 22, 26, *34*
Hughes, K. P., 168, *185*
Hume, D., 21, *34*
Hurd, T. L., 55, 57, *72*
Hyde, J. S., *140*, 181, *184*

Ibrahim, F. A., 258, *267*
Ivey, A. E., 206, *224*

Jaggar, A. M., 20, 27, 29, 30, *34*, 37, 38,
    41, 46, 47, *53*, 170, *185*, 241,
    245
Jakobsen, J. R., 30, *34*
Jenkins, Y., *15*
Jennings, B., 254, *267*
Jensen, P. S., 135, *140*
Johnson, L., *140*
Johnson, N. G., 3, 5, *15*, 171, 205, *224*,
    251, 259, *268*
Jones, A., 79, *99*
Jones, J. H., 250, *267*
Jones, J. J., 233–235, *245*
Jones, S., 55, *72*, *73*
Jones, S. G., 148–150, *163*
Jordan, A. E., 63, *72*, 238, *245*, 257,
    258, *267*
Juntunen, C. L., 194, *200*

Kahle, B., 153, *163*
Kahoe, S., 171, *185*, *267*
Kallman, E. A., 146, *163*
Kant, I., 21, *34*, 126, 128, *141*
Kantrowitz, B., 144, 157, *163*
Kaplan, A., 5, *14*, *32*, *52*, *71*, *162*, 192,
    200, 199, *245*
Kaschak, E., 5, *14*, *32*, *52*, *71*, *162*, 192,
    199, *200*, *245*
Kassin, S. M., 114, *122*
Keefe, S., 217, *223*
Keele, S. W., 113, *123*
Keita, G. P., *201*, 228, *245*
Keith-Spiegel, P., 131, *141*, 167, 169,
    171, *185*
Kendler, H. H., 235, 236, *245*
Ketcham, K., 105, 112, 114, *122*
Kiechel, K. L., 114, *122*
Kiesler, S., 149, *165*
Killen, M., 128, *141*

Kim, B. C., 215, *223*
Kimmel, E., 168, 170, 171, 172, *185*,
    261, *267*
King, D. K., 206, *223*
King, J. E., 60, 66, *72*
Kitayama, S., 210, *223*
Kitchener, K. S., 6, 7, 13, 18, 29, *34*,
    37–40, 45, 46, 49, 51, *53*, 80,
    169, 171, *185*, 226, 238, 239,
    240, 243, *245*, 258, 261, *267*
Kitzinger, C., 55, *74*, 82, *99*
Koehn, D., 59, *72*
Kohlberg, L., 128, *141*
Koocher, G. P., 129, 131, *141*, 254, *267*
Kramarae, C., 144, 145, *163*, *165*
Kravetz, D., 194, 196, *200*
Krumboltz, J. D., *200*
Kulberg, J., 102, 110, *123*
Kuther, T., 129, *140*
Kvale, S., 236, *245*

LaFrance, M., 168, *185*
Laird, M., 234, *245*
Larned, A. G., 25, *32*
Larsen, C., 4, 6, *15*, 47, 49, *54*, 198,
    200
Law, S. A., 151, *162*
Lea, M., 144, 148, 149, 155, *163*, *165*
Leichtman, M. D., 106, *123*
Lerman, H., 4, 6, 8, 12, *15*, 25, 26, *34*,
    37, 38, 41, 43, *53*, 63, *72*, 91,
    99, 148, 150, 153, *163*, 189–192,
    195, 198, *200*, *201*
Lerner, G., 88, *99*, 232, *245*
Lerner, K., 171, *185*, *267*
Lesk, M., 153, *163*
Levensen, H., 168, *186*
Levine, R. J., 129, *141*
Lichtenberg, J., 194, *200*
Liljestrand, P., 194, *200*
Lindsay, D. S., 109, *122*
Liss-Levinson, N., 192, *200*
Lock, A., 210, *222*
Loftus, E. F., 105, 106, 107, 111, 112,
    114, *122*
Lonner, W. J., 208, *223*
Lopez, I. F. H., 57, *72*
Lorde, A., 25, *34*, 206, *223*
Lugones, M. C., 47, *54*
Luke, C., 70, *72*

Perkins, D. V., 167, *185*
Perkins, R., 82, 83, 99
Pezdek, K., 107, 115, *122*
Phillips, E., 5, *14, 32, 52, 71, 162, 199,*
 245
Pojman, L. P., 257, *267*
Polonsky, S., *122*
Poole, D. A., 109, *122*
Pope, K. S., 103, 106–109, 113, 117,
 121, 122, 168, *186*
Porter, N., 4, 6, 8, 12, *15,* 25, 26, *34,* 37,
 43, *53,* 63, *72,* 91, 99, 148, 150,
 153, *163,* 189–192, 195, 198,
 200
Posner, M. I., 113, *123*
Powell, L. C., 57, *71*
Pressman, B., 214, *224*
Prilleltensky, I., 29, 30, *34,* 129, 138,
 141, 235, 236, *246*
Puka, B., 22, 26, 30, *34*
Punzo, V. A., 257, *268*

Quina, K., 6–8, 10, 13, 101, 102, 110,
 123, 138, 143–145, 149, *164,*
 261
Quinn, S. C., 250, *268*

Radan, A., 20, *34,* 220, *223*
Rafaeli, S., 144, *165*
Raimy, V. C., 249, *268*
Raman, T. V., 152, *164*
Ramirez, M., 205, *224*
Ramos, N., 233, *245*
Raphael, P., 255, *268*
Rau, M. B., 129, *140*
Rave, E. J., 4, 6, *15,* 198, *200*
Rawlings, E., *201*
Raymond, J., 19, 24, 25, *34, 35*
Reay, D., 55, *73*
Reid, E. M., 151, 154, 155, *164*
Rest, J. R., 46, *54*
Reyes, C., 194, *200*
Rheingold, H., 144, 146, *164*
Rice, J. K., *201*
Richardson, M. S., 38, *54*
Ricoeur, P., 129, *141*
Ridley, C. R., 218, *224*
Rigby, D. N., 38, 41, *53*
Riger, S., 236, *246*

Roades, L., 168, *186*
Robb, C., 59, *73,* 170, *186,* 209, 210,
 224
Robertson, M. K., *15*
Robinson, D., 181, *186*
Robitschek, C. G., 192, *200*
Robson, R., 82, 99
Rocchio, L., *201*
Rochlin, M, 193, *200*
Roe, C., 107, *122*
Roediger, D., 57, *73*
Roediger, H. L., 107, 113, *123*
Roman, L., 60, *73*
Romenesko, K., 144, *164*
Root, M. P., 215, *224,* 227–229, *246*
Rose, L., 146, *164*
Rose, S., 168, *186*
Rosenberg, F., 168, *184*
Rosendahl, S. A., 128, 134, *140*
Rosenthal, R., 129, *141*
Rosenwald, L., 111, *122*
Rosewater, L. B., 77, 86, 96, 99, *100,*
 201
Rosewater, R., 6, *15*
Ross, W. D., 51, *54*
Rothenberg, P. S., 170, *185*
Rowan, C. T., 229n, 230, 243, *246*
Ruddick, S., 19, 20, 23, *35*
Russell, M, 192, *200*
Russo, N., 228, *245*

Sagan, D., 154, *164*
Saliba, P. A., 194, *200*
Salter, A., 109, 117, *123*
Sampson, E. E., 206, *224*
Sanchez, R., 157, *164*
Sanchez, W., 227, *246*
Sanchez-Hucles, J., 11, *15*
Sanders, C. J., 259, *268*
Scaltsas, P. W., 19, 21, 22, *35*
Scane, J., 56, *73*
Schatzow, E., 106, 116, *121*
Scheurich, J., 57, *73*
Schmidt, L., 29, *34,* 46, *54,* 226, *246,*
 257, *267*
Schneider, H. G., 127, *139*
Schrewsbury, C. M., 168, *186*
Schroeder, H. E., 193, *199*
Sears, D. O., 132, *141*
Seaver, W. B., 129, *139*
Seigfried, C. H., 128, *141*

SUBJECT INDEX

Childhood sexual abuse, 91. *See also* False
   memory controversy
Christian Coalition, 159
CMC. *See* Computer-mediated communication
Coercion power, 173
Colearning, 129–130. *See also* Mutual
   teaching–learning process
Collectivism, 210–211, 215
Commercialism, 254–255
Community
   cyberspace and, 146–147, 161
   moral, expansion of, 242–243
   virtue ethics and, 258–259
Computer-mediated communication
   (CMC)
   context analysis and, 10
   cyberspace revolution and, 143–144
   feminist ethics and, 146–149
   gender and, 144–146
Confidentiality
   adolescent risk research and,
      134–137
   cyberspace and, 155–156
Consequentialist stance. *See* Act–
   utilitarian moral ideology
Consultation, in forensic practice, 93–94
Contested memory debate. *See* False memory controversy
Context analysis, 9–11
   See also Multiculturalism
   ethical decision making and, 238,
      241
   feminist theory and, 5, 28–29,
      260–261
   self-disclosure by therapists and,
      194–198
Cornell University, 157–158
Council of Medical Specialty Societies,
   257
Critical–evaluative level of decision making, 238–239
Critical thinking, 149, 160, 182
Cultural context, and therapy. *See* Multiculturalism
Cyberspace
   abuses and, 156–158
   activism and, 158–161
   empowerment and, 159–161
   exaptation of feminist ethics to,
      146–149

exploitation in, 159–160
feminist ethical issues and, 149–161
feminist resources in, 144, 145
gender in, 144–146
growth of CMC and, 143–144
power dynamics and, 10
structure of, 158–159

Deception research, 130–134
Dehoaxing, 130, 131, 133
Denial, and battering, 216
Deontological perspective, 127–128
Dignity, 169
Disclosure, and research guidelines, 136–
   137. *See also* Self-disclosure
Discriminatory distortions, 7, 11–12, 229.
   See also Hate speech
   feminist theory and, 6, 26–27,
      259–260
Disempowerment, 41
Diversity
   See also Multiculturalism; Antiracist
      ethic, and forensic practice
   feminist theory and, 5, 243, 259–
      260, 264
   language of, 56
   U.S. demographics and, 229–230
   voice and, 175–178
Domestic violence
   forensic practice and, 84–87
   multiculturalism and, 212–221

Education, as feminist role
   See also Antiracist pedagogy; Ped-
      agogy
   cyberspace and, 159–160
   forensic practice and, 79, 80, 87,
      94–95
Education, equal access to, 42
Empowerment
   See also Power dynamics
   cyberspace and, 150–153
   as ethical imperative, 41
   forensic practice and, 79–82, 90, 91,
      92
   pedagogy and, 171, 172–175
Equal protection, and hate speech, 233,
   235
Essentialism, danger of, 11, 92

Ethical decision making.
    See also Feminist ethics; Principle
        ethics; Virtue ethics
    elements of, 168–169
    hate speech and, 237–241
    intuitive vs. critical–evaluative lev-
        els in, 238–239
    models of, 169–170
    pedagogy and, 168–169
    therapy and, 197–198
Ethical risk, 179
Ethic of care, 19–23, 169
    See also Relational feminism
    discriminatory distortions and, 26
    individualism and, 30
    pedagogy and, 50–51, 66
    scientist–citizen dilemma and, 128
Ethnocentrism, 12. See also Context anal-
        ysis; Discriminatory distortions;
        U.S. cultural context
Excellence, 169
Experiences of women, moral significance
        of. See also Objectivity
    models of ethical decision making
        and, 170
    as theme in feminist ethics, 4, 5, 6–
        7, 19–23, 261
Expert power, 172
Expert testimony. See Forensic practice

Faculty–student relationship, 178–181
Fairness. See Justice
Fallacy of is to ought, 134
False memory controversy
    conflicting values in researchers and,
        110–111
    current state of knowledge about,
        104–105
    empirical evidence and, 106–107
    feminist ethical critique and,
        108–115
    feminist science and, 8, 101–120
    forensic practice and, 91
    individual cases and, 105
    logical arguments and, 105–106
    misrepresentations and, 109–110
    nature of, 103–107
    overgeneralization of laboratory data
        and, 112–115
    population studies and, 105, 106

as scientist vs. therapist debate, 110,
    112
struggle for authority and, 108–109
Feminine, as construction, 30
Feminine vs. feminist ethic, 22
Feminism
    definition of, 205–207
    dilemma of hate speech for, 232–233
    disputes within, 18–19, 264
    integration with multiculturalism,
        203–221
    theory building process and, 5
    underlying assumptions of, 207–209
Feminist consciousness
    definition of, 5, 232
    feminist theory and, 5, 12–13, 23,
        24, 232
    forensic practice and, 83–84
    paternalism and, 240
Feminist critique
    See also Social transformation
    expansion of, 259–260
    false memory controversy and,
        108–115
    pedagogy and, 57–58, 59–60
Feminist ethics
    core tenets of, 3, 5–6
    link between virtue ethics and,
        256–264
    nature of, 17–19
    themes in, 4, 6–13, 19–32
Feminist practice
    See also Antiracist pedagogy; Foren-
        sic practice; Multiculturalism;
        Pedagogy; Science; Therapeutic
        practice
    defined, 4
    multiculturalism and, 203–205,
        206–207
Feminist Therapy Institute (FTI)
    Code of Ethics, 10–11, 41, 42, 49,
        79, 189–190, 195
    Ethical Guidelines for Feminist Ther-
        apists, 11, 149–150
    feminist theory and, 6, 26
Fidelity, principle of, 40, 43–44, 169, 239
First Amendment, 233–235
Flaming, 155
Forensic practice
    conflicts of interest and, 111
    consultation strategies in, 93–94

Mentoring, 48–59
Mexican American culture, 213–214,
    216–217
Moral
    absolutes, 28–29
    action. See Action toward social
        justice
    ambiguity, and deception research,
        130–131
    exclusion, 13, 231, 241, 242
    inclusion, 242, 244
    sentiment, 21
Mother–child relationship, as paradigma-
    tic, 22
Multicultural counseling and therapy
    (MCT), 208
Multiculturalism and feminism, integra-
    tion of, 203–221
    definition of multiculturalism and,
        205–207
    flexibility and, 219–221
    navigation of borderland and,
        214–221
    parameters of borderland and,
        209–214
    self-awareness and, 218–219
    underlying assumptions and,
        207–209
    understanding the cultural context
        and, 214–217
    U.S. cultural oppression and, 218
Mutual teaching–learning process, 170–
    171, 178–181. See also Co-
    learning

Narrative, and feminist ethics, 27
National Alliance, 239–240
National Conference on Education and
    Training in Feminist Practice
    (Boston College, 1993), 3, 4, 10,
    195
N., M. L. (vignette), 212–213, 214
Nonmaleficence, principle of, 39, 40–41,
    169, 239–240

Objectivity, 8, 253, 261
    See also Science
    forensic practice and, 77–78, 79–80,
        81–82
    recovered memories and, 110–111
Other-regarding virtues, 257, 262, 264

Participant perspectives
    adolescent risk research and,
        135–137
    deception research and, 130–134
    relational ethics and, 129–130
Patriarchal ethics
    definition of harm and, 240
    legal system and, 79
    Western feminism and, 209–210
Pedagogy
    See also Antiracist pedagogy
    context analysis and, 10
    cross-racial dialogue and, 69–70
    ethical challenges in, 7, 10, 37–52
    ethical principles and, 39–44, 169,
        170–171
    feminist ethical dilemmas and,
        171–183
    feminist ethics and, 37–39
    feminist virtues and, 7, 47–51
    mutual teaching–learning process
        and, 170–171, 178–181
    power dynamics and, 10, 41, 48–49,
        171, 172–175, 181
    scientist–participant relationship
        and, 137–138
    social transformation and, 13, 58,
        59–60, 172, 181–183
    traditional concerns and, 167–168,
        183
    voice and, 171, 175–178
Personal as political, 5, 30
Personhood. See Identity
Planned Parenthood, 226–227
Playboy magazine, 227, 240
Portland, OR, 227
Postmodernism, 28–29
Power dynamics, 9–11
    See also Empowerment; Reward
        power; Coercion power
    complementary relationships and,
        138
    context and, 28–29
    context-derived asymmetries and,
        137–138
    cyberspace and, 10, 148–149
    false memory debate and, 116–117
    feminist vision and, 260–261,
        264–265
    pedagogy and, 10, 41, 48–49, 171,
        172–175, 181
    scientist–participant relationship
        and, 137–138

Self-regarding virtues, 257, 262
Self-silencing, 175–176
Separatism, 24–26, 83
Sexual harassment
    forensic practice and, 81–82, 84,
        88–89
    psycholegal assessment and, 96
Sexual orientation, and self-disclosure,
    194
Silencing, 117
Simpson, O. J., 84–87
Social justice noise, 58. *See also* Social
    justice
Social transformation
    See also Action toward social justice;
        Advocacy; Feminist critique
    cyberspace and, 147–149, 153,
        158–161
    ethical principles and, 41–42
    feminist theory and, 5, 6, 12–13, 232
    forensic practice and, 84, 86
    science and, 118
Sociopolitical context. *See* Context
Solidarity, being in, 58, 68–69
Southern Poverty Law Center, 226, 235,
    239
Stacy v. Williams, 234
Standpoint theory, 26–27
State of Washington v. Yvonne Wanrow,
    79
Subjective knowledge, 8–9, 21, 23–26,
    78, 253. *See also* Experiences of
    women, moral significance of;
    Standpoint theory
Sweezy v. New Hampshire, 234

Texaco, 241–242, 244
Theory Group, 3, 26, 195
    tenets of feminist practice and, 3,
        5–6
Therapeutic practice
    empowerment as ethical imperative
        in, 41
    power dynamics and, 10–11, 189,
        195, 218–219, 252–253
    revolutions in, 101–102
    self-disclosure in, 189–198
    social change and, 147
    therapist as role model and,
        195–196
    values and, 78, 196

Trauma theory, and hate speech,
    227–229
Trustworthiness, 48–49
Truth
    See also False memory controversy
    forensic practice and, 76
    uncertainty about, and science, 104,
        108–109
    universal, 28–29

U.S. Armed Forces, 242, 244
U.S. Constitution, 233–235, 239
U.S. cultural context
    demographics and, 229–230
    feminism and, 209–210
    oppressive forces in, and multicultur-
        alism, 218
Universal truth, 28–29
University of Wisconsin, 227, 238–239
Utilitarianism, 242

Values
    forensic practice and, 77–83, 92–93
    pedagogy and, 181–183
    science and, 8
    therapy and, 78, 196
    virtue ethics and, 46–47, 263
Verbal violence. *See* Hate speech
Vices, virtues as, 51
Vietnamese culture, 212–213, 214–214
Violence. *See* Domestic violence; Hate
    crime; Hate speech
Virtue ethics, 13, 29–30, 46, 238,
    241–243
    dangers of, 258
    faculty–student relationship and,
        47–51
    feminist dialogue and, 261–264
    link between feminist ethics and,
        256–264
    self- vs. other-regarding virtues and,
        262
Virtuous agents, 243
Voice
    computer-mediated communication
        and, 144, 155, 159–160, 161
    feminist presence in psychology and,
        255–256
    feminist thought and, 5, 20, 251
    hate speech and, 232–233

ABOUT THE EDITOR

Mary M. Brabeck, PhD, is a professor in the Department of Counseling, Developmental, and Educational Psychology and dean of the Peter S. and Carolyn A. Lynch School of Education at Boston College. She earned her PhD from the University of Minnesota in 1980, is a licensed psychologist, and is a fellow of the American Psychological Association (APA; Division 35, Psychology of Women; Division 52, International Psychology). Her research interests include ethical sensitivity and the moral self, professional ethics, and intellectual and ethical development. She has published over 60 book chapters, essays, and journal articles and edited *Who Cares? Theory, Research and Educational Implications of the Ethic of Care* (Praeger, 1989). She has been an active member of Division 35 of APA and has served as task force chair and fellows committee chair for the division.